ABOVE THE WAR FRONTS

ABOVE THE WAR FRONTS

The British Two-Seater Bomber Pilot and
Observer Aces, The British Two-Seater
Fighter Observer Aces, and the Belgian,
Italian, Austro-Hungarian and
Russian Fighter Aces 1914–1918

Norman L R Franks
Russell Guest & Gregory Alegi

GRUB STREET · LONDON

Published by
Grub Street
The Basement
10 Chivalry Road
London SW11 1HT

Copyright © 1997 Grub Street, London
Text copyright © 1997 Norman Franks, Russell Guest and Gregory Alegi

British Library Cataloguing in Publication Data

Franks, Norman L. R. (Norman Leslie Robert), 1940-
  Above the War Fronts: a complete record of the British two-seater bomber pilot and observer aces,
  the British two-seater fighter observer aces, and the Belgian, Italian, Austro-Hungarian and
  Russian fighter aces, 1914-1918
    1. World War, 1914-1918 — Aerial operations. 2. Fighter pilots — Biography.
    I. Title. II. Guest, Russell. III. Alegi, Gregory.
    940.4'4'0922

ISBN 1 898697 56 6

Typeset by Pearl Graphics, Hemel Hempstead
Printed and bound by Biddles Ltd, Guildford and King's Lynn

ACKNOWLEDGEMENTS

As with the other books in this series we have been lucky enough to receive help from many people, some unhappily no longer with us. We wish, however, to thank everyone and especially the following friends and colleagues, past and present.

August Blume, Jack Bruce/Stu Leslie photo collection, Hal Giblin, Bob Lynes, John Lyons, Gerald Muir, Walter Pieters, Keith Rennles, Stewart Taylor, Barry Videon, the late Jean Alexander, the late Jim Kerr, the late Martin O'Connor.

The Italian Section could not have been compiled without the co-operation of the Italian Air Force's Historical Office, in particular Lt Col Carlo Fejer de Buk and Maresciallo Arcangelo Mastrangeli of the Archives Section. Over the years help has also come from Gianclaudio Polidori, Franco Briganti, Maurizio Longoni, Baldassare Catalanotto, Paolo Varriale, Antonio Iozzi and Roberto Gentilli.

Help is gratefully acknowledged from the Ufficio Storica della Stato Maggiore Aeronautica, Rome; Museo Caproni, Rome-Trento; Archivio Centrale della Stato, Rome; The Public Records Office, Kew, England.

Contents

Introduction

Volume Four of the WW1 aces series brings the now familiar and accepted format of the previous three books to cover the other nations in the conflict: Italy, Belgium, Austria-Hungary and Russia. To this has been added, by demand, the extension of the appendices in *Above the Trenches* which only listed the names and scores of the British two-seat corps and bomber pilots who were deemed aces, their observers, and the two-seater fighter observers who flew in FE2s, 1½ Strutters, and Bristol Fighters.

To some extent, the scores of these and other aces seem of less concern than their brief biographies, for it has always been the intention to put some flesh on the bones, so that at least some background knowledge of the WW1 aces adds something to the cold, impersonal lists of names and numbers.

Bearing some of this in mind we have made the conscious decision, as we did with *Above the Trenches*, to list all victories achieved by the two-seater men when they flew together. While it is accepted that in WW1 pilots were credited with their own claims, plus those scored by their observers, and observers themselves credited only with their own actual claims, and not those of the pilot, the victory lists show all claims while the observer was in 'residence'. Their Air War, of course, was covered in *Above the Trenches* and readers are referred to that book for information on the air war over France, etc.

The reason to include Austro-Hungarian and Russian aces, despite recent excellent books in which their stories are told, is that it was felt right to have their brief biographies and scores listed in order to round out the series without leaving any nation out. It is very much acknowledged that the two books in question, namely the late Dr. Martin O'Connor's marvellous *Air Aces of the Austro-Hungarian Empire 1914-1918*, originally published in 1986 and republished in 1994 by Flying Machines Press, and *The Imperial Russian Air Service* by Alan Durkota, Thomas Darcey and Victor Kulikov, (Flying Machines Press), 1995, cover their subject in much greater detail than that recorded here. Readers who wish to learn more about Austro-Hungarian and Russian aces, their squadrons and their air wars, are recommended, most highly, to read these two books which really should grace the bookshelves of any serious historian or enthusiast on WW1 fighter pilots.

Norman Franks, who has been involved in all four volumes of the aces series, fully acknowledges Russell Guest's involvement with his knowledge and penchant for discovering who-got-who, and of course, Gregory Alegi, who brings new and much detailed information and knowledge of the Italian pilots, squadrons and their air war into the English language for the first time.

All three authors also acknowledge the orginal research into the Belgian aces by Walter Pieters, who is planning his own book on all Belgian fighter pilots who served in WW1.

PART ONE
ABOVE THE BRITISH WAR FRONTS

CHAPTER ONE

Two-seat Fighter Observer Aces

AGABEG Ivan Wilmot Frank   Lieutenant   88 SQN

From London, born 21 September 1896. Commissioned into the 2nd Battn. of the South Lancashire Regiment in March 1916 and went to France in November 1916. Seconded to the RFC 18 May 1918 and served with 88 Squadron, effective 15 September. Shot up in E2533, 3 October, with Captain E C Johnston, but neither was harmed.

	1918			BF2b				
1	2 Oct	Fokker DVII	(a)	E2412	88	La Bassée	0815	DES
2	„	Fokker DVII	(a)	„	„	„	0820	DES
3	3 Oct	Fokker DVII	(b)	E2533	„	Meurchin	1730	DES
4	7 Oct	Fokker DVII	(a)	E2412	„	Annapes	0635	DES
5	30 Oct	Fokker DVII	(a)	E2533	„	Havinnes	0855	DES(F)
6	4 Nov	Fokker DVII	(c)	E2412	„	Faucoumont	1308	DES

Total: 6 destroyed.

Pilots: (a) Lt C Findlay; (b) Capt E C Johnston; (c) Lt C E Lacoste.

AGELASTO Cyril John   Lieutenant   59, 43 & 20 SQNS

Born 9 March 1897, he lived in West Hampstead pre-war. Joining the RFC he was made second lieutenant on 5 August 1916 and went to 59 Squadron on 29 January 1917. Temporary second lieutenant (General List) on probation, 17 June 1917, he then served with 43 Squadron on Sopwith 1½ Strutters in 1917 and later with 20 Squadron flying BF2b fighters. Confirmed as Lieutenant 1 June 1918.

	1917			Sop 1½				
1	23 Jul	Albatros DV	(a)	A8247	43	NE Lens	1745	OOC
				BF2b				
2	13 Nov	Albatros DV	(b)	B883	20	SE Houthulst	1500	DES
	1918							
3	22 Jan	Albatros DV	(c)	B883	„	Dadizeele	1117	DES
4	25 Jan	Albatros DV	(d)	C4836	„	Stadenberg	1240	OOC
5	„	Albatros DV	(d)	„	„	„	1240	DES
6	30 Jan	Albatros DV	(d)	C4826	„	W Zedeighem	1425	DES
7	4 Feb	Albatros DV	(e)		„	Roulers	1415	OOC
8	5 Feb	Albatros DV	(e)	C4605	„	N Staden	1130	OOC
9	„	Albatros DV	(e)	„	„	„	1130	OOC

Total: 4 destroyed, 5 out of control = 9.

Pilots: (a) 2/Lt J H G Womersley; (b) Lt W Beaver; (c) Sgt H O Smith; (d) 2/Lt D M McGoun; (e) 2/Lt D G Cooke.

ALLEN Laurence William   Lieutenant   48 SQN

From Coventry, born 14 September 1892. Served with the Royal Warwickshire Regiment, Territorial Force, and seconded to the RFC as second lieutenant on 11 April 1917. Wounded in action with 48 Squadron 24 May 1917, flying with Captain J H T Letts, in BF2a (A3350). Military Cross gazetted 26 May 1917. In 1922 he was a Class 'A' reservist, and in 1926, Class 'C', but relinquished his commission that September. On 17 February 1926 he had been slightly injured in a crash at Whitby aerodrome, flying a Wolf, G-EDHJ.

	1917			BF2a				
1	5 Apr	Albatros DIII	(a)		48	Douai	pm	OOC
2	9 Apr	Albatros DIII	(b)		„	E Arras	pm	DES
3	„	Albatros DIII	(b)		„	„	pm	OOC

	1918								
4	12 Apr	Albatros DIII	(c)		„				OOC
5	13 Apr	Albatros DIII	(d)		„	Vitry-en-Artois	pm		DES
6	„	Albatros DIII	(d)		„	„	pm		OOC
7	22 Apr	Albatros DIII	(a)		„	Vitry-en-Artois			OOC
				BF2b					
8	12 May	Albatros DIII	(e)	A7106	„	Izel	1930		OOC
9	24 May	2-seater	(e)	A3350	„	Vitry	1515		OOC
10	16 Jun	Albatros DIII	(f)	A7107	„	Fresnes-les-Montauban	0730		DES

Total: 1 & 2 shared destroyed, 4 & 3 shared out of control = 10.
Pilots: (a) Capt A M Wilkinson; (b) Wilkinson and shared with Lt J H T Letts/Lt H G Collins; (c) Wilkinson and shared with 2/Lt W O B Winkler/2/Lt E S Moore; (d) Wilkinson and shared with Lt J W Warren/2/Lt H B Griffith; (e) Capt J H T Letts; (f) 2/Lt R L Curtis.

ANSELL Arnold Edward   Lieutenant   48 SQN

From Laindon, Essex, a former electrical engineer and a married man, he was born on 23 August 1896. Served in the 1/24th Battn. the London Regiment before joining the RFC in November 1917. Joined 48 Squadron. Shot up flying with 2/Lt T G Jackson in BF2b A7114, 24 April 1918 but neither man was harmed. Left the service on 3 March 1919 but in September 1924 joined the RAFO as a pilot officer whilst living in Winchester, Hants. Flying Officer in 1925, he relinquished his commission in September 1933 being a 'C' Class reservist in July 1935.

	1918			BF2b					
1	9 May	Pfalz DIII	(a)	A7128	48	Vauvillers	1545		DES
2	„	Pfalz DIII	(a)	„	„	„	1545		OOC
3	30 May	Albatros DV	(b)	C877	„	Bray	1745		DES
4	2 Jul	Pfalz DIII	(c)	D8061	„	Mericourt	2000		OOC
5	7 Jul	Pfalz DIII	(d)	D7909	„	SW Proyart	1130		DES(F)

Total: 3 destroyed, 2 out of control = 5.
Pilots: (a) 2/Lt T G Jackman; (b) Capt L A Payne; (c) 2/Lt E N Griffiths; (d) Capt C R Steele.

ANTCLIFFE Ernest   Sergeant   88 SQN

Born 12 October 1898, he served as a private with the 270th Infantry Battn. prior to joining the RFC. No.86267, Antcliffe flew in BF2b machines with 88 Squadron which he joined in June 1918, and won the DFM, gazetted on 3 June 1919.

	1918			BF2b					
1	25 Jun	Fokker DVII	(a)	C4880	88	Thorout	1115		DES(F)
2	29 Jul	Fokker DVII	(b)	C821	„	Bois Grenier	1830		OOC
3	31 Jul	Fokker DVII	(b)	„	„	Zelobes	1200		DES(F)
4	11 Aug	Fokker DVII	(c)	„	„	Combles	1145		DES
5	„	Fokker DVII	(c)	„	„	„	1145		OOC
6	1 Sep	Fokker DVII	(b)	„	„	E Becelaère	1910		DES(F)
7	30 Oct	Fokker DVII	(d)	C922	„	N Beclers	0900		DES

Total: 5 destroyed, 2 out of control = 7.
Pilots: (a) Lt J P West; (b) Capt A Hepburn; (c) Lt C R Poole; (d) Lt V Voss.

BARNES William Thomas   2nd Lieutenant   11 SQN

From Sutton, Surrey, born 10 March 1892, he served with the Royal Fusiliers. Commissioned 10 June 1917 and joined 11 Squadron RAF on 15 August 1918. On the 30th he and his pilot, Lt C R Smythe, were badly shot up by AA fire over Bourlon Wood but Smythe flew D7981 back safely.

	1918			BF2b					
1	22 Aug	Fokker DVII	(a)	D7981	11	Bapaume	0740		DES
2	29 Aug	Fokker DVII	(a)	„	„	Bourlon Wood	1830		OOC
3	4 Sep	Fokker DVII	(a)	B8941	„	S St Hilaire	1045		DES(F)

4	16 Sep	Fokker DVII	(b)	D7978	„	Cambrai	1850	DES
5	„	Fokker DVII	(b)	„	„	S Cambrai	1900	DES
6	17 Sep	Fokker DVII	(b)	„	„	N Cambrai-E Wasnes	1055	DES
7	1 Oct	Fokker DVII	(a)	E2573	„	S Le Cateau	0820	DES(F)
8	„	Fokker DVII	(a)	„	„	S Le Cateau	0825	OOC
9	3 Oct	Fokker DVII	(a)	B8941	„	NE Cambrai	1800	OOC

Total: 6 destroyed, 3 out of control = 9.
Pilots: (a) Lt C R Smythe; (b) Lt B S B Thomas.

BEALES Walter   Sergeant   48 SQN

From Grimsby, (2565) Beales was the son of Alderman W S Beales of the town's Borough Council. Joined the RFC as a despatch rider in December 1914. He received the 1914-15 Star. He then flew with 48 Squadron as an observer. Wounded in the hand on 28 March 1918, while a corporal, flying with Captain W L Wells in C4701, he nevertheless claimed one German out of control and drove off others. Awarded the DCM in April 1918, gazetted 26 June, for this action and for assisting in bringing down two other machines sometime later. His Bristol was also shot-up twice; on 23 March he and Wells claimed two victories, and he claimed three on 9 May, when a sergeant, and flying with Captain C G D Napier. Came down on this latter date, possibly after a combat with Jasta 46. After the war he became an undertaker at Weelsby Grove, Grimsby, and in WW2 was commissioned in the RAFVR, commanding a gliding school. Later he commanded the local Air Training Corps unit. He retired to Goxhill where he died in 1962, aged 68.

	1918			BF2b				
1	21 Mar	Pfalz DIII	(a)	C4707	48	SW Honnecourt	1420	DES
2	23 Mar	LVG C	(a)	„	„	NE Ham	1155	DES
3	„	LVG C	(a)	„	„	Matigny	1625	DES
4	„	Pfalz DIII	(a)	„	„	„	1625	DES
–	28 Mar	Scout		C4701				OOC
5	1 Apr	Albatros DV	(b)	„	„	Quesnil	1745	OOC
6	25 Apr	Rumpler C	(c)	C814	„	E Harbonnières	1705	DES
7	9 May	Fokker DrI	(d)	C4750	„	Wiencourt-Mericourt	1540	OOC
8	„	Fokker DrI	(d)	„	„	„	1550	OOC
9	„	Pfalz DIII	(d)	„	„	„	1600	OOC

Total: 5 destroyed, 4 out of control = 9.
Pilots: (a) Capt W L Wells; (b) 2/Lt C L Glover; (c) Lt R H Little; (d) Capt C G D Napier.

BENGER William Joseph   Sergeant   20 SQN

From Ewell in Surrey, Rifleman Benger served with 20 Squadron in 1917. Injured in a crash on 25 June (A6511) after being brought down by AA fire. As Sergeant Benger (88288) was shot down on 17 October 1917, along with his pilot, Lieutenant A G V Taylor (A7271). Both were taken prisoner but died of their wounds soon afterwards. They were shot down by Leutnant Theodor Quandt of Jasta 36. Benger's Military Medal was gazetted on 20 October 1917. He was 22 years old and has no known grave.

	1917			BF2b				
1	25 Sep	Albatros DV	(a)	A7255	20	E Gheluvelt	1835	OOC
2	27 Sep	Albatros DV	(b)	A7245	„	Moorslede	1300	DES(F)
3	3 Oct	Albatros DV	(c)	A7271	„	Wervicq	1500	OOC
4	11 Oct	Albatros DV	(d)	B1122	„	Moorslede	0715	DES(F)
5	„	Albatros DV	(d)	„	„	„	0715	OOC

Total: 2 destroyed, 2 & 1 shared out of control = 5.
Pilots: (a) Lt J P Dalley and shared with Sgt F Hopper/Capt L W Burbidge in B1111; (b) 2/Lt W Durrand; (c) 2/Lt A G V Taylor; (d) Lt H G E Luchford.

BENJAMIN Maurice Arthur Captain 48 SQN

Born in London on 10 July 1883 he was working in South Africa before the war, listed as a theatrical manager. Joined the Royal Flying Corps, Special Reserve, in April 1917, confirmed as a second lieutenant 9 March 1917, full lieutenant 1 August. Military Cross recommended on 15 May for actions on 25 and 27 April, gazetted 18 July 1917 which noted four victories as at the award date. Undertook flying training, gaining RAC ticket No.5883 on 3 February 1918. Became a temporary Captain on 1 August 1918 while an instructor in England. Granted a permanent commission one year later, he was posted to the unemployed list on 12 October 1919.

	1917			BF2a				
1	6 Apr	EA	(a)		48	Douai		OOC
2	9 Apr	2-seater	(a)		„	E Arras	am	DES
3	23 Apr	Albatros DIII	(b)		„	Vimy		OOC
4	25 Apr	Albatros DIII	(a)		„	E Arras		DES
5	27 Apr	2-seater	(c)		„	Vitry-SW Douai		DES
				BF2b				
6	26 May	Albatros DIII	(d)	A7119	„	SW Douai	1945	DES
7	„	Albatros DIII	(d)	„	„	„	1945	OOC
8	15 Jun	Albatros DIII	(e)	A7117		Fampoux	1940	OOC

Total: 3 & 1 shared destroyed, 2 & 2 shared out of control = 8.
Pilots: (a) Lt W T Price; (b) Price and shared with Lt F P Holliday/Capt A H W Wall, Lt R B Hay/?, Lt W O B Winkler/2/Lt E S Moore; (c) Price and shared with Lt R B Hay/?; (d) Lt J W Warren; (e) Lt H M Fraser and shared with Lt H J Pratt/Lt H Owen, A7116.

BIRMINGHAM Thomas James Lieutenant 22 SQN

Born Hastings, Sussex, 13 January 1885 (gave his year of birth as 1887 when he joined the RFC) and became a motor mechanic. Emigrated to Canada with his wife in 1910. Between 1910-15 he was a self-employed motor engineer in Janzen, Saskatchewan. Enlisted into the 2nd Division Supply Column, CEF, April 1915 and served in the Ypres sector. Transferring to the RFC he was commissioned Second Lieutenant 12 February 1918 and when posted to a night bombing squadron created such a 'stink' that his CO put in an application for him to go to 22 Squadron. Confirmed in rank as an officer observer, 20 July. Was shot about on 2 September, flying with Lt H H Beddow (D7908) with whom he shared all victories, during a combat with a Fokker DVII, but they survived. Returned to Home Establishment on 23 October and left the service on 14 June 1919. Returned to farm in Janzen and in the 1930's moved to the west coast. Died 12 November 1965, in the Shaughnessy Veterans' Hospital, Vancouver.

	1918			BF2b				
1	13 Aug	Pfalz DIII		E2499	22	Auberchicourt	1100	OOC
2	„	Pfalz DIII		„	„	„	1100	OOC
3	16 Aug	Pfalz DIII		D7908	„	Lille	1035	DES
4	„	Pfalz DIII		„	„	„	1035	DES
5	22 Aug	Halberstadt C	(a)	—	„	NE Bailleul	1910	DES
6	27 Aug	Fokker DVII		D7908	„	Vitry	0630	OOC
7	2 Sep	Fokker DVII		„	„	Arras-Cambrai Road	0915	DES

Total: 4 destroyed, 3 out of control = 7.
(a) Shared with Capt W F J Harvey/Capt D E Waight and Lt I O Stead/2/Lt W A Cowie.

BLAICKLOCK George Walter Lieutenant 45 SQN

Born Montreal, Canada, 7 December 1891. Served with the 148th Battn., CEF from 14 December 1915 and transferred to the RFC 9 March 1917. Posted overseas on 11 April, joining 45 Squadron, with whom he served until 1 September. Returned to Canada and became an instructor with the RAF there, on photography and Lewis gun. Refused pilot training and became depressed after the war. Died in July 1977.

	1917			Sop 1½				
1	20 May	Albatros DIII	(a)	A8268	45	Lille	1630	DES(F)
2	,,	Albatros DIII	(a)	,,	,,	,,	1630	DES(F)
3	31 May	Albatros DV	(b)	A8295	,,	Comines	1900	OOC
4	7 Jul	Albatros DV	(c)	A1031	,,	Menin	0930	OOC
5	22 Jul	Albatros DV	(c)	A8304	,,	Menin	1035	OOC

Total: 2 destroyed, 3 out of control = 5.
Pilots: (a) Sgt E A Cook; (b) 2/Lt R M Findlay; (c) 2/Lt E F Crossland.

BOOTHROYD Clement Graham   Lieutenant   20 SQN

From Yesmond, Newcastle-on-Tyne, born 25 August 1899, he lived in Halifax, Yorkshire, pre-war. Clem Boothroyd won the DFC flying with 20 Squadron in 1918, gazetted in February 1919. His citation recorded eight victories and a raid carried out on 23 October, during which he and his pilot were attacked by 15 enemy fighters, he and his pilot each destroying one. Transferred to the reserve in 1922 and relinquished his commission in December 1926.

	1918			BF2b				
1	2 Jul	Fokker DVII	(a)	C843	20	Dadizeele-Gheluwe	0840	DES
2	11 Aug	Balloon	(a)	C987	,,	S Heule	1345	DES
3	20 Sep	Fokker DVII	(b)	D7915	,,	E Longchamps	1020	DES
4	,,	Fokker DVII	(b)	,,	,,	N Longchamps	1025	OOC
5	23 Sep	Fokker DVII	(c)	E2340	,,	NE St Quentin	1820	DES
6	25 Sep	Fokker DVII	(b)	E2568	,,	Estres	1830	DES(F)
7	27 Sep	Fokker DVII	(b)	E2470	,,	W Bernot	1030	DES
8	29 Sep	Fokker DVII	(b)	,,	,,	Lehaucourt	1030	DES
9	23 Oct	Fokker DVII	(d)	E2407	,,	SW Noyelles	1510	DES
10	,,	Fokker DVII	(d)	,,	,,	E Preux	1515	DES
11	30 Oct	Fokker DVII	(d)	,,	,,	S Avesnes	1205	DES
12	,,	Fokker DVII	(d)	,,	,,	,,	1205	DES

Total: 10 destroyed, 1 out of control, 1 balloon = 12.
Pilots: (a) 1/Lt E W Sweeney USAS; (b) Lt M McCall; (c) Lt A D Kiernander; (d) Capt H P Lale.

BROOKE George Ai   Lieutenant   45 SQN

A married man from St Martins, Jersey, Channel Islands, he attended Sheffield University OTC. Transferred from the Machine Gun Corps to the 4th South Staffordshire Regiment, Special Reserve, and then seconded to the RFC. Flying Officer Observer from 25 July 1917, not long after he joined 45 Squadron. On 28 July, he was observer to the future ace M B Frew and was shot-up by Max Müller of Jasta 28, crashing on the aerodrome on their return (A1031). On 23 August Brooke was once more in a shot-about Sopwith (A1048) after a combat with an Albatros Scout, this time with 2/Lt E D Clarke. After four victories he went to 20 Squadron and brought his score to 7. An instructor in 1918, he was posted to 55 Squadron in January 1919 but left the service in March.

	1917			Sop 1½				
1	16 Jul	Albatros DV	(a)	A1020	45	Polygon Wood	0910	DES
2	28 Jul	Albatros DV	(a)	A8228	,,	S Comines	1700	DES
3	10 Aug	Albatros DV	(a)	A1013	,,	E Comines	1830	OOC
4	23 Aug	Albatros DV	(b)	A1048	,,	Bellewarde Lake	0915	OOC
				FE2d				
5	11 Sep	Albatros DV	(c)	A6458	20	N Wervicq	1430	OOC
				BF2b				
6	8 Nov	Albatros DV	(d)	A7193	,,	Staden	1300	DES
7	22 Dec	Albatros DV	(e)	A7255	,,	Moorslede	1415	DES

Total: 4 destroyed, 3 out of control = 7.
Pilots: (a) Lt M B Frew; (b) 2/Lt E D Clarke; (c) Lt A G V Taylor; (d) Lt J C Kirkpatrick; (e) Lt R M Makepeace.

BRUCE NORTON John   Lieutenant   62 SQN

From Newcastle-on-Tyne, born 31 March 1895, he was commissioned into the 4th West Yorks on 11 November 1917. A married man, his wife's wartime address was in Westminster, London. During a low patrol on 27 March 1918, he and his pilot, 2/Lt H N Arthur, were brought down by ground fire (B1305) near Mailly and had to abandon their Bristol near the front line. Went into hospital on 3 July and returned to England. Left the service on 11 June 1919.

	1918			BF2b				
1	20 Mar	EA	(a)		62			OOC
2	„	EA	(a)		„			OOC
3	21 Mar	Albatros DV	(a)		„			DES
4	3 May	Albatros DV	(b)	C4709	„	S Armentières	1100	DES(F)
5	„	Albatros DV	(b)	„	„	„	1100	OOC

Total: 2 destroyed, 3 out of control = 5.
Pilots: (a) 2/Lt H N Arthur; (b) Capt H Rees-Jones.

BUNTING Stanton William   2nd Lieutenant   22 SQN

Bunting came from Ealing, West London and had been a cadet with the 13th OCB, Middlesex Regt. A second lieutenant on probation in the RFC, 29 August 1917, full Lieutenant 13 June 1918. Operated with 22 Squadron which he joined on 11 December 1917. He was wounded on 5 March 1918 during a combat with German fighters near Lens. His pilot, Lt S A Oades (with whom he shared all victories) was also wounded; their propellor was also shot off (B1168). Medically fit only for ground duties afterwards, he left the service on 5 February 1919.

	1918		BF2b				
1	30 Jan	2-seater	B1152	22	E La Bassée	1140	OOC
2	17 Feb	Albatros DV	„	„	N Douai	1445	DES
3	18 Feb	Albatros DV	„	„	E La Bassée	1140	OOC
4	26 Feb	Albatros DV	„	„	Douai	1030	DES(F)
5	„	Albatros DV	„	„	E La Bassée	1140	OOC
6	5 Mar	2-seater	B1168	„	Lens	1535	DES
7	„	Albatros DV	„	„	„	1545	OOC

Total: 3 destroyed, 4 out of control = 7.

BURBIDGE Leslie William   Captain   20 SQN

Born 10 March 1891, his home address when he joined the RFC was Le Havre, France, being fluent in French and Italian, the son of the Rev. E O Burbidge. Between 1910-14 he worked with a ship building company in St Helens, Lancs, then joined the Army Service Corps and became an Honorary Captain. Transferring to the RFC, he flew with 20 Squadron from September 1917. Returning to HE on 21 February 1918, he rejoined the Squadron in September and received the DFC, gazetted on 8 February 1919. On 23 October 1918, flying with his usual pilot, Captain T C Traill, they collided with another Bristol while returning home, losing part of the right-hand plane, which sent their machine into a spin, Burbidge gallantly climbed out onto the lower wing to counter the spin and they had partly recovered before they hit the ground. Catapulted into the ground, Burbidge broke his nose and bit through his tongue. In 1919 he served once more with 20 Squadron, then 22 Squadron, and 12 Squadron at Cologne, Germany, but left the RAF on 23 October 1919.

	1917			BF2b				
1	25 Sep	Albatros DV	(a)	B1111	20	E Gheluvelt	1835	OOC
2	2 Oct	Albatros DV	(b)	A7164	„	Dadizeele	1150	OOC
3	„	Albatros DV	(b)	„	„	„	1155	OOC
4	13 Nov	Albatros DV	(c)	A7253	„	Becelaère	1500	OOC
5	5 Dec	Albatros DV	(c)	A7298	„	Oostnieuwkerke	1250	OOC
	1918							
6	29 Sep	Fokker DVII	(d)	E2370	„	N St Quentin	1025	DES

Total: 1 destroyed, 4 & 1 shared out of control = 6.
Pilots: (a) Sgt F Hooper, and shared with Lt J P Dalley/Sgt W J Benger in A7255; (b) Sgt F Hooper; (c) Lt R K Kirkman; (d) Lt T C Traill.

CAMBRAY William Charles   Lieutenant   20 SQN

From Herne Hill, south-east London, born 12 November 1894, he worked in insurance between 1912-14. Following service with the London Regiment, Territorial Force, seeing action in France, Bill Cambray transferred to the RFC in 1916 and flew in FEs with 20 Squadron in 1917, qualifying as an observer on 13 June with seniority from 26 March. Awarded the Military Cross, gazetted 17 September 1917 after at least four victories. Surviving his period at the front he was returned to Home Establishment on 9 October, left the service on 22 April 1919, and did not fly again until 1967!

	1917			FE2d				
1	31 May	Albatros DIII	(a)	A6430	20	Comines	1920	DES
2	17 Jun	Albatros DIII	(b)	A6516	,,	Houthem	2030	DES
3	18 Jun	Albatros DV	(c)	,,	,,	E Quesnoy	1315	DES
4	17 Jul	Albatros DV	(d)	,,	,,	Polygon Wood	1955	DES
5	16 Aug	Albatros DV	(d)	,,	,,	SE Polygon Wood	1100	OOC
				BF2b				
6	21 Sep	Albatros DV	(e)	A7428	,,	Becelaère	1100	OOC

Total: 4 destroyed, 2 out of control = 6.
Pilots: (a) Lt D C Cunnell; (b) Lt B Strange; (c) Lt A N Solly; (d) Capt F D Stevens; (e) Lt H G E Luchford.

CAULFIELD-KELLY Edward T   2nd Lieutenant   45 SQN

From County Galway, Ireland, he was educated at Trinity College, Dublin between June 1913 and 1914. After serving with the 9th Royal Dublin Fusiliers (6/3 Leinster Regt), transferred to the RFC General List on 21 May 1917, as a temporary lieutenant. By this time he had been with 45 Squadron since 5 April. On 28 May, he was wounded and returned to England two days later. In 1919 he trained as a pilot and was granted a short service commission as a flying officer on 12 September.

	1917			Sop 1½				
1	9 May	Albatros DIII	(a)	A8225	45	NW Seclin	1700	DES
2	24 May	Albatros DIII	(b)	A8269	,,	Zonnebeke	1945	DES(F)
3	,,	Albatros DIII	(b)	,,	,,	,,	1945	OOC
4	27 May	Albatros DIII	(c)	A1016	,,	Menin	0630	OOC
5	28 May	Albatros DV	(b)	A8269	,,	Comines	1345	DES(F)

Total: 2 & 1 shared destroyed, 2 out of control = 5.
Pilots: (a) 2/Lt W A Wright, and shared with Lt G H Cock/2/Lt J T G Murison A8260; (b) 2/Lt Wright; (c) Lt G H Cock.

CHAMBERS Percival V G   2nd Lieutenant   62 SQN

First served with the 5th Battn. of the South Staffordshire Regiment, enlisting in 1914, and was wounded four times. Commissioned on 28 March 1917 and later seconded to the RFC. Joined 62 Squadron on 28 December 1917, and confirmed as an observer on 5 April 1918, having teamed up with Captain T L Purdom with whom he shared all victories. On 26 June he was invalided home with appendicitis. Left the service on 1 May 1919.

	1918		BF2b				
1	21 Mar	Albatros DV	62				DES
2	,,	EA	,,				OOC
3	23 Mar	Albatros DV	,,				DES(F)
4	26 Mar	EA	,,				DES
5	,,	EA	,,				OOC
6	28 Mar	EA	,,		Sailly	1005	OOC

7	21 Apr	Fokker DrI	(a)		„	SE Estaires	0945	DES
8	3 May	Albatros C	B1216		„	N Merville	1100	DES
9	„	Albatros C	„		„	S Armentières	1100	OOC
10	15 May	2-seater			„	Pozières	1745	DES
11	17 May	Fokker DVII	„		„	Armentières	1045	OOC
12	„	2-seater	„		„	„	1045	OOC

Total: 5 & 1 shared destroyed, 6 out of control = 12.
(a) shared with Lt W E Staton/Lt J R Gordon.

CHILTERN Thomas Sydney   2nd Lieutenant   88 SQN

Born County Durham, 10 February 1898. Became an electrician before joining the RFC by way of the General List, being commissioned on 3 January 1918. Went to France in April and assigned to 88 Squadron.

	1918			BF2b				
1	29 Jun	Fokker DVII	(a)	C774	88	NW Dixmude	2010	DES(F)
2	„	Fokker DVII	(a)	„	„	Ghistelles	2012	DES
3	31 Jul	Pfalz DIII	(b)	D8062	„	Fromelles	0915	OOC
4	15 Sep	Fokker DVII	(b)		„	E Seclin		OOC
5	27 Sep	Fokker DVII	(b)	E2451	„	Lambersart	0755	OOC
6	4 Oct	Fokker DVII	(b)	„	„	Quesnoy	1145	OOC

Total: 2 destroyed, 4 out of control = 6.
Pilots: (a) Lt W A Wheeler; (b) Lt G F Anderson; second victory on 29 June shared with Capt K R Simpson/ Sgt C Hill, C983, Lt R J Cullen/2/Lt E H Ward, D8062, Lt K B Conn/2/Lt B H Smyth, C787.

CLAYE Hugh   Captain   62 SQN

Claye was born on 22 June 1890. A pre-war soldier, Claye had become a lieutenant in June 1912. Saw service with the 5th Notts & Derby Regiment, Territorial Force, promoted temporary captain 21 May 1915, and seconded to the RFC 16 March 1918. His rank of Captain was confirmed in April, effective from 27 January. Joined 62 Squadron in December 1917 and went to France with them in January 1918. Teamed up with Captain G F Hughes and together they scored 62's first combat victory on 21 February 1918, although their Bristol Fighter was shot about (C4630). All of Claye's subsequent victories were scored while flying with Hughes. Claye, flying with Lt H A Clarke, was brought down and captured on 19 May, in BF2b No.C4630 'J'. They were claimed by flak and Ltn August Delling of Jasta 34, but the flak unit was given the credit. Repatriated 30 December 1918. A married man, he lived in Farleyfield with his wife and left the service on 10 April 1919. He was also an Honorary Captain with the 5th Battn. Sherwood Forresters.

	1918			BF2b				
1	21 Feb	2-seater		C4630	62	Armentières-Ploegsteert		DES
2	10 Mar	Albatros DV			„			DES(F)
3	„	Albatros DV			„			OOC
4	11 Mar	Fokker DrI			„			OOC
5	13 Mar	Pfalz DIII		C4630	„	E Cambrai	1030	OOC
6	„	Fokker DrI		„	„	„	1030	DES
7	12 Apr	Albatros DV			„	E Estaires	1420	OOC
8	„	LVG C			„	Auchy-La Bassée	1500	DES(F)
9	22 Apr	Fokker DVII			„	Nieppe Forest	1300	OOC
10	„	Fokker DVII			„	„	1300	OOC
11	10 May	Rumpler C			„	Combles-Péronne	1835	OOC

Total: 4 destroyed, 7 out of control = 11.

COLLINS Valentine St Barbe   Lieutenant   45, 48 & 22 SQNS

Born London 2 January 1894, his aunt was Lady Buckingham. Educated at Wellington College, Berkshire, he joined the RFC in October 1916 but was injured on 29 November 1916, flying Sopwith 1½ Strutters with 45 Squadron. In 1917 he served with 48 Squadron in France before returning to England in December 1917. He was then assigned to 22 Squadron in mid-1918. Killed in action on 2 September 1918, flying with Captain Brian Laidley Dowling, from Sydney, Australia, on an early morning OP in D7790. They have no known grave.

	1917			BF2b				
1	4 Sep	Albatros DV	(a)	A7224	48	Middlekerke-Ostende	1900	OOC
2	27 Sep	Albatros DV	(a)	A7226	„	Pervyse	1830	DES
3	„	Albatros DV	(a)	„	„	„	1845	OOC
	1918							
4	28 Jun	Fokker DrI	(b)	C989	22	N Estaires	1015	DES
5	10 Jul	Fokker DrI	(b)	„	„	Lille	0945	OOC
6	8 Aug	Pfalz DIII	(c)	D7894	„	S Douai	1030	OOC
7	10 Aug	Fokker DVII	(c)	„	„	SW Péronne	1810	DES
8	„	Fokker DVII	(c)	„	„	„	1810	DES
9	21 Aug	Fokker DVII	(c)	E2454	„	Albert-Cambrai	1945	OOC
10	27 Aug	Fokker DVII	(c)		„	Senlemont	1400	OOC

Total: 4 destroyed, 6 out of control = 10.
Pilots: (a) 2/Lt W D Bostock; (b) Lt F G Gibbons; (c) Lt L W King.

COOPER Arthur Cyril   Lieutenant   48 SQN

From Hambleton, Rutland, born 24 December 1894. Commissioned into the 18th Battn. of the London Regiment prior to transferring to the RFC. Served with 48 Squadron from 23 October 1917 and returned to Home Establishment on 22 March 1918. Posted to Egypt in May 1918, he was attached to the 64th Naval Wing in June, and was at the Seaplane Stations at Alexandria and Kantara. Returned home in March 1919 and left the service on 4 April.

	1917			BF2b				
1	21 Oct	Albatros DV	(a)	B1134	48	Clemskerke	1245	OOC
	1918							
2	3 Jan	Albatros C	(b)	B1187	„	Gouy-Le Catelet	1130	OOC
3	1 Mar	2-seater	(b)	B1190	„	Joncourt	1010	OOC
4	„	Albatros DIII	(b)	„	„	SE St Quentin	1030	OOC
5	8 Mar	Albatros DV	(b)	„	„	Bohain	1040	OOC
6	„	Albatros DV	(b)	„	„	„	1555	OOC
7	11 Mar	Pfalz DIII	(c)	B1269	„	SE St Quentin	1300	OOC

Total: 7 out of control.
Pilots: (a) Lt R Dodds; (b) Capt N C Millman; (c) 2/Lt R J Smethan-Jones.

COWELL John J   Sergeant   20 SQN

From County Limerick, Eire, Sergeant (78171) Cowell was a very experienced observer, winning the DCM (on 11 June) as well as the MM and Bar. His Military Medal was gazetted on 27 October 1916, the Bar on 27 September 1917 with the DCM on 18 July 1917. Became a pilot and returned to his former squadron in 1918. Killed in action 30 July 1918 with Corporal Charles William Hill in the rear cockpit of E2471, claimed by Ltn Fritz Röth of Jasta 16b, south of Ypres.

	1917			FE2d				
1	5 May	Albatros DIII	(a)	A6400	20	Poelcapelle	1710	OOC
2	13 May	2-seater	(b)	A6412	„	Reckem airfield	1040	DES
3	20 May	Albatros DIII	(a)	„	„	Menin	0920	OOC
4	25 May	Albatros DIII	(a)	A6415	„	Wervicq	0850	OOC
5	26 May	Albatros DIII	(a)	„	„	Comines	1030	OOC
6	„	Albatros DIII	(a)	„	„	SE Ypres	2010	DES(F)
7	2 Jun	Albatros DIII	(c)	A6480	„	Gheluvelt	0945	DES

8	29 Jun	Albatros DV	(d)	A6376	„	Becelaère	1610	OOC
9	12 Jul	Albatros DV	(d)	„	„	E Ploegsteert Wood	1700	DES
10	„	Albatros DV	(d)	„	„	„	1715	OOC
11	17 Jul	Albatros DV	(e)	A6468	„	Polygon Wood	1945	DES(F)
12	„	Albatros DV	(e)	„	„	28Q 28	1950	DES
13	20 Jul	Albatros DV	(d)	A6376	„	Wervicq	0955	OOC
14	22 Jul	Albatros DV	(d)	„	„	Menin-Wervicq	1650	OOC
15	28 Jul	Albatros DV	(d)	„	„	E Messines	1845	OOC
	1918			BF2b				
16	29 Jul	Fokker DVII	(f)	E2471	„	NW Wervicq	2010	OOC

Total: 6 destroyed, 10 out of control = 16.

Pilots: (a) 2/Lt R E Conder; (b) 2/Lt M P Scott; (c) 2/Lt R M Trevetham; (d) 2/Lt O H D Vickers; (e) Lt C R Richards; (f) Obs. Cpl C Hill.

CRITCHLEY Roland   2nd Lieutenant   22 SQN

From Lytham St Anne's, Lancashire, Critchley was living in Fairhaven, Blackpool when war came. He joined the RFC General List in April 1917 and was commissioned on 23 October. With 22 Squadron, his pilot, with whom he shared all his victories, was Sergeant E J Elton DCM MM. Confirmed in his rank on 8 February 1918 he was killed in action on 2 April in combat with Fokker Triplanes of Jasta 11 south of Albert. His pilot on this occasion was 2/Lt F Williams and they were flying A7286.

	1918			BF2b				
1	16 Mar	Albatros DV		B1162	22	Carvin	1030	DES
2	„	Albatros DV		„	„	„	1045	DES(F)
3	18 Mar	Albatros DV		„	„	Carvin	1030	DES
4	26 Mar	Pfalz DIII		„	„	E Albert	1245	DES
5	29 Mar	2-seater		„	„	Rosières	1530	DES
6	„	2-seater		„	„	Lihons	1535	DES
7	„	2-seater		„	„	Vauvillers	1540	DES

Total: 7 destroyed.

CROWE Henry George   Lieutenant   20 SQN

Born 11 June 1897, Donnybrook, Dublin. Interested in early flight he became secretary of a school aviation club formed at St Helen's School. Educated in England at Colwyn Bay and then Cheltenham Public School in 1911. Returned to Ireland in 1913 and to Trinity College, Dublin to study engineering, also joining the OTC. Commissioned into the 18th Reserve Battn. Royal Irish Regiment in Dublin in July 1916, 'Hal', as he was known, went to France in September and with the 6th Battn. saw action in the Battle of Messines and at Passchendaele in 1917. Crowe was attached to the RFC on 5 September but his application for pilot training was turned down due to the shortage of observers. Joined 20 Squadron in November. The award of a Military Cross came in April 1918, gazetted on 26 July 1918, noting many low level bomb raids and successful combats. He and Major J A Dennistoun were shot down by AA fire on 1 April 1918 but survived (A7240), while on the 12th, he and Lt D G Cooke were lucky to survive a Special Mission, returning with their BF2b badly shot about (C4605). When he left the Squadron he had been shot down six times in 11 days. Learnt to fly at the end of the war and posted to Ireland with 106 Squadron at Fermoy in April 1919, serving there for two years, during which time he took his Aero Certificate No.7911 dated 25 November 1920 and given a permanent commission in 1921. Remained in the RAF, serving with 39 Squadron in Iraq 1925-27 and 14 Squadron in Amman 1927-28 before attending the Staff College in 1929. Commanded 23 Squadron at Biggin Hill in 1933-35, and during the Abyssinian crisis in 1935, he reformed 74 Squadron on Malta, becoming its CO. He was a Wing Commander by 1936, and Group Captain in January 1940. Sent to India in 1942, he mostly commanded 223 Group at Peshawar. Retired with the rank of Air Commodore, CBE, 28 December 1945 and became a JP. Helped with the RAF Association and RAF Benevolent Fund on retiring to Thornton-le-Dale, North Yorkshire, where he died peacefully on 26 April 1983.

	1918			BF2b				
1	13 Jan	2-seater	(a)	B1122	20	N Moorslede	1425	DES
2	22 Jan	Albatros DV	(b)	A7256	,,	W Roulers	1110	OOC
3	,,	Albatros DV	(b)	,,	,,	S Moorslede	1115	DES(F)
4	28 Mar	Fokker DrI	(c)	B1191	,,	Albert	0830	OOC
5	21 Apr	Albatros DV	(b)	C4749	,,	N Wervicq	1100	OOC
6	3 May	Fokker DrI	(b)	,,	,,	SE Hollebeke	1720	DES(F)
7	,,	Albatros DV	(b)	,,	,,	SE Ypres	1730	OOC
8	8 May	Fokker DrI	(b)	,,	,,	Comines-Wervicq	1650	DES

Total: 4 destroyed, 4 out of control = 8.
Pilots: (a) 2/Lt T Colville-Jones; (b) 2/Lt D G Cooke; (c) 2/Lt E Lindup.

CUBBON Francis Richard   Captain   20 SQN

Born in London on 26 November 1892 but living in Poona, India, pre-war, Cubbon joined the Yorks and Lancs Regiment and also served with the 72nd Punjabis (Indian Army) and then the Royal Warwickshire Regiment. Seconded to the RFC in October 1916, be became a flying officer observer on 23 May 1917, with seniority from 8 April. Served with 20 Squadron from April, teaming up with Lt, later Captain, F J H Thayre to become a highly successful duo on FE2s. Both were killed in action on 9 June 1917 following a hit by AA fire (A6430). Cubbon was 24. Although a message was dropped by the Germans confirming their death, the men have no known graves. Cubbon received the MC and Bar, both gazetted on 18 July, the actual awards being made on 11 May and 16 May 1917.

	1917			FE2d				
1	24 Apr	Albatros DIII	(a)	A6392	20	W Ledeghem	0720	DES
2	,,	Albatros DIII	(a)	,,	,,	,,	0720	OOC
3	29 Apr	Albatros DIII		A6430	,,	E Menin	1705	DES(F)
4	,,	Albatros DIII		,,	,,	E Zillebeke	1710	DES(F)
5	1 May	Albatros C		,,	,,	Ploegsteert Wood	1120	DES(F)
6	3 May	Albatros DIII		,,	,,	Moorslede	1720	DES
7	,,	Albatros DIII		,,	,,	Westroosebeke	1725	DES
8	5 May	Albatros DIII		,,	,,	Poelcapelle	1700	DES(F)
9	,,	Albatros DIII		,,	,,	Houthem	1720	DES(F)
10	,,	Albatros DIII	(b)	,,	,,	,,	1730	DES
11	12 May	Albatros DIII		,,	,,	Tournai	0810	OOC
12	13 May	Albatros DIII		,,	,,	Gheluvelt	1045	DES
13	,,	Albatros DIII		,,	,,	,,	1045	DES
14	23 May	Albatros DIII		,,	,,	Zandvoorde	1510	DES
15	,,	Albatros DIII		,,	,,	NE Ploegsteert	1515	OOC
16	25 May	Albatros DIII		,,	,,	Reckem	0730	DES
17	,,	Albatros DIII		,,	,,	Wervicq	0900	DES(F)
18	27 May	Albatros C		,,	,,	Ypres	0730	DES
19	,,	Albatros DIII		,,	,,	,,	0735	DES
20	5 Jun	Albatros DIII		,,	,,	Houthem	1700	DES
21	7 Jun	Albatros DIII		,,	,,	Coucou	0810	DES

Total: 17 & 1 shared destroyed, 3 out of control = 21.
Pilots: (a) Lt R E Johnson; All the others with Capt F H Thayre; (b) shared with 2/Lts G C Heseltine/F G Kydd, A5747.

DAVIES Clive William   2nd Lieutenant   48 SQN

From Newgate Cross, London, born 21 September 1895. Pre-war he was a master stevedore and contractor with the family business in the Regent's Canal Docks and when war came he joined the 1/7th Battn. Royal Scots. Served with 48 Squadron from 12 June until 4 August 1918. Left the RAF on 5 February 1919.

	1918			BF2b				
1	12 Apr	Pfalz DIII	(a)	C4886	48	W Moreuil Wood	1040	DES
2	25 Jun	Fokker DVII	(a)	C786	„	Foucaucourt-Rosières	1145	OOC
3	27 Jun	Fokker DVII	(a)	C808	„	E Lamotte	1800	DES
4	24 Jul	Fokker DVII	(b)	F6094	„	Foucaucourt	0730	OOC
5	„	Fokker DVII	(b)	„	„	„	0730	OOC

Total: 2 destroyed, 3 out of control = 5.
Pilots: (a) 2/Lt F C Ransley; (b) Capt H A Oaks.

DAVIES Llewelyn Crichton   Lieutenant   22 & 105 SQNS

Formally with the 3rd Cameronians (2/Lt Scottish Rifles), Davies is believed to have come from Glasgow. Served in 22 Squadron 1917 where he was involved in five victories with his pilot, Captain C M Clement, although slightly wounded on 11 March. Received the MC and returned to Home Establishment. He then went to 105 Squadron in November but was severely injured in a crash in DH4 B5495 on 13 March 1918 and died three days later.

	1917			FE2b				
1	6 Apr	Albatros DIII	(a)		22	St Quentin	0800	DES
2	8 Apr	Albatros DIII	(b)	A5461	„	Regny	0700	DES
3	5 Jun	Albatros DV		„	„	NW Lesdains	0715	DES
4	„	Albatros DV		„	„	„	0715	OOC
				BF2b				
5	29 Jul	2-seater		A7174	„	Tortequesne	0650	DES(F)

Total: 2 & 2 shared destroyed, 1 out of control = 5.
(a) shared with Capt Gladstone/1AM H Friend, Lt J V Aspinall/2/Lt M K Parlee, Lt J F Day/2/Lt J K Campbell;
(b) shared with Capt L W Beale/Lt G G Bell, Lt J F Day/Lt Taylor, Lt Furlonger/Lt W C Lane, Lt H G Spearpoint/2/Lt J K Campbell.

DEIGHTON Ernest Arthur   Sergeant   20 SQN

Born at Masham, Yorkshire, 28 May 1889. Enlisted in the RFC on 15 March 1917 as a MT driver (67051), his address being given as Cheltenham, Glos. Volunteered for observer duties with the rank of Corporal Mechanic. Flew with Captain W Beaver, and together they were forced down on 13 June, in C889, by an Albatros DV but unharmed. Also flew with Lts Capel, Lindup and Weston. Slightly injured on 15 July, Deighton returned to the UK. The award of the DCM was made on 7 June 1918, gazetted on 3 October. Died 5 December 1957, whilst residing in Bournemouth, Hampshire.

	1918			BF2b				
1	11 Apr	2-seater	(a)	C4616	20	S Armentières	1515	DES
2	9 May	Albatros DV	(b)	C817	„	E Warneton-Comines	1330	DES
3	16 May	Albatros DV	(c)	C4763	„	Wervicq	1830	DES
4	19 May	Pfalz DIII	(c)	„	„	Armentières	1035	OOC
5	„	Pfalz DIII	(c)	„	„	Nr Armentières	1035	DES(F)
6	„	Pfalz DIII	(c)	„	„	N Frelinghien	1040	DES
7	27 May	Albatros DV	(b)	C889	„	NE Armentières	1125	DES(F)
8	„	Fokker DrI	(b)	„	„	„	1130	OOC
9	„	Fokker DrI	(b)	„	„	„	1135	DES
10	29 May	Fokker DrI	(b)	„	„	Bac St Maur	1825	DES
11	31 May	Pfalz DIII	(d)	C850	„	S Armentières	1850	DES
12	13 Jun	Albatros DV	(b)	C889	„	NW Armentières	0800	OOC
13	17 Jun	Pfalz DIII	(a)	C4604	„	N Comines	0740	OOC
14	„	Pfalz DIII	(a)	„	„	NE Gheluvelt	0755	DES
15	23 Jun	Pfalz DIII	(a)	„	„	Laventie	0930	DES

Total: 11 destroyed, 4 out of control = 15.
Pilots: (a) Lt L H T Capel; (b) Capt W Beaver; (c) Lt D J Weston; (d) Lt E H Lindup.

DIGBY-WORSLEY Bruce   2nd Lieutenant   88 SQN

Born Tunbridge Wells, Kent, 8 February 1896. A married man, he served in the ranks of the 5th Gloucester Regiment, 16th Middlesex Regiment and the 5th King's Own Surrey Borderers between September 1914 and August 1917, going to France in May 1915. Seconded to the RFC General List, he was commissioned on 3 January 1918 and returned to France in April, assigned to 88 Squadron. All victories with Lt K B Conn except numbers 5 through 11, which were with Lt C Findlay.

	1918			BF2b				
1	5 Jun	Albatros DV		C787	88	Messines	2015	DES
2	„	Albatros DV		„	„	„	2015	DES
3	1 Jul	Fokker DVII		„	„	W Westroosbeke	1945	DES(F)
4	„	Fokker DVII		„	„	„	1945	OOC
5	30 Jul	Pfalz DIII		C4061	„	Richebourg	1035	OOC
6	6 Aug	Fokker DVII		„	„	Ploegsteert	1045	DES(F)
7	11 Aug	Fokker DVII		„	„	Clery	1135	OOC
8	„	Fokker DVII		„	„	„	1135	OOC
9	„	Fokker DVII		„	„	Mericourt	1700	DES(F)
10	„	Fokker DVII		„	„	„	1700	OOC
11	12 Aug	Fokker DVII		„	„	E Biaches	1005	DES
12	5 Sep	Fokker DVII		E2216	„	NE Armentières	1845	OOC
13	16 Sep	Fokker DVII		„	„	NE Harbourdin A/F	1750	DES
14	„	Fokker DVII		„	„	„	1750	DES
15	20 Sep	Fokker DVII		„	„	Quesnoy	0750	OOC
16	„	Fokker DVII	(a)	„	„	SE Quesnoy	0755	DES

Total: 8 & 1 shared destroyed, 7 out of control = 16.
(a) shared with Capt E C Johnston/Lt W I N Grant, Lt C R Poole/Sgt C Hill.

DOUGLAS Percy   2nd Lieutenant   11 SQN

From Great Sutton, Chester, Douglas was a second lieutenant with the Army Service Corps prior to joining the RFC in August 1917. Flew with 11 Squadron, and returned home on 26 March 1918. Was with the School of Air Gunnery in May and No.4 TDS in July. Left the RAF on 11 April 1919. All his victories were scored with Second Lieutenant J S Chick, five in one running fight on 12 March.

	1918		BF2b				
1	12 Mar	2-seater	C4847	11	S Cambrai	1115	OOC
2	„	Fokker DrI	„	„	S Caudry	1145	OOC
3	„	Fokker DrI	„	„	Caudry	1150	OOC
4	„	Fokker DrI	„	„	„	1155	OOC
5	„	Fokker DrI	„	„	„	1155	OOC
6	13 Mar	Albatros DV	„	„	S Cambrai	1345	OOC
7	15 Mar	Albatros DV	A7153	„	Rumilly	1115	OOC
8	„	Albatros DV	„	„	„	1115	DES(F)

Total: 1 destroyed, 7 out of control = 8.

DRAISEY Arthur Stuart   Lieutenant   20 SQN

From Brentford, Middlesex, born 21 November 1899, he was a junior clerk at Euston Railway Station, London, between 1915-17. Joined the RFC as an observer and flew with 20 Squadron. All his victories were scored with Lieutenant F G Harlock. Awarded the Russian Order of St Stanislas, 2nd Class with Swords.

	1918		BF2b				
1	1 Jul	Fokker DrI	C873	20	N Tourcoing	1850	OOC
2	13 Aug	Fokker DVII	C4718	„	Quesnoy	1915	DES
3	20 Sep	Fokker DVII	E2258	„	Mesnil	1000	DES(F)

4	„	Fokker DVII		„	„	„	1015	DES
5	25 Sep	Fokker DVII		E2340	„	Magny	1820	DES
6	„	Fokker DVII		„	„	Lehaucourt	1021	DES
7	27 Sep	Fokker DVII		E2338	„	NE Marcy	1030	DES

Total: 6 destroyed, 1 out of control = 7.

EASTON H E 2nd Lieutenant 20 SQN

From Brondesbury Park, north-west London. Served with the 9th Battn. of the London Regiment before joining the RFC. Flew with 20 Squadron, which he joined on 8 March 1918; injured 26 March 1918. Left the service on 19 January 1919. All victories scored while flying with Wilfred Beaver.

	1918		BF2b					
1	3 Jan	Albatros DV	B883	20	NE Moorslede	1545	DES
2	6 Jan	Albatros C	„	„	Houthulst Forest	1210	OOC
3	3 Feb	Albatros DV	B1156	„	Roulers-Menin	1245	DES(F)
4	4 Feb	Albatros DV		„	Roulers	1415	OOC
5	5 Feb	Albatros DV	B1156	„	N Staden	1130	OOC
6	„	Albatros DV	„	„	„	1130	OOC
7	16 Feb	2-seater	C4826	„	Menin	1140	OOC
8	23 Mar	Albatros DV	B1114	„	Menin-S Roncq	1220	DES

Total: 3 destroyed, 5 out of control = 8.

EDWARDS Harold Leslie 2nd Lieutenant 20 SQN

Born Franktown, Ontario, Canada, 28 April 1893, he became a chauffeur. Enlisted in the 130th Battn, CEF, 16 December 1915 and served in France and Belgium with the 38th Battn. before being wounded on 8 April 1917. Awarded the Military Medal 26 May. Discharged from CEF 1 June 1918, he transferred to the RAF and joined 20 Squadron on 27 July 1918, but was wounded (a bullet in the lungs) on 21 October. Of his 21 victories, 19 were scored in one month, or to be exact, on nine days that month, including four triples and two doubles. Awarded the DFC. After the war he became a car salesman. Died in Toronto 15 June 1951.

	1918			BF2b				
1	30 Jul	Fokker DVII	(a)	D7915	20	NE Bailleul	1930	DES(F)
2	21 Aug	Fokker DVII	(b)	E2158	„	N Menin	1920	DES
3	5 Sep	Fokker DVII	(c)	E2467	„	SE Cambrai	1520	DES
4	6 Sep	Fokker DVII	(c)	E2181	„	St Quentin	0845	DES(F)
5	„	Fokker DVII	(c)	„	„	„	0845	DES(F)
6	7 Sep	Fokker DVII	(c)	„	„	NE St Quentin	1810	DES
7	15 Sep	Fokker DVII	(d)	E2154	„	St Quentin	1120	DES
8	„	Fokker DVII	(d)	„	„	„	1120	OOC
9	16 Sep	Fokker DVII	(d)	„	„	NE St Quentin	0815	DES
10	„	Fokker DVII	(d)	„	„	NW St Quentin	0820	DES
11	„	Fokker DVII	(d)	„	„	St Quentin	0821	DES
12	23 Sep	Fokker DVII	(e)	E2213	„	NE St Quentin	1815	DES
13	„	Fokker DVII	(e)	„	„	„	1818	DES(F)
14	„	Fokker DVII	(e)	„	„	„	1820	OOC
15	24 Sep	Fokker DVII	(f)	E2536	„	SE St Quentin	1600	DES
16	25 Sep	Fokker DVII	(f)	„	„	NE St Quentin	1815	DES
17	„	Fokker DVII	(f)	„	„	„	1815	DES(F)
18	„	Fokker DVII	(f)	„	„	E Bellenglise	1820	DES
19	29 Sep	Fokker DVII	(f)	„	„	N St Quentin	1020	OOC
20	„	Fokker DVII	(f)	„	„	„	1025	DES
21	„	Fokker DVII	(f)	„	„	„	1025	DES

Total: 17 & 1 shared destroyed, 3 out of control = 21.
Pilots: (a) Lt P T Iaccaci; (b) Lt J H Colbert; (c) Capt H P Lale; (d) Lt W M Thomson; (e) Lt N S Boulton; (f) Capt G H Hooper. Victory No.10 was shared with Lts A R Strachan/D M Calderwood, C951.

ELDON Horace George   Lieutenant   88 SQN

From Dorset, born 6 April 1897. A laboratory assistant and a married man by 1918, he had joined the London Regiment and went to France on 17 May 1917 having been commissioned on 28 March. Transferred to the RFC in March 1918 and left 88 Squadron in 1919.

	1918			BF2b				
1	5 Sep	Fokker DVII	(a)	C821	88	N Douai	1900	OOC
2	„	Fokker DVII	(a)	„	„	Armentières	1901	DES(F)
3	6 Sep	Fokker DVII	(a)	„	„	N Douai	1845	OOC
4	24 Sep	Fokker DVII	(a)	„	„	Harbourdin	1010	DES(F)
5	4 Oct	Fokker DVII	(b)	„	„	SE Lille	1745	DES

Total: 3 destroyed, 2 out of control = 5.
Pilots: (a) Capt A Hepburn; (b) Lt I G Fleming.

ELLIOTT Thomas   2nd Lieutenant   62 SQN

From Gateshead, Co. Durham, born 17 March 1898, pre-war he was a clerk with Raine & Co, in Newcastle till he joined the colours in April 1916. Joined 62 Squadron on 12 March 1918 and often flew with Captain G E Gibbons. Was with No.1 School of Air Gunnery in late 1918 and left the service on 21 February 1919.

	1918			BF2b				
1	22 May	LVG C	(a)	C4633	62	NW Merville	0800	DES
2	1 Aug	EA	(b)		„	W Douai		OOC
3	3 Aug	Pfalz DIII	(b)		„	N Merville		OOC
4	13 Aug	2-seater	(b)	E2457	„	Bullecourt	1025	DES
5	22 Aug	Fokker DVII	(b)	„	„	W Pronville	0740	DES
6	„	Fokker DVII	(b)	„	„	„	0741	DES(F)
7	1 Sep	Fokker DVII	(c)	F2218	„	E Cambrai	1330	DES(F)
8	3 Sep	Fokker DVII	(b)	E2457	„	N Cambrai	1845	OOC
9	„	Fokker DVII	(b)	„	„	„	1845	OOC
10	4 Sep	Fokker DVII	(b)	„	„	Abancourt-N Cambrai	0930	DES
11	„	Fokker DVII	(b)	„	„	N Cambrai	0932	OOC

Total: 6 destroyed, 5 out of control = 11.
Pilots: (a) 2/Lt W K Swayze; (b) Capt G E Gibbons; (c) Lt C Allday.

FINLAY Garfield   Lieutenant   1 AFC SQN

Born Glebe, Sydney, Australia, 7 September 1893, he also lived in West Perth, Western Australia and became a wool-classer pre-war. Joined the Australian Light Horse on 21 January 1915; sergeant, October 1915, and commissioned in March 1917. Transferred to the Australian Flying Corps in July. Served in Palestine with 1 AFC Squadron and was awarded the DFC, gazetted 8 February 1919, the citation noting an action on 22 August 1918 in company with his pilot Lt A R Brown, bringing down a two-seater inside Allied lines. Began pilot training in October 1918. In WW2 was a Wing Commander in the RAAF.

	1917			RE8				
1	29 Nov	Albatros DIII	(a)		1	SW Samaria	0830	OOC
	1918			BF2b				
2	27 Mar	AEG C	(b)		„	Kissir, S Amman	0710	FTL/DES
3	3 May	2-seater	(c)	B1149	„	SW Suweilah	0700	FTL/DES
4	9 May	Rumpler C	(d)	C4623	„	Jenin A/F	1515	FTL/DES
5	27 Jun	AEG C	(e)	B1149	„	El Kutrani	0645	DES
6	28 Jun	Albatros DV	(f)	„	„	Amman	0630	DES(F)
—	3 Jul	AEG C	(e)		„	Lubban		dam
7	28 Jul	Rumpler C	(g)	B1284	„	N Wadi Fareh	1200	FTL/DES
8	22 Aug	LVG C	(e)		„	Ramleh	1315	CAPT

Total: 3 & 3 shared destroyed, 1 captured, 1 out of control = 8.
Pilots: (a) Lt R A Austin; (b) Lt J M Walker and shared with Capt D W Rutherford/Lt J McElligott; (c) Lt A R Brown and shared with Lt G V Oxenham/Lt H A Leach, B1225; (d) Lt G C Peters; (e) Lt A R Brown; (f) Lt S A Nunan; (g) Brown and shared with Lt C S Paul/Lt W J A Weir.

FLETCHER Ronald Malcolm   2nd Lieutenant   22 SQN

Born 22 February 1899. Attached to the RAF from the 30th Training Reserve Battn. in November 1917, he joined 22 Squadron. As sergeant (P22398) Fletcher, won the DFM, gazetted on 2 November 1918, the citation noting seven victories since 21 May. All victories in company with his pilot Lieutenant S F H 'Siffy' Thompson MC DFC. Became a flight cadet in 1918 and commissioned in October, but left the service on 28 February 1919. In WW2 he held a RAFVR wartime commission, for service with the Air Training Corps, from March 1941.

	1918		BF2b				
1	16 May	Pfalz DIII	B1213	22	Douai	1005	DES
2	"	Pfalz DIII	"	"	"	1005	DES
3	"	Pfalz DIII	"	"	"	1015	DES
4	21 May	Pfalz DIII	"	"	SW Vitry	1015	DES
5	"	Pfalz DIII	"	"	"	1015	OOC
6	22 May	Albatros DV	"	"	Hancourt	1030	DES
7	25 May	Albatros DV	"	"	W Carvin	1130	DES(F)
8	1 Jun	Albatros C	C929	"	Erquinghem	1915	DES
9	"	Albatros DV	"	"	"	1915	DES
10	2 Jun	Pfalz DIII	"	"	NE Lens	1030	DES(F)
11	"	Pfalz DIII	"	"	"	1030	OOC
12	5 Jun	Albatros DV	"	"	S Laventie	1030	DES
13	"	Albatros DV	"	"	"	1030	DES
14	"	Pfalz DIII	"	"	NE La Bassée	1915	OOC
15	23 Jun	Pfalz DIII	"	"	La Bassée	2045	OOC
16	"	Pfalz DIII	"	"	"	2045	OOC
17	8 Aug	Fokker DrI	E2477	"	Dechy	1040	DES
18	13 Aug	Fokker DrI		"	Arras-Cambrai Rd	1130	DES
19	"	Fokker DVII		"	SE Douai	1135	OOC
20	"	Fokker DVII		"	"	1140	DES
21	27 Aug	Fokker DVII	E2477	"	Senlemont	1400	OOC
22	"	Fokker DVII	"	"	"	1400	OOC
23	2 Sep	Fokker DVII	"	"	Haynecourt	1115	DES
24	5 Sep	Fokker DVII	E2243	"	Douai	1700	DES(F)
25	"	Fokker DVII	"	"	"	1700	OOC
26	24 Sep	Fokker DVII	"	"	Cambrai	1700	OOC

Total: 16 destroyed, 10 out of control = 26.

FYSH Wilmot Hudson   Lieutenant   67 & 1 AFC SQNS

Born Tasmania, 7 January 1895. A wool-classer pre-war, he joined the 3rd Light Horse Regiment and served at Gallipoli. In July 1916 he was with the Machine Gun Section, and commissioned in January 1917. Transferred to the Australian Flying Corps in Palestine on 6 July and with 1 AFC received the DFC, gazetted 8 February 1919. Immediately after the war he helped survey the route for the Ross-Smith brothers' flights and the following year became a founder of QANTAS Airlines. Flew on air mail routes over Queensland in 1922, and by the 1930's had become Managing Director of Qantas in Brisbane and later became Chairman of Quantas Empire Airways Ltd. Was a AFRAeS and FRGS (Aust); Knighted KBE in 1953. President of IATA 1960-61 and in later life an author, living in Sydney. Died 6 April 1974.

	1918			BF2b				
1	23 Jan	Albatros DV	(a)	A7237	1	SE Bireh	0800	OOC
2	3 Aug	Albatros C	(b)	B1223	"	NE Ez Duba	1210	DES
3	31 Aug	LVG C	(c)	C4623	"	Rantieh	1430	CAPT

| 4 | „ | LVG C | (c) | „ | „ | E Kalkilieh | 1440 | DES |
| 5 | 14 Sep | Rumpler C | (d) | „ | „ | E Jenin | 1130 | FTL/DES |

Total: 1 & 2 shared destroyed, 1 captured, 1 out of control = 5.

Pilots: (a) Capt S W Addison; (b) Lt P J McGinness and shared with Lt E P Kenny/Lt L W Sutherland, C4626; (c) Lt McGinness; (d) McGinness and shared with Lt D R Dowling/Lt E A Mulford, B1223.

GASS Charles George   Lieutenant   22 SQN

From Chelsea, London, born in April 1898. Leaving school he joined the 2/24th London Regiment in France as a sergeant, and commissioned into the 17th Battn. in October 1917. Transferred to the RFC late 1917 and was posted to 22 Squadron on 26 March 1918, where he teamed up with Lt Alfred Atkey. Awarded the MC in May 1918 and returned to UK in August. On one occasion their top wing was hit by shrapnel and Gass had to climb out on one of the lower wings to balance the machine, Atkey having only rudder and elevator control. Assigned to pilot training, the war ended before this was achieved. He left the service on 11 April 1919. With 39 victories, in company with his various pilots, he was the top scoring gunner/observer in WW1. In his latter years he lived in south London.

	1918			BF2b				
1	22 Apr	Albatros DV	(a)	B1136	22	E Merville	0840	OOC
2	7 May	D	(b)	B1164	„	E Arras	1845	DES(F)
3	„	D	(b)	„	„	„	1845	DES(F)
4	„	D	(b)	„	„	„	1845	DES
5	„	D	(b)	„	„	„	1850	DES
6	„	D	(b)	„	„	„	1855	DES
7	8 May	DFW C	(c)	B1253	„	Cuincy, NW Douai	1845	DES
8	9 May	D	(b)	„	„	Lille	0940	DES(F)
9	„	D	(b)	„	„	„	0940	OOC
10	„	D	(b)	„	„	„	0940	OOC
11	„	Pfalz DIII	(b)	„	„	N Douai	1840	DES
12	„	Pfalz DIII	(b)	„	„	„	1840	DES(F)
13	15 May	Pfalz DIII	(b)	„	„	NW Lille	1020	OOC
14	„	Pfalz DIII	(b)	„	„	„	1020	OOC
15	19 May	Albatros C	(b)	C4747	„	S Douai	1040	DES
16	„	LVG C	(b)	„	„	W Lille	1845	OOC
17	„	LVG C	(b)	„	„	„	1845	OOC
18	20 May	Halberstadt C	(b)	„	„	Lille-Armentières	1045	OOC
19	„	Halberstadt C	(b)	„	„	„	1100	OOC
20	„	Halberstadt C	(b)	„	„	„	1115	OOC
21	22 May	Albatros DV	(b)	B1253	„	SE Arras	1030	DES
22	„	DFW C	(b)	„	„	Armentières-Merville	1915	OOC
23	27 May	Pfalz DIII	(b)	„	„	NE Lens	2000	DES
24	„	Pfalz DIII	(b)	„	„	Meurchin	2000	OOC
25	„	Pfalz DIII	(b)	„	„	NE Lens	2000	OOC
26	30 May	Pfalz DIII	(b)	„	„	Armentières	1940	DES
27	„	Pfalz DIII	(b)	„	„	S Armentières	1942	OOC
28	31 May	Pfalz DIII	(b)	„	„	Armentières	1030	OOC
29	„	Pfalz DIII	(b)	„	„	„	1030	OOC
30	2 Jun	2-seater	(b)	„	„	NE Lens	1015	OOC
31	„	2-seater	(b)	„	„	„	1015	OOC
32	5 Jun	Halberstadt C	(d)	C961	„	S Laventie	1030	DES
33	„	Albatros DV	(d)	„	„	„	1030	OOC
34	26 Jul	Fokker DrI	(a)	D7896	„	Laventie	0900	OOC
35	8 Aug	Albatros DV	(c)	E2454	„	Douai	1030	OOC
36	„	Pfalz DIII	(e)	„		NE Vitry	1040	DES(F)
37	10 Aug	Fokker DVII	(c)	„	„	SW Péronne	1810	DES
38	„	Fokker DVII	(c)	„	„	„	1810	DES
39	13 Aug	Fokker DVII	(c)	„	„	Auberchicourt	1120	OOC

Total: 16 & 1 shared destroyed, 22 out of control = 39.
Pilots: (a) Lt S F H Thompson; (b) Lt A C Atkey; (c) Lt J E Gurdon; (d) Lt E C Bromley; (e) Lt Gurdon and shared with Capt W F J Harvey/Capt D E Waight, 2466.

GILROY Eric Charlton   Lieutenant   11 SQN

Born Clinton, Ontario, Canada, on 21 August 1897, his parents died when he was a child and was brought up by his sister. Enlisted into the 3rd Canadian Mounted Rifles on 31 December 1914 and served in France 1915-16 before transferring to the RFC in February 1917. Discharged from CEF 12 August on being commissioned in the Imperial Army. Joined 11 Squadron on 21 November 1917, remaining until being hospitalized on 20 July 1918. Thought to have died in the 1930s.

	1918			BF2b				
1	15 Mar	Albatros DV	(a)	C4845	11	Rumilly	1115	OOC
2	9 May	Pfalz DIII	(b)	„	„	S Albert	1220	OOC
3	„	Pfalz DIII	(b)	„	„	„	1220	OOC
4	15 May	2-seater	(b)	C797	„	Brebières	0600	DES(F)
5	„	Fokker DrI	(b)	„	„	SE Albert	1720	DES
6	„	Pfalz DIII	(b)	„	„	„	1721	DES
7	„	Fokker DrI	(b)	„	„	„	1722	OOC

Total: 3 destroyed, 4 out of control = 7.
Pilots: (a) Capt L R Wren; (b) Lt J S Chick.

GILSON William Thompson   Lieutenant   20 SQN

From south-west London, born 9 September 1896, he was educated at King's College, Wimbledon, between 1908-10, and then at the Collge Jean d'Arc, Lille, France, 1912-13. Served initially with the Royal Naval Air Service. Commissioned 29 October 1916 and became a flying officer observer with the RFC on 19 December 1917 by which time he was in France with 20 Squadron. Left the service on 10 October 1919.

	1916			FE2d				
1	16 Nov	Albatros DII	(a)	A29	20	Abeele	1100	OOC
2	„	Albatros DII	(a)	„	„	„	1130	OOC
	1917							
3	25 Jan	Halberstadt D	(b)	A32	„	Menin	1510	DES
4	26 Jan	Albatros DII	(c)	A31	„	Westroosbeke	1550	DES
5	26 May	Albatros DIII	(d)	A6431	„	Comines-Quesnoy	1035	DES

Total: 3 destroyed, 2 out of control = 5.
Pilots: (a) Capt R S Maxwell; (b) Lt T C H Lucas; (c) Lt J K Stead; (d) Lt D C Cunnell.

GLADMAN Cyril William   Lieutenant   11 SQN

From Berkhampsted, Herts, born 22 April 1897, he was working in Chelmsford as an electrical engineer pre-war. Commissioned into the 8th Royal West Surrey Regiment in June 1917 prior to joining the RFC. Served with 11 Squadron from 19 March 1918, but was wounded in action 14 August 1918 flying with Lt E S Coler, in Bristol Fighter D7912, being forced to land after combat with an enemy fighter. All victories shared with Eugene Coler in just two air fights. Left the service on 23 April 1919.

	1918			BF2b				
1	9 May	Pfalz DIII		C792	11	Albert-Comines	1220	OOC
2	„	Pfalz DIII		„	„	„	1220	OOC
3	„	Pfalz DIII		„	„	„	1220	OOC
4	13 Aug	Fokker DVII		D7912	„	Péronne	0840	DES(F)
5	„	Fokker DVII		„	„	„	0840	OOC
6	„	Fokker DVII		„	„	„	0841	OOC

| 7 | „ | Fokker DVII | „ | „ | „ | 0842 | DES(F) |
| 8 | „ | Fokker DVII | „ | „ | „ | 0842 | DES(F) |

Total: 3 destroyed, 5 out of control = 8.

GODFREY Frank   Captain   20 SQN

From Godalming, Surrey, born 16 August 1889, he had been an accountant and assistant secretary to Alderman E Bridger JP in Godalming between 1902-14. After serving with the 19th Battn. of the Middlesex Regiment (2nd Public Works Pioneers), he was seconded to the RFC. Flew with 20 Squadron from 3 March 1918, with whom he received the DFC, gazetted on 3 August 1918, the citation mentioning eight victories. All claims in company with Captain T P Middleton. Returned to Home Establishment on 22 September 1918, he left the service on 25 April 1919.

	1918			BF2b				
1	17 Apr	Albatros DV		C4699	20	SE Hazebrouck	1400	DES
2	„	Albatros DV		„	„	„	1400	OOC
3	3 May	Albatros DV		„	„	S Ploegsteert Wood	1055	DES
4	„	Albatros DV		„	„	Le Touquet	1055	OOC
5	8 May	Albatros DV		„	„	SE Bailleul	0845	DES
6	„	Fokker DrI		„	„	E Dranoutre	0930	DES
7	8 Jun	Pfalz DIII		C951	„	SE Comines	1720	DES
8	„	Pfalz DIII		„	„	„	1725	DES
9	12 Jun	Albatros DV		„	„	E Zillebeke Lake	1910	DES(F)
10	30 Jun	Fokker DrI		„	„	E Comines	0730	DES
11	„	Pfalz DIII		„	„	W Wervicq	0750	DES
12	29 Jul	Fokker DVII		„	„	S Gheluwe	1950	DES

Total: 10 destroyed, 2 out of control = 12.

GORDON John Rutherford   Lieutenant   62 SQN

Born 18 June 1895, in Gilberton, South Australia, of a distinguished political family. Served with the 10th Battn. AIF at Gallipoli, first as a sergeant, then commissioned on 4 August 1915. Invalided out of the AIF following typhoid and joined the AFC in Australia. Began pilot training but failed, so became an observer. Posted to 62 Squadron on 25 December 1917 and went to France on 20 January 1918. Often flying with Captain W E Staton MC DFC, with whom he scored all his victories, he was awarded the Military Cross. This appeared in the London Gazette on 22 June 1918, the citation noting five victories and numerous ground attack sorties. Returned to HE on 17 June and began pilot training again in July, transferring back to the AFC on October. Became a pilot post-war and stayed in the RAAF; in WW2 he was a Wing Commander. Died 11 December 1978.

	1918			BF2b				
1	21 Mar	Fokker DrI			62			DES(F)
2	26 Mar	EA			„			DES
3	„	EA			„			DES
4	„	EA			„			OOC
5	1 Apr	Albatros DV		C4619	„	Bouchoir	1700	OOC
6	21 Apr	Fokker DrI	(a)		„	SE Estaires	0945	DES
7	3 May	Albatros DV		C4619	„	S Armentières	1130	DES
8	„	2-seater		„	„	SE Ploegsteert Wood	1140	DES
9	22 May	LVG C		C874	„	N Laventie	0800	DES
10	29 May	LVG C		„	„	Aubigny	1915	OOC
11	30 May	2-seater		„	„	Arras-Cambrai	1345	OOC
12	2 Jun	Fokker DrI		„	„	S Pozières	1945	DES
13	5 Jun	Pfalz DIII		„	„	Douai	1645	DES(F)
14	„	Pfalz DIII		„	„	NW Douai	1650	DES
15	8 Jun	Pfalz DIII		„	„	SE Bray	1745	OOC

Total: 9 & 1 shared destroyed, 5 out of control = 15.
(a) shared with Capt T L Purdom/2/Lt P V G Chambers.

GORDON-BENNETT Richard   Lieutenant   20 SQN

From London, born 2 March 1900, he lived in Westminster, and was educated at St.George's College, Weybridge. Commissioned into the Household Battn. and transferred to the RFC in February 1918. Operating with 20 Squadron, he was wounded in action on 25 September 1918. Returned to hospital in England in October and left the service on 27 February 1919.

	1918			BF2b				
1	29 Jul	Fokker DVII	(a)	E2452	20	Gheluwe	1955	OOC
2	3 Sep	Pfalz DIII	(b)	D7915	„	Havrincourt Wood	1750	DES
3	„	Pfalz DIII	(b)	„	„	„	1750	OOC
4	24 Sep	Fokker DVII	(a)	E2252	„	W Busigny	1600	OOC
5	25 Sep	Fokker DVII	(a)	„	„	NE St Quentin	1820	DES(F)

Total: 2 destroyed, 3 out of control = 5.
Pilots: (a) Lt T C Traill; (b) 1/Lt C R Oberst USAS.

GRANT Walter Irving Newby   Lieutenant   88 SQN

An Australian and former bank clerk, Grant was born on 28 August 1899. Joined the RFC 23 January 1918 and was commissioned on 14 August. He was the son of Lt Col W F N Grant, 4th (Reserve) Northamptonshire Regiment, which was based at Crowborough in 1918.

	1918			BF2b				
1	4 Sep	Fokker DVII	(a)	C4867	88	Seclin	0900	DES(F)
2	„	Fokker DVII	(a)	„	„	Phalempin	0915	OOC
3	„	Fokker DrI	(a)	„	„	Provin	0930	OOC
4	20 Sep	Fokker DVII	(b)		„	SE Quesnoy	0755	DES
5	23 Oct	Fokker DVII	(c)	E2481	„	Beclers	1710	DES
6	„	Fokker DVII	(c)	„	„	„	1711	DES(F)
7	30 Oct	Fokker DVII	(d)	E2412	„	Beclers	0855	DES(F)

Total: 4 & 1 shared destroyed, 2 out of control = 7.
Pilots: (a) Capt E C Johnston; (b) Lt K B Conn and shared with Capt E C Johnston/2/Lt B Digby-Worsley E2216 and Lt C R Poole/Sgt C Hill C922; (c) Lt A Williamson; (d) Lt A H Berg.

GRIFFITH Hugh Bradford   Captain   20, 11, 48 SQNS

A Canadian from Montreal, born 20 March 1893, the son of a doctor, Griffith was an Arts student at McGill University in 1914. Left to join No.6 Canadian Field Ambulance, serving with them in France from September 1915 to September 1916. Commissioned into the RFC in October 1916, he served his probation with 20 Squadron, helping Captain Norman to perfect his Norman Gunsight. Back in England he then went to 11 Squadron from 9 November but scored no victories. Transferred to 48 Squadron on 17 March 1917, although he later said he went to 48 after its débâcle with Jasta 11. He remained with this unit until 30 April. Was with No.1 School of Aerial Gunnery, Hythe, as assistant Wing instructor from May 1917 and became temporary captain on 1 January 1918. Returned to Canada in December to instruct at No.4 SMA in Toronto and then Texas. Demobilised on 1 April 1919, having been Mentioned for Valuable Service. After WW1 he sold life insurance and died in April 1974.

	1917			BF2a				
1	5 Apr	Albatros DIII	(a)	A3325	48	Douai	1000	OOC
2	9 Apr	2-seater	(b)	„	„	Lens	am	DES
3	„	Albatros C	(b)	„	„	„	am	OOC
4	13 Apr	Albatros DIII	(c)	„	„	Vitry-en-Artois	pm	DES
5	„	Albatros DIII	(c)	„	„	„	pm	OOC

Total: 2 destroyed, 3 out of control = 5.
Pilots: (a) Lt P Pike; (b) Capt A M Wilkinson; (c) Lt J W Warren.

HALL John Herbert   Sergeant   22 SQN

As Sergeant Mechanic (No.93913) volunteered for observer duties with 22 Squadron. In January 1919 he received the Decoration Militaire from the Belgian Government. The Albatros DVa (7265/17) brought down in Allied lines on 9 July became G/1/10, and was from MFJ III.

	1918			BF2b				
1	5 Jun	Albatros DV	(a)	A7243	22	S Laventie	1030	OOC
2	„	Pfalz DIII	(a)	„	„	Fromilly	1915	DES(F)
3	9 Jul	Albatros DV	(b)	D7896	„	N La Bassée	1100	DES
4	„	Albatros DV	(b)	„	„	W Steenwerck	1130	CAPT
5	27 Aug	Fokker DVII	(b)		„	Senlemont	1400	OOC

Total: 2 destroyed, 1 captured, 2 out of control = 5.
Pilots: (a) Lt J E Gurdon; (b) Lt T W Martin.

HARDCASTLE Ernest   Lieutenant   20 SQN

From Dudley Hill, Bradford, born 31 December 1898, and pre-war worked for the Bradford Chamber of Commerce. Hardcastle, aged 19, transferred from the King's Own Yorkshire Light Infantry to the RFC in August 1917. Sailed to France on 18 April 1918 and posted to 20 Squadron. He eventually teamed up with Victor Groom. He was slightly injured in a crash on 8 July, going to No.9 VAD at St Omer, but returned to the Squadron. Hospitalized in September, he received the DFC, gazetted 2 November 1918. This referred to two actions, both with Victor Groom, one against 25 enemy aircraft in which they shot down two, and a second against 12 when they again claimed two kills. Left the service on 13 February 1919. Served in the RAF 1940-45, at the night flying OTU at Cranfield, near Bedford. Retired to Bexhill, Sussex, in 1971, but died in November 1973.

	1918			BF2b				
1	8 May	Fokker DrI	(a)		20	NW Wervicq	1645	DES(F)
2	14 May	Albatros DV	(a)	C4764	„	E Zillebeke Lake	1845	DES
3	„	2-seater	(a)	„	„	SW Polygon Wood	1850	DES
4	17 May	Albatros DV	(b)		„	E Armentières	1715	OOC
5	19 May	Pfalz DIII	(a)		„	S Calonne	1030	OOC
6	31 May	Pfalz DIII	(c)		„	N Comines	1850	OOC
7	1 Jun	Pfalz DIII	(a)	C4764	„	NW Comines	0630	DES
8	„	Pfalz DIII	(a)	„	„	„	0630	DES
9	17 Jun	Pfalz DIII	(d)	C4672	„	NW Armentières	0745	DES
10	30 Jun	Fokker DVII	(e)	A8716	„	NW Menin	0730	DES
11	30 Jul	Fokker DVII	(a)	D7939	„	Bailleul	1930	DES(F)
12	„	Fokker DVII	(a)	„	„	„	1930	DES(F)

Total: 9 destroyed, 3 out of control = 12.
Pilots: (a) Lt V E Groom; (b) Capt D G Cooke; (c) Lt A T Iaccaci; (d) Lt L M Price; (e) Capt H P Lale.

HARRIES Thomas Montagu   Lieutenant   45, 24 SQNS

(Observer with six victories, then an SE5 pilot gaining four more. See *Above the Trenches* for full details.)

HAYWARD George Searle Lomax   2nd Lieutenant   22 SQN

Initially served in the Royal West Kent Regiment, becoming a lance corporal, and later commissioned second lieutenant on 28 September 1916. Seconded to the RFC, he flew with 22 Squadron and won the Military Cross. This was gazetted on 26 July 1918, noting five victories. Often flew with Captain Weare.

	1917			BF2b				
1	29 Nov	2-seater	(a)		22	Lambersart, NW Lille	1125	DES
2	6 Dec	Albatros DV	(a)	„	„	Habourdin	1115	OOC

	1918							
3	6 Mar	Albatros DV	(b)	B1162	„	Douai	1400	OOC
4	„	Albatros DV	(b)	„	„	SE Douai	1410	DES
5	11 Mar	Albatros DV	(b)	B1152	„	Vendville-Faches	1425	DES
6	„	Albatros DV	(b)	„	„	Lille	1430	OOC
7	13 Mar	Pfalz DIII	(b)	B1162	„	SW Lille	1615	DES
8	„	Pfalz DIII	(b)	„	„	„	1620	DES
9	16 Mar	Pfalz DIII	(c)	C4808	„	Oignes	1045	OOC
10	„	Pfalz DIII	(c)	„	„	„	1100	OOC
11	„	Albatros DV	(c)	„	„	Beaumont	1115	DES
12	18 Mar	Albatros DV	(d)	C4631	„	Carvin	1015	OOC
13	24 Mar	Albatros DV	(d)	C4828	„	Cherisy	1115	DES
14	„	Albatros DV	(d)	„	„	Vis-en-Artois	1120	DES
15	26 Mar	Pfalz DIII	(d)	B1217	„	E Albert	1245	OOC
16	„	Pfalz DIII	(d)	„	„	„	1245	DES
17	29 Mar	Albatros DV	(d)	B1164	„	Guillancourt	1545	OOC
18	2 Apr	Albatros DV	(d)	„	„	Vauvillers	1645	DES
19	„	Fokker DrI	(d)	„	„	„	1645	DES(F)
20	12 Apr	Pfalz DIII	(d)	B1253	„	SW Sailly	1455	DES
21	„	Pfalz DIII	(d)	„	„	„	1455	DES
22	„	Pfalz DIII	(d)	„	„	Sailly	1500	DES
23	22 Apr	Albatros DV	(d)	„	„	E Merville	0940	OOC
24	„	Albatros DV	(d)	„	„	„	0940	OOC

Total: 14 destroyed, 10 out of control = 24.
Pilots: (a) 2/Lt W G Pudney; (b) Sgt E J Elton; (c) Lt W L Wells; (d) 2/Lt F G C Weare.

HEDLEY John Herbert   Captain   20 SQN

Born 19 July 1889, he was living in North Shields with his wife pre-war. Served with the Lincoln Regiment (17th Labour Company) before transferring to the RFC General List. Made temporary captain on 13 April 1917. Was with 62 Squadron in England in October 1917, then joined 20 Squadron on 6 November 1917, and often flew with Sgt F Johnson and Captain R K Kirkman. With the latter was brought down on 27 March 1918, by Karl Gallwitz of Jasta 2, and taken prisoner (B1156). For many years they were noted as being brought down by Manfred von Richthofen but this was not the case. Hedley had received the French Croix de Guerre, gazetted 28 April 1918, recommended on 12 March for four destroyed, four out of control and one balloon deflated. Repatriated from Germany on 13 December 1918.

	1917			BF2b				
1	5 Dec	Albatros C	(a)	A7144	20	Dadizeele	0925	OOC
2	10 Dec	Albatros DV	(a)	„	„	E Staden	0915	OOC
3	22 Dec	Albatros DV	(a)	„	„	Roulers	1400	DES(F)
4	„	Albatros DV	(a)	„	„	„	1420	OOC
	1918							
5	4 Jan	Albatros DV	(b)	A7255	„	Menin	1200	OOC
6	4 Feb	Balloon	(c)		„	28K 5c	1055	DES
7	„	Albatros DV	(c)		„	„	1100	DES
8	17 Feb	Pfalz DIII	(a)	B1177	„	Moorslede	1120	OOC
9	„	Pfalz DIII	(a)	„	„	W Moorslede	1130	DES
10	23 Mar	Albatros DV	(d)	B1156	„	E Wervicq	1210	DES(F)
11	„	Albatros DV	(d)	„	„	E Menin	1212	OOC

Total: 4 & 1 balloon destroyed, 6 out of control = 11.
Pilots: (a) Sgt F Johnson; (b) 2/Lt R M Makepeace; (c) 2/Lt T Colville-Jones; (d) Capt R K Kirkman.

HERRING Robert Samuel   Lieutenant   48 SQN

From Hunstanton, Norfolk, born 13 October 1897. After serving with the 1/16th Battn. of the London Regiment (Royal Fusiliers), Territorial Force as a second lieutenant, transferred into the RFC in August 1917. Joined 48 Squadron on 20 November and was wounded in action on 26 March 1918. Awarded the Military Cross, gazetted 22 June, the citation noting four victories and helping in valuable recce sorties and photo ops. Returned to England on 4 April and on 23 January 1919 was injured in an aero accident. Relinquished his RAF commission and joined the 20th Battn. London Regiment as a lieutenant.

	1918			BF2b				
1	25 Jan	Albatros DIII	(a)	B1187	48	NE St Quentin	1425	OOC
2	28 Jan	Rumpler C	(b)	B1193	,,	Beaurevoir	1240	OOC
3	9 Feb	Albatros DV	(c)	C4628	,,	S Guise	1200	OOC
4	16 Mar	Albatros DV	(d)	B1181	,,	Bellicourt-Bellenglise	1210	OOC
5	,,	DFW C	(d)	,,	,,	,,	1211	OOC

Total: 5 out of control
Pilots: (a) Lt H W Elliott; (b) 2/Lt F C Ransley; (c) 2/Lt H H Hartley; (d) Lt P Burrows.

HILL Charles   Sergeant   88 SQN

Born Huddersfield, 16 November 1898. Enlisted into the army 9 April 1917, serving with the 16th Battn. of the Durham Light Infantry. Seconded to the RFC in November 1917. Had a narrow escape on 29 June 1918 on being brought down by enemy aircraft in C983, along with Captain K R Simpson, by Alexandre Zenses, a German Marine pilot of MFJ II.

	1918			BF2b				
1	29 Jun	Fokker DVII	(a)	C983	88	Ghistelles	2010	DES
2	31 Jul	Fokker DVII	(b)	D8064	,,	Estaires-Merville	0945	OOC
3	11 Aug	Fokker DVII	(c)	,,	,,	Barleux, SW Péronne	1610	OOC
4	5 Sep	Fokker DVII	(d)	D7942	,,	Armentières	1845	DES
5	20 Sep	Fokker DVII	(b)	C922	,,	SE Capinghem	0750	DES
6	,,	Fokker DVII	(e)	,,	,,	SE Quesnoy	0755	DES
7	30 Oct	Fokker DVII	(f)	E2506	,,	Herquegnies	0930	DES

Total: 3 & 2 shared destroyed, 2 out of control = 7.
Pilots: (a) Capt K R Simpson and shared with Lt R J Cullen/2/Lt E H Ward, D8062, Lt K B Conn/2/Lt B H Smyth, C787, Lt W A Wheeler/2/Lt T S Chiltern, C774; (b) Lt C R Poole; (c) Capt Simpson; (d) Lt V Voss; (e) Poole and shared with Lt K B Conn/Lt W I N Grant, Capt E C Johnston/2/Lt B Digby Worsley, E2216; (f) Lt J Baird.

HILL Richard Frank   2nd Lieutenant   20 SQN

Born at Jarvis Bank, Crowborough, Sussex, 28 April 1899, he was living in Brighton pre-war. A student at Charterhouse School (Weekites) between September 1912 and April 1917 he left and joined the RFC. Commissioned second lieutenant on probation 4 May 1917 and confirmed a flying officer observer on 25 August. Joined 20 Squadron in July and often flew with Captain Luchford. Awarded the Military Cross in October 1917, at the same time as his pilot. Returned to HE at the end of that month. In 1918 he was with 107 Squadron and No. 3 TDS in England. Died of appendicitis on 17 September following two operations and is buried in High Hurstwood Cemetery, Sussex.

	1917			FE2d				
1	19 Aug	Albatros DV	(a)	A6456	20	Comines	1700	OOC
				BF2b				
2	9 Sep	Albatros DV	(b)	A7215	,,	Becelaère	1315	OOC
3	11 Sep	Albatros DV	(b)	,,	,,	E Menin	1400	OOC
4	25 Sep	Albatros DV	(b)	B1122	,,	E Gheluvelt	1830	DES
5	28 Sep	Albatros DV	(b)	,,	,,	Menin	1230	DES(F)
6	,,	Albatros DV	(b)	,,	,,	,,	1230	DES
7	1 Oct	Albatros DV	(b)	,,	,,	SE Roulers	1445	DES

Total: 4 destroyed, 3 out of control = 7.
Pilots: (a) 2/Lt C B Simpson; (b) Lt H G W Luchford.

HILLS John 2nd Lieutenant 20 SQN

From Oldfield Park, Bath, born 26 October 1897, he was a draughtsman/engineer from 1912 until he joined the RFC. Served initially as a probationer with the Squadron before being commissioned as a flying observer. He was taken prisoner of war and wounded on 14 August 1918, with his pilot, Lt D E Smith being killed. They were shot down by Ltn Schramm of Jasta 56 near Wervicq, the German's first victory.

	1918			BF2b				
1	16 Jun	Pfalz DIII	(a)	C859	20	S Comines	1915	DES
2	2 Jul	Pfalz DIII	(a)	„	„	SE Ypres	0845	OOC
3	25 Jul	Fokker DVII	(a)	C4672	„	Comines Canal	0850	DES
4	„	Fokker DVII	(a)	„	„	Comines	0855	OOC
5	„	Fokker DVII	(b)	„	„	Comines Canal	0855	DES(F)
6	30 Jul	Fokker DVII	(c)	D7897	„	Bailleul	1930	OOC
7	11 Aug	Balloon	(d)	E2467	„	W Courtrai	1340	DES

Total: 2 and 1 shared destroyed, 1 balloon, & 3 out of control = 7.
Pilots: (a) Lt D E Smith; (b) Smith and shared with Capt H P Lale/2/Lt F J Ralph (C4718) and Lt W M Thomson/Sgt J D C Summers (C843); (c) Lt J Purcell; (d) Capt H P Lale.

HINES G F Sergeant 62 SQN

Served with 62 Squadron but was shot down and taken prisoner, together with his pilot, 2/Lt P S Manley, in C944, on 27 September 1918. All victories shared with Patrick Manley.

	1918			BF2b				
1	15 Sep	EA			62	Marquion	1705	OOC
2	16 Sep	Fokker DVII			„			OOC
3	17 Sep	Fokker DVII			„			OOC
4	24 Sep	Fokker DVII			„	E Cambrai		DES
5	„	Fokker DVII			„	„		DES(F)

Total: 2 destroyed, 3 out of control = 5.

HOARE Edward Sergeant 88 SQN

From Acton Vale, West London, Hoare volunteered for observer duties while a 1st Class Air Mechanic. Was wounded in action on 17 August 1918 while still a private (in E2183), but was promoted to Sergeant (215955). Received the DFM, gazetted on 1 January 1919.

	1918			BF2b				
1	28 Jun	Halberstadt C	(a)	C4720	88	Houthulst Forest	2000	DES(F)
2	„	Halberstadt C	(a)	„	„	„	2000	DES
3	1 Jul	Fokker DVII	(b)	„	„	W Westroosbeke	1945	OOC
4	6 Aug	Fokker DVII	(a)	„	„	Ploegsteert	1045	OOC
5	11 Aug	Fokker DVII	(a)	C787	„	Combles	1130	DES(F)
6	„	Fokker DVII	(a)	E2183	„	Herbecourt	1615	OOC
7	14 Aug	Fokker DVII	(a)	„	„	Dompierre	1745	OOC

Total: 3 destroyed, 4 out of control = 7.
Pilots: (a) Lt A Williamson; (b) Lt C Foster.

HODGKINSON William 2nd Lieutenant 62 SQN

From Ainsdale, near Southport, born 10 April 1897, he lived at 23 Shore Road. A student at the University School, Southport from 1913 he left to join the 2/6th King's Liverpool Regiment prior to transferring to the RFC in December 1917. Joined 62 Squadron on 12 March 1918. Killed in action 9 October 1918, along with his pilot, Captain L Campbell (E2256), brought down by Paul Bäumer of Jasta 2, his 43rd and final victory. Hodgkinson was buried at Preseau, France.

	1918			BF2b				
1	12 Apr	Albatros DV			62	E Estaires	1425	OOC
2	3 Aug	EA			,,			OOC
3	8 Aug	EA			,,			OOC
4	12 Aug	EA			,,			DES
5	9 Oct	Fokker DVII		E2256	,,	Preseau		DES

Total: 2 destroyed, 3 out of control = 5.

HOLMES W N   Sergeant   62 SQN

Sergeant (66635) Holmes came from Selby, Yorkshire. He and his pilot, 2/Lt J W Symons, crashed into a shell hole on 17 March 1918, trying to force land after being hit by AA fire in C4632. Awarded the Military Medal, gazetted on 12 June 1918.

	1918				BF2b			
1	11 Mar	Fokker DrI	(a)		62			DES(F)
2	13 Mar	Albatros DV	(a)	C4609	,,	Cambrai	1040	OOC
3	24 Mar	Albatros DV	(a)		,,	Nurlu-Lieramont		DES
4	12 Apr	Albatros DV	(b)	B1336	,,	Allennes	1420	DES
5	,,	Albatros DV	(b)	,,	,,	N Chemy	1425	DES
6	19 May	Fokker DVII	(c)		,,	NW Douai	1815	OOC
7	2 Jun	Fokker DrI	(d)	C953	,,	S Pozières	1945	OOC
8	8 Jul	Fokker DrI	(e)	D7899	,,	NW Carvin	0710	OOC

Total: 4 destroyed, 4 out of control = 8.
Pilots: (a) 2/Lt S W Symons; (b) Sgt F Johnson; (c) Capt T L Purdom; (d) Lt D A Savage; (e) Capt W E Staton.

HOY Campbell Alexander   Lieutenant   20 SQN

Served with the Northern Cyclist Battn., Territorial Force before being seconded to the RFC. Commissioned 17 June 1917. Awarded the Military Cross, gazetted 17 September 1917, the citation noting four German aircraft shot down. On 25 May he and his pilot, 2/Lt J H Baring-Gould, who was wounded, were shot down by Ltn A Hanko of Jasta 28w, Hoy being injured (FE A6366). His usual pilot was Lt R M Trevethan.

	1917				FE2d			
1	29 Jun	Albatros DV	(a)	A6547	20	Becelaère	1610	DES
2	2 Jul	Albatros DV	(b)	A6523	,,	Comines-Houthem	1245	OOC
3	7 Jul	Albatros DV	(b)	A6528	,,	Wervicq	1900	DES(F)
4	17 Jul	Albatros DV	(b)	A6512	,,	Polygon Wood	1955	DES
5	22 Jul	Albatros DV	(b)	A6528	,,	Menin-N Wervicq	1650	DES(F)
6	27 Jul	Albatros DV	(b)	,,	,,	Lille-Menin	eve	OOC
7	28 Jul	Albatros DV	(b)	,,	,,	Kezelbars	0915	OOC
8	8 Aug	Albatros DV	(b)	,,	,,	E Messines	1030	OOC
9	,,	Albatros DV	(b)	,,	,,	,,	1040	DES
10	9 Aug	Albatros DV	(c)	A5147	,,	Polygon Wood	1815	OOC

Total: 5 destroyed, 5 out of control = 10.
Pilots: (a) Lt J R Patterson; (b) 2/Lt R M Trevathan; (c) Capt A N Solly.

HUNT Hubert Cecil   Sergeant   22 SQN

Sergeant Mechanic (6434). Won the DFM in September 1918 while serving with 22 Squadron, the award being gazetted on 2 November.

	1918				BF2b			
1	28 May	2-seater	(a)	C4894	22	Merville-La Bassée	1110	OOC
2	8 Aug	Fokker DVII	(b)	E4706	,,	Brebières	1045	DES
3	,,	Fokker DVII	(b)	,,	,,	,,	1045	DES(F)

4	16 Aug	2-seater	(c)	F5824	„	Fresnoy	1100	DES
5	25 Aug	Pfalz DIII	(c)	C1035	„	W Péronne	1830	DES
6	„	Fokker DrI	(c)	„	„	Maricourt	1835	DES
7	„	Pfalz DIII	(c)	„	„	W Maricourt	1835	OOC
8	31 Aug	Fokker DVII	(c)	F5824	„	SE Vitry	1710	OOC

Total: 5 destroyed, 3 out of control = 8.
Pilots: (a) Lt C W M Thomson; (b) Lt T H Newsome; (c) Lt C E Hurst.

JACKMAN B   2AM   48 SQN

Usual observer to Captain B E Baker MC, 48 Squadron, 1917. On 29 November Baker and Jackman were probably in combat with Jasta 26 who had two pilots wounded in this area.

	1917			BF2b				
1	9 Sep	Albatros DV	(a)	A7213	48	Middlekerke	1615	OOC
2	11 Nov	Albatros DIII	(b)	A7170	„	NE Dixmude	1510	OOC
3	„	Albatros DIII	(b)	„	„	E Dixmude	1515	OOC
4	12 Nov	Albatros DIII	(c)	B1115	„	Dixmude	1550	OOC
5	29 Nov	Albatros DV	(b)	A7170	„	Houthulst	1445	OOC
6	29 Nov	Albatros DV	(b)	„	„	Amersvelde-Zarren	1530	FTL

Total: 1 Forced To Land, 5 out of control = 6.
Pilots: (a) 2/Lt E G H C Williams; (b) Capt B E Baker; (c) 2/Lt I R Mees.

JENKS Archibald Nathaniel   Lieutenant   20 SQN

Born Coaticook, Port Quebec, Canada, 14 October 1889, and educated at McMaster and McGill Universities. Enlisted in the McGill University Hospital and in 1915 transferred to the 13th Battn. of the Royal Horse Guards. Joined the RFC on 15 March 1917 and served with 20 Squadron from 16 May to 9 October. Returned to Canada as an instructor. After WW1 set up a dentistry practice. He committed suicide after shooting his wife in 1938, having suffered mental problems following the war.

	1917			FE2d				
1	26 May	Albatros DIII	(a)	A6469	20	Comines	1030	DES
2	29 Jun	Albatros DV	(a)	A6431	„	Becelaère	1610	OOC
3	2 Jul	Albatros DV	(a)	„	„	Comines-Houthem	1245	DES(F)
4	6 Jul	Albatros DV	(b)	A6516	„	Comines	1830	OOC
5	22 Jul	Albatros DV	(a)	A6512	„	Menin-Wervicq	1900	OOC
6	28 Jul	Albatros DV	(a)	A3	„	NE Tourcoing	1830	OOC
7	21 Sep	Albatros DV	(c)	B1892	„	Becelaère	1100	OOC

Total: 2 destroyed, 5 out of control = 7.
Pilots: (a) Capt H L Satchell; (b) Capt F D Stevens; (c) 2/Lt W Durrand.

JOHNSON Frank   Sergeant   22, 20 & 62 SQNS

From Kettering, Northants, he was born in Oldham, 26 December 1896. As acting Sergeant (6391), he flew with 22 Squadron 1916-17, initially as a corporal, and was recommended for the DCM on 13 February. This was confirmed and his award was gazetted on 26 April, the citation noting a Pfalz crashed, and an Albatros out of control, while on previous occasions he had destroyed four enemy aircraft and driven down three out of control. Later trained as a pilot, RAC ticket number 4531, 21 April 1917, and joined 20 Squadron, bringing his score to 13 before going to 62 Squadron where he added three more kills to his tally. A Bar to his DCM came in May 1918.

	1916			FE2b				
1	24 Sep	D	(a)	4924	22	Epehy	1635	OOC
2	16 Oct	Albatros DI	(b)	4855	„	Gueudecourt	1440	OOC
3	22 Nov	Albatros DI	(c)	7706	„	Bancourt	1330	OOC

	1917							
4	4 Feb	Albatros DII	(d)	7697	„	Haplincourt	1345	DES
				BF2b				
5	11 Oct	Albatros DIII	(e)	B1130	20	Moorslede	0715	OOC
6	3 Dec	Albatros DV	(f)	A7214	„	Wervicq	1215	OOC
7	5 Dec	Albatros DV	(g)	A7144	„	Dadizeele	0925	OOC
8	10 Dec	Albatros DV	(g)	„	„	E Staden	0915	DES
9	22 Dec	Albatros DV	(g)	„	„	Roulers	1400	DES
10	„	Albatros DV	(g)	„	„	„	1420	OOC
	1918							
11	25 Jan	Albatros DIII	(h)	C4604	„	Staden	1230	OOC
12	17 Feb	Pfalz DIII	(g)	B1117	„	Moorslede	1120	OOC
13	„	Pfalz DIII	(g)	„	„	W Moorslede	1130	DES
14	27 Mar	EA	(i)		62			OOC
15	12 Apr	Albatros DV	(j)	B1136	„	Allennes	1420	DES
16	„	Albatros DV	(j)	„	„	N Chemy	1425	DES

Total: 6 destroyed, 9 & 1 shared out of control = 16.
Pilots: (a) 2/Lt A Cropper; (b) 2/Lt C S Duffas; (c) 2/Lt N H Tolhurst; (d) Capt H R Hawkins; Observers: (e) Lt N M Sanders; (f) 2/Lt S H P Masding; (g) Capt J H Hedley; (h) 2/Lt D H Prosser; (i) Sgt C Brammer; (j) Sgt W N Holmes.

JONES John H   Sergeant   22 SQN

Believed to have come from Tenbury. Served with 22 Squadron and won the DFM, gazetted 3 June 1919. Injured 18 January 1918.

	1917			BF2b				
1	5 Dec	2-seater	(a)	B1164	22	N Roulers	1520	DES(F)
2	6 Dec	Albatros DV	(a)	„	„	Harbourdin	1115	DES
	1918							
3	18 Feb	2-seater	(b)	C4808	„	Seclin	1400	OOC
4	11 Mar	Albatros DV	(b)	A7286	„	Lomme	1420	OOC
5	„	Albatros DV	(b)	„	„	Ligny	1425	OOC
6	20 May	Pfalz DIII	(c)	C901	„	NW Estaires	1850	DES
7	21 May	LVG C	(c)	„	„	SW Vitry	1015	OOC
8	„	LVG C	(c)	„	„	„	1015	OOC
9	22 May	Albatros DV	(c)	„	„	SE Arras	1030	OOC
10	26 May	Albatros DV	(c)	„	„	SE Armentières	1945	OOC
11	31 May	Pfalz DIII	(d)	A7243	„	SW Armentières	1030	OOC
12	„	Pfalz DIII	(d)	„	„	„	1030	DES
13	„	Pfalz DIII	(e)	„	„	SE	1915	OOC
14	1 Jun	Balloon	(d)	C842	„	Neuf Berquin	1040	DES
15	2 Jun	Pfalz DIII	(e)	C901	„	NE Lens	1030	OOC

Total: 4 destroyed, 10 out of control, 1 balloon = 15.
Pilots: (a) 2/Lt S A Oades; (b) 2/Lt S H Wallage; (c) Capt W J Mostyn; (d) 2/Lt C H Dunster; (e) 2/Lt F G Gibbons.

JONES Percy Griffith   2nd Lieutenant   20 SQN

From Mold, Flint, North Wales, he initially served with the Royal Engineers. Transferring to the RFC in November 1917 he served briefly with 2 Squadron in March 1918, then with 20 Squadron from 27 April, but was killed in action on 2 July 1918, aged 29. Buried at Longuenesse, France.

	1918			BF2b				
1	15 May	Albatros DV	(a)		20	Wervicq	1115	OOC
2	„	Albatros DV	(a)		„	„	1115	OOC
3	29 May	Fokker DrI	(b)	C856	„	W Armentières	1840	OOC
4	30 Jun	Fokker DVII	(b)	C938	„	N Comines	0730	OOC
5	2 Jul	Pfalz DIII	(b)	B1344	„	SE Gheluvelt	0840	DES(F)

Total: 1 destroyed, 4 out of control = 5.
Pilots: (a) Lt R G Bennett; (b) Lt T C Traill.

KEMP George Hubert   2nd Lieutenant   20 SQN

Native of Charlton, London (Kent), where he resided at 30 Wyndcliffe Road, Kemp originally served with the 15th Battn. of the Durham Light Infantry. Commissioned 26 May 1918. Flew with 20 Squadron but was killed in action on 1 June 1918, aged 20. Buried at Longuenesse (St Omer) Souvenir Cemetery, France. All victories scored with his pilot, Lt W M Thomson, who survived Kemp's last air fight.

	1917		BF2b				
1	9 May	Albatros DV	C4851	20	W Comines	1330	DES
2	14 May	Albatros DV	C859	„	Wervicq-Zillebeke	1845	CAPT
3	17 May	Albatros DV	„	„	E Armentières	0815	DES
4	„	Albatros DV	„	„	Armentières	0816	OOC
5	18 May	Pfalz DIII	„	„	S Merville	1140	OOC
6	19 May	Pfalz DIII	C843	„	Estaires	1045	DES
7	21 May	Albatros DV	„	„	Warneton	0835	DES(F)
8	29 May	Albatros DV	„	„	Bac St Maur	1830	OOC
9	31 May	Pfalz DIII	„	„	Bois Grenier	1850	DES
10	„	Albatros DV	„	„	Armentières	1855	OOC
11	1 Jun	Albatros DV	„	„	Comines	0630	DES
12	„	Albatros DV	„	„	„	0635	DES

Total: 7 destroyed, 1 captured, 4 out of control = 12.

KIRK Walter Alister   Lieutenant   1 AFC SQN

From Lismore, New South Wales, although he was born in Belfast, Northern Ireland on 6 August 1887. A peacetime engineer, he enlisted into the 2nd Australian Light Horse from August 1914 in the machine-gun section. Sergeant 1915 but reduced to private soon afterwards. Commissioned 18 December 1916. To aviation training 5 July 1917 and then transferred to the Australian Flying Corps in October. Flew as observer to Ross Smith in 1918, and was awarded the DFC, gazetted 8 February 1919. Flight Lieutenant in RAAF WW2. Died Orange, NSW, 6 June 1961.

	1918			BF2b				
1	27 Mar	AEG C	(a)	1		Amman	0745	FTL/DES
2	„	AEG C	(a)	„		„	0800	FTL/DES
3	22 May	Albatros DV	(b)	B1299	„	N Nablus	0645	OOC
4	11 Jun	Rumpler C	(c)	„	„	N Tul Keram	0615	FTL/DES
5	19 Jun	Rumpler C	(b)	„	„	Jericho-Damie	0605	FTL/DES
6	17 Jul	Albatros DV	(b)	„	„	Wadi el Auja	0640	DES
7	„	Albatros DV	(b)	„	„	„	0640	DES

Total: 6 destroyed, 1 out of control = 7.
Pilots: (a) Lt E S Headlam; (b) Capt R M Smith; (c) Smith and shared with Lt E G C Stooke/Lt L P Kreig, B1226.

KNIGHTS Sidney Arthur William   Lieutenant   62 SQN

Seconded to the RFC following service with the 13th Battn. Yorks and Lancs Regiment, with whom he won the Military Cross, gazetted 11 December 1916, and Mentioned in Despatches. This was for an exploit in a raid on the German trenches. On 10 March 1918 he joined 62 Squadron but was hospitalised on 10 July. In August he was with the School of Aviation in England and at the Armament School in October; he was demobilised on 18 March 1919. Died 1 April 1968, the 50th Anniversary of the RAF, while living in Bury St Edmunds with his wife. All victories with Lt G E Gibbons MC DFC.

	1918		BF2b					
1	12 Mar	Fokker DrI			62	NE Nauroy	1100	OOC
2	17 Mar	EA			„			OOC
3	3 May	Albatros DV	C779		„	N Armentières	1145	DES
4	„	Albatros DV	„		„	„	1145	DES
5	„	Fokker DrI	„		„	„	1145	DES
6	22 May	LVG C	C919		„	W Laventie	0805	DES
7	28 May	Fokker DVII	„		„	Menin-Armentières	1915	DES(F)
8	„	Rumpler C	„		„	La Creche-Steenwerck	1945	OOC

Total: 5 destroyed, 3 out of control = 8.

KNOWLES F J   Corporal   111 SQN

From Nairn, on the Moray Forth, Scotland. Serving with Treble One Squadron in the Middle East, firstly as a Second Air Mechanic (403944). He received the Military Medal in 1918, gazetted on 10 April and promoted to corporal. Usually flew with Captain R M Drummond. One of their victims on 12 December may have been Ltn Heinrich Deilmann, who was killed.

	1917			BF2b				
1	12 Dec	Albatros DV	(a)	A7202	111	Tul Keram	1030	OOC
2	„	Albatros DV	(a)	„	„	NW Tul Keram	1035	DES
3	„	Albatros DV	(a)	„	„	Wadi el Auja	1045	DES
4	14 Dec	Albatros DV	(a)	„	„	N Beisan	0945	DES
5	28 Dec	2-seater	(b)	A7192	„	Nebulus Valley	1600	FTL/DES
	1918							
6	17 Jan	2-seater	(c)	„	„	Kalkilieh	0920	DES
7	18 Jan	2-seater	(d)	A7198	„	Jaffa-Arsuf	1130	DES

Total: 5 & 1 shared destroyed, 1 out of control = 7.
Pilots: (a) Capt R M Drummond; (b) Lt C R Davidson; (c) Lt A L Fleming; (d) Lt Fleming and shared with Lts D B Aitken and L A J Barbe, A7196.

KYDD Frederick Joseph   Lieutenant   20 SQN

From Frodsham, Cheshire, born 15 May 1892. A medical student at Liverpool University, from 1912 till August 1914, he served in the King's Liverpool Regiment, Territorial Force, until seconded into the RFC on 3 May 1917 and commissioned with seniority from 15 February. Returned to Home Establishment on 11 August and in July 1918 he was an instructor at No.1 School of Armament. Left the RAF on 2 February 1919.

	1917			FE2d				
1	5 May	Albatros DIII	(a)	A5147	20	Houthem	1730	DES
2	„	Albatros DIII	(a)	„	„	Houthem-Hollebeke	1730	OOC
3	9 May	Albatros DIII	(b)	A6445	„	N Menin	1325	DES
4	12 Jun	Albatros DIII	(c)	A6354	„	Zandvoorde	1215	OOC
5	3 Jul	Albatros DV	(d)	A6516	„	Becelaère	c1600	OOC

Total: 2 destroyed, 3 out of control = 5.
Pilots: (a) 2/Lt G C Heseltine; (b) 2/Lt H B Howe; (c) Lt A N Solly; (d) Capt F D Stevens.

LEARMOND George Victor   2nd Lieutenant   20 SQN

From Glasgow, born 20 June 1897, he went to Dudhope School, Dundee between 1910 and 1913. With the 12th Battn. Highland Light Infantry, he was commissioned on 27 June 1917. He received a Mention in Despatches and left the service on 16 May 1919. Enlisted into the army in July 1927. All his victories were shared with Lt G E Randell, except No.5, shared with Capt H P Lale.

	1918		BF2b				
1	24 Jul	Fokker DVII	D8086	20	N Wervicq	2015	DES
2	14 Aug	Pfalz DIII	„	„	Dadizeele	1815	OOC
3	3 Sep	Fokker DVII	E2249	„	S Havrincourt Wood	1745	OOC
4	5 Sep	Fokker DVII	„	„	SE Cambrai	1521	OOC
5	3 Oct	Fokker DVII	E2588	„	E Mericourt	1005	OOC
6	3 Nov	Fokker DVII	E2429	„	SW Berlainmont	1330	DES
7	9 Nov	Fokker DVII	„	„	SE Beaumont	1130	OOC
8	10 Nov	Fokker DVII	„	„	W Louerval	1100	DES
9	„	Fokker DVII	„	„	„	1135	DES(F)

Total: 4 destroyed, 5 out of control = 9.

LEWIS Thomas Archibald Mitford Stuart   Lieutenant   20 SQN

From Edenbridge, Kent, born 26 June 1894. Served with the Royal West Kent Regiment, Territorial Force and then transferred to the RFC in October 1916, commissioned as a flying officer observer General List in April 1917. Began duty with 20 Squadron on 15 May and on 5 June he and Lieutenant H L Satchell, in A6469, shot down Karl Emil Schäfer, leader of Jasta 28 (30 victories). Lewis was wounded in action 27 July 1917, his pilot, Lt G T W Burkett, also being wounded (FE2d A6512). Lewis was hit in the leg by a phosphorus bullet and, taken to No.53 CCS, had to have the leg amputated. The award of a MC was made on 6 August, gazetted 9 January 1918. The citation recorded his final fight, noting that despite his serious injury he continued to engage the enemy whilst lying on his back. He later became an admin. officer in 1918 attached to Air Ministry. Left the service on 1 August 1920. After the war he was known as T Stuart Lewis. In the 1930's he was living in Hythe, Kent, and was a Director of the Cinque Ports Flying Club. In 1941 he was a flight lieutenant with the RAFVR for work with the Air Training Corps. Died 21 June 1961.

	1917			FE2d				
1	29 Apr	Albatros DIII	(a)	A6412	20	Courtrai-Ypres	1725	DES
2	23 May	Albatros DIII	(b)	„	„	Zandvoorde	1045	OOC
3	26 May	Albatros DV	(b)	„	„	Comines-Quesnoy	1045	OOC
4	5 Jun	Albatros DV	(c)	A6469	„	Becelaère-Zandvoorde	1435	DES(F)
5	27 Jul	Albatros DV	(d)	A6512	„	Menin	eve	DES
6	„	Albatros DV	(d)	„	„	E Menin	eve	DES

Total: 4 destroyed, 2 out of control = 6.
Pilots: (a) 2/Lt E J Smart; (b) Capt H G White; (c) Lt H L Satchell; (d) 2/Lt G T Burkett.

LIBBY Frederick   Captain   23, 11, 43, 25 SQNS

From Sterling, Colorado, USA, born 15 July 1891, Libby became famous for gaining 14 victories as both an observer and later a pilot, winning the MC. His full biography and victory list can be found in both *Above the Trenches* and *Over the Front*. Died in Los Angeles, 9 January 1970.

LIGHT Alan Douglas   Lieutenant   48 SQN

From Finchley, London, born 31 July 1891. Joined up in March 1915 and became a Second Lieutenant with the 13th Middlesex Regiment, commissioned 10 November 1916. Served in France with the 7th Londons and then the 17th Middlesex, and finally with the 14th Trench Mortar Battery, receiving a Mention in Despatches. Transferred to the RFC in April 1917, confirmed as a Flying Officer Observer on 3 June 1917, and noted as a full lieutenant from 26 August 1918. Initially served with 11 Squadron from May, then 48 Squadron. While flying with 48 he was injured in a crash on 4 June, and on 11 September 1917, returning from a night sortie in search of Gothas, a crash left him with concussion and a head wound. Returned to England and on leaving hospital volunteered for pilot training, but instead was sent to become an airship pilot. He became 3rd officer on a North Sea type non-rigid airship, NS8, flying on convoy protection sweeps where he remained until the war's end. Left the RAF on 11 June 1919. He went out to Malaya where he became a rubber planter but rejoined the RAF in WW2, flying as an air gunner with 209 Squadron, Coastal Command.

	1917			BF2b					
1	7 Jul	Albatros DV	(a)	A7129	48	S Vitry	0550	DES	
2	13 Jul	Albatros DIII	(b)	A7115	„	Snaeskerke-Slype	0940	DES	
3	21 Aug	Albatros DV	(c)	A7213	„	W Westende	1940	DES(F)	
4	22 Aug	Albatros DV	(c)	„	„	SW Ostend	0900	DES	
5	„	Albatros DV	(c)	„	„	Slype-Westende	0915	DES	
6	2 Sep	Albatros DV	(d)	A7170	„	E Dixmude	0930	OOC	
7	„	Albatros DV	(e)	„	„	SE Dixmude	0935	OOC	
8	9 Sep	Albatros DV	(a)	A7216	„	Middlekerke-Slype	1615	OOC	

Total: 5 destroyed, 2 & 1 shared out of control = 8.
Pilots: (a) Capt J T Milne; (b) Lt O J F Scholte; (c) Lt R D Coath; (d) Lt K R Park and shared with 2/Lt R L Curtis/ 2/Lt D P F Uniacke, A7224; (e) Lt Park.

LINDFIELD H   2AM   48 SQN

Survived several months as an observer with 48 Squadron, flying with a variety of pilots, assisting in the destruction of six German scouts.

	1917			BF2b					
1	12 Jul	Albatros DIII	(a)	A7112	48	Ghistelles	1845	OOC	
2	22 Aug	Albatros DIII	(b)	A7153	„	S Ghistelles	1945	DES	
3	5 Sep	Albatros DV	(c)	A7182	„	4 miles off Ostende	1200	DES	
4	9 Sep	Albatros DV	(c)	A7220	„	Middlekerke-Slype	1615	OOC	
5	12 Sep	Albatros DV	(d)	A7216	„	Ostende	1950	OOC	
6	13 Nov	Albatros DV	(e)	A7227	„	NE Ostende	1510	OOC	

Total: 2 destroyed, 4 out of control = 6.
Pilots: (a) 2/Lt G Colledge; (b) Lt H E T Crocker; (c) Lt K R Park; (d) Lt E G H C Williams; (e) Lt W A McMichael.

LLOYD WILLIAMS John Jordan   Captain   111 SQN

After serving with the Denbigh Yeomanry, commissioned 26 July 1913, he was made full lieutenant on 15 December 1914 and captain 1 June 1916. With the RFC he served in Egypt and the Middle East with 111 Squadron during two periods, 31 August 1917 to 29 January 1918 and then, following pilot training, from 15 June to 24 November 1918. Awarded the MC on 24 October 1917, gazetted 23 April 1918, for three victories. The Gazette records his name as Captain J J L Williams.

	1917			BF2b					
1	8 Oct	Albatros DIII	(a)	A7194	111			CAPT	
2	15 Oct	Albatros DIII	(a)	„	„	Shellah-Sharia	0825	DES	
3	30 Oct	2-seater	(b)	„	„	NW Khalusa	0945	CAPT	
4	6 Nov	Rumpler C	(b)	„	„	Um Dabkel	1045	FTL/DES	
5	8 Nov	Albatros DIII	(b)	„	„	Muleikat	1300	DES(F)	

Total: 3 destroyed, 2 captured = 5.
Pilots: (a) 2/Lt R C Steele; (b) Capt A H Peck.

LOWE Reginald   2nd Lieutenant   62 SQN

From Birch Vale, near Stockport, he was commissioned into the Notts and Derby Regiment, transferring into the RAF in 1918. With 62 Squadron, which he joined in July, he had two close encounters with enemy aircraft, on 4 and 16 September 1918. He was with Lt R O Schallaire (E2128) on the former date, being shot about, while on the 16th his pilot, 2/Lt C H Moss was wounded during a fight with a Fokker DVII, but he flew them home. Joined 22 Squadron on 29 July 1919.

	1918			BF2b				
1	22 Aug	Fokker DVII	(a)	E2182	62	Bourlon-Inchy	0745	OOC
2	4 Sep	Fokker DVII	(a)	„	„	Marq, N Cambrai	0930	DES
3	15 Sep	EA	(a)		„	Marquion	1705	DES
4	16 Sep	Fokker DVII	(b)		„			DES
5	1 Nov	Fokker DVII	(c)		„			OOC

Total: 3 destroyed, 2 out of control = 5.
Pilots: (a) Lt R Schallaire; (b) Lt C H Moss; (c) Capt P J Long.

MASDING Stanley Henry Percy   2nd Lieutenant   20 SQN

From Bridgewater, Somerset. Commissioned into the 1st Battn. the Monmouth Regiment prior to joining the RFC in August 1917. Joined 62 Squadron on 18 October, then moved to 20 Squadron. Later in 1918 he was serving at Biggin Hill, Kent. Left the RAF 10 March 1919.

	1917			BF2b				
1	3 Dec	Albatros DV	(a)	A7214	20	Wervicq	1215	OOC
	1918							
2	4 Jan	Albatros DV	(b)		„	Menin	1106	DES
3	17 Feb	Pfalz DIII	(c)	C4826	„	Moorslede	1130	OOC
4	19 May	Pfalz DIII	(d)	C4749	„	Estaires	1025	DES(F)
5	„	Pfalz DIII	(d)	„	„	Laventie	1030	DES

Total: 3 destroyed, 2 out of control = 5.
Pilots: (a) Sgt F Johnson; (b) 2/Lt G D Jooste; (c) 2/Lt D M McGoun; (d) Capt D G Cooke.

MASON Jack   Sergeant   11 SQN

Corporal and later Sergeant (103364) Mason flew with 11 Squadron 1917-18 gaining five combat victories. Awarded the Military Medal in October 1917.

	1917			BF2b				
1	8 Jul	Albatros DIII	(a)	A7143	11	Bohain	1900	OOC
2	14 Aug	Albatros DV	(b)	A7124	„	Brebières	1315	OOC
3	21 Oct	Albatros DV	(b)	„	„	Boiry	1045	DES(F)
4	„	Albatros DV	(b)	„	„	Lecluse	1048	OOC
5	„	Albatros DV	(b)	„	„	„	1048	DES

Total: 2 destroyed, 3 out of control = 5.
Pilots: (a) Capt R Raymond-Barker; (b) Lt R F S Mauduit.

MATHER M B   Corporal   20 SQN

Awarded the DCM on 19 March 1918, gazetted 1 May, while serving with 20 Squadron. Service No. 20624.

	1917			BF2b				
1	2 Dec	Albatros DV	(a)	B883	20	SE Passchendaele	1030	DES
2	5 Dec	Albatros DV	(a)	„	„	Dadizeele	0925	OOC
	1918							
3	4 Feb	Albatros DV	(b)		„	Menin-Roulers Rd	1415	DES(F)
4	„	Albatros DV	(b)		„	„	1415	OOC
5	17 Feb	Pfalz DIII	(c)	C4641	„	Westroosbeke	1130	DES
6	9 Mar	Albatros DV	(d)	B1191	„	S Menin	0800	OOC
7	„	Albatros DV	(d)	„	„	„	0800	OOC
8	25 Apr	Albatros DV	(a)	B817	„	N Ploegsteert Wood	1930	DES(F)

Total: 4 destroyed, 4 out of control = 8.
Pilots: (a) 2/Lt W Beaver; (b) Lt R G Bennett; (c) 2/Lt E Lindup; (d) 2/Lt L H T Capel.

McCORMACK G   Captain   22 SQN

Served with the Royal Irish Rifles, and gazetted an honorary lieutenant from 22 August 1918. Flew in 22 Squadron until wounded in action 24 September 1918, having attained the rank of honorary Captain. All claims made whilst flying with Lieutenant C W M Thomson.

	1918			BF2b				
1	3 Sep	Pfalz DXII		F5820	22	Sailly-Saillisel	0700	DES
2	5 Sep	Fokker DVII		„	„	Douai	1700	OOC
3	17 Sep	Fokker DVII		C1045	„	SW Douai	1830	DES
4	„	Fokker DVII		„	„	Brebières	1840	OOC
5	24 Sep	Fokker DVII		C1035	„	Cambrai	1700	OOC

Total: 2 destroyed, 3 out of control = 5.

McDONALD James   Lieutenant   22 SQN

From Renfrew, Scotland, born 23 July 1899. Between June 1915 and July 1917 he was a civil servant, working for the Post Office Savings Bank in London. Once old enough to enlist, he became an observer with 22 Squadron in April 1918 and usually flew with Captain F G Gibbons. Returned to England on 11 September and left the service on 26 May the following year. DFC gazetted 3 December 1918.

	1918			BF2b				
1	31 May	Albatros DV	(a)	C4835	22	Neuve Chapelle	1030	DES(F)
2	2 Jun	Albatros DV	(a)	„	„	SE La Bassée	1015	OOC
3	„	Albatros C	(a)	„	„	„	1015	OOC
4	23 Jun	Fokker DVII	(b)	C989	„	E La Bassée	2015	OOC
5	„	Fokker DVII	(b)	„	„	„	2015	OOC
6	9 Jul	Albatros C	(c)	C4888	„	N Bois de Phalempin	1110	DES(F)
7	27 Aug	Fokker DVII	(d)	E2454	„	Douai	1345	OOC
8	5 Sep	Fokker DVII	(d)	„	„	„	1700	OOC

Total: 2 destroyed, 6 out of control = 8.
Pilots: (a) 2/Lt L W King; (b) Lt J E Gurdon; (c) Capt G W Bulmer; (d) Lt F G Gibbons.

McROBERT Leslie Harrison   2nd Lieutenant   11 SQN

From West Hartlepool, born 22 August 1898. Educated at his local high school and at Newcastle Grammar, between 1905 and September 1916, at which time he was a Royal Fusiliers cadet. Joined the RFC in March 1917 and commissioned second lieutenant on 4 April 1917. Flying Officer Observer from 9 May 1917, having joined 11 Squadron in France. Returned to HE in March 1918.

	1917			BF2b				
1	27 Jun	2-seater	(a)	A7124	11	S Monchy	1120	DES
2	6 Jul	Albatros DV	(a)	„	„	Dury	2025	DES
3	8 Jul	Albatros DV	(a)	„	„	Montigny	2020	OOC
4	18 Aug	Albatros DV	(a)	„	„	Douai	0630	OOC
5	17 Oct	Albatros DV	(b)	A7275	„	Sensée Canal-Cambrai	1030	OOC
6	„	Albatros DV	(b)	„	„	„	1035	OOC

Total: 2 destroyed, 4 out of control = 6.
Pilots: (a) Lt A J P Lynch; (b) Lt R F S Mauduit.

MERCHANT Alexander Walker   Captain   48 SQN

Born on 27 April 1894, he hailed from Winchmore Hill, London, N21, living at 'Burgoyne', Elm Park Road, his parents living in Muswell Hill. Was a housing agent and warehouseman in the family business from May 1914 until he joined the colours in August 1915. Inns of Court OTC 11 October 1915, No.11 OCB. 20th London Regiment TF, 4 September 1916 and transferred to the RFC in April 1917. Commissioned with the RFC 19 June 1917. Flying with Lt Keith

Park on 24 July, their BF2b (A7176) was shot about in combat with an Albatros DIII but they survived. Invalided back to England later and was with 2 TDS at the beginning of 1918. Left the service on 6 January 1919.

	1917			BF2b				
1	27 May	Albatros DIII	(a)	A7119	48	SW Douai	1945	DES
2	,,	2-seater	(a)	,,	,,	,,	1945	OOC
3	3 Jun	Albatros DIII	(a)	A7112	,,	E Douai	1050	OOC
4	18 Jun	Albatros DV	(a)	A7102	,,	S Rumaucourt	1430	DES
5	29 Jun	Albatros DIII	(b)	A7118	,,	Brebières	2000	OOC
6	6 Jul	Albatros DV	(b)	,,	,,	E Cambrai	0930	DES
7	13 Jul	Albatros DIII	(c)	A7106	,,	Slype	0915	OOC
8	24 Jul	Albatros DIII	(d)	A7176	,,	off Ravensyde	1740	OOC

Total: 3 destroyed, 5 out of control = 8.
Pilots: (a) Lt T P Middleton; (b) Lt O J F Scholte; (c) Lt R D Coath; (d) Lt K R Park.

MERRITT Horace Ernest   Lieutenant   62 SQN

From Bow, East London, he was born on 15 May 1898. Following service in France with the 1/8th Battn. Northumberland Fusiliers, Territorial Force, he was seconded to the RFC in 1917, joining 62 Squadron on 28 December. Flew as observer to Lt E T Morrow, and with him had to abandon their BF2b (C4613) near the front lines on 28 March 1918, after being brought down by machine-gun fire while trench strafing east of Villers Bretonneux during the German March offensive. Went into hospital on his 20th birthday but a few days later was with 2 ASD until he returned to 62 on 8 June. On the 29th he went to 59 CCS and then into the 20th General Hospital, but on 13 August once more returned to his Squadron. Went to England on 3 September and on 26 February 1919 returned to the 5th Battn. of his old Regiment.

	1918			BF2b				
1	13 Mar	Fokker DrI	(a)	C4619	62	Cambrai	1030	OOC
2	,,	Albatros DV	(a)	,,	,,	,,	1030	OOC
3	26 Mar	EA	(b)		,,			DES
4	3 May	Albatros DV	(b)	C796	,,	S Armentières	1120	DES
5	,,	Albatros DV	(b)	,,	,,	,,	1120	DES
6	9 May	Pfalz DIII	(c)	C4859	,,	NE La Bassée		DES
7	,,	Pfalz DIII	(c)	,,	,,	,,		OOC
8	16 Jun	Pfalz DIII	(d)	C919	,,	SE Montdidier	0800	OOC
9	24 Jun	LVG C	(e)	A7215	,,	Harnes	0730	DES

Total: 5 destroyed, 4 out of control = 9.
Pilots: (a) 2/Lt W E Staton; (b) Lt E T Morrow; (c) Lt C H Arnison; (d) Lt G M Yuill; (e) Lt L W Hudson.

MILLS Alfred   Lieutenant   20 SQN

From Belfast, Northern Ireland, born 26 June 1897, he attended Campbell College, Belfast between 1908-14. Saw service with the 13th Reserve Battn., Argyll and Sutherland Highlanders before joining the RFC in November 1917. As an honorary lieutenant, won the DFC, gazetted 2 August 1918, the citation noting his excellent marksmanship while serving with 20 Squadron, commencing 7 April. Was brought down by machine-gun fire but survived, along with 2/Lt L Campbell, on 24 March (B1122). Also shot up on 6 September in E2470, but again was unharmed. Was hospitalised at the beginning of October 1918, at the Prince of Wales Hospital and left the service on 12 February 1919. In 1924 he was remanded at Marylebone on a charge of theft, and then deprived of his DFC following a term of three months imprisonment.

	1918			BF2b				
1	9 May	Fokker DrI	(a)		20	W Lille	1650	DES(F)
2	22 May	LVG C	(b)	C856	,,	Wytschaete-St Eloi	0705	DES
3	,,	Albatros DV	(b)	,,	,,	Warneton	1840	OOC
4	29 May	Albatros DV	(b)	C951	,,	Bac St Maur	1830	OOC
5	30 May	Pfalz DIII	(b)	,,	,,	NW Lille (into a canal)	1720	DES

6	„	Pfalz DIII	(b)	„	„	W Macquart	1720	DES
7	31 May	Pfalz DIII	(b)	„	„	SW Armentières	0740	DES
8	„	Pfalz DIII	(c)	B1168	„	Armentières	1850	DES(F)
9	24 Jul	Fokker DVII	(a)	C4672	„	N Comines	2000	DES
10	3 Sep	Fokker DVII	(d)	E2470	„	Havrincourt Wood	1745	DES
11	6 Sep	Fokker DVII	(d)	„	„	Cambrai-Péronne	0830	DES
12	„	Fokker DVII	(d)	„	„	St Quentin	0850	OOC
13	15 Sep	Hannover CL	(b)	„	„	Harly, SE St Quentin	1750	DES
14	20 Sep	Fokker DVII	(b)	E2246	„	Rouvroy	1030	DES
15	„	Fokker DVII	(b)	„	„	„	1032	DES

Total: 12 destroyed, 3 out of control = 15.
Pilots: (a) Lt L M Price; (b) Capt T P Middleton; (c) Lt W M Thomson; (d) Lt J H Colbert; (d) Lt P T Iaccaci.

MITCHELL Leslie Edwin   2nd Lieutenant   62 SQN

From Leytonstone, Essex, born 19 March 1894. Between 1910-14 he was a self-employed engineer. Joined the RFC in August 1917, and in July the following year became an observer with 62 Squadron. Gained all victories with Lieutenant W E Staton MC DFC, but was killed on 29 September 1918, aged 24, flying with Lt R H O'Reilly in E2509. They may have been hit by a shell, but their BF2b was certainly seen falling to pieces over Dury. Buried at Rumaucourt, France.

	1918		BF2b					
1	12 Aug	EA			62			DES
2	„	EA			„			OOC
3	13 Aug	Fokker DVII			„	Bullecourt	1025	OOC
4	22 Aug	Fokker DVII		D7899	„	Pronville	0745	DES(F)
5	3 Sep	Fokker DVII		„	„	SE Marquion	1830	DES
6	4 Sep	Fokker DVII		„	„	Marquette, N Cambrai	0930	OOC
7	15 Sep	Pfalz DXII			„	Marquion	1705	CAPT
8	24 Sep	Fokker DVII			„	E Cambrai		OOC

Total: 3 destroyed, 1 captured, 4 out of control = 8.

MOORE Ernest Stanley   2nd Lieutenant   48 SQN

From Hull, he was born in 1870, and pre-war he was an assistant surveyor with the Post Office engineers, working in Port Harcourt, Nigeria. Joining the colours, he was with the 7th OCB, then the RFC from August 1916, being commissioned into the General List on 10 May 1917 with seniority from 9 March. Trained with 62 Squadron in England prior to being sent to 48 Squadron on 27 February 1917, going with them to France on 18 March. Prisoner of war 11 May 1917 during combat with Jasta 11, probably shot down by Ltn Lothar von Richthofen. His pilot, 2/Lt W O B Winkler was killed (A7111). Repatriated at the end of December 1918, he left the service on 5 March 1919 with the rank of Honorary Lieutenant.

	1917			BF2a				
1	12 Apr	Albatros DIII	(a)		48			OOC
2	23 Apr	Albatros DIII	(b)		„	Vimy		OOC
3	24 Apr	Albatros DIII	(c)		„	Cagnicourt		OOC
4	2 May	Albatros DIII	(d)	A3348	„	Brebières-Biache	1930	OOC
5	„	Albatros DIII	(d)	„	„	„	1935	OOC
6	„	Albatros DIII	(d)	„	„	„	1940	DES
				BF2b				
7	9 May	LVG C	(e)	A7110	„	Vitry-Noyelles	0820	DES

Total: 1 & 1 shared destroyed, 2 & 3 shared out of control = 7.
Pilots: (a) Lt W O B Winkler, and shared with Capt A M Wilkinson/Lt L W Allen; (b) Winkler and shared with Lt F P Holliday/Capt A H W Wall, Lt R B Hay/?, Lt W T Price/Lt M A Benjamin; (c) Winkler and shared with Holliday/Wall, Hay/?; (d) Winkler; (e) 2/Lt W T Price and shared with Holliday/Wall, A7108.

MOORE Hugh Fitzgerald   Lieutenant   22 SQN

From Scotland, born 17 February 1898, he emigrated to Canada somewhere between 1910 and 1912. Served with the 18th Reserve Battn. CEF (44th Canadian Infantry of Manitoba Regt.). Arrived in England in April and went to France in August, seeing action on the Lens and Somme Fronts. Commissioned in the field 1 July 1917. Once in the RFC he became an observer and joined 22 Squadron in October. After gaining five victories he was hospitalised between 3-13 March 1918 and again on 22 April, then invalided back to England in April. Washed out as pilot material, he became an instructor at the School of Air Gunnery on 1 June and later saw duty with No.41 TDS until 1919, relinquishing his commission in June. As far as is known he did not return to Canada after the war.

	1918			BF2b				
1	25 Jan	Albatros DIII	(a)	A7236	22	Emmerin	1340	OOC
2	18 Feb	2-seater	(a)	A7251	„	Seclin	1400	OOC
3	24 Mar	Albatros DV	(b)	A7286	„	SE Arras	1305	DES
4	„	Albatros DV	(b)	„	„	„	1305	OOC
5	25 Mar	Albatros DV	(b)	„	„	St Leger	0825	DES
6	30 Mar	Balloon	(b)	C4894	„	NE Albert		DES

Total: 2 destroyed, 3 out of control, 1 balloon = 6.
Pilots: (a) Lt W L Wells; (b) 2/Lt W F J Harvey.

MORGAN Josiah Lewis   Lieutenant   22 SQN

From Caerphilly, Wales, he transferred to the RFC from the South Wales Borderers on 10 October 1917. Posted to 22 Squadron on 13 January 1918 he returned to HE on 4 April. Awarded the MC in April 1918, gazetted 26 July, the citation recording many low level strafing attacks and successful air combats. An instructor with No.6 School of Aviation, he left the service on 11 April 1919. All victories with Lt H F Davison, except 18 March, scored with Lt W F J Harvey.

	1918		BF2b				
1	6 Mar	Albatros DV	B1152	22	Douai	1400	OOC
2	8 Mar	Albatros DV	„	„	Lille-Douai	1245	OOC
3	„	Albatros DV	„	„	„	1245	OOC
4	„	Pfalz DIII	„	„	Douai	1310	DES
5	13 Mar	Pfalz DIII	„	„	Annoeullin	1615	DES(F)
6	18 Mar	Albatros DV	C4808	„	Carvin	1030	DES(F)
7	25 Mar	Albatros DV	A7243	„	N Havrincourt Wood	0800	OOC
8	26 Mar	Pfalz DIII	„	„	E Albert	1245	DES(F)
9	27 Mar	Fokker DrI	B1164	„	Montauban	1130	OOC
10	„	Fokker DrI	„	„	SE Albert	1135	DES
11	29 Mar	2-seater	A7243	„	SE Hangard	1530	DES
12	„	Rumpler C	„	„	E Bervillers	1610	OOC

Total: 6 destroyed, 6 out of control = 12.

MURISON John Thompson Guy   Lieutenant   45 SQN

From Muswell Hill, North London, born 16 February 1889, he became a pharmaceutical chemist until war began. Joined the London Scottish Regiment and went to France where he became entitled to the Mons Star. The London Scottish were the first territorial unit to see action in the war. Following service with the Machine Gun Corps, transferred to the RFC General List on 22 April 1917, commissioned with seniority from 2 February. Joined 45 Squadron on 22 April 1917, and commissioned temporary lieutenant from 1 May. Flew as Geoffrey Cock's observer, sharing his five victories with him. In November 1917 he was with 199 (N) Training Squadron, and trained as a pilot in 1918. Left the service on 26 April 1919. His wife notified Air Ministry of his sudden death in March 1936.

	1917			Sop 1½				
1	6 Apr	Albatros DI		A1075	45	Lille	1030	DES
2	7 May	SS DI		A8260	„	Don-Lille	1830	OOC
3	9 May	Albatros DIII		„	„	NW Seclin	1650	DES
4	„	Albatros DIII	(a)	„	„	„	1700	DES
5	16 Jun	Albatros DV		A1016	„	Warneton	1800	OOC

Total: 2 & 1 shared destroyed, 2 out of control = 5.
(a) shared with 2/Lt W A Wright/2/Lt E T Caulfield-Kelly, A8225.

MUSTARD Ernest Andrew   Lieutenant   1 AFC SQN

Born Oakleigh, Melbourne, Australia, 21 September 1893 and lived in Fitzroy, Victoria while employed on the railways. Joined the Signals Service, as a corporal with the 1st Signals Troop in Egypt and later with the 29th Australian Battn. at Gallipoli. Transferred to the Australian Flying Corps in 1917. Known as 'Pard' he often flew with Ross Smith with 1 AFC Squadron in Palestine, scoring all victories with him. Received the DFC, gazetted 8 February 1919, and was also a recipient of the Order of the Nile, 4th Class. After the war he changed his name to Mustar, qualified as a pilot and flew with the RAAF. Made the first aerial survey of the Great Barrier Reef. Left the air force and set up flying service in New Guinea. Became a Group Captain in the RAAF during WW2. Died in Queensland, whilst on holiday, 10 October 1971.

	1918			BF2b				
1	7 May	2-seater	(a)	B1229	1AFC	Jenin	1515	DES(F)
2	22 Sep	2-seater	(b)	„	„	Mufrak-Nabib	1000	FTL/DES
3	„	Pfalz DIII		„	„	Mufrak	1030	FTL/DES
4	„	Pfalz DIII		„	„	„	1030	FTL/DES
5	„	Pfalz DIII		„	„	„	1030	FTL/DES

Total: 3 & 2 shared destroyed = 5.
(a) shared with Lt A V Tonkin/Lt R A Camm B1276; (b) shared with Lt E S Headlam/Lt W H Lilly B1286.

NEWLAND Arthur   Sergeant   20 SQN

From Enfield Wash, born in 1886, Newland served with 20 Squadron from 1AM to Acting Sergeant Mechanic (67162). Received the DFM in July 1918 while still a private, London Gazette 21 September, and a Bar as Sergeant gazetted 3 December, noting six German aircraft crashed in August 1918. He was the only RAF airman to win a Bar to the DFM in WW1. Often flew with the two American Iaccaci brothers. Newland was with the London Postal Service after the war and, upon his retirement in 1959, received the Imperial Service Medal. Lived in the Edmonton area where he died in early 1964 aged 77.

	1918			BF2b				
1	18 May	Fokker DrI	(a)		20	SW Nieppe	1140	OOC
2	19 May	Pfalz DIII	(b)	C859	„	S Vieux Berquin	1040	DES
3	22 May	2-seater	(b)		„	Bailleul	0705	DES
4	27 May	Pfalz DIII	(b)	B1114	„	SW Neuve Eglise	1215	DES
5	31 May	Pfalz DIII	(a)	B1122	„	E Merville	0745	DES(F)
6	„	Albatros DV	(a)	„	„	S Merville	0800	DES
7	8 Jun	Pfalz DIII	(b)	C892	„	NE Wervicq	1720	DES
8	17 Jun	Pfalz DIII	(b)	„	„	Houthem	0715	DES
9	30 Jun	Pfalz DIII	(b)	„	„	W Halluin	0730	DES
10	14 Aug	Pfalz DIII	(c)	D7993	„	Dadizeele	1820	DES
11	„	Pfalz DIII	(c)	„	„	„	1822	DES
12	21 Aug	Pfalz DIII	(d)	„	„	Menin	1910	DES
13	„	Fokker DVII	(d)	„	„	Gheluwe	1915	DES(F)
14	„	Pfalz DIII	(c)	„	„	Wadizeele	1915	DES
15	22 Aug	Fokker DVII	(e)	E2158	„	E Comines	0840	DES
16	6 Sep	Fokker DVII	(b)	E2213	„	Cambrai-St Quentin	0830	OOC
17	„	Fokker DVII	(b)	„	„	„	0855	DES

18	15 Sep	Fokker DVII	(b)	„	„	S Lesdin	1115	DES
19	„	Fokker DVII	(b)	„	„	S Morcourt	1120	DES
20	16 Sep	Fokker DVII	(b)	„	„	W Lesdin	0825	DES
21	27 Sep	Fokker DVII	(b)	„	„	S Fontaine	1030	DES
22	„	Fokker DVII	(b)	„	„	N Bernot	1030	OOC

Total: 18 & 1 shared destroyed, 3 out of control = 22.
Pilots: (a) Lt P T Iaccaci; (b) Lt A T Iaccaci; (c) Capt D Latimer; (d) Latimer and shared with Capt H P Lale/2/Lt F J Ralph (E2467) and Lt J H Colbert/2/Lt H L Edwards (E2158); (e) Lt G E Randall.

NOBLE Walter   Lieutenant   20 SQN

Born 15 October 1885, he came from Stowmarket, Suffolk. Pre-war he was a tea planter in India between 1911-15, but returned to see service with the 9th Battn. of the Essex Regiment prior to transferring to the RFC in September 1917. Flew with 20 Squadron from 28 December, and although slightly injured on 18 February, completed his period of front line duty by 10 July. Awarded the DFC, which was gazetted on 2 August 1918 for successfully destroying enemy aircraft. On 12 September he was sent to 79 Squadron in France as the unit's recording officer (RO) and in July 1919 held an administrative post with 43 Squadron. Left the RAF on 30 November 1919. In 1920 his book *With a Bristol Fighter Squadron* was published, reprinted in 1977.

	1918			BF2b					
1	25 Jan	Albatros DV	(a)	B1177	20	SE Staden	1225	DES
2	„	Albatros DV	(a)	„	„	„	1226	OOC
3	4 Feb	Albatros DV	(a)		„	Menin-Roulers Road	1415	OOC
4	17 Feb	Pfalz DIII	(b)	B1209	„	NW Menin	1125	OOC
5	30 May	Pfalz DIII	(a)	C979	„	Lille Citadel	1725	DES
6	31 May	Albatros DV	(a)	C4699	„	Estaires	0740	OOC
7	13 Jun	Albatros DV	(c)	B1122	„	NNW Armentières	0800	OOC
8	17 Jun	Pfalz DIII	(c)	„	„	Houthem	0755	DES
9	30 Jun	Pfalz DIII	(a)	B1307	„	Wervicq	0730	DES
10	„	Pfalz DIII	(a)	„	„	„	0732	OOC
11	„	Pfalz DIII	(a)	„	„	NE Wervicq	0735	OOC
12	2 Jul	Fokker DVII	(a)	B1168	„	Gheluvelt-Menin	0845	DES

Total: 5 destroyed, 7 out of control = 12.
Pilots: (a) 2/Lt D J Weston; (b) 2/Lt L P Roberts; (c) Lt P T Iaccaci.

NOEL Tom Cecil   Lieutenant   20 SQN

From Oakham, Rutland, born 12 December 1897. A student at Eton College, he first saw service as an officer with the 3rd King's Own Scottish Borderers before joining the RFC. Won the MC with the KOSB, gazetted 9 January 1918, for conspicuous gallantry in action, and a Bar, gazetted 16 September 1918, for sharing seven German aircraft destroyed and three out of control with his pilot over a four day period. He was still only 20 years old when he was killed on 22 August. Flying with Captain D Latimer MC DFC, they were shot down in combat with Ltn Willi Negben of Jasta 7, coming down near Westroosbeke, Latimer being taken prisoner (D7993). Tom Noel was buried at Perth (China Wall), Zillebeke, Belgium. His first two victories were while flying with Captain N V Harrison and then Lt R G Bennett; the rest while with Denis Latimer.

	1918			BF2b				
1	19 Jan	Albatros DV		20	SW Roulers	1120	OOC
2	27 Mar	Albatros DV	C4641	„	W Cappy	1100	DES
3	21 Apr	Albatros DV	B1232	„	N Wervicq	1100	OOC
4	8 May	Albatros DV	C856	„	SE Wervicq	1320	DES(F)
5	„	Fokker DrI		„	Comines	1640	DES(F)
6	„	Fokker DrI		„	SE Wervicq	1640	OOC
7	„	Fokker DrI		„	„	1641	OOC

8	14 May	Albatros DV		,,	,,	Wervicq	1845	DES
9	,,	Albatros DV		,,	,,	Zillebeke	1850	CAPT
10	15 May	Pfalz DIII		,,	,,	NW Lille	1045	OOC
11	,,	Fokker DrI		,,	,,	Comines-Ypres	1115	DES
12	18 May	Pfalz DIII		,,	,,	Comines	0700	DES
13	,,	Pfalz DIII		,,	,,	NE Nieppe Forest	1140	OOC
14	,,	Pfalz DIII		,,	,,	Merville	1145	OOC
15	20 May	Albatros DV		,,	,,	NE Moorseele	1130	DES(F)
16	,,	Albatros DV		,,	,,	Coucou airfield	1135	DES
17	1 Jun	Pfalz DIII		C892	,,	Comines	0630	DES
18	9 Jun	Pfalz DIII		,,	,,	,,	0915	DES
19	17 Jun	Fokker DVII	(a)	C987	,,	Boesinghe	0745	OOC
20	30 Jun	Pfalz DIII		,,	,,	Comines	0730	DES
21	1 Jul	Fokker DrI		,,	,,	Menin	1845	OOC
22	14 Jul	Fokker DVII	(b)	,,	,,	SE Ypres	0900	OOC
23	,,	Fokker DVII		,,	,,	,,	0900	OOC
24	19 Jul	Fokker DVII		,,	,,	N Comines	0845	DES

Total: 12 destroyed, 1 captured, 9 and 2 shared out of control = 24.
(a) shared with Lt W M Thomson/Pbr F J Ralph, C843; (b) shared with Lt A T Iaccaci/2/Lt R W Turner.

NOSS Arthur Rex Hurden   2nd Lieutenant   48 SQN

From Crouch End, north London, Noss was commissioned into the HAC before transferring into the RFC in March 1917. Served with 48 Squadron from June 1917, often flying as observer to Captain K R Park MC. Recommended for the Military Cross on 19 August 1917 for actions on the 17th. This was approved and gazetted on 9 January 1918 for a fight in which one enemy aircraft was shot down and three driven down out of control after two other squadron aircraft had been put out of action. Injured in a landing accident on 15 September in A7217 flown by Second Lieutenant E B Corry and died of his injuries the next day; buried at Zuydcoote, France.

	1917			BF2b				
1	26 May	Albatros DIII	(a)	A7117	48	SE Douai	1945	OOC
2	11 Jun	2-seater	(b)	A7137	,,	Vitry	1100	DES
3	12 Aug	Albatros DIII	(c)	A7176	,,	S Slype	1045	OOC
4	16 Aug	DFW C	(c)	A7182	,,	Slype	1130	OOC
5	17 Aug	Albatros DV	(c)	,,	,,	W Slype	0655	OOC
6	,,	Albatros DV	(c)	,,	,,	,,	0655	DES
7	,,	Albatros DV	(c)	,,	,,	off Slype	0715	OOC
8	,,	Albatros DV	(c)	,,	,,	Slype	0725	OOC
9	25 Aug	Albatros DV	(c)	A7213	,,	S Slype	2000	DES(F)

Total: 3 destroyed, 6 out of control = 9.
Pilots: (a) Lt H M Fraser; (b) 2/Lt H Smithers; (c) Lt K R Park.

O'TOOLE William   2nd Lieutenant   48 SQN

Born 30 December 1893, he came from Sutton, Surrey. A married man, he worked on the London Underground from December 1912 until late 1914. Transferred to the RFC from the 4th Reserve Battn. of the Royal Irish Fusiliers on 2 April 1917 on secondment. Joined 48 Squadron on 19 June and returned to Home Establishment on 6 September. Underwent pilot training at Reading but was injured in an accident on 14 January 1918. However, by May he was with 56 Training Squadron. A year later he was assistant adjutant with 4 Comm. Squadron at Felixstowe and left the service on 14 October. In the early 1920s he was living in Cheam, Surrey.

	1917			BF2b				
1	3 Jul	Albatros DV	(a)	A7153	48	Quéant	0930	OOC
2	27 Jul	DFW C	(b)	A7108	,,	Westende	1650	OOC
3	20 Aug	Albatros DV	(c)	A7216	,,	Ghistelles	1915	DES

4	„	Albatros DV	(c)	„	„	„	1915	OOC
5	21 Aug	Albatros DV	(d)	„	„	E Westende	0745	OOC
6	„	Albatros DV	(d)	„	„	„	0745	OOC
7	„	Albatros DV	(c)	„	„	„	1945	DES
8	25 Aug	Albatros DV	(c)	„	„	Westkerke	1210	OOC

Total: 2 destroyed, 6 out of control = 8.
Pilots: (a) 2/Lt A G Riley; (b) Capt F P Holliday; (c) Capt J T Milne; (d) Lt K R Park.

OWEN Hugh 2nd Lieutenant 48 SQN

Born on 3 August 1892. Living in Wheathampstead, Hertfordshire, he became an actor in May 1910, believed to be under the name of Matheson Lang, but this ended at the end of 1912. When war came he joined the East Kent Regiment and was the company Lewis Gun officer in his Battalion. Transferring to the RFC, he served with 48 Squadron, often flying as Keith Park's observer. He left the RAF on 7 March 1919.

	1917			BF2b				
1	20 May	Albatros DIII	(a)	A7108	48	Brebières	1230	OOC
2	15 Jun	Albatros DIII	(b)	A7116	„	Fampoux	1945	OOC
3	16 Jun	Albatros DIII	(c)	„	„	Estrée	1050	OOC
4	25 Aug	Albatros DV	(c)	A7217	„	Westkerke	1210	OOC
5	31 Aug	Albatros DV	(c)	„	„	Zarren	0905	OOC
6	14 Sep	Albatros DV	(d)	A7227	„	N Dixmude	1845	OOC
7	„	Albatros DV	(d)	„	„	S Dixmude	1950	DES(F)

Total: 1 destroyed, 4 & 2 shared out of control = 7.
Pilots: (a) Lt H J Pratt and shared with Capt B E Baker/Lt R N W Jeff A7112; (b) Pratt and shared with Lt H M Fraser/Lt M A Benjamin A7117; (c) Lt Pratt; (d) Lt K R Park.

PARLEE Medley Kingdon 2nd Lieutenant 22 SQN

Born Stanley, York County, New Brunswick, Canada, 31 May 1888 he was a Rhodes Scholar. Enlisted in the 28th Battn. CEF on 23 October 1914 and went to France in September 1915. Transferred to the RFC in October 1916. Joined C Flight 22 Squadron on 7 November 1916. Later trained as a pilot and became an instructor at the School of Special Flying towards the end of the war, in Canada. Schoolteacher post-war, retiring after WW2, he died in a house fire in 1966. His older brother, George William Hugh Parlee, also an observer, was killed with 5 Squadron on 20 August 1918.

	1917			FEb2				
1	4 Feb	Albatros DII	(a)	A5461	22	Rocquigny	1400	DES
2	6 Apr	Albatros DIII	(b)		„	St Quentin	0800	DES
3	8 Apr	Albatros DIII	(b)		„	Regny	0700	DES
4	13 Apr	Albatros DII	(b)	4983	„	Itancourt	1830	DES
5	9 May	Albatros DIII	(a)	A5461	„	Honnecourt	1545	OOC
6	„	Albatros DIII	(a)		„	SW Lesdains	1550	DES

Total: 5 destroyed, 1 out of control = 6.
Pilots: (a) Lt C M Clement; (b) Lt J V Aspinall. Victory No.2 shared with Capt Gladstone/1AM Friend, Capt C M Clement/2/Lt L G Davies, Lt J F Day/2/Lt J K Campbell.

PARRY Samuel Lieutenant 62 SQN

A married man, his home address was given as The Shepherd's Arms, Cwmaman, Aberdare, Glamorgan. Following service with the Royal Engineers, Parry joined the RFC and was sent to 62 Squadron on 28 December 1917, going with them to France on 20 January 1918. Killed in action on 3 May 1918, (Bristol Fighter C4859) although his pilot, Lt C H Arnison, was unhurt. Buried at Huby-St Leu, France.

	1918			BF2b					
1	27 Mar	EA	(a)		62				OOC
2	„	EA	(a)		„				OOC
3	„	EA	(a)		„				DES
4	12 Apr	Albatros DV	(b)	C4859	„	E Estaires		1420	OOC
5	21 Apr	Pfalz DIII	(b)	„	„	Estaires-Lille		1000	OOC
6	„	Pfalz DIII	(b)	„	„	„		1000	OOC
7	3 May	Albatros DV	(b)	„	„	E Armentières		1115	OOC
8	„	Albatros DV	(b)	„	„	„		1116	OOC
9	„	Albatros DV	(b)	„	„	„		1117	DES(F)

Total: 2 destroyed, 7 out of control = 9.
Pilots: (a) 2/Lt H C M Nangle; (b) 2/Lt C H Arnison.

PLATEL Sidney Henri   1AM   11 SQN

Observer with 11 Squadron in 1917, service No.25362. Shot up and forced to land in Third Army lines, 31 October 1917 and had a toe shot off. His pilot was Sgt T F Stephenson (with whom he shared all victories), and their BF2b (A7235) could not be salvaged.

	1917			BF2b				
1	23 Sep	Albatros DV		A7209	11	Vitry	1625	OOC
2	20 Oct	Albatros DV		„		NW Cambrai	1640	OOC
3	„	Albatros DV		„		„	1640	OOC
4	31 Oct	Albatros DV		A7235		Fresse	1530	DES(F)
5	„	Albatros DV		„		„	1530	DES

Total: 2 destroyed, 3 out of control = 5.

POTTER Frank A   Sergeant   20 SQN

From Leyton, Essex, Frank Potter (No.P2425) served with 20 Squadron and won the Military Medal in July 1917. After a combat on 27 July the FE2d he and his pilot, Lt H W Joslyn were flying — A6415 — was hit by AA fire, and their undercarriage collapsed on landing but they survived unhurt. Potter was badly injured on 5 September and died on the 10th. He was buried at Bailleul Cemetery, having been promoted to Sergeant (93971). His first victory was scored while flying with Lt N V Harrison, the remainder with Lt H W Joslyn.

	1917			BF2b				
1	16 Jun	Albatros DIII		A6415	20	NE Ypres	2030	OOC
2	29 Jun	Albatros DV		„		Houthem	1315	DES(F)
3	2 Jul	Albatros DV		„		Comines-Houthem	1245	OOC
4	7 Jul	Albatros DV		„		Wervicq	1900	OOC
5	22 Jul	Albatros DV		A6548		Menin-Wervicq	1645	DES(F)
6	27 Jul	Albatros DV		A6415		Menin	c2020	OOC
7	28 Jul	Albatros DV		A6429		Kezelbars	0915	OOC

Total: 2 destroyed, 5 out of control = 7.

POWELL Leslie Archibald   Lieutenant   11 SQN

From Redland, Bristol, he was born on 27 June 1896. Pre-war he was a journalist with the *Western Daily Press* between 1913-14. Saw service with the 8th Battn. of the Gloucester Regiment before transferring to the RFC in May 1917, becoming a temporary second lieutenant (General List) in July. Joined 11 Squadron on 16 July and was the usual observer to the Canadian ace, Andrew McKeever, with whom he shared all his victories except No.7 (Capt G H Hooper). Received the MC and Bar, in September and December respectively, both gazetted in January 1918, the same month he returned to Home Establishment. Returned to the army in January 1920.

	1917							
1	7 Jul	Albatros DV		A7194	11	S Vitry	2030	DES
2	„	Albatros DV		„	„	„	2032	OOC
3	„	Albatros DV		„	„	Monchy	2040	OOC
4	5 Aug	Albatros DV		A7159	„	Quéant	1950	DES
5	„	Albatros DV		„	„	„	1950	DES(F)
6	„	Albatros DV		„	„	„	2000	OOC
7	11 Sep	Albatros DV			„	Cagnicourt	1845	OOC
8	23 Sep	Albatros DV		A7159	„	Vitry	1625	OOC
9	„	Albatros DV		„	„	„	1625	OOC
10	2 Oct	Albatros DV		A7121	„	Douai-Cambrai	1810	DES(F)
11	16 Oct	Albatros DV		A7159	„	Brebières	1020	DES
12	„	Albatros DV		„	„	Douai	1025	DES
13	31 Oct	Albatros DV		A7153	„	Fresse	1600	OOC
14	„	Albatros DV		„	„	„	1600	DES
15	„	Albatros DV		„	„	„	1600	OOC
16	30 Nov	Albatros DV		A7258	„	S Cambrai	1150	DES
17	„	Albatros DV		„	„	„	1150	DES
18	„	Albatros DV		„	„	„	1155	DES
19	„	Albatros DV		„	„	„	1155	DES

Total: 11 destroyed, 8 out of control = 19.

PROCTOR Thomas   Sergeant   88 SQN

As private and then a sergeant (212137), this 31 year old from Belfast, County Antrim, NI, flew with 88 Squadron in 1918 until his death in combat on 27 September 1918. He and his pilot, Lt C Foster, were on a Special Mission in E2153 and were shot down near Abancourt by Vfw Fritz Classen of Jasta 26. Proctor has no known grave.

	1918			BF2b				
1	31 May	Albatros DV	(a)	C821	62	Ostende	1950	OOC
2	2 Jun	Albatros DV	(a)	„	„	Middlekerke-Ostende	1935	DES(F)
3	11 Aug	Fokker DVII	(b)	C852	„	NW Péronne	1145	DES
4	„	Fokker DVII	(b)	„	„	„	1145	DES
5	19 Aug	Fokker DrI	(c)	E2153	„	Bauvin-Douai	1025	OOC

Total: 3 destroyed, 2 out of control = 5.
Pilots: (a) Capt A Hepburn; (b) Lt A R Stedman; (c) Lt A Williamson.

PURVIS W C   2nd Lieutenant   45 & 20 SQNS

Flew Sopwith 1½ Strutters with 45 Squadron between 22 June and 1 September 1917, then transferred to 20 Squadron when 45 equipped with Camels. Brought his score to five that month.

	1917			Sop 1½				
1	16 Jul	Albatros DV	(a)	A8298	45	Polygon Wood	1640	DES(F)
2	11 Aug	Albatros DV	(a)	A1053	„	Comines	1915	OOC
3	23 Aug	Albatros DV	(a)	„	„	Bellewarde Lake	0915	OOC
				BF2b				
4	11 Sep	Albatros DV	(b)	A7193	20	E Menin	1400	DES
5	27 Sep	Albatros DV	(b)	A7255	„	Moorslede	1300	DES

Total: 3 destroyed, 2 out of control = 5.
Pilots: (a) Lt K B Montgomery; (b) 2/Lt F F Babbage.

RALPH Francis James   2nd Lieutenant   20 SQN

Born 9 December 1892, he was living with his wife in Turlanton, Leicester pre-war where he was a draughtsman with the Co-op Gas Company, 1910-15. Ralph was commissioned on 12 February 1918 and flew with 20 Squadron on 18 April 1918, winning the DFC (gazetted 2 November). He was wounded on 10 May during an air fight, although his pilot, Lt D E Smith, flew him back to base (C4851). Returning to duty later, he was killed in action on 3 September. This time his pilot flew back with his lifeless body. He was 25 years old and was buried at Villers Bretonneux Cemetery, France.

	1918			BF2b					
1	9 May	Fokker DrI	(a)		20	W Lille	1650	DES(F)
2	31 May	Albatros DV	(b)	C4604	„	N Laventie	0730	DES
3	9 Jun	Pfalz DIII	(c)	C843	„	Comines-Houthem	0945	DES
4	17 Jun	Fokker DVII	(d)	„	„	Boesinghe	0745	OOC
5	26 Jun	Pfalz DIII	(e)	D8090	„	Armentières	1900	OOC
6	25 Jul	Fokker DVII	(f)	C4718	„	N Comines	0850	DES
7	„	Fokker DVII	(g)	„	„	Comines	0855	DES(F)
8	14 Aug	Fokker DVII	(f)	E2467	„	Dadizeele	1820	OOC
9	21 Aug	Pfalz DIII	(f)	„	„	NE Gheluwe	1910	DES
10	„	Albatros DV	(f)	„	„	Gheluwe	1915	OOC
11	„	Fokker DVII	(h)	„	„	„	1915	DES(F)
12	„	Fokker DVII	(f)	„	„	W Menin-Roulers Rly	1917	DES
13	3 Sep	Fokker DVII	(f)	E2181	„	S Havrincourt Wood	1745	OOC

Total: 6 & 2 shared destroyed, 5 out of control = 13.
Pilots: (a) Lt D E Smith; (b) Lt L H T Capel; (c) Lt W M Thomson; (d) Thomson, and shared with Capt D Latimer/Lt T C Noel C987; (e) Lt P T Iaccaci; (f) Capt H P Lale; (g) Lale, and shared with Lt W M Thomson/Sgt D D C Summers (C843) and Lt D E Smith/Pbr J Hills (C4672); (h) Lale, and shared with Capt D Latimer/Sgt A Newlands (D7993) and Lt J H Colbert/2/Lt H L Edwards (E2158).

REED V　　Corporal　　48 SQN

All except victory number one was scored whilst sitting behind Second Lieutenant J A W Binnie, 48 Squadron, 1917, Reed being one of the original gunner/observers that went to France with this unit in April.

	1917			BF2a				
1	4 May	2-seater	(a)	A3347	48	Pelves	1615	DES
				BF2b				
2	15 Jun	Albatros DIII		A7123	„	SW Douai	1940	OOC
3	„	Albatros DIII	(b)	„	„	N Vitry	2020	DES(F)
4	13 Jul	Albatros DIII		A7151	„	Slype	0940	DES(F)
5	28 Jul	Albatros DV	(c)	A7123	„	Ghistelles-Zevecote	0815	DES(F)
6	19 Aug	Albatros DV		A7220	„	Ostende	0650	OOC
7	22 Aug	Albatros DV		„	„	Ghistelles	0900	DES(F)
8	26 Aug	Albatros DV		„	„	W Middlekerke	0830	DES
9	„	Albatros DV		„	„	Wiskerke-Leffinghe	0830	OOC

Total: 3 & 3 shared destroyed, 3 out of control = 9.
Pilots: (a) 2/Lt H Smithers and shared with Capt J H T Letts/2/Lt L Speller A3350; (b) 2/Lt J A W Binnie and shared with Capt B E Baker/Lt H Munro A7149; (c) Binnie and shared with Capt Baker/Lt G R Spencer A7170.

ROBERTSON John Henry　　Lieutenant　　48 SQN

Although noted as having an Edinburgh address, Robertson served in the Welsh Regiment, commissioned 20 January 1917, seniority 23 July 1916, until he transferred to the RFC General List on 6 November 1917. Served with 48 Squadron from 2 September 1917 but was wounded on 11 March 1918 and died the same day. Buried at Roye, France.

	1918			BF2b				
1	3 Jan	Albatros DV	(a)	A7229	48	St Quentin	1210	OOC
2	8 Mar	Albatros DV	(b)	A7114	„	Busigny	1050	DES
3	„	Albatros DV	(b)	„	„	„	1050	OOC
4	„	Albatros DV	(b)	„	„	S Bohain	1600	OOC
5	11 Mar	Fokker DrI	(b)	„	„	St Quentin	1255	OOC

Total: 1 destroyed, 4 out of control = 5.
Pilots: (a) Capt K R Park; (b) 2/Lt H H Hartley.

ROBSON Charles Crichton   Lieutenant   11 SQN

From Edinburgh, Scotland, Robson saw service with the 12th Regiment of the Royal Scots (2/Lt) before transferring to the RFC General List in September 1917 as a temporary lieutenant. Posted to 11 Squadron on 19 December 1917, proceeding to France the next day, teaming up with Lt H W Sellers. Their victory on 21 March was over Ludwig Hanstein, ace and commander of Jasta 35b. Awarded the Military Cross. Shot down on 15 May and made a prisoner, but Sellers was killed (C845). They were claimed by Josef Mai of Jasta 5 over Bouchou. His MC was gazetted on 22 June, noting a successful long range reconnaissance mission despite difficult weather conditions. Robson was a prisoner at Karlsruhe and repatriated in December 1918; left the service on 28 February 1919. All victories with Herbert Sellers.

	1918			BF2b					
1	12 Mar	LVG CVI		C4673	11	Doignes	1440	DES(F)
2	13 Mar	Albatros DV		„	„	Oisy	1400	OOC
3	15 Mar	Albatros DV		„	„	Rumilly	1115	OOC
4	18 Mar	Albatros DV		„	„	N St Quentin	1100	OOC
5	21 Mar	Albatros C		„	„	Morchies	1615	DES
6	„	Albatros DV	(a)	„	„	„	1615	DES(F)
7	2 Apr	Fokker DrI		„	„	SE Albert	1820	OOC
8	15 May	Fokker DrI	(b)	„	„	Mametz	1720	OOC

Total: 3 destroyed, 5 out of control = 8.
(a) Ludwig Hanstein, Jasta 35b; (b) shared with Capt J V Aspinall/Lt de la Cour.

RUDKIN John   2nd Lieutenant   88 SQN

From Grantham, Lincolnshire. Born 22 June 1898, he was with the 4th Reserve Dragoon Regiment in 1917. Commissioned 8 July 1917. Joined 88 Squadron in April 1918. Life-long friend of his pilot, Edgar Johnston, with whom he shared all his WW1 victories. Died in the 1970s.

	1918			BF2b				
1	18 May	Albatros DV		C4867	88	N Langemarck	0730	OOC
2	„	Albatros DV		„	„	„	0735	DES(F)
3	8 Jun	Albatros DV			„	E Couckelaere		OOC
4	1 Jul	Fokker DVII		C4867	„	W Westroosebeke	1945	OOC
5	8 Aug	Fokker DrI		E2458	„	Provin	1030	OOC
6	„	Fokker DrI		„	„	„	1030	DES
7	11 Aug	Fokker DVII		„	„	Rancourt	1130	DES
8	„	Fokker DVII		„	„	„	1135	OOC
9	13 Aug	Fokker DVII		D8064	„	Provin	1610	OOC
10	19 Aug	Fokker DrI	(a)	C4867	„	Oignies	1030	OOC

Total: 3 destroyed, 6 & 1 shared out of control = 10.
(a) shared with Lt K B Conn/2/Lt B H Smyth E2216.

SAYERS Edward Harper   Sergeant   20 SQN

From Merton, south London, Sayers was a 2AM, later a sergeant (12315), flying with 20 Squadron in 1917. On 24 April he and 2/Lt E O Perry survived being shot down by Vfw J Wirtz of MFJ I in FE2d A6403 over Polygon Wood. However, he was not so lucky on the 30th; after being hit by AA fire he and Lt D Y Hay (A5143) fell out of control and crashed north of Poperinghe, both men being injured. AA damaged his FE again on 8 June (A1965) but his pilot 2/Lt W Durrand got them back home safely. On 31 May, he was notified of the award of the French Medaille Militaire. Trained as a pilot upon posting to HE. Killed in an accident on 17 July 1918 in a Pup (B5992), colliding with another Pup, whilst serving with the Manston Pilot Pool.

	1917			FE2d				
1	7 Apr	Albatros DII	(a)	A29	20	Tourcoing	1830	OOC
2	24 Apr	Albatros DIII	(b)	A6403	„	Becelaère	0755	DES(F)
3	2 May	Albatros DIII	(c)	A6431	„	Comines	1115	DES(F)
4	5 Jun	Albatros DIII	(c)	A6414	„	Wervicq	0800	DES(F)
5	8 Jun	Albatros DIII	(d)	A1965	„	Comines	0745	DES(F)

Total: 4 destroyed, 1 out of control = 5.
Pilots: (a) 2/Lt S N Pike; (b) Lt E O Perry; (c) Lt D C Cunnell; (d) 2/Lt W Durrand.

SCARAMANGA James John   Lieutenant   20 & 22 SQNS

From Redhill in Surrey, born 25 July 1898, he also lived at Buckingham Gate, south-west London. Scaramanga volunteered to be a pilot in 1916, but did not achieve his aim so became an observer. Qualified as such he was posted to 20 Squadron on 28 December, with the rank of second lieutenant effective the next day. He was wounded on 11 April 1918, his pilot, Major J A Dennistoun also being wounded. They were forced to land through hits from machine-gun fire, after which their BF2b (B1275) was destroyed by shell fire. On recovery he was posted to 22 Squadron on 6 June 1918 but was wounded again on 10 July, in an air fight. Flying with Lt J E Gurdon he was severely wounded and became unconscious. With Gurdon also wounded and an EA on their tail, he came round and with his one good arm shot down the attacker. He died soon after they landed and was buried at Aire. He was just short of his 20th birthday. All victories with Lt Gurdon except the first two, scored with Lt D G Cooke and Lt D Latimer.

	1918			BF2b				
1	9 Mar	Albatros DV		C4605	20	S Comines	0800	OOC
2	13 Mar	Pfalz DIII		C4615	„	Comines-Wervicq	1255	OOC
3	19 Jun	Fokker DVII		C989	22	SE Armentières	2020	DES
4	„	Fokker DVII		„	„	„	2020	DES
5	„	Fokker DVII		„	„	„	2020	OOC
6	27 Jun	Fokker DrI		„	„	„	1850	OOC
7	1 Jul	Pfalz DIII		„	„	Armentières	1940	OOC
8	4 Jul	Fokker DVII		„	„	Noyelles, N Seclin	1920	DES
9	9 Jul	DFW C		„	„	N La Bassée	1100	DES
10	10 Jul	Pfalz DIII		C1003	„	Armentières-Lille	0930	DES
11	„	Pfalz DIII		„	„	„	0930	OOC
12	„	Pfalz DIII		„	„	„	0930	OOC

Total: 5 destroyed, 7 out of control = 12.

SCOTT Laurence Henry   Captain   20 SQN

Born 9 March 1896, he came from Balham, south London. Attended the City of London School between 1908-13 and then a year with the University of Paris, France. Flew with 20 Squadron in 1916-7 following service with the 8th Middlesex Regiment, Territorial Force. The award of the Military Cross was made in October 1916, gazetted on 25 November. The citation related how he and his pilot chased an enemy aircraft six miles into enemy held territory and eventually shot it down. Became Assistant Instructor in Gunnery from 13 July and made temporary Captain on 7 November. Left the service on 20 April 1919. All victories with Captain G R M Reid.

	1916			FE2b				
1	29 Jul	Rumpler C		A22	20	Zandvoorde	1215	DES
2	31 Jul	LVG C		„	„	Ypres	1135	DES
3	31 Aug	Fokker D		A19	„	Langemarck	1025	OOC
4	24 Sep	Fokker D	(a)	A39	„	Rumbeke	1210	DES
5	16 Oct	LVG C		„	„	Dadizeele	0905	OOC
6	21 Oct	Fokker D		„	„	Comines	1200	DES

Total: 3 & 1 shared destroyed, 2 out of control = 6.
(a) shared with Lt A D Pearce/2/Lt W F Findlay, A19.

SHANNON Christopher James   Sergeant   22 SQN

From Stamford Hill, London, Shannon often flew as observer to Capt F G Gibbons. He was awarded the DFM late in 1918 and his service No. was 237756.

	1917			BF2b				
1	21 Aug	Fokker DVII	(a)	C1040	22	N Cambrai	1945	OOC
2	2 Sep	Fokker DVII	(b)	D7894	„	Haynecourt	1115	DES
3	„	Fokker DVII	(b)	„	„	„	1115	DES
4	16 Sep	Fokker DVII	(b)	E2454	„	Quesnoy Wood	1530	OOC
5	27 Sep	Fokker DVII	(b)	F6040	„	Sensée Canal-Cambrai	0730	OOC

Total: 2 destroyed, 3 out of control = 5.
Pilots: (a) Lt T W Martin; (b) Lt F G Gibbons.

SMITH William Watson   Lieutenant   139 SQN

Saw service in Italy with 139 Squadron on Bristol Fighters but was wounded on 30 July 1918. He and his pilot, Lt W C Simon (C999) were in action with Albatros Scouts and two-seaters. Smith was wounded again on 30 October during a combat and also injured in a crash on 7 November. He was awarded the DFC, gazetted 8 February 1919.

	1918			BF2b				
1	4 Jul	Albatros DIII	(a)	C999	139	Levico	1030	OOC
2	15 Jul	Albatros DIII	(b)	C997	„	Cortesano	0800	DES
3	17 Jul	Albatros DV	(b)	C994	„	Nemo		DES
4	30 Jul	Albatros DIII	(a)	C999	„	Motta	0630	DES(F)
5	„	Albatros DIII	(a)	„	„	„	0630	DES(F)
6	„	2-seater	(a)	„	„	Torre de Mosta	0635	DES
7	„	2-seater	(a)	„	„	Caorle	0635	DES
8	„	Albatros DIII	(a)	„	„	„	0635	DES(F)

Total: 7 destroyed, 1 out of control = 8.
Pilots: (a) Lt W C Simons; (b) Lt H C Walters.

SMYTH Bertram Hutchinson   Lieutenant   88 SQN

Born 5 September 1894, he and his family were living in Buenos Aires, Argentina, where he was employed as a statistics clerk with the Buenos Aires Pacific Railway between May 1912 and February 1916. Coming to England he was commissioned into the 10th Battn. of the Gloucester Regiment. Transferred to the RFC in February 1918 he was sent to 88 Squadron on 16 April where he remained until returned to HE on 12 September. On 1 March 1919 he returned to the 3rd Battn. of his former regiment.

	1918			BF2b				
1	28 Jun	Halberstadt C	(a)	C787	88	Houthulst Forest	2000	DES(F)
2	29 Jun	Fokker DVII	(a)	„	„	Ghistelles	2010	DES
3	„	Fokker DVII	(b)	„	„	„	2010	DES
4	14 Aug	Fokker DVII	(c)	E2153	„	Dompierre	1745	DES(F)
5	19 Aug	Fokker DVII	(a)	E2216	„	Oignies	1025	OOC
6	„	Fokker DrI	(d)	„	„	„	1030	OOC
7	4 Sep	Fokker DrI	(c)	E2153	„	Seclin	0900	OOC
8	„	Fokker DrI	(c)	„	„	Provin	0930	OOC

Total: 4 destroyed, 4 out of control = 8.
(a) Lt K B Conn; (b) shared with Capt K R Simpson/Sgt C Hill C983, Lt W A Wheeler/2/Lt T S Chiltern C774; (c) Lt C Foster; (d) shared with Capt E C Johnston/2/Lt J Rudkin C4867.

SUTHERLAND Leslie William   Lieutenant   1 AFC SQN

Born Murrumbeena, Melbourne, Victoria, Australia, 17 December 1892. A peacetime carpenter, he saw service with the Australian Signals Service and Light Horse, being Mentioned in Despatches on 6 September 1916. Transferred to the Australian Flying Corps in 1917. Flew in

Bristol Fighters in Palestine with No.1 AFC Squadron in 1918 and won the MC, gazetted on 18 July 1918, having previously been awarded the DCM. He later became a pilot in the RAAF and wrote the book *Aces and Kings*, an unofficial history of 1 AFC Squadron. Died 24 October 1967.

	1918			BF2b				
1	3 Jan	Albatros DIII	(a)	C4623	1AFC	E Arran-Mukeibik	0920	DES
2	22 Jul	Rumpler C	(b)	„	„	S Beit Lid	0615	DES
3	30 Jul	Rumpler C	(c)	C4626	„	Wadi el Auja	0710	FTL/DES
4	3 Aug	2-seater	(c)	„	„	NW Afuleh	1130	FTL/DES
5	„	2-seater	(c)	„	„	Leijun	1145	OOC
6	„	2-seater	(d)	„	„	NE Ez Daba	1210	DES
7	23 Sep	DFW C	(c)	„	„	NW Deraa	0715	FTL/DES
8	28 Sep	DFW C	(c)	„	„	Damascus A/F	0815	FTL/DES

Total: 6 & 1 shared destroyed, 1 out of control = 8.
Pilots: (a) Lt R A Austin; (b) Lt A V Tonkin; (c) Lt E P Kenny; (d) Kenny and shared with Lt J P McGinness/ Lt H Fysh B1223.

TENNANT James   Lieutenant   20 SQN

Born 27 February 1896, he came from Newton Stewart, Dumfries, Scotland. In 1910 he joined the local branch of the Clydesdale Bank then moved to London in 1913, working for the London and Provincial Bank. Served as a private in the London Regiment (almost certainly the 14th Battn). Commissioned into the 3/4th Cameron Highlanders on 2 November 1915 and went to France attached to the Liverpool Scottish Regiment, 7 September 1916. Mentioned in Despatches, gazetted 29 November 1916 and won the Military Cross, gazetted 4 June 1917. Transferred to the RFC, qualifying as a Flying Officer Observer on 7 July 1917. Full Lieutenant 1 September. Flew with 20 Squadron from 7 July 1917 and had a lucky escape on 16 August being brought down by AA fire whilst flying with Lt Harry Luchford (FE2d A6448). Was an assistant adjutant in 1918 in England, and served with 51 and 143 Squadrons. Served again with the RAF in WW2, 1939-40.

	1917			FE2d				
1	9 Jun	Albatros DIII	(a)	A6427	20	N Wervicq-E Ploegsteert	1900	OOC
2	13 Jun	Albatros DIII	(b)	A6516	„	Houthem	0845	OOC
3	3 Jul	Albatros DV	(b)	A6547	„	Becelaère	1500	DES
4	6 Jul	Albatros DV	(b)	A6512	„	Comines	1830	OOC
5	„	Albatros DV	(b)	„	„	„	1830	OOC
6	16 Aug	2-seater	(b)	A6448	„	Menin	1145	OOC
7	17 Aug	Albatros DV	(b)	B1897	„	Houthem	1445	DES

Total: 2 destroyed, 5 out of control = 7.
Pilots: (a) 2/Lt B Strange; (b) Lt H G E Luchford.

THOMPSON Louis Mark   Lieutenant   62 SQN

A Canadian from Balgonie, Saskachewan, Lou was born in Toronto on 22 October 1888, although the date in the RFC records shows 1892. In his teens he moved to the Canadian Prairies with his family and was a self employed grain broker in Saskatchewan pre-war. Joined the CEF and became a sergeant in the 18th Canadian reserve Battn. in France before transferring to the RFC in September 1917. He joined 62 Squadron on 13 March 1918 but was slightly wounded on 21 April. He and his pilot, Lt D A Savage were hit by AA fire near Armentières and crashed, Savage also being injured (B1234). Thompson was recommended for the DFC on 23 August 1918. This followed an incident the previous day, his Canadian pilot, Capt E T Morrow was wounded in combat with a Fokker DVII and their BF2b — C895 — caught fire. Morrow fainted and they spun down, Thompson using a fire extinguisher to fight the flames. Morrow came round and managed a forced landing near Ficheux, but flames again started up. Thompson pulled Morrow from the cockpit to safety. Morrow had to have his lower left leg amputated.

Both men were recommended for the DFC but only Morrow received one. Thompson was invalided out of the service on 7 September 1918. After the war he returned to his broker job and then worked in the farm implement business in the USA until he retired to Altoona, Florida in 1971, where he died a couple of years later.

	1918			BF2b					
1	26 Mar	EA	(a)	B1302	62	E Nurlu		OOC
2	12 Apr	Pfalz DIII	(a)	B1234	„	Estaires	1420	OOC
3	„	Albatros DV	(a)	„	„	Aubers	1515	OOC
4	21 Apr	Albatros DV	(a)	„	„	W Lille	0945	DES
5	„	Pfalz DIII	(a)	„	„	„	0950	DES
6	10 Aug	Pfalz DIII	(b)	C895	„	SW Péronne	1130	OOC
7	„	Pfalz DIII	(b)	„	„	„	1131	OOC
8	22 Aug	Fokker DVII	(b)	„	„	Pronville	0745	OOC
9	„	Fokker DVII	(b)	„	„	„	0745	DES

Total: 3 destroyed, 6 out of control = 9.
Pilots: (a) Lt D A Savage; (b) Lt/Capt E T Morrow.

THOMSON George   Lieutenant   22 SQN

Born in England, 3 October 1896, his family emigrated to Celista, British Columbia, Canada in 1910. Worked as a clerk in Revelstone, BC 1911-13. The youngest of six boys, he enlisted at Kamloops in 1914, aged 17, whilst living in Notch Hill, BC. Went overseas with the 30th Battn CEF and served at Ypres in April 1915 and was drafted into the famous 15th Battn. (48th Highlanders of Canada). Saw action at all the major battles: Festaubert, Givenchy and Ploegsteert. Following a year's service with the Canadians he received a commission and was gazetted to the 7/8th King's Own Scottish Borderers and was twice wounded with them. Thomson joined the RFC in October 1917 and on 19 March 1918 was with 22 Squadron. The award of the DFC was gazetted on 21 September, noting 9 victories in his citation. Returned to HE on 12 August and commenced pilot training at No.1 School of Aviation. Left the service on 9 April 1919, as an Honorary Lieutenant and returned to Canada but did not stay long in the country. His first three victories were scored whilst flying with Lt S H Wallage, the rest with W F J Harvey.

	1918			BF2b				
1	8 May	Pfalz DIII	C795	22	N La Bassée	1900	DES
2	15 May	DFW C	„	„	La Bassée	1040	OOC
3	„	2-seater	„	„	„	1045	OOC
4	20 May	Balloon	B1209	„	Bailleul	1700	DES
5	„	Balloon	„	„	„	1705	DES
6	22 May	DFW C	C776	„	Merville-Estaires	1925	OOC
7	26 May	Albatros DV	C842	„	Armentières-Lille	1945	OOC
8	28 May	2-seater	C4631	„	La Bassée	1100	DES
9	„	2-seater	„	„	Richebourg	1105	DES
10	10 Jul	Fokker DrI	C1040	„	SE Lille	0915	DES
11	„	Fokker DrI	„	„	„	0920	DES
12	20 Jul	Fokker DVII	C989	„	S Lille	0900	DES
13	„	Fokker DVII	„	„	„	0915	DES
14	„	Fokker DVII	„	„	„	0930	OOC

Total: 9 destroyed, 5 out of control = 14.

THORNTON Anthony Joseph Hill   2nd Lieutenant   22 SQN

Born 24 November 1898. Made temporary Second Lieutenant RFC General List, on probation on 1 October 1917. Flying with 22 Squadron, which he joined on 11 December, he flew with J E Gurdon, taking part in the famous 'two versus twenty' fight on 7 May 1918, over Arras. He returned to Home Establishment in July and left the service on 9 February 1919.

	1918			BF2b					
1	2 Apr	Fokker DrI		B1162	22	W Vauvillers	1615	DES
2	"	Fokker DrI		"	"	"	1615	DES
3	7 May	D		B1253	"	E Arras	1845	DES(F)
4	"	D		"	"	"	1845	DES
5	"	D		"	"	"	1846	DES

Total: 5 destroyed.

TINSLEY William   Lieutenant   88 SQN

From East Ham, Essex, Bill Tinsley was born on 28 April 1895. Between July 1912 and September 1914 he worked as a clerk with the Portland Cement Company in London. When war came he joined the 13th London Regiment before transferring to the RFC in February 1918. Went to 88 Squadron on 25 March where he remained until posted to HE on 12 September. Left the service on 25 April 1919.

	1918			BF2b					
1	2 Jun	Albatros DV	(a)		88	Ostende	1945	OOC
2	29 Jul	Fokker DVII	(a)	D7942	"	Bois Grenier	1830	OOC
3	31 Jul	Pfalz DIII	(a)	"	"	S Merville	1000	DES(F)
4	11 Aug	Fokker DVII	(a)	"	"	Barleux	1610	OOC
5	12 Aug	Fokker DVII	(a)	"	"	La Chapellette	1000	OOC
6	29 Aug	Fokker DVII	(b)	D8064	"	E Lille	0815	OOC
7	6 Sep	Fokker DVII	(c)	E2474	"	N Douai	1845	OOC

Total: 1 destroyed, 6 out of control = 7.
Pilots: (a) Lt W G Westwood; (b) Lt W A Wheeler; (c) Lt J P Findlay.

TOLMAN Clifford John   Lieutenant   22 SQN

From Whippingham, Isle of Wight, born 5 November 1896, Cliff Tolman served with the 1st Hampshire Yeomanry prior to joining the RFC in March 1918. Flew with 22 Squadron but was killed in action 27 September 1918, aged 21. He was lost together with his pilot, Captain S F H Thompson, east of Cambrai in BF2b E2477. Thompson had brought his own score to 30 that morning but was killed with Tolman in the afternoon. Tolman has no known grave. All victories scored with Lt F C Stanton except the last one.

	1918			BF2b					
1	10 Jul	Pfalz DIII		D8089	22	S Lille	1015	DES
2	"	Pfalz DIII		"	"	"	1015	DES
3	"	DFW C		"	"	"	1030	OOC
4	13 Aug	Fokker DVII		"	"	Auberchicourt	1120	DES
5	"	Fokker DVII		"	"	"	1120	DES(F)
6	21 Aug	2-seater		E2500	"	Albert	1945	OOC
7	27 Aug	Fokker DVII		"	"	SE Senlemont	1400	OOC
8	27 Sep	Halberstadt C		E2477	"	N Noyelles	0720	DES

Total: 5 destroyed, 3 out of control = 8.

TRAILL James H   Lieutenant   1 SQN AFC

Born 8 July 1895, Bligh, Cassilis, New South Wales, he was a Stationhand before the war and initially served in the Signals Service until transferring to the Australian Flying Corps. Joined 1 AFC in Palestine and usually flew as observer to Lt G C Peters. Awarded the DFC.

	1918			BF2b					
1	15 Apr	Albatros DV	(a)	C4623	1 AFC	Taiyibeh	1150	OOC
2	29 May	Rumpler C	(b)	"	"	Nablus	0815	DES
3	24 Jul	Rumpler C	(c)	B1278	"	Majdal Yaba	0530	DES
4	24 Aug	Pfalz DIII	(a)	"	"	Bir el Hanuta	0815	DES

5	„	LVG C	(a)	„	„	„	0815	DES
6	22 Sep	DFW C	(a)	„	„	Um Es Surab	1700	DES

Total: 5 destroyed, 1 out of control = 6.
Pilots: (a) Lt G C Peters; (b) Peters and shared with Lt E C Stooke/Lt W J A Weir, B1280; (c) Peters and shared with Lt J M Walker/Lt H A Letch B1222.

TRANTER Alexander   2nd Lieutenant   88 SQN

From Burghead, Scotland, born 7 June 1896. An engineer, he joined the 4th Seaforth Highlanders on 3 March 1913 and saw action in France from 1 May 1915. Transferred to the RFC on 4 February 1918 and after training, was posted to 88 Squadron in September where he remained until 1919.

	1918			BF2b				
1	14 Oct	Fokker DVII	(a)		88	E Lille		OOC
2	18 Oct	Fokker DVII	(b)	E2339	„	NW Tournai	1300	OOC
3	„	Fokker DVII	(b)	„	„	„	1300	DES
4	30 Oct	Fokker DVII	(c)	„	„	Peruwelz-N Warchin	0920	DES(F)
5	„	Fokker DVII	(c)	„	„	„	0920	DES(F)
6	4 Nov	Pfalz DXII	(d)	C821	„	Faucoucourt	1300	DES
7	„	Pfalz DXII	(d)	„	„	„	1300	DES

Total: 5 destroyed, 2 out of control = 7.
Pilots: (a) Capt W G Westwood; (b) Lt R H Hammer; (c) Capt K R Simpson; (d) Capt A Hepburn.

TUFFIELD Thomas Cecil Silwood   Lieutenant   48 SQN

Born 17 February 1893, his father was employed in Bombay, India. Transferred to the RFC General List from the 16th Battn. of the Welsh Regiment in 1917 and sent to 48 Squadron. Confirmed as a full lieutenant, Flying Officer Observer, 22 May 1918. Returned to Home Establishment in June, returning to the Squadron four days before the Armistice. He later served with 99 Squadron, flying DH9a machines and was with the Army of Occupation in 1919. Flying with 2/Lt W J Tremellen in F978, on 15 February, carrying mail, they crashed on landing at Morville but were unharmed. However, the pair were less fortunate on 4 March, in F1031. Flying mail once more, their machine stalled in strong wind and nose dived into the ground, both men being seriously injured. Left the service on 1 October 1919 but in 1934 he was with Auxiliary Force of India, Rifle Rangers.

	1917			BF2b				
1	21 Jul	Albatros DV	(a)	A7153	48	Slype	1800	OOC
2	22 Aug	Albatros DV	(b)	A7222	„	Ghistelles	0905	OOC
3	3 Sep	Albatros DV	(b)	„	„	N Dixmude	0815	OOC
4	„	Albatros DV	(b)	„	„	„	0815	DES(F)
5	11 Sep	DFW C	(c)	A7220	„	Dixmude	1015	OOC
6	11 Nov	Albatros DV	(d)	B1134	„	E St George	1510	OOC

Total: 1 destroyed, 4 & 1 shared out of control = 6.
Pilots: (a) Lt R Dodds, and shared with Capt B E Baker/Lt G R Spencer A7107, Lt R D Coath/2/Lt H Tanner A7164; (b) Lt Dodds; (c) 2/Lt J A W Binnie; (d) Lt N C Millman.

TURNER Ronald William   2nd Lieutenant   20 SQN

Born 17 November 1897, he came from York, where he worked as a carpenter and joiner for five years prior to WW1. Served with the Yorkshire Regiment prior to joining the RFC in December 1917. Won the DFC, gazetted 2 November 1918, which recorded six victories, two in one fight. He was invalided to a London hospital on 9 August and later served with the School of Air Gunnery 1918-19, then with 50 TDS in 1919. Left the service on 1 June 1919.

	1918			BF2b				
1	18 May	Pfalz DIII	(a)	B1168	20	N Neuf Berquin	1140	DES
2	4 Jul	Albatros DV	(b)	C951	„	W Veldhoek	1620	DES

3	„	Albatros DV	(b)	„	„	„	1630	OOC
4	„	Albatros DV	(b)	„	„	NE Zillebeke Lake	1640	DES
5	10 Jul	Fokker DVII	(b)	D7919	„	E Zillebeke Lake	0920	DES
6	„	Fokker DVII	(b)	„	„	„	0920	OOC
7	14 Jul	Fokker DVII	(c)		„	SE Ypres	0900	OOC
8	24 Jul	Fokker DVII	(a)	D7951	„	N Comines	2000	DES
9	29 Jul	Fokker DVII	(a)	„	„	NW Wervicq	2010	DES

Total: 6 destroyed, 2 & 1 shared out of control = 9.
Pilots: (a) Lt J H Colbert; (b) Lt P T Iaccaci; (c) Lt A T Iaccaci, and shared with Capt D Latimer/Lt T C Noel, C987.

TYRRELL William Upton   Lieutenant   22 SQN

Transferred to the RAF from the 3rd Reserve Battn. Royal Irish Rifles, in which he held a commission, and had served since November 1915. Became an honorary lieutenant observer on 29 August 1918 whilst flying with 22 Squadron from 1 September. Returned to England on 14 March 1919, he was with 205 Squadron briefly but returned to 22 on 19 December. Rejoined the Irish Rifles on 27 June 1919.

	1918			BF2b				
1	5 Sep	Fokker DVII	(a)	D7998	22	Douai	1700	OOC
2	24 Sep	Fokker DVII	(b)	F5823	„	Mesnières-Crevecourt	1700	DES
3	„	Fokker DVII	(b)	„	„	„	1700	OOC
4	26 Sep	Fokker DVII	(c)	C1035	„	Cambrai-Arras Road	1300	DES
5	„	Fokker DVII	(c)	„	„	„	1315	DES
6	27 Sep	Fokker DVII	(d)	E2517	„	Oisy-le-Verger	0730	DES

Total: 3 & 1 shared destroyed, 2 out of control = 6.
Pilots: (a) Lt H H Beddow; (b) Lt L C Rowney; (c) Lt C W M Thomson; (d) Rowney and shared with Lt C W M Thomson/Lt L R James, F5820.

UMNEY John Howard   2nd Lieutenant   22 SQN

Born on 11 April 1898, his parents lived in Sloane Square, London. By the time he joined the RFC he was living with his wife in Reading, Berkshire. An RFC cadet he was commissioned on 3 January 1918 into the General List, and went to 22 Squadron on 11 April. Won the MC, gazetted 16 September, the citation noting five victories in recent operations. He had a spell in hospital in July and returned to Home Establishment on 5 September. Left the RAF on 17 January 1919.

	1918			BF2b				
1	6 May	Albatros DV	(a)	C4747	22	Roeux	1845	OOC
2	8 May	2-seater	(a)	„	„	SE Arras	1005	DES
3	9 May	Pfalz DIII	(a)	„	„	N Douai	1840	OOC
4	16 May	Pfalz DIII	(a)	„	„	Douai	1005	DES
5	„	Pfalz DIII	(a)	„	„	„	1015	DES
6	22 May	Albatros DV	(a)	A7243	„	SE Arras	1030	OOC
7	30 May	Pfalz DIII	(a)	C961	„	Armentières	1940	OOC
8	31 May	Pfalz DIII	(a)	„	„	Laventie	1915	OOC
9	1 Jun	Pfalz DIII	(b)	„	„	Erquinghem	1915	DES
10	„	Pfalz DIII	(b)	„	„	„	1915	DES
11	2 Jun	2-seater	(a)	„	„	E Lens	1015	OOC
12	„	2-seater	(a)	„	„	„	1015	OOC
13	25 Aug	Pfalz DIII	(c)	C978	„	Péronne	1830	OOC

Total: 5 destroyed, 8 out of control = 13.
Pilots: (a) Lt E C Bromley; (b) Lt F G Gibbons; (c) Lt O StG Harris.

UNIACKE Desmond Percival Fitzgerald   2nd Lieutenant   48 SQN

Born 18 December 1895. Lived at Millfield House, Oak Place, Upminster, Essex. Transferred to the 1st Irish Rifles (second lieutenant) from the Royal Inniskillen Fusiliers, and seconded to the RFC in May 1917. Confirmed as an observer in August he flew with 48 Squadron from June. Shot down, wounded and taken prisoner, 21 September 1917, by Hermann Göring of Jasta 27, his pilot, Lt R L Curtis, being killed. Their BF2b No.A7224 was seen going down over Roulers. All victories with Curtis.

	1917			BF2b					
1	3 Jul	2-seater		A7149	48	Quéant	0910	OOC
2	5 Jul	Albatros DV		A7153	„	Bapaume	2020	OOC
3	7 Jul	Albatros DV		A7107	„	Vitry	0550	DES
4	28 Jul	Albatros DIII		A7121	„	Ghistelles	0815	OOC
5	16 Aug	Albatros DV		A7151	„	St Pierre-Capelle	1955	DES(F)
6	„	Albatros DV		„	„	„	1955	OOC
7	20 Aug	Albatros DV		A7224	„	Ghistelles	2005	OOC
8	22 Aug	Albatros DV		„	„	Ostende	0907	DES
9	„	Albatros DV		„	„	„	0907	OOC
10	2 Sep	Albatros DV	(a)	„	„	E Dixmude	0930	OOC
11	5 Sep	DFW C		A7170	„	Middlekerke	0840	OOC
12	14 Sep	Albatros DV		A7224	„	Ghistelles	1640	DES
13	17 Sep	2-seater	(b)	„	„	Leke	0915	OOC

Total: 4 destroyed, 7 & 2 shared out of control = 13.
(a) shared with Lt K R Park/2/Lt A D Light A7170; (b) shared with Sgt J Oldham/2AM W Walker A7222.

VESSEY John Arthur   Lieutenant   45 SQN

From Rochdale, Lancashire, he was a probationary second lieutenant in the General List from 27 January 1917, with seniority from 15 October 1916. Flew with 45 Squadron until killed in a collision on 12 June 1917. Buried at Hazebrouck. All victories whilst flying with Captain G Mountford except number one, scored with Second Lieutenant C W Carleton.

	1917			Sop 1½				
1	7 May	Albatros DIII		A8216	45	Lille	1750	OOC
2	25 May	Albatros DIII		A1099	„	Dadizeele	1100	OOC
3	„	Albatros DIII		„	„	„	1100	OOC
4	27 May	Albatros DIII		A8299	„	Roulers	1115	OOC
5	31 May	Albatros DV		„	„	Comines	1320	OOC

Total: 5 out of control.

WADDINGTON Melville Wells   Lieutenant   20 SQN

Born Toronto, Canada, 21 December 1895. Enlisted in the Canadian Field Artillery and commissioned in March 1916. Transferred to the RFC in England on 16 April 1917 and joined 20 Squadron on 18 June, serving until 6 December. Returned to Canada as an instructor on 13 February 1918. Worked as a real estate and insurance salesman post-war and died from a second heart attack, 14 August 1945.

	1917			FE2d				
1	29 Jun	Albatros DV	(a)	A6498	20	Houthem	1330	OOC
2	6 Jul	Albatros DV	(b)	„	„	Comines	1830	DES(F)
3	17 Jul	Albatros DV	(c)	A6548	„	Polygon Wood	1955	OOC
4	21 Jul	Albatros DV	(c)	„	„	Menin	1850	OOC
5	27 Jul	Albatros DV	(c)	A1956	„	N Menin	2015	DES(F)
6	„	Albatros DV	(c)	„	„	„	2020	OCC
7	16 Aug	Albatros DV	(a)	A3	„	Zonnebeke	0905	OOC
				BF2b				
8	3 Sep	Albatros DV	(a)	A7214	„	Menin-Wervicq	1010	DES(F)
9	5 Sep	Albatros DV	(a)	A7203	„	W Lille	1117	OOC
10	11 Sep	Albatros DV	(a)	A7214	„	E Menin	1010	DES

11	17 Oct	Albatros DV	(a)	A7255	„	Zonnebeke	0840	OOC
12	„	Albatros DV	(a)	„	„	NE Zonnebeke	0845	OOC

Total: 4 destroyed, 8 out of control = 12.
Pilots: (a) Lt R M Makepeace; (b) 2/Lt M McCall; (c) Lt H G E Luchford.

WAIGHT Dennis Edward   Captain   22 SQN

Born 15 February 1895, he came from London, and attended Beevors House, Aldenham School between 1911 and 1913. Joined the 12/13th Northumberland Fusiliers before transferring to the RFC in March 1918. He was awarded the Military Cross while serving with the Northumberland Fusiliers, gazetted on 3 June 1918. Flew as an observer with 22 Squadron. (A third forename — Francis — shown in the *London Gazette* is incorrect.) In 1919 his address was given as St John's Wood, North London.

	1918			BF2b				
1	10 Jul	Pfalz DIII	(a)	D7896	22	Lille	1000	OOC
2	8 Aug	Pfalz DIII	(b)	E2466	„	NE Vitry	1040	DES
3	„	Pfalz DIII	(c)	„	„	„	1040	DES(F)
4	11 Aug	Fokker DVII	(b)	„	„	SE Armentières	1935	OOC
5	13 Aug	Rumpler C	(b)	„	„	NW Cambrai	1100	DES
6	„	Pfalz DIII	(b)	„	„	„	1100	OOC
7	14 Aug	2-seater	(b)	„	„	SW Lille	1050	OOC
8	16 Aug	Pfalz DIII	(b)	„	„	SE Lille	1045	DES
9	21 Aug	2-seater	(b)	„	„	Ervillers	1410	OOC
10	22 Aug	Halberstadt C	(d)		„	NE Bailleul	1910	DES
11	31 Aug	Fokker DVII	(e)	F4820	„	Douai	1710	DES
12	4 Nov	Pfalz DXII	(f)	E2454	„	NW Bavay	1415	OOC

Total: 4 & 2 shared destroyed, 6 out of control = 12.
Pilots: (a) Lt T W Martin; (b) Capt W F J Harvey; (c) Harvey and shared with Capt J E Gurdon/2/Lt C G Gass, E2454; (d) Harvey and shared with Lt I O Stead/2/Lt W A Cowie, Lt H H Beddow/Lt T J Birmingham; (e) Lt I O Stead; (f) Capt S H Wallage.

WALKER William   2nd Air Mechanic   48 SQN

From Hull, Bill Walker served with 48 Squadron in 1917. On 17 September, flying with Sergeant J Oldham (A7222) he was wounded in the neck but continued to engage German fighters, and was then hit in the leg by an explosive bullet, above the knee. Recommended for the DCM on 19 September the award was gazetted on 17 November. His service number was 94311.

	1917			BF2b				
1	12 Aug	Albatros DV	(a)	A7164	48	Slype	1045	OOC
2	„	Albatros DV	(a)	„	„	„	1045	DES
3	17 Aug	Albatros DV	(b)	A7115	„	Ostende	1025	DES
4	4 Sep	Albatros DV	(b)	A7217	„	„	1900	OOC
5	17 Sep	2-seater	(c)	A7222	„	Leke	0915	OOC

Total: 2 destroyed, 2 & 1 shared out of control = 5.
Pilots: (a) Lt R D Coath; (b) Sgt W H Roebuck; (c) Sgt J Oldham, and shared with Lt R L Curtis/Lt D P F Uniacke, A7224.

WALL Anthony Herbert William   Captain   48 SQN

A Londoner, born 17 June 1888, he became a journalist with the *Daily Mail* in 1911. His first experience of flying was that same year, and he also travelled extensively in Europe, Africa and America. When the war started he saw service with the Belgian Army for the first six months. Transferred to the RFC from the 17th Battn. of the Middlesex Regiment. With 48 Squadron he was observer to Captain Fred Holliday with whom he shared all his victories. His MC was gazetted on 18 July 1917 for actions on the 13, 24 April and 9 May, and he was recommended for a Bar on 26 June for actions on the 15th. He was on the Committee of Imperial Defence at the end of September 1918, assigned special duties in connection with RAF history. He became an OBE (Military Division) on 1 January 1919, and left the service on 18 October 1919.

	1917			BF2a				
1	6 Apr	EA			48	NE Arras		OOC
2	23 Apr	Albatros DIII			„	Vimy		DES
3	„	Albatros DIII	(a)		„	„		OOC
4	24 Apr	2-seater			„	SE Arras		DES
5	„	Albatros DIII	(b)		„	Cagnicourt		OOC
				BF2b				
6	9 May	LVG C	(c)	A7108	„	Vitry-Noyelles	0820	DES
7	„	Albatros DIII		„	„	E Vitry	1725	OOC
8	„	Albatros DIII		„	„	„	1730	OOC
9	„	Albatros DIII		„	„	„	1735	OOC
10	11 May	Albatros DIII		„	„	Fresnes	1605	DES
11	„	Albatros DIII		„	„	SW Izel-le-Esquerchin	1605	OOC
12	3 Jun	Albatros DIII		„	„	Plouvain	1920	DES
13	14 Jun	Albatros DIII		„	„	Arleux	2015	DES
14	„	Albatros DIII		„	„	„	2020	OOC
15	15 Jun	Albatros DIII		„	„	Etaing	1945	OOC
16	3 Jul	Albatros DV		„	„	Haucourt	1840	OOC

Total: 5 & 1 shared destroyed, 8 & 2 shared out of control = 16.
(a) shared with Lt W O B Winkler/2/Lt E S Moore, Lt R B Hay/?, 2/Lt W T Price/Lt M A Benjamin; (b) shared with Winkler/Moore, Hay/?; (c) shared with 2/Lt W T Price/2/Lt E S Moore A7110.

WARD Edward Henry   2nd Lieutenant   88 SQN

Born 14 December 1897 he came from Cleethorpes, Lincolnshire and pre-war had been an engineering apprentice in Grimsby from May 1914 to 1915. Served initially with the East Yorkshire Regiment, then the 1st North Midland Brigade of the RFA. Attached to the RFC in February 1918, he became a temporary second lieutenant observer on 23 July, effective from 6 July. Posted to 88 Squadron on 25 March he went with this unit to France on 16 April. On 18 May 1918, he and his pilot, Lt Cullen (with whom he shared all his victories), had to force land near the trenches after an air fight and killed a Frenchman whilst landing on a road. Briefly hospitalised on 6 July he became dangerously ill in October and was invalided back to England in December. Relinquished his commission on 25 February 1919, he returned to the RFA on 30 July 1920.

	1918			BF2b				
1	15 May	Albatros DIII		C780	88	Ghistelles	0635	DES
2	18 May	Albatros DV		„	„	Zandvoorde	0800	OOC
3	29 Jun	Fokker DVII		D8062	„	W Ghistelles	2010	DES
4	„	Fokker DVII	(a)	„	„	Ghistelles	2010	DES
5	„	Fokker DVII		„	„	W Ghistelles	2011	DES

Total: 3 & 1 shared destroyed, 1 out of control = 5.
(a) shared with Capt K R Simpson/Sgt C Hill C983, Lt K B Conn/2/Lt B H Smyth C787, Lt W A Wheeler/2/Lt T S Chiltern C774.

WEAR Albert Edward   2nd Lieutenant   20 SQN

From Bowers Park, Middlesex (53 Middleton Rd), the son of a Minister, Frank Fowler Wear, he served with the Royal Fusiliers. Joined the RFC and flew with 20 Squadron in 1917. Wear was in the fight on 6 July in which Manfred von Richthofen was wounded and brought down, flying with Lt C R Richards (A6448). Killed in an accident, 11 September 1917 and was buried at Longuenesse, France. All victories with Richards.

	1917			FE2d					
1	14 Jun	Albatros DIII		A6498	20	Becelaère	1200	OOC	
2	17 Jun	2-seater		A6431	„	Zonnebeke	0720	DES(F)	
3	6 Jul	Albatros DV		A6498	„	Wervicq	1030	OOC	
4	7 Jul	Albatros DV		„	„	Becelaère	1400	OOC	
5	17 Jul	Albatros DV		„	„	Menin	1030	OOC	
6	„	Albatros DV		„	„	„	1040	DES	
7	10 Aug	2-seater		B1890	„	Polygon Wood	0840	OOC	
8	„	Albatros DV	(a)	„	„	Wervicq	0900	OOC	
9	16 Aug	Albatros DV		„	„	E Passchendaele	0915	OOC	

Total: 2 destroyed, 6 & 1 shared out of control = 9.
(a) shared with Capt A N Solly/2/Lt J Cawley (A5147) and Lt D Y Hay/2/Lt M Tod (A6456).

WEIR William James Alexander   Lieutenant   1 AFC SQN

Born Leichhardt, Sydney, NSW, Australia, 4 April 1891, he was a plantation overseer on the island of Fiji pre-war. Joined the 6th Australian Light Horse in September 1914, corporal October, sergeant March 1915 and commissioned 1 June 1917. Transferred to the Australian Flying Corps on 21 January 1918, full lieutenant 13 July. Served in Palestine with 1 AFC Squadron and won the DFC, gazetted on 8 February 1919, the citation mentioning attacks on enemy cavalry on 14 August (with Lt C S Paul). Posted back to Australia in November 1918, in the 1930s he was living in Fiji, working as a plantation overseer once more.

	1918			BF2b					
1	23 May	Albatros DV	(a)	C4627	1AFC	Nablus	0700	OOC	
2	„	Albatros DV	(a)	„	„	„	0715	FTL/DES	
3	29 May	2-seater	(b)	B1280	„	Nablus	0815	DES	
4	13 Jun	Rumpler C	(a)	C4627	„	N Nablus	0430	DES	
5	28 Jul	Rumpler C	(c)	„	„	N Wadi Farah	1200	FTL/DES	
6	16 Aug	Rumpler C	(a)	„	„	Kefr Kaddum	0830	DES	

Total: 3 & 2 shared destroyed, 1 out of control = 6.
Pilots: (a) Lt C S Paul; (b) Paul and shared with Lt G C Peters/Lt J H Traill C4623; (c) Lt E G C Stooke and shared with Capt A R Brown/Lt G Finlay B1284.

WHITE Victor Rodney Stokes   Lieutenant   45 & 20 SQN

Served with the 3rd Reserve Battn. of the Staffordshire Regiment, Special Reserve, prior to being seconded to the RFC, having won the MC. Flew Sopwith 1½ Strutters with 45 Squadron, then BF2bs with 20 Squadron. Awarded Bar to his MC. MC Gazetted 26 May 1917 as a forward observation officer, the citation noting that he ". . . constantly moved about in the open under very heavy fire and obtained most valuable information." The Bar was gazetted on 6 April 1918 noting several successful air combats.

	1917			Sop 1½					
1	13 Jul	Albatros DIII	(a)	A1016	45	E Polygon Wood	1715	OOC	
				BF2b					
2	25 Sep	Albatros DV	(b)	B1126	20	Becelaère	1830	DES(F)	
3	17 Oct	Albatros DV	(c)	B1138	„	Dadizeele	1000	DES	
4	18 Oct	Albatros DV	(c)	„	„	Houthem-Tenbrielen	0845	DES	
5	„	DFW C	(c)	„	„	Dadizeele	0900	DES	
6	21 Oct	LVG C	(c)	„	„	Menin	1530	DES	

Total: 5 destroyed, 1 out of control = 6.
Pilots: (a) Capt G H Cock; (b) 2/Lt N V Harrison; (c) Capt H G E Luchford.

WILLIAMS Percy Stanley   2nd Lieutenant   22 SQN

A married man, he came from Barnes, south-west London, being commissioned into the 21st London Regiment. Transferred to the RFC in September 1917 and posted to 22 Squadron at the beginning of December. Returned to Home Establishment 31 May 1918 and in August was attached to Air Ministry for duty with Colonel Monckton at Cambridge. Left the service on 20 March 1919. All victories with Lt G W Bulmer, except the first, while observer to Lt W L Wells.

	1918			BF2b				
1	13 Mar	Albatros DV		A7286	22	W Emmerin	1630	DES
2	16 Mar	Pfalz DIII		C4810	„	Hénin-Liétard	1030	OOC
3	„	Pfalz DIII		„	„	„	1030	OOC
4	23 Mar	Albatros DV		A7251	„	Bussy	1100	DES
5	8 May	Pfalz DIII		C4888	„	Brebières	1015	DES
6	16 May	Balloon		„	„	E Neuf Berquin	1045	DES
7	17 May	2-seater		„	„	Villers, SE Douai	1200	DES

Total: 5 destroyed, 2 out of control = 7.

WOODBRIDGE Albert Edward   Lieutenant   20 SQN

Flew as observer in 20 Squadron during the summer of 1917, often as observer to Capt D C Cunnell. On 6 July, during an action with Jasta 11, he claimed four out of control victories, one possibly being flown by Manfred von Richthofen, who force landed with a head wound. Woodbridge himself was wounded on 31 July but returned, the squadron having replaced its FE2s with BF2b machines. He later became a pilot himself (RAC No.5696 29 Dec 1917) and after the war spent some time in civil aviation before rejoining the RAF. In 1927 he was serving as a pilot with 58 Squadron at Worthy Down. Later went to the Middle East but was killed in a night landing crash at Jask, Persia, flying a mail plane, on 7 September 1929.

	1917			FE2d				
1	6 Jul	Albatros DV	(a)	A6512	20	Wervicq	1030	OOC
2	„	Albatros DV	(a)	„	„	„	1030	OOC
3	„	Albatros DV	(a)	„	„	„	1030	OOC
4	„	Albatros DV	(a)	„	„	„	1030	OOC
				BF2b				
5	17 Oct	DFW C	(b)	A7141	„	Wervicq-Menin	0925	DES
6	27 Oct	Albatros DV	(b)	A7298	„	SW Roulers	1310	DES
7	8 Nov	Albatros DV	(b)	A7253	„	NE Houthulst Forest	1330	DES

Total: 3 destroyed, 4 out of control = 7.
Pilots: (a) Capt D C Cunnell; (b) 2/Lt W Durrand.

CHAPTER TWO

Two-seat Corps and Bomber Pilot Aces

ASBURY Edward Dannett   Captain   49 SQN

From Enfield, north London, Asbury was born in Blackheath, SE London, on 9 June 1899. Between 1913-16 he attended Malvern School, Worcester. Joined the RFC and gazetted a 2/Lt on 1 December 1917. Posted to 49 Sqn from No. 31 TDS on 7 May 1918. Temporary Captain from 13 Sept 1918. Killed in action on 24 September 1918 along with his observer, 2/Lt B T Gillman. They had taken off at 2.50 pm to attack Baulnoye Junction and fell in combat with EA on the return journey west of Fort de Mormal, in DH9 E8869; they have no known graves. They were shot down by either Ltn Otto Löffler of Jasta 2 or Ltn Josef Mai of Jasta 5.

	1918			DH9				
1	10 Jun	Albatros DV	(a)	C6140	49	Assainvillers	0500	OOC
2	„	Albatros DV	(a)	„	„	„	0502	OOC
3	29 Jun	Albatros DV	(a)	„	„	W Lille	1400	DES(F)
4	25 Jul	Fokker DVII	(a)	„	„	Mont Notre Dame	1900	OOC
5	25 Aug	Fokker DVII	(b)		„	Bourlon Wood	1900	OOC

Total: 1 destroyed, 4 out of control = 5.
Obs: (a) 2/Lt W N Hartley; (b) Lt R A V R Sherk.

ASHFIELD Lionel Arthur   Lieutenant   202 SQN

From Bury St Edmunds, Suffolk, born 1 August 1898, he lived in Frant, Sussex. Attended Marlborough College, Wiltshire, between 1912-17, before joining the RNAS on 29 April 1917. Became a flight sub lieutenant 29 August then joined 2 Naval Squadron on 15 November, which later became 202 Squadron RAF. Won the DFC, the citation noting 62 ops, 17 combats and five victories, although not all the latter can be found. In combat with EA on 27 June 1918 Ashfield had his observer — Lt N H Jenkins DSM — wounded in action near Middelkerke, 5pm, flying DH4 A7868. Killed in action 16 July 1918, with Lt M G English, again in A7868, near Ostende, claimed by Flgm Hans Goerth, of MFJ III. Buried at Ramscapelle Road, nr Nieuport, Belgium.

	1918			DH4			
1	18 May	Scout	(a)	A7868	202	Bruges	OOC
2	31 May	EA	(b)	D8402	„	Ostende	OOC
3							
4							
5							

Obs: (a) AGL. Allen; (b) Lt Russell.

ATKINSON Rupert Norman Gould   Captain   10, 98 AND 206 SQNS

Atkinson was born on 17 July 1896, in Shanghai, China, where his father was a leading merchant. Educated at Marlborough but before he was due to attend Cambridge, joined the colours with the Middlesex Regiment in 1914. Commissioned in December, he went to Cameroon, West Africa, spending nine months attached to the West African Regt. Invalided home in April 1916, he transferred to the RFC and obtained his Aero Club Certificate, No. 3646, on 28 September 1916 and was gazetted a pilot as from 1 November. Served initially with 10 Squadron for a year, from late 1916 and awarded an Immediate MC in November 1917 (gazetted 7 March 1918). Rested, he then went to 98 Squadron in January and went to France with this unit until June. After another brief rest he returned to France, taking over the senior flight commander post with 206 Squadron. Received an Immediate DFC in September (gazetted 2 November), and also the Belgian Croix de Guerre. A Bar to his DFC was gazetted on 4 June 1919 but by this date he was dead. Arriving home on leave from Germany in February 1919 he became a victim of the influenza epidemic and died on 7 March — the day he had been due to return to his Squadron. He had over 1,000 hours combat flying!

	1918			DH9					
1	19 May	Fokker DrI	(a)	B7657	98	NW Roulers	0645	DES(F)
2	„	Pfalz DIII	(a)	„	„	NW Roulers	0645	DES(F)
3	30 Aug	Fokker DVII	(b)	D1718	206	Nieppe	1115	DES
4	4 Sep	Balloon	(b)	„	„	Frelinghien	0700	DES
5	14 Oct	Fokker DVII	(c)	D569	„	Lendelede	1440	DES(F)

Total: 5 destroyed = 5.
Obs: (a) Lt E A Shaw; (b) 2/Lt W T Ganter; (c) 2/Lt J B Blamford.

BARBOUR Robert Lyle McKendrick   Lieutenant   205 SQN

Served with the King's Own Scottish Borderers before joining the RFC. Assigned to 205 Squadron from April 1918 to February 1919 and carried out over 40 raids and 45 recce sorties with 205 to win the DFC, recommended on 13 October, and gazetted on 8 February 1919, the citation noting 29 raids and 47 photo ops. On 9 October he was driven back during a sortie but later recrossed lines. Engaged again by Fokker DVIIs, he shot down one which was seen to crash. He remained in the RAF.

	1918			DH4					
1	7 Jul	Scout	(a)	D8412	205	Warfusée-Abancourt	1130	OOC
2	31 Jul	Pfalz DIII	(a)	A7985	„	Marcelcave	2000	DES(F)
3	11 Aug	Pfalz DIII	(b)	„	„	Péronne	0800	DES
				DH9a				
4	29 Sep	Fokker DVII	(c)	F1014	„	Montbrehain	1340	DES
5	3 Oct	Fokker DVII	(c)	„	„	Neuville	1640	DES
6	9 Oct	Fokker DVII	(c)	„	„	Busigny	0830	DES

Total: 5 destroyed, 1 out of control = 6.
Obs: (a) 2/Lt J H Preston; (b) Sgt F G Manning; (c) Capt M F M Wright.

BARTLETT Charles Philip Oldfield   Major   5N/205 SQN

Born in Weston-Super-Mare, Somerset, on 3 January 1889, he spent his early years in the Cotswolds, son of Canon Bartlett, Rector of Willersey, near Broadway and later vicar of Minsterworth, Gloucestershire. Joined the RNAS 1916, gaining Royal Aero Club Certificate No. 3118, on 21 June 1916. Flew with 5N/205 Squadron between 1916-18 and recorded 101 sorties, winning the DSC and Bar. Hospitalised between April to September 1918 following the effects of his operational service, he was, however, made temporary major on 12 July. Remained in the RAF till 1932, six years being spent as adjutant at RAF Manston, School of Technical Training with the rank of squadron leader. Re-employed as a civilian adjutant at Ruislip and in 1936 became bursar at Bryanston School, Dorset and later at St Dunstan's Training Centre for the Blind till 1945. His nephew, Nigel Weir, was a fighter pilot in the Battle of Britain, won the DFC but was killed in action on 7 November 1940. Philip Bartlett retired to Cheltenham after WW2 and died in March 1986.

	1917			DH4					
1	2 Jul	Albatros DV	(a)	N5967	5N	Zeebrugge	1230	OOC
	1918							
2	30 Jan	Albatros DV	(b)	N6001	„	Engel airfield	1330	OOC
3	18 Mar	Albatros DV	(b)	N5961	„	Beaurevoir	1102	OOC
4	21 Mar	Fokker DrI	(b)	N6000	„	Honnecourt	1804	OOC
5	27 Mar	Albatros DV	(b)	„	„	Fontaine	1045	OOC
6	28 Mar	Fokker DrI	(b)	N6001	„	Raincourt	c1000	DES

| 7 | „ | Fokker DrI | (b) | „ | „ | „ | | c1000 | DES |
| 8 | „ | Fokker DrI | (b) | „ | „ | „ | | c1000 | DES |

Total: 3 destroyed, 5 out of control = 8.
Obs: (a) AGL. S D Sambrook; (b) AGL. W Naylor.

BOWMAN Clifford   Captain   49 SQN

Cliff Bowman came from Thornton-le-Fyfe, via Preston, born 26 March 1899. Joined the General List of the RFC on 4 April 1917 and commissioned on 21 June 1917. After training he joined 49 Squadron in England, then No.19 TS until early December, at which time he was sent to 110 Squadron at Sedgeford. He left this unit at the end of January 1918 (having also attended the WT School at Biggin Hill) and returned to 49 Squadron on 14 February, which had now moved to France. At this time he had 47½ flying hours. Bowman had six victories credited to him and his observers, for which he received the DFC on 25 August, gazetted 2 November, noting he had flown more than 50 raids, mostly as leader, and in two raids on one day, his formation had downed four German aircraft. Left the RAF in February 1919.

	1918			DH9				
1	11 Jun	Albatros DV	(a)	D7201	49	Cuvilly	1500	DES
2	8 Aug	Fokker DVII	(b)	D3052	„	Bethencourt	1820	OOC
3	9 Aug	Fokker DVII	(b)	„	„	Falvy	0630	OOC
4	„	Fokker DVII	(b)	„	„	Marchélepot	1700	OOC
5	11 Aug	Fokker DVII	(a)	D7201	„	Cuvilly	1500	OOC
6	24 Sep	Pfalz DIII	(c)	D3052	„	Bavai	1705	OOC

Total: 1 destroyed, 5 out of control = 6.
Obs: (a) Lt V Gordon; (b) Lt P T Holligan; (c) 2/Lt C B Edwards.

CARBERY Douglas Hugh Moffatt   Captain   52, 9 & 59 SQNS

Born Ambala, India 26 March 1894, he was educated at King's School, Bruton, Somerset, having travelled to England in 1913 upon the death of his father. He then went to the RMA at Woolwich, being commissioned in August 1914. In France he served with the 96th Battery, then with the RHA before returning to the 96th until wounded in May. Was wounded a second time in July. Transferred to the RFC on 20 April 1916 (RAC Cert. No. 3383, 31 July 1916). Joined 52 Squadron in 1916, and after a tour of duty became a flight commander with 9 Squadron. Became an instructor with No.15 TS, then returned to France to join 59 Squadron in August 1918. MC gazetted 26 March 1917, DFC gazetted 3 Dec 1918. After the war he served with 31 Squadron in India from March 1919, being awarded a Bar to his DFC gazetted 12 July 1920, for service in Afghanistan. Rejoined the Royal Artillery in 1920 and saw considerable service in India. In WW2 he served in West Africa and later in Burma. Retired as Brigadier 1946, he lived in Lanner, Cornwall until his death in April 1959.

	1917			RE8				
1	25 Jan	2-seater	(a)	A81	52	Morlancourt	1230	CAPT
				BE2e				
2	14 Feb	Albatros DIII	(b)	6755	„	St Pierre V	1350	OOC
	1918			RE8				
3	30 Aug	Fokker DVII	(c)	B5892	59	Beugnâtre	1120	OOC
4	8 Sep	Halberstadt C	(c)	C2337	„		0635	DES
5	24 Sep	Halberstadt C	(d)	C2407	„	Gonnelieu	1810	DES
6	28 Sep	Halberstadt C	(c)	C2537	„	La Vacquerie	0700	DES

Total: 3 destroyed, 1 captured, and 2 out of control = 6.
Obs: (a) 2/Lt H A D MacKay; (b) 2/Lt M A S Vaile; (c) Lt J B V Clements; (d) Lt R N Ireland.

CHALMERS Robert   2nd Lieutenant   205 SQN

From Glasgow, born 17 October 1898. Before war service he worked as a shipping clerk for the Canadian Pacific Railway from Glasgow, 1914-17. Becoming a pilot with the RAF, Chalmers served with 205 Squadron from 3 April 1918 and flew over 60 raids and 15 recce missions before being hospitalised on 22 October. Left the RAF on 26 February 1919.

	1918			DH4					
1	3 May	Pfalz DIII	(a)	D8401	205	Chaulnes-Rosières	1545	DES(F)
2	„	Pfalz DIII	(a)	„	„	„	„	OOC
3	17 May	Albatros DV	(b)	D9255	„	W Chaulnes	1605	DES(F)
4	20 May	Pfalz DIII	(b)	D9260	„	Rosières	0825	OOC
5	10 Aug	Pfalz DIII	(b)	A7587	„	Brie Bridge	1540	OOC
6	11 Aug	Pfalz DIII	(b)	„	„	W Péronne	0756	OOC

Total: 1 & 1 shared destroyed, 3 & 1 shared out of control = 6.
Obs: a/b. 2/Lt S H Hamblin; (a) shared with Capt E Dickson/AGL. C V Robinson D9232, Lt G E Siedle/AGL. C V Middleton A8071, Lt W B Elliott/2/Lt J A Whalley N6009, 2/Lt J C Wilson/Sgt S M MacKay D9241, Lt W Grossart/Sgt P L Richards A7811, Lt C J Heywood/Sgt S F Langstone D9238, Lt Fox/Lt C F Amber D8412, Capt J Gamon/2/Lt W H Scott N6004, Lt R Scott/2/Lt T A Humphrey D9243.

CLARKE William Henry   Lieutenant   205 SQN

From Harrogate, Yorkshire, born 11 September 1894. A pre-war motor engineer between 1910-14, he was a sergeant (54243) in the Royal Engineers prior to serving with the RFC from June 1917. Commissioned in September, he became a pilot and joined 205 Squadron on 18 May 1918. Flew over 40 raids and 30 recce sorties. He and his observers claimed five victories. Left the RAF on 19 March 1919.

	1918			DH4				
1	10 Aug	Fokker DVII	(a)	A7573	205	Brie Bridge	1540	OOC
2	11 Aug	Pfalz DIII	(b)	D8387	„	Péronne	0800	OOC
3	„	Fokker DVII	(a)	D9233	„	Biaches	1910	OOC
4	13 Aug	Pfalz DIII	(a)	D9265	„	Péronne	1110	OOC
5	21 Aug	Fokker DVII	(a)	D9277	„	NE Bethencourt	1505	DES

Total: 1 destroyed, 3 & 1 shared out of control = 5.
Obs: a/b. 2/Lt C N Witham; (b) shared with Lt E H Johnson/Lt H F Taylor A8029.

DARVILL George William Francis   Captain   18 SQN

Darvill was born on 26 October 1898, at Petersfield. A farmer pre-war, he joined the RFC (GL) and was commissioned a second lieutenant on probation on 20 April 1917; RAC Certificate No.4973, 13 July 1917 (Hendon). Served briefly with 9 Squadron from October, going to France in December but then went to 18 Squadron, flying DH4s, on 13 January 1918, and became acting Captain and flight commander on 18 August 1918. Received the MC, gazetted 3 June 1918 and the DFC in August 1918, gazetted 2 November, for 44 raids, many as leader, and for shooting down a Fokker when he single-handedly attacked three, despite his observer's gun being out of action. Left the service on 12 September 1919, but applied to join the RAFVR in September 1939 whilst living in Ramsden, Petersfield.

	1918			DH4				
1	10 Mar	Albatros DV	(a)	B9435	18	Allenes	1215	OOC
2	19 May	Albatros DV	(b)		„	Douai	1200	OOC
3	21 May	Albatros DV	(c)	A8034	„	Douai	1045	DES
4	8 Jul	Fokker DVII	(d)	A7815	„	Hénin-Liétard	0830	DES
5	28 Jul	Fokker DVII	(d)	„	„	Vitry	0735	OOC
6	9 Aug	Fokker DVII	(e)	„	„	W Douai	1050	OOC
7	12 Aug	Fokker DVII	(f)	F5857	„	W Somain	1100	OOC
8	4 Sep	Fokker DVII	(d)	A7815	„	Cantin	0750	DES(F)
9	„	Fokker DVII	(d)	„	„	Aubigny-au-Bac	0755	DES(F)

Total: 4 destroyed, 3 & 2 shared out of control = 9.
Obs: (a) Sgt A Pollard; (b) Lt E Collis, and shared with Capt A G Waller/Lt Ayres, 2/Lt A Green/2/Lt F Lolly;
(c) 2AM L Vredenberg; (d) Lt W N Miller; (e) Lt J Fenwick, and shared with Capt H R Gould/2/Lt E Jinman,
Lt J Gillanders/Lt McCall, Lt A Pickin/Lt Hutchinson, Lt E Peskett/2/Lt W Clark, Lt Snook/Lt Aslin, Lt Kearney/
Lt Buckner; (f) Lt J Fenwick.

DICKSON Euan   Captain   5N/205 SQN

Born in Sheffield on 31 March 1892, he became an engineer and in late 1912 went to New
Zealand to work as a foreman in an automobile gear cutting shop, but he returned in 1915 to
join the RNAS, gaining RAC Certificate No.3966 dated 12 December 1916. Posted to 10 Naval
Squadron on 31 March 1917, he was then sent to 5 Naval on 29 April. Saw considerable service
with 5 Naval, which later became 205 Squadron RAF. Won the DSC on 16 November for raids
on Thourout and Varssenaere, and a Bar in March 1918. The DFC came in July, as well as
the French Croix de Guerre with Bronze Star. His DFC citation, gazetted 21 September 1918,
recorded that ". . . since 17 April 1918 he has led 84 bomb raids . . ." Apart from 14 days leave
and a short stay in hospital, by August 1918 Dickson had been in France continually since April
1917 and had been on some 180 raids. He was sent back to England, his war flying over. Leaving
the service in July 1919 he returned to New Zealand and joined the Canterbury Aviation
Company in Christchurch and on 25 August 1920, became the first person to fly across Cook
Strait, which separates North and South islands of New Zealand. Thereafter he remained in
aviation for the next ten years, pioneering many mail routes over New Zealand's South Island.
In 1930 he returned to engineering in Auckland, rising to company chairman of the Eden Motor
Co, until he retired in 1964. He died in Auckland on 10 March 1980.

	1917			DH4				
1	8 Dec	Albatros DV	(a)	N5962	5N	Aertrycke A/F	1140	OOC
	1918							
2	17 Feb	Albatros DV	(b)	N6000	„	off Ostende	1210	OOC
3	18 Feb	Albatros DV	(b)	„	„	St Pierre Capelle	1300	OOC
4	16 Mar	Albatros DV	(c)	A7739	„	Bohain-Le Catelet	1100	DES
5	18 Mar	Albatros DV	(c)	A7620	„	Beaurevoir	1054	OOC
6	27 Mar	Albatros DV	(d)	„	„	Rainecourt	1530	DES
7	28 Mar	Pfalz DIII	(d)	„	„	Foucaucourt	0950	OOC
8	6 Apr	Pfalz DIII	(c)	A7739	205	Abancourt	1550	OOC
9	22 Apr	Fokker DrI	(e)	„	„	Chaulnes	1615	OOC
10	23 Apr	Fokker DrI	(e)	„	„	Chaulnes	1940	OOC
11	3 May	Pfalz DIII	(e)	D9237	„	Chaulnes-Rosières	1542	OOC
12	„	Pfalz DIII	(e)	„	„	„	1545	DES(F)
13	„	Pfalz DIII	(f)	„	„	„	1545	OOC
14	18 May	Albatros DV	(f)	D9238	„	W Chaulnes	1130	DES(F)

Total: 3 & 1 shared destroyed, 9 & 1 shared out of control = 14.
Obs: (a) AGL. Shaw; (b) AGL. W Naylor; (c) FSL W H Scott; (d) FSL Stewart; (e) AGL. V Robinson; (f) AGL.
C V Robinson and shared with eight other crews.

DODDS Roy Edward   Captain   106 & 103 SQNS

Born in Buffalo, New York State, 19 July 1891. Joined the RFC in Canada in 1917, leaving for
the UK on 24 December and commissioned. Went to 106 Squadron in England, then to
103 Squadron in France on 26 May 1918, serving until the end of the war, first with C Flight,
then OC B Flight from 30 September. DFC recommended 24 October and gazetted 8 February
1919 for 60 raids, often as leader, and photo ops. with three EA destroyed (sic), his observers
claiming four more. His usual observer was Lt Irving Benfield Corey DFC, a Canadian. In all
he carried out at least 64 sorties. Car salesman post war in Detroit, USA. Link Trainer Instructor
RCAF WW2. Died 1966.

	1918			DH9				
1	4 Jul	Pfalz DIII	(a)	C6150	103	La Bassée	2030	OOC
2	10 Aug	Fokker DVII	(b)	„	„	Péronne	1815	OOC
3	„	Fokker DVII	(b)	„	„	Péronne	1815	OOC
4	11 Aug	EA	(b)	„	„	Estaires		OOC
5	„	EA	(b)	„	„	„		OOC
6	25 Aug	EA	(b)	„	„			OOC
7	30 Oct	Fokker DVII	(b)	E8884	„	Mainvault	0955	OOC

Total: 7 out of control = 7.
Obs: (a) 2/Lt J B Russell; (b) 2/Lt I B Corey.

DRINKWATER Arthur Thomas   Captain   57 & 40 SQNS

Born 3 February 1894 in Queenscliff, Victoria, Australia. Joined the RFC in November 1916, being commissioned on 19 March the following year. Flying DH4s with 57 Squadron in 1917, he and his observers claimed six victories. After a period in England he became a fighter pilot, returning to France in August 1918 to fly with 40 Squadron as a flight commander, raising his personal score to nine. Drinkwater received the DFC, gazetted 3 June 1919.

	1917			DH4				
1	18 Aug	Albatros DV	(a)	A2138	57	Courtrai	1920	OOC
2	20 Aug	Albatros DV	(a)	A2132	„	Houthulst Forest	1130	OOC
3	21 Sep	Albatros DV	(a)	A7581	„	Dadizeele	1050	DES
4	„	Albatros DV	(a)	„	„	„	1051	DES
5	12 Nov	Albatros DV	(a)	A7424	„	SE Houthulst	1145	OOC
6	„	Albatros DV	(a)	„	„	„	1145	OOC
	1918			SE5a				
7	17 Sep	Fokker DVII		E5982	40	SE Cambrai	0955	OOC
8	1 Oct	Halberstadt C		E5527	„	N Cambrai	1245	DES
9	9 Oct	Fokker DVII		E4036	„	NE Cambrai	0740	OOC

Total: 3 destroyed, 6 out of control = 9.
Obs: (a) Lt F T S Menendez.

EDGLEY D E   Sergeant   57 SQN

Flew DH4s with 57 Squadron in 1918, he and his observers claiming six victories. He was brought down twice: on 8 August and again on 1 September, his observer being wounded on the second occasion. Both actions were with German fighters. Service No.99978, he had previously been an RFC ground mechanic before requesting pilot training.

	1918			DH4				
1	8 Aug	Fokker DVII	(a)	D8382	57	Moislains A/F	0805	OOC
2	29 Aug	Fokker DVII	(b)	„	„	Marquion	1830	OOC
3	1 Sep	Fokker DVII	(b)	„	„	Cambrai	1345	DES(F)
4	„	Fokker DVII	(b)	„	„	Cambrai	1345	OOC
5	5 Sep	Fokker DVII	(c)	F5828	„	Marcoing	1125	OOC
6	16 Sep	Fokker DVII	(d)	„	„	Havrincourt Wood	0955	OOC

Total: 1 destroyed, 5 out of control = 6.
Obs: (a) 2/Lt F C Craig; (b) Sgt N Sandison; (c) Sgt J H Bowker; (d) Sgt A Lovesay.

ELLIOTT William Boyd   Captain   103 & 205 SQNS

A Canadian, born in St Catherine's, Ontario, 26 August 1898, he joined the RFC in Canada and sailed to the UK in December 1917 to join 103 Squadron on the 12th. Joined 205 Squadron on 7 April 1918 with whom he was promoted to Captain on 20 June. He had completed nearly 100 bomb raids by 22 August, at which date he was hospitalized with typhoid, but recovered. His DFC was awarded in September. After the war he became a mechanical engineer, later being Vice President of a major tool company in Canada. He also helped found the St Catherine's Flying Club in his home town. Died 27 March 1979.

	1918			DH4				
1	22 Apr	Fokker DrI	(a)	A7561	205	Chaulnes	1620	OOC
2	3 May	Pfalz DIII	(b)	N6009	„	Chaulnes	1545	DES(F)
3	„	Pfalz DIII	(b)	„	„	Chaulnes	1545	OOC
4	15 May	Pfalz DIII	(c)	A7561	„	Chaulnes	1020	OOC
5	20 May	Pfalz DIII	(d)	„	„	Mericombe	0830	DES(F)

Total: 2 shared destroyed, 2 & 1 shared out of control = 5.
Obs: (a) AM G Smith; (b) 2/Lt J A Whalley, and shared with eight other crews; (c) 2/Lt H P Bennett; (d) Sgt P L Richards, and shared with seven other crews.

FOX-RULE Gordon   Captain   49 SQN

From Southminster, Essex, born 16 August 1898. Attended Eastbourne College between January 1914 and December 1916, and spoke Portuguese and Brazilian. Flew bombers with 49 Squadron from January 1918, becoming a Captain and flight commander on 15 May. Awarded the DFC, gazetted 21 September, which noted 30 bomb raids and ten photo sorties. On one occasion he bombed a bridge from 100 feet then attacked troops along the river bank. Engaged by several German fighters, his observer was wounded but he succeeded in driving them off and landed at a French airfield to seek aid for his wounded colleague. Shortly after his return to Home Establishment on 14 August, he received the French Croix de Guerre. Turned down a permanent commission but took a short service commission in October 1919. However, in June 1921 he was forced to resign through ill health contracted in the service.

	1918			DH4				
1	8 Mar	Rumpler C	(a)	A7705	49	Brebières	1315	OOC
2	10 Mar	LVG C	(a)	„	„	Marquion	1400	OOC
				DH9				
3	7 Jun	Albatros DV	(b)	D5576	„	Flavy-le-Martel	1045	OOC
4	10 Jun	Albatros DV	(b)	D1715	„	Assainvillers	0440	DES(F)
5	„	Albatros DV	(b)	„	„	„	0440	OOC
6	25 Jul	Fokker DVII	(c)	„	„	Fismes	1900	OOC
7	9 Aug	Fokker DVII	(d)	„	„	Marchélepot	1700	OOC

Total: 1 destroyed, 6 out of control = 7.
Obs: (a) 2/Lt P T Holligan; (b) Lt E H Tredcraft; (c) Lt R A V R Scherk; (d) 2/Lt S P Scott.

GAMMON Richard John   Captain   104 SQN

Gammon rose to flight commander with 104 Squadron Independent Force in 1918, flying DH9 bombers. He was credited with five victories by September. Awarded the DFC, gazetted 2 November 1918, the citation mentioning an attack on Mannheim on 7 September. His usual observer was Lt Percival Ewart Appleby, with whom he shared all his victories.

	1918			DH9				
1	1 Jul	Albatros DV		C6264	104	Metz	0720	DES
2	1 Aug	Pfalz DIII			„	Boulay A/F	0845	DES
3	7 Sep	Hannover C		C6264	„	Saverne	1230	DES
4	„	Pfalz DIII		„	„	Vosges	1400	DES
5	15 Sep	Pfalz DIII		„	„	Verny-Sonvigny	1105	DES

Total: 5 destroyed = 5.

GAMON John   Captain   5N/205 SQN

Born 25 July 1898, Parkgate, Cheshire. Joined the RNAS five days after his 18th birthday, and became a probationary FSL on 13 June 1917. Served with 4 Naval Squadron on fighters from 14 July. Ditched a Camel off Calais on 24 July (N6368), after becoming lost in sea mist. Gamon then moved to 5 Naval on 18 August (flight lieutenant 1 January 1918) and flew DH bombers in 1917-18, completing almost 100 raids. Gamon received the DSC, gazetted 7 June 1918, his citation referring to an action on 30 March, whilst returning from a raid. Attacked by three

Fokker Triplanes, he shot down one and drove off the other two. He was wounded on 17 June 1918, in DH4 D9277, being hit by AA fire. His observer on this sortie was the squadron commander, Stan Goble. Gamon fainted but luckily Goble, being a pilot, was able to regain control after their machine had fallen on fire for 1,000 feet. Despite another attack, by a Pfalz Scout, Goble got them back over the lines and to their base. In later life Gamon lived in his home town of Chester.

	1917			DH4				
1	8 Dec	Albatros DV	(a)	N6004	5N	Aertrycke A/F	1150	OOC
	1918							
2	30 Mar	Fokker DrI	(b)	„	„	Villers Bretonneux	0912	DES
3	23 Apr	Fokker DrI	(c)	„	„	Chaulnes	1950	DES(F)
4	„	Pfalz DIII	(c)	„	„	Chaulnes	1950	DES
5	3 May	Pfalz DIII	(d)	„	205	Chaulnes	1545	DES(F)
6	„	Pfalz DIII	(d)	„	„	Chaulnes	1545	OOC
7	20 May	Pfalz DIII	(e)	„	„	Mericombe	0830	DES(F)

Total: 4 & 1 shared destroyed, 2 out of control = 7.
Obs: (a) AGL. Winter; (b) S/Lt F H Stringer; (c) Lt R Scott; (d) Lt R Scott, and shared with eight other crews; (e) Sgt J Jones.

GILLANDERS John Gordon   Lieutenant   18 SQN

A Canadian from London, Ontario, Gillanders was born 26 August 1895. He volunteered for the RFC in Canada, where he trained, coming to England to join 103 Squadron. Went to France and posted to 18 Squadron on 14 March 1918 and received the DFC on 23 August, gazetted 2 November 1918, for 29 raids, 16 photo ops and 36 recce sorties plus numerous air fights. He became OC C Flight on 15 August. Returning to his home town he practised law and eventually became a judge of the High Ontario Court. He died of cancer in 1946, ironically while committee chairman for the 'Investigation of Cancer Remedies'.

	1918			DH4				
1	28 Jul	2-seater	(a)	A7907	18	Esquerchin	0720	DES
2	„	Fokker DVII	(a)	„	„	„	0730	DES
3	31 Jul	Pfalz DIII	(a)		„	Brebières	1050	DES
4	„	Pfalz DIII	(a)		„	„	1050	DES
5	9 Aug	Fokker DVII	(b)		„	W Douai	1050	OOC

Total: 4 destroyed, 1 shared out of control = 5.
Obs: (a) 2/Lt E Walker; (b) Lt McCall, and shared with Capt H R Gould/2/Lt E Jinman, Lt G W F Darvill/ Lt J Fenwick, Lt A Pickin/Lt Hutchinson, Lt E Preskett/2/Lt W Clark, Lt Snook/Lt Aslin, Lt Kearney/Lt Buckler.

GOULD Herbert Ruska   Captain   18 SQN

From Bedfont, Middlesex, born 23 December 1891, Gould was employed in London working for the Mexican Oil Company between 1912-14. Joining the RFC in April 1917, he served with 18 Squadron in 1918 and won the Military Cross, gazetted on 16 September. He was made captain and flight commander on 24 June but was killed in action on 14 August, along with his observer, 2/Lt E W F Jinman, flying DH4 A7903. It is possible they were shot down by Uffz Georg Staudacher of Jasta 1, the German's first confirmed victory although he identified it as a BF2b. Gould has no known grave.

	1918			DH4				
1	26 Mar	Albatros DV	(a)	A7989	18	Bihucourt	1730	DES
2	12 Apr	Pfalz DIII	(b)		„	Estaires	1025	DES(F)
3	„	Pfalz DIII	(b)		„	„	1025	OOC
4	9 May	Pfalz DIII	(b)	A8000	„	Estaires	1150	OOC
5	31 Jul	Pfalz DIII	(c)		„	Douai	1050	OOC
6	9 Aug	Fokker DVII	(c)		„	W Douai	1050	OOC

Total: 1 & 1 shared destroyed, 3 & 1 shared out of control = 6.

Obs: (a) Lt J M Brisbane; (b) Capt M S E Archibald, with victories 2 & 3 shared with Lt F J Morgan/Sgt M B Kilroy, Capt A G Waller/Lt Waugh, Lt A C Atkey/Lt Hammond; (c) 2/Lt E Jinman, with victory No.6 shared with Lt J Gillanders/Lt McCall, Lt G W F Darvill/Lt J Fenwick, Lt A Pickin/Lt Hutchinson, Lt E Preskett/2/Lt W Clark, Lt Snook/Lt Aslin, Lt Kearney/Lt Buckner.

GREEN William Edward   Captain   57 SQN

From Ipswich, born 20 October 1898 he joined the RFC in June 1917. Confirmed as Second Lieutenant in August 1917, Bill Green flew with 57 Squadron from 29 September and won the DFC. Gained his 8th victory on 29 August although he was shot up by a Fokker biplane; neither he nor his observer, Lt A M Brown MC, was hurt (DH4 D9262). Made temporary captain on 2 July and his DFC was gazetted on 3 December, noting him as a courageous pilot, brilliant leader and a fine example to his unit. He was at RAF Biggin Hill in March 1918 and left the service on 22 February 1919.

	1918			DH4				
1	6 Jan	Albatros DV	(a)	A7904	57	Lichtervelde	1200	OOC
2	24 Jan	Fokker DrI	(b)	A2161	„	NW Roulers	1130	DES(F)
3	„	Albatros DV	(b)	„	„	„	1130	OOC
4	3 Feb	Albatros DV	(b)	A7674	„	Menin	1245	OOC
5	31 Mar	Pfalz DIII	(b)	A7904	„	Bapaume	1115	OOC
6	10 Aug	Fokker DVII	(c)	D9262	„	Bray-Péronne	1830	OOC
7	„	Fokker DVII	(c)	„	„	„	1830	OOC
8	29 Aug	Fokker DVII	(d)	„	„	Ytres	0800	OOC
9	19 Sep	Fokker DVII	(d)	D8419	„	Havrincourt	1725	OOC

Total: 1 destroyed, 8 out of control = 9.
Obs: (a) 2/Lt E H Wilson; (b) 2/Lt H S Gros; (c) 2/Lt C G Smith; (d) Lt A M Barron MC.

GROSSART William   Captain   205 SQN

From Dumfries, Scotland, born 26 May 1896, he attended Trinity Academy, Edinburgh prior to joining the RFC in February 1918. Served with 205 Squadron until December 1918, during which time he carried out over 40 bomb raids and 70 recce sorties. Of these, 27 and 25 respectively were made during the summer of 1918, for which he received the DFC in September. His final victory was scored by the novel method of dropping a bomb on the Pfalz as it flew below his bomber! Left the service on 12 April 1919 and later lived in Midlothian. Joined the RAFVR on 1 June 1940.

	1918			DH4				
1	3 May	Pfalz DIII	(a)	A7811	205	Chaulnes	1545	DES(F)
2	„	Pfalz DIII	(a)	„	„	„	1545	OOC
3	15 May	Pfalz DIII	(a)	„	„	„	1030	OOC
4	20 May	Pfalz DIII	(b)	„	„	Mericombe	0830	DES(F)
5	11 Aug	Pfalz DIII	(c)	D8421	„	Péronne	1328	DES

Total: 1 & 1 shared destroyed, 2 & 1 shared out of control = 5.
Obs: (a) Sgt P L Richards, and victories 1 & 2 shared with eight other crews; (b) Lt A R Crosthwaite, and shared with seven other crews: (c) 2/Lt J B Leach.

HALL David Sidney   Captain   57 SQN

From Helensburgh, Dumbarton, Scotland, Hall served with the 9th Argyle and Sutherland Highlanders before transferring to the RFC. By 1917 he was flying DH4 bombers and had become A Flight commander. He won the MC, gazetted 6 April 1918, for his actions on 2 October (two kills by him, two by his observer) but by then he had been killed. On 20 November 1917, the first day of the Battle of Cambrai, he and his observer, Lt E P Hartigan, took off at 0945 hrs and failed to return. Their wrecked machine, A7586, was found at Les Alleux where they had been killed in a crash. Hall was 25 years old.

	1917			DH4				
1	27 Jul	Albatros DV	(a)	B3964	57	Houthulst Forest	1730	OOC
2	2 Oct	Albatros DV	(b)	A7568	„	Roulers	1335	OOC
3	„	Albatros DV	(b)	„	„	„	1336	DES(F)
4	„	Albatros DV	(b)	„	„	„	1337	OOC
5	„	Albatros DV	(b)	„	„	„	1340	DES
6	28 Oct	Albatros DV	(b)	„	„	W Roulers	1230	OOC

Total: 2 destroyed, 4 out of control = 6.
Obs: (a) 2/Lt N M Pizey; (b) 2/Lt E P Hartigan.

HARKER Howard Redmayne   Captain   57 SQN

From Manchester, born in Prestwich on 12 May 1891. Educated at Rossell School, and then, having obtained a BSc with 1st Class Honours in engineering at Manchester University, he joined the experimental department of the Royal Aircraft Factory at Farnborough in February 1913, only leaving in April 1916 to join the RFC. Becoming a pilot, Harker flew FEs and DHs with 57 Squadron during 1916-17, winning the Military Cross, gazetted on 9 January 1918. The citation recorded that he had been with his unit for nearly a year and had flown numerous bomb raids and photo reconnaissance sorties. Became temporary captain and flight commander in April 1917 — A Flt — serving until he returned to Home Establishment on 31 August. In 1918 he was with 31 TS, as acting squadron commander from March. He was Mentioned in Despatches for valuable service, gazetted 27 May 1919. However, by this date his death had occurred, on 27 February 1919 in Tidworth Barracks Hospital, Hampshire, a victim of the massive influenza epidemic that swept Europe at this time. He is buried in Manchester Southern Cemetery.

	1917			FE2d				
1	24 Mar	Albatros DII	(a)	A1954	57	E Lens	1145	OOC
				DH4				
2	18 Jun	Albatros DIII	(b)	A7455	„	S Houthulst	0645	DES
3	17 Jul	Albatros DV	(c)	A7492	„	Roulers	1830	OOC
4	28 Jul	Albatros DV	(b)	„	„	Ingelmunster	1810	OOC
5	21 Aug	Albatros DV	(b)	A7568	„	Ledeghem-Menin	1815	DES

Total: 2 destroyed, 3 out of control = 5.
Obs: (a) 2/Lt V D Fernauld; (b) Lt/Capt W E B Barclay MC; (c) Sgt A G Broad.

HEYWOOD Cyril Justin   Lieutenant   5N/205 SQN

Heywood came from Hagley, Stourbridge, born 21 July 1899. Joined the RNAS on 20 September 1917, and after flying with the DH4 School at Manston in February 1918, went to France in March. He flew nearly 100 bomb raids and 20 recce sorties while serving with his Squadron. On 5 July 1918, with 2/Lt E A Dew in the back seat, they were attacked by five Pfalz Scouts. While Heyward engaged one, Dew fought off two more before being seriously wounded in the leg but shot down one scout in flames. Dew then passed out, falling over the dual control stick, which put the DH4 into a steep dive. Heywood had great difficulty in regaining control, but he did so and flew his wounded observer back home. Heywood was taken ill on 6 October 1918 and saw out the war in hospital.

	1918			DH4				
1	3 May	Pfalz DIII	(a)	D9238	205	Chaulnes	1545	DES(F)
2	„	Pfalz DIII	(a)	„	„	„	1545	OOC
3	20 May	Pfalz DIII	(a)	„	„	Mericombe	0830	DES(F)
4	5 Jul	Pfalz DIII	(b)	„	„	S Bray	1956	DES(F)
5	13 Aug	Fokker DVII	(a)	„	„	Péronne	1100	DES
6	15 Sep	Fokker DVII	(a)	F990	„	Busigny	1520	OOC

Total: 2 & 2 shared destroyed, 2 out of control = 6.
Obs: (a) Sgt F S Langstone; victories 1, 2 & 3 shared with several other crews; (b) 2/Lt E A Dew.

HOME-HAY Jeffrey Batters   Captain   104 SQN

Jeff Home-Hay was born in Alloa, Scotland, 31 January 1890, but emigrated to Canada with his widowed mother, three sisters and two brothers shortly before WW1. Commissioned into the 7th Reserve Battn., of the Argyll and Sutherland Highlanders he transferred to the RFC. Took his Royal Aero Club Certificate, No.3209, on 10 July 1916 and was gazetted a temporary lieutenant on 1 February 1917. Won the MC, gazetted 26 July 1917, for artillery observation work with 53 Squadron over ten months beginning February 1917. In May 1918 he joined 104 Squadron Independent Force, winning the DFC, which was gazetted on 21 September 1918. Brought down on a raid to Mannheim on 22 August 1918, the day the Squadron suffered its most severe losses of the war, together with his observer, Sergeant W T Smith DCM MM; both became prisoners. In 1919 he began farming in Canada but in 1920 was called to take part in the first Trans-Canada flight from Halifax to Vancouver. He later made regular runs between Winnipeg, Saskatoon, Moose Jaw and Regina with Prairie Airways. In later years he was, at one stage, the oldest pilot in the north still actively flying. He retired to his farm at Kelington, Saskatchewan in 1952 where he died in the summer of 1956.

	1918			DH9				
1	30 Jun	Albatros DV	(a)		104	nr Landau	0740	DES
2	6 Jul	EA	(a)	C2960	,,	Metz	0845	OOC
3	11 Aug	Scout	(b)		,,	Karlsruhe	0910	OOC
4	12 Aug	Fokker DVII	(a)		,,	Saverne	0715	DES
5	13 Aug	Pfalz DIII	(b)		,,	Corny	1545	DES
6	,,	Pfalz DIII	(b)		,,	S Corny	1545	DES
7	15 Aug	Pfalz DIII	(b)		,,	Château Salins	1830	OOC

Total: 4 destroyed, 3 out of control = 7.
Obs: (a) Lt C C Blizard; (b) Sgt W T Smith.

JOHNSEN Olans Charles William   Captain   98 SQN

From Bromley, Johnson was born on 25 October 1889. A married man, he served with the 1/4 London Brigade, RFA, from April 1913 and when war came he went to France on 3 October 1915 until wounded on 1 November 1916. Transferred to the RFC on 28 February 1917 and after pilot training he was retained as an instructor and flight commander. Finally posted to 98 Squadron, via No. 1 Air Depot in 1918. Awarded the French Croix de Guerre in 1918 and his DFC was gazetted 8 February 1919.

	1918			DH9				
1	11 Jul	Pfalz DIII	(a)	D1731	98	Don	0730	OOC
2	18 Jul	Albatros DV	(a)	C6349	,,	Fère-en-Tardenois	0805	DES
3	20 Jul	Fokker DrI	(a)	,,	,,		1950	DES(F)
4	30 Aug	Fokker DVII	(b)	D3169	,,	Somain	1815	OOC
5	16 Sep	Fokker DVII	(c)	,,	,,	Oisy	1045	OOC

Total: 2 destroyed, 3 out of control = 5.
Obs: (a) Capt G H Whitfield; (b) 2/Lt A H Fuller; (c) 2/Lt C H Thompson.

JOY Ernest Graham   Major   49, 57 & 205 SQNS

Although born in Alabama, USA, on 2 November 1891, he was a Canadian. A lawyer in Toronto, he enlisted on 24 July 1915 and by March 1916 was a Major with the 74th Battn. Canadian Expeditionary Force. Joy then transferred to the RFC and on 9 May 1917 was sent to 49 Squadron but within a couple of weeks went to 23 Squadron. The next month he was posted to 57 Squadron, operating until 21 August, when he returned to the UK. In September 1918 he went to 205 Squadron, flying at least 12 raids by the war's end. Awarded the DFC in 1919. Returning home he returned to his law practice and served in the Canadian Army in WW2. Died in Toronto 21 June 1993. Signed himself E Graham Joy.

	1917			DH4				
1	28 Jul	Albatros DV	(a)	A7537	57	Ingelmunster	1830	OOC
2	„	Albatros DV	(a)	„	„	„	1830	OOC
3	16 Aug	Albatros DV	(a)	A7563	„	Houthulst	1745	OOC
4	17 Aug	Albatros DV	(a)	„	„	Menin	0730	OOC
5	„	Albatros DV	(a)	„	„	Menin	0730	OOC
6	„	Albatros DV	(a)	„	„	W Menin	0732	OOC
7	20 Aug	Albatros DV		A7564	„	E Ypres	1115	OOC
	1918			DH9a				
8	4 Nov	Fokker DVII	(b)	F1025	205	Mauberge	1535	DES

Total: 1 destroyed, 7 out of control = 8.
Obs: (a) Lt F Leathley; (b) 2/Lt L A Drain.

KEATING James Alfred   1st Lieutenant   49 SQN

Born 4 December 1897, in Chicago, USA, he also resided at Fort Lauderdale, Florida. A married man, he joined the US Air Service and was attached to 49 Squadron RAF on 26 May 1918. His five August victories were scored in conjunction with his observer during two actions over two days. Both he and his observer, 2/Lt Edward Arthur Simpson, also a married man, from London, who had served with the Royal Irish Fusiliers, were awarded the DFC, Keating later also receiving the American DSC and Silver Star. Served as a Colonel in WW2. He died on 2 October 1976.

	1918			DH9				
1	22 Jul	Fokker DVII			49	Sergy	1820	OOC
2	8 Aug	Pfalz DIII		D3165	„	Bethencourt	1835	DES(F)
3	9 Aug	Fokker DVII		C2202	„	Marchélepot	0630	DES(F)
4	„	Fokker DVII		„	„	Ablaincourt	0630	DES(F)
5	„	Fokker DVII		„	„	Soyecourt	0640	OOC
6	„	Fokker DVII		„	„	Lamotte	0645	OOC

Total: 3 destroyed, 2 out of control = 5.

KEEBLE Noel   Captain   1 WING, 202 SQN

Born 6 April 1891, Keeble, a married man who lived in Andover, Hants, joined the RNAS on 2 August 1915 and served at Eastbourne with Farmans and Curtiss JN3s, then in No.1 Naval Wing, Dunkirk, in late 1915, flying Short S.38s and BE2c machines as a FSL. Flying a Nieuport 10 two-seater as a scout, he forced a German seaplane to land on the sea on 25 January 1916. He operated on scouts for most of the year, claiming a second victory in October. He had a narrow escape on 12 November in Pup N5189, suffering engine failure over the sea chasing another seaplane, but was saved by a French patrol boat. By 1918 he was a flight commander with 202 Squadron RAF flying Airco DH4s on recce and artillery sorties for the Navy along the North Sea coast of Belgium. He was awarded the DSC, DFC and Bar, claiming four more victories with his usual observer, Captain E B C Betts. His DFC was gazetted on 21 September 1918; his citation recorded over 1,000 photos taken and eight aircraft destroyed. He also received the French Croix de Guerre in late 1916. Died 4 June 1963.

	1916			Nieuport				
1	25 Jan	Seaplane		3178	1Wg	off Nieuport	0800	FTL
				Pup				
2	23 Oct	Seaplane		N5183	„	off Ostende	1600	DES
	1918			DH4				
3	5 Jun	Pfalz DIII	(a)	A7446	202	N Easen	1200	DES
4	10 Aug	Fokker DVII	(a)	„	„	Bruges	1425	OOC
5	16 Sep	Pfalz DIII	(a)	„	„	Lissewerghe	1100	DES
6	„	Fokker DVII	(a)	„	„	Dudzeele	1125	DES(F)

Total: 4 destroyed, 1 out of control, 1 force to land = 6.
Obs: (a) Capt E B C Betts DSC DFC.

LALLY Conrad Tolendal   Lieutenant   25 SQN

Born Toronto, 3 April 1888. When he enlisted in the CEF, he was the Mayor of Wainwright, Alberta. Joined the RFC in Canada and went to England where he was briefly with 28 TS Squadron in England, then went to France to join 25 Squadron on 11 April 1917 as a Captain. He and his observer, Lt J E Cole, were shot down and wounded on 8 December but survived. Lally had been hit in the back by a spent bullet but he was back with the Squadron ten days later. Leaving the Squadron on 18 December, Lally returned to England and received the MC on 1 December 1917, for 32 raids and 42 recce sorties and a Bar was awarded in February 1918. For his services in England in 1918 he was awarded the AFC on 1 November. Lally returned to Canada but died shortly after the end of the war.

	1917			FE2d				
1	7 Jun	Albatros DIII	(a)	A6417	25	W Lille	0700	OOC
2	"	Albatros DIII	(a)	"	"	"	0705	DES
				DH4				
3	5 Aug	Albatros DV	(b)	A7477	"	Perenchies	1730	DES
4	3 Sep	Albatros DV	(b)	"	"	Quesnoy	0940	OOC
5	"	Albatros DV	(b)	"	"	Douai	1930	OOC

Total: 2 destroyed, 3 out of control = 5.
Obs: (a) 2/Lt L F Williams; (b) 2/Lt B L Blackett.

LE MESURIER Thomas Frederick   Flight Commander   5N, 11N/211 SQNS

From 'Michwood', Merton Park, Surrey, England, born on 16 February 1897, he was educated at Rutlish School and Hurstpierpoint College. Served with the RNAS from 23 July 1915, gaining his Aero Certificate No.2753 at the Central Flying School on 17 March 1916, and flew from Dunkirk later in the year. He was twice Mentioned in Despatches, for raids on Ghistelles and St Denis Westrem aerodromes in September 1916. Promoted to flight lieutenant at the end of the year, he joined 5 Naval Squadron in February 1917, and he was made an acting flight commander in May, rank confirmed at the end of June. His first DSC came after flying 14 bomb raids and numerous fighter patrols, and in August he was again Mentioned in Despatches after bombing Snelleghem airfield. His second DSC came on 1 August. After his first tour of duty with 5N, he was assigned to 11 Naval, which became 211 Squadron in April 1918. He was killed on 26 May 1918 along with his observer, 2/Lt R Lardner, flying DH9 D1693, which was either hit by AA fire or broke up in the air over Pervyse. He was only 21 years old but had been awarded the DSC and two Bars for his service and recommended for squadron commander. He was buried at Dunkirk.

	1917			DH4				
1	3 Jun	Albatros DIII	(a)	N5967	5N	W Brugge	0500	OOC
2	5 Aug	Albatros DIII	(b)	"	"	Snelleghem A/F	1800	DES
3	"	Albatros DIII	(b)	"	"	Dixmude	1802	OOC
4	19 Aug	Albatros DV	(b)	N6005	"	SW Ostende	0600	OOC
5	11 Sep	Albatros DV	(b)	N5968	"	Sparappelhoek	1100	OOC
6	15 Oct	Albatros DV	(b)	N5967	"	E Dixmude		OOC
7	21 Oct	Albatros DV	(b)	"	"	Houttave A/F		OOC

Total: 1 destroyed, 6 out of control = 7.
Obs: (a) FSL R G StJohn; (b) AGL. H S Jackson.

LUPTON Charles Roger   Captain   5N/205 SQN

From Roundhay, Leeds, born 27 January 1898, 'Luppy' had joined the Royal Navy 20 July 1916, and as a flight sub-lieutenant with the RNAS, gained his Aero Club Certificate (No.3734) on 14 September. Flying DH4s with 5N Squadron he completed over 60 bomb raids, winning the DSC and Bar. On 17 April 1917 he was shot up by fighters (in N6000) and force landed with his rudder controls out of action. He ended up in Plymouth Hospital with a dislocated right hip and facial injuries but later returned to duty. Acting flight commander 2 January 1918. His DSC was for a raid on Thorout Rail Station and Varssenaere on 26 October 1917, and the Bar was gazetted on 7 June 1918, noting four successful and damaging low bombing raids flown on 26 March, during the German March offensive. He was killed in action on 9 May 1918, along with his observer, Gnr. Albert George Wood (aged 19), both being buried at Vignacourt.

	1917			DH4				
1	28 Sep	Albatros DV	(a)	N6009	5N	Blankenberghe		OOC
2	8 Dec	Albatros DV	(a)	N6000	„	Aertrycke A/F	1100	OOC
	1918							
3	22 Mar	Albatros DV	(b)	N6009	„	SW Vendhuille	1520	OOC
4	6 Apr	Fokker DrI	(b)	„	205	NE Villers Bretonneux	1540	DES(F)
5	7 Apr	Pfalz DIII	(b)	N6000	„	Lamotte	1350	OOC

Total: 1 destroyed, 3 & 1 shared out of control = 5.
Obs: (a) AGL. Smith, with victory No.2 shared with FSL J Gamon/AGL. Winter N6004; (b) AGL. A G Wood.

MacGREGOR Andrew   Captain   57 SQN

Andrew MacGregor was born 25 October 1897, Glen Gyle, Crieff, Scotland. Transferred to the RFC from the Argyll and Sutherland Highlanders. Flew with 57 Squadron in 1918, becoming a Captain on 10 August and commanding 'C' Flight. Won the DFC, gazetted on 5 April 1919, for an action on 14 August 1918 during a bomb raid. They were attacked by several German fighters, and from one, which MacGregor's observer shot down, the pilot was seen to take to a parachute. His second 'flamer' on 5 September also had the German pilot taking to his parachute. In 1919 he went to Egypt to join 47 Squadron, then posted to 55 Squadron in July, operating over Iraq and Kurdistan. In 1921 he was attached to the Desert Survey Flight at Amman and helped create the Cairo-Baghdad air route. Served in Egypt and again in Iraq between 1923-24, and Kurdistan again in 1927. Staff College 1927-28; Squadron Leader 1932, Wing Commander in 1937, having been made an MBE while serving in the Sudan and Palestine. Air Ministry in 1940 and then SASO 4 Group 1940-42; AOA North Africa 1942-44 (Air Commodore) and Assistant Commandant at the RAF Staff College 1944. AOC 28 Group 1945-46 (CBE) and AOA HQ Fighter Command 1946-49. Other awards: Légion d'Honneur and Officer of the Legion of Merit (USA) 1944; Commander Order of the Crown of Belgium, 1948; Croix de Guerre. Retired from the RAF with the rank of Air Vice-Marshal CB CBE, in 1949, and lived in Crieff until his death on 24 October 1983.

	1918			DH4				
1	31 Jul	Fokker DVII	(a)	D8398	57	Quéant	1110	OOC
2	8 Aug	Fokker DVII	(a)	„	„	Moislains A/F	0810	OOC
3	14 Aug	Fokker DVII	(a)	D8419	„	SE Roisel	1040	DES(F)
4	4 Sep	Fokker DVII	(b)	„	„	Bourlon Wood	1000	OOC
5	5 Sep	Fokker DVII	(b)	„	„	W Marcoing	1125	OOC
6	„	Fokker DVII	(b)	„	„	Avesnes-le-Sec	1605	DES(F)

Total: 2 destroyed, 4 out of control = 6.
Obs: (a) Lt J F D Tanqueray; (b) Sgt J Grant.

MINOT Laurence   Captain   16 & 57 SQNS

Minot, born in Upper Norwood, south-east London on 21 July 1896, gained his Royal Aero Club Certificate on 8 July 1915 (No.1409). Flew with 16 Squadron from February 1916, becoming a flight commander in July. Went briefly to 7 Squadron before being rested. Posted to 57 Squadron as a supernumerary in 1917, he took over B Flight after Captain N G McNaughton MC was killed on 24 June. The 'flamer' on 3 July was the machine flown by the leader of Jasta 10, Oberleutnant Albert Dossenbach, 15 victories. Minot was himself killed in action on 28 July along with his observer, 2/Lt S J Leete, in combat with fighters of Jasta 6 over Oostroosebeke, at 5.55 pm, flying A7540.

	1917			DH4					
1	3 Jul	Albatros DV	(a)	A7487	57	Zonnebeke	1225	OOC
2	,,	Albatros DV	(a)	,,	,,	,,	1225	DES(F)
3	7 Jul	Albatros DV	(b)	,,	,,	NE Ypres	0830	OOC
4	27 Jul	Albatros DV	(a)	B3963	,,	Houthulst	1730	OOC
5	,,	Albatros DV	(a)	,,	,,	,,	1730	OOC
6	,,	Albatros DV	(a)	,,	,,	,,	1730	OOC

Total: 1 destroyed, 5 out of control = 6.
Obs: (a) Lt A F Britton; (b) 1AM Goffe.

O'LIEFF Percy Henry   2nd Lieutenant   1 & 55 SQNS

Born Banbury, Oxon, 8 May 1895. Gained his Royal Aero Club Certificate, No.4610, whilst an RFC 1st Air Mechanic, on 28 April 1917. He had previously been an observer with No.1 Squadron in 1916, scoring two victories, one being confirmed, his pilot being Second Lieutenant Vernon Castle, the famous dancer. Commissioned and a fully fledged pilot, he returned to France and joined 55 Squadron, where he and his gunners claimed a further four victories. Taken prisoner on 5 April 1918, in A7553, over Luxemburg, during a bomb raid. Renewed his flying licence on 24 May 1939.

	1916			MS					
–	8 Sep	Fokker E	(a)		1	Ypres	eve	DD
1	27 Nov	2-seater	(b)		,,	Vlamertinghe	1230	DES
	1917			DH4					
2	3 Oct	Albatros DV	(c)	A7592	55	Courtrai	0800	DES(F)
	1918								
3	24 Mar	Albatros DV	(d)	,,	,,	Mannheim	1245	DES
4	,,	Albatros DV	(d)	,,	,,	,,	1250	OOC
5	,,	Albatros DV	(d)	,,	,,	,,	1250	OOC

Total: 3 destroyed, 2 out of control = 5.
Pilot: (a) 2/Lt T M B Newton; (b) 2/Lt V W Castle; Observer: (c) Cpl A Walters; (d) 2/Lt S R Wells.

PEARSON Laurence Herbert   Lieutenant   202 SQN

Born in Nottingham, 10 March 1899. Having joined the Royal Navy, Pearson chose to fly, transferred to the RNAS on 8 July 1917 and took his Royal Aero Club Certificate on 15 September 1917 (No.5322). Once qualified as a flying officer, he proceeded to France, joining 202 Squadron on 18 January 1918 where he saw out the war. He was shot down twice in June, on the 4th and on the 27th. On the first date he force landed on the beach near Fort Mardycke (A7930) with his rudder shot away, and on the second he force landed near Middlekerke after being attacked by five scouts (A8025).

	1918			DH4					
1	4 Jun	Scout	(a)	A7930	202	Zeebrugge	1930	OOC
2	,,	Scout	(a)	,,	,,	,,	1930	OOC
3	27 Jun	Pfalz DIII	(b)	A8025	,,	Ostende	1520	OOC
4	14 Aug	Fokker EV	(b)	A7632	,,	Nieuport	1135	OOC
5	16 Sep	Pfalz DXII	(b)	,,	,,	Lisseweghe	1105	OOC
6	,,	Fokker DVII	(b)	,,	,,	Dudzeele	1125	DES(F)

Total: 1 destroyed, 5 out of control = 6.
Obs: (a) AGL S E Allatson; (b) 2/Lt E Darby DSM.

PITHEY Croye Rothes   Lieutenant   12 SQN

From Natal, South Africa, Pithey was born on 19 August 1895. Between June 1916 and May 1917 he was an accounts clerk in Johannesburg (and spoke fluent Zulu), from where he joined the RFC. Flew RE8s with 12 Squadron in 1918, whom he joined on 17 April, having earlier gone to 52 Squadron but then had to go into hospital. Along with his observer, Lieutenant Hervey Rhodes, they became the highest scoring RE8 crew of the war, and both received the DFC and Bar. Their run of extraordinary skill and not a little luck came to an end on 27 September after both were wounded in combat, Pithey having been slightly wounded earlier, on 24 April. In April 1919 he was with 106 Squadron, then received a permanent commission on 1 August, joining 105 Squadron in October. Pithey was killed en-route to Ireland with 2 Squadron in a Bristol Fighter crash on 21 February 1920, flying from Chester to Baldonnell. Rhodes later became Lord Rhodes and was Lord Lieutenant of Lancashire; he died on 11 September 1987.

	1918			RE8				
1	7 May	Balloon			12			DES
2	4 Jun	Balloon			,,		0845	DES
3	7 Jun	Pfalz DIII	B7715		,,	Sheet 57c B8	0920	DES
4	,,	Pfalz DIII	,,		,,	,,	0920	OOC
5	,,	Pfalz DIII	,,		,,	,,	0920	OOC
6	21 Aug	Fokker DVII	E47		,,	Behaignes	1130	OOC
7	23 Aug	LVG C			,,	Boyelles	1740	DES(F)
8	28 Aug	DFW C	F6097		,,	E St Léger	0945	DES
9	30 Aug	Fokker DVII	,,		,,	Bullecourt	1650	DES(F)
10	3 Sep	LVG C	,,		,,	Lagnicourt	1715	DES

Total: 5 destroyed, 3 out of control, 2 balloons = 10.

PUGH John Edward   Captain   25 SQN

Born 29 April 1890, Great Soughall, Chester, England. Went to Canada in 1913 and became a civil servant with Indian Affairs. Enlisted as a Trooper in the 9th Canadian Reserve Battn. while living in Cardston in 1914 and was commissioned into the 49th Battn. on 10 July 1916, then serving with the 19th Alberta Dragoons in England and France until wounded on the Somme on 16 September. Seconded to the RFC on 26 May 1917 and after training went to 25 Squadron on 2 October. Became a flight commander in the spring of 1918 and returned to the UK on 12 June, having won the DFC. After instructing he returned to Alberta, Canada to resume his career. He later became Deputy of Indian Affairs. Died from an aneurysm on 28 May 1966.

	1918			DH4				
1	13 Jan	Scout	(a)	A7609	25	La Jardinet	1150	OOC
2	27 Mar	SS DIII	(b)	A7913	,,	Foucaucourt	1510	OOC
3	8 May	Pfalz DIII	(c)	,,	,,	Thorout	0810	DES
4	,,	Pflaz DIII	(c)	,,	,,	,,	0820	OOC
5	5 Jun	Rumpler C	(d)	,,	,,	E Albert	0930	DES

Total: 2 destroyed, 3 out of control = 5.
Obs: (a) 2/Lt O S Hinson; (b) Sgt A H Muff; (c) 2/Lt W Dixon; (d) Lt S C Eschmann.

ROULSTONE Alexander   Captain   25 & 57 SQNS

From Nottingham, born 10 October 1890, Alex Roulstone was commissioned into the 12th Battn. Notts and Derby Regiment. Transferred to the RFC in August 1916 and became temporary lieutenant in the General List on 7 July 1916. Saw service with 25 Squadron, joining this unit on 23 March 1917, on FEs, and later a flight commander in July. Posted to Home Establishment on 4 September he went as a flight commander to 57 Squadron on DH4s, on 27 February 1918. Recommended for the MC on 22 July 1917, gazetted 19 September, he was wounded on 17 March 1918, together with his observer, 2/Lt W C Venmore, flying a DH4 A7901, whilst they shot down Oblt Hans Bethge, commander of Jasta 30. Invalided back to England he was a flight commander with 110 Squadron in 1919, then 100 Squadron until he left the service on 18 March 1920. After the war he lived in Loughborough.

	1917			FE2b					
1	6 Apr	Albatros DIII	(a)	7686	25	E Givenchy	1030	DES(F)
2	24 Apr	Albatros DIII	(a)	5347	,,	Billy-Montigny	1750	DES
3	21 May	Albatros DIII	(b)	A6381	,,	La Bassée	1630	OOC
				DH4				
4	20 Jul	Albatros DV	(c)	A7482	,,	NW Habourdin	0745	OOC
5	22 Jul	Albatros C	(c)	,,	,,	Douai	0900	OOC
6	22 Aug	Albatros DV	(d)	A7547	,,	SE Carvin	0815	DES(F)
	1918							
7	13 Mar	Albatros DV	(e)	A7901	57	E Ledeghem	1230	OOC
8	17 Mar	Albatros DV	(f)	,,	,,	N Menin	1130	OOC

Total: 3 destroyed, 5 out of control = 8.
Obs: (a) 2/Lt E G Green; (b) Lt H Cotton; (c) 2/Lt L F Williams; (d) 2/Lt D W T Fox; (e) Lt D F V Page; (f) 2/Lt W C Venmore.

SMITH George Henry Benjamin   Lieutenant   104 SQN

From Camberwell, south-east London, born 20 August 1899. A clerk in the family business during 1916-17, he was commissioned temporary second lieutenant 20 January 1918. Flew operations with No.104 Squadron, Independent Force, in 1918, where his usual observer was Sergeant W Harrop MM. Both were taken prisoner on a raid to Mannheim on 22 August, the Squadron suffering its worst losses of the war on this day, seven DH9s failing to return. Smith's machine was C2179. Repatriated on 9 December he left the RAF on 12 February 1919.

	1918			DH9				
1	1 Aug	Pfalz DIII	(a)		104	Boulay A/F	0815	DES
2	12 Aug	Pfalz DIII	(a)		,,	Saverne	0715	DES
3	,,	Albatros DV	(a)		,,	,,	0715	DES
4	,,	EA	(a)		,,	,,	0715	OOC
5	15 Aug	EA	(a)		,,	Delm	1830	OOC

Total: 3 destroyed, 2 out of control = 5.
Obs: (a) Sgt W Harrop.

SPURLING Arthur Rowe   Lieutenant   49 SQN

From Bermuda, born 19 May 1896. Joined the RFC and gained his Royal Aero Club Certificate on 21 August 1917 (No.5148) and made second lieutenant with effect from 29 July. Trained with 89 Squadron, 40 TDS and 121 Squadron before joining 49 Squadron in France in 1918. Awarded the DFC in August. Becoming lost in cloud on 23 August, Spurling nearly landed on a German airfield by mistake but was attacked by a Fokker just as he noticed several German fighters below him. He and his observer, Sgt F W Bell, fought their way out and back, seeing three fighters burning on the ground and then drove off a two-seater on the return journey to the lines.

	1918			DH9				
1	25 Jul	Fokker DVII	(a)	D3056	49	Mont Notre Dame	1900	OOC
2	23 Aug	Fokker DVII	(a)	,,	,,	Lens	1915	DES(F)
3	,,	Fokker DVII	(a)	,,	,,	,,	1915	DES
4	,,	Fokker DVII	(a)	,,	,,	,,	1915	OOC
5	,,	Fokker DVII	(a)	,,	,,	,,	1915	DES(F)
6	,,	Fokker DVII	(a)	,,	,,	,,	1915	DES

Total: 4 destroyed, 2 out of control = 6.
Obs: Sgt F W Bell.

STEWART David Arthur   Captain   20 & 18 SQNS

As a Second Air Mechanic, Stewart gained two victories flying as an observer in FE2b 'pushers' in 1916. With the rank of corporal, he gained his Royal Aero Club Certificate on 7 December

1916 (No.3958) and was flying with 18 Squadron in the autumn of 1917, operating DH4 bombers. Promoted to Captain in May 1918, he received the MC and Bar, gazetted on 22 April and 22 June, followed by the DFC in August.

	1916			FE2b				
1	1 Aug	Fokker EIII	(a)	A13	20	Moorslede	1600	DES
2	3 Aug	Scout	(b)	A23	„	Ypres	1010	DES
	1918			DH4				
3	6 Jan	Albatros DV	(c)	A7653	18	Valenciènnes	1205	OOC
4	6 Mar	Pfalz DIII	(c)	A7797	„	Pont-à-Vendin	1115	DES
5	„	Pfalz DIII	(c)	„	„	„	1115	OOC
6	„	Albatros DV	(c)	„	„	„	1115	OOC
7	„	Albatros DV	(c)	„	„	„	1115	OOC
8	10 Mar	Pfalz DIII	(d)	A7799	„	Carvin	1245	OOC
9	15 Mar	Pfalz DIII	(e)	A8038	„	Avelin	1255	DES
10	25 Mar	2-seater	(f)	„	„	Loupart Wood	1715	DES
11	27 Mar	Fokker DrI	(f)	A7800	„	SW Albert	1130	DES
12	28 May	Albatros DV	(f)	A8038	„	W Douai	1140	DES
13	30 May	Pfalz DIII	(g)	„	„	Neuve Chapelle	1300	DES
14	„	Pfalz DIII	(g)	„	„	Richebourg	1305	OOC
15	17 Jun	Pfalz DIII	(f)	„	„	Hulloch	0845	DES
16	„	Pfalz DIII	(f)	„	„	Loos	0850	OOC

Total: 9 destroyed, 7 out of control = 16.
Pilots: (a) Lt D H Dabbs; (b) Capt R S Maxwell; Obs: (c) 2/Lt H W N Mackay; (d) Sgt C Beardmore; (e) Sgt A Pollard; (f) Capt L I Collins; (g) Lt W Miller.

STOKES Claude Harry   Captain   57 SQN

From Blackheath, south-east London, born 16 March 1884, he was living with his wife in Lewisham when he joined the RFC Special Reserve in June 1916. However, between 1910-16 his profession was that of mechanical engineer, working in Rhodesia with an ore reduction unit, with gas and steam engines. After pilot training served with 41 Squadron, which he joined on 15 October 1916 but he was injured five days later and returned to England. For most of 1917 he was an instructor. Then served with 57 Squadron, having become a captain on 2 January 1918. On 29 October 1918 his DH4, D8398, was hit by AA fire over Mauberge at 1430 hrs. Stokes was badly injured and died on 7 November. His observer, 2/Lt L H Eyles was taken prisoner. Stokes was 34 years old and was buried at Erquelinnes, Belgium. His DFC was gazetted on 1 January 1919 and he was Mentioned in Despatches on 3 June.

	1918			DH4				
1	19 Jun	Pfalz DIII	(a)	D8398	57	Bapaume	1930	OOC
2	23 Jun	Fokker DVII	(b)	„	„	Le Transloy	1510	OOC
3	16 Sep	Fokker DVII	(c)	„	„	Havrincourt Wood	1215	OOC
4	„	Fokker DVII	(c)	„	„	„	1215	OOC
5	21 Sep	Fokker DVII	(c)	„	„	N Fontaine-Notre Dame	1835	OOC

Total: 5 out of control = 5.
Obs: (a) Capt J H Bowler; (b) 2/Lt T C Danby; (c) Lt R D Bovill.

STUBBS John Stevenson   Captain   103 SQN

Came from Aintree, Liverpool and was educated at St Bees, Cumberland, between 1909-10 and was later commissioned into the Territorial Reserve, becoming a Captain in the 3rd South Lancs Regt. Went to France early in the war and was therefore entitled to the Mons Ribbon; also saw service in Egypt. Transferring to the RFC, Stubbs became a pilot and eventually joined 27 Squadron in 1917. He was wounded in action on 9 May. Later he was sent to 103 Squadron in May 1918, serving till the Armistice. He commanded C Flight and together with his usual observer, 2/Lt John Bernard Russell, received the DFC, gazetted on 2 November 1918. The citation recorded 51 raids and recce sorties. On the same date the London Gazette recorded the award of the Air Force Cross to Stubbs. He had two narrow escapes with 103, firstly on 20 May during an attack on a kite balloon at Seclin, he and 2/Lt C C Dance being forced down in DH9 C6179, and on 30 October. On this date in combat with Fokker DVIIs, Stubbs made his 8th and final claim but was brought down in D550, with Lt C G Bannermann, but both survived unharmed. In all he flew almost 90 sorties, of which 78 were over the lines.

	1918			DH9				
1	20 May	Balloon	(a)	C6179	103	Seclin	1100	DES
2	6 Jun	Fokker DVII	(a)	„	„	Fretoy, SW Ham	1620	DES(F)
3	„	Fokker DVII	(a)	„	„	„	1620	OOC
4	4 Jul	Pfalz DIII	(a)	C6150	„	La Bassée	2030	OOC
5	31 Jul	EA	(b)	„				OOC
6	„	„	(b)	„				OOC
7	25 Aug	Fokker DVII	(b)	D3274	„	S Armentières	1115	OOC
8	„	Fokker DVII	(b)	„	„	SE Armentières	1115	DES
9	30 Aug	Fokker DVII	(a)	D3162	„	E Bac St Maur		OOC
10	6 Sep	Fokker DVII	(c)	„	„	W St André	1130	DES
11	30 Oct	Fokker DVII	(c)	D550	„	Montreuil	1430	DES

Total: 5 destroyed, 6 out of control = 11.
Obs: (a) 2/Lt C C Dance; (b) 2/Lt J B Russell; (c) 2/Lt C G Bannermann; victories 2 & 3 shared with 2/Lt C H Henderson/2/Lt C E Eddy, D5569 and Lt I W Leiper/Pvt J Buffery, D1007.

TURNER Francis McDougall Charlewood   Captain   55 & 57 SQNS

Born 17 March 1897 he came from Clapham, south London. Educated at Marlborough College from 1910 to 1915, he joined the RFC Special Reserve on 3 January 1916, and after seeing action with No.55 Squadron, winning the MC in the summer of 1917, Turner transferred to 57 Squadron in September. His MC was gazetted on 9 January 1918, the citation noting many photo ops and bomb raids, at least 24 of the latter having been led by him. He was also the first officer to carry out a lone Squadron long-range recce sortie. With 57, he was awarded the DFC during the summer of 1918 although he was slightly injured on 8 August while on a low bombing sortie, being attacked by a Fokker DVII over Moislains. His Canadian observer, 2/Lt H S Musgrove was unhurt; they were flying DH4 D8398. Turner was also Mentioned in Despatches. On the 9th he and Lt H E W Bryning were injured in a crash flying D8428, Turner giving the other man some dual instruction. Coming in to land they hit a tree, wrecking the machine and putting themselves in hospital. Turner's DFC was gazetted on 2 November, and he was noted as a brilliant leader. The citation also recorded a raid that was attacked by 20 Fokker biplanes, but he continued with some low-level bombing and when singled out by three enemy fighters, he shot down one of them. He relinquished his commission in 1920 due to ill-health. In January 1940 he applied to serve with the RAFVR.

	1917			DH4				
1	13 Aug	Albatros DV	(a)	B3962	55	Roulers	0815	OOC
2	„	Albatros DV	(a)	„	„	SE Roulers	0820	OOC
	1918							
3	1 Apr	Fokker DrI	(b)	A7901	57	Irles	1145	DES(F)
4	„	Fokker DrI	(b)	„	„	„	1145	DES
5	„	Fokker DrI	(b)	„	„	„	1145	OOC
6	28 Jul	Fokker DVII	(c)		„	Vaulx-Vraucourt	1720	OOC
7	8 Aug	Fokker DVII	(d)	D8419	„	Moislains A/F	0815	DES

Total: 3 destroyed, 3 & 1 shared out of control = 7.
Obs: (a) 2/Lt R deR Brett; (b) 2/Lt A Leach; (c) Sgt S G Sowden, and shared with Lt W J Pitt/2/Lt T C Danby and Lt E M Coles/Sgt McDonald; (d) 2/Lt H S Musgrove.

WALLER Albert Gregory   Captain   18 SQN

From Banagher, Ireland. Saw service with the Army Service Corps, becoming a temporary captain with effect from 28 March 1916. Transferred to the RFC General List and took his Royal Aero Club Certificate on 3 December 1916, No.4015. Served with 55 Squadron from 15 November 1917 until 12 February 1918, becoming a flight commander on this latter date. Then went to 18 Squadron in 1918 also as a flight commander. Waller was awarded the MC, gazetted 16 September 1918, for 15 bomb raids, 22 low bombing attacks and recce flights, plus eight photographic sorties, as well as accounting for five enemy aircraft. Became a communications pilot attached to the Air Ministry in the summer of 1918, and was then second in command of 22 TDS. Left the service on 3 February 1919.

	1918			DH4				
1	6 Mar	Albatros DV	(a)	A7798	18	Carvin	1125	OOC
2	10 Mar	Albatros DV	(a)	A7770	„	Carvin-Fromelles	1215	OOC
3	15 Mar	Pfalz DIII	(b)	A8076	„	Avelin	1245	OOC
4	12 Apr	Pfalz DIII	(c)		„	Estaires	1025	DES(F)
5	„	Pfalz DIII	(c)		„	„	1025	OOC
6	14 May	Fokker DVII	(d)	A8000	„	Merville	1800	DES
7	16 May	Fokker DrI	(d)	A8041	„	Neuf Berquin	1350	OOC
8	19 May	Albatros DV	(e)		„	Douai	1200	OOC
9	25 May	Albatros DV	(e)		„	Courrières	1130	OOC
10	30 May	Fokker DVII	(f)	A8018	„	Bac St Maur	2030	DES(F)
11		Fokker DVII	(f)	„	„	„	2050	OOC

Total: 2 & 1 shared destroyed, 7 & 1 shared out of control = 11.
Obs: (a) Sgt M B Kilroy; (b) Lt J M Brisbane; (c) 2/Lt J Waugh, and shared with Lt F J Morgan/Sgt M B Kilroy, 2/Lt H R Gould/Capt M S E Archibald, Lt A C Atkey/Sgt H Hammond; (d) Capt F T R Kempster; (e) 2/Lt Ayres; (f) 2/Lt B J Blackett; victory No.8 shared with 2/Lt A Green/2/Lt F Loly and 2/Lt G Darville/Lt E Collis.

WARREN Leslie Reginald   Captain   6N/206 SQN

Les Warren was another RN officer who transferred to the Royal Naval Air Service (8 April 1917), taking his Royal Aero Club Certificate on 20 August 1917, No.5194. He was born in Leamington Spa, 21 January 1899 and educated at Uppingham School 1912-17. Flew with 6 Naval Squadron, joining this unit on 9 January 1918 with a total of 58 flying hours. This became 206 Squadron RAF in April 1918, and he rose to flight commander and won the DFC. This was gazetted on 21 September, recording 46 bomb raids, of which he had led 14, plus photographic sorties and five long range recce missions. His Flight had only suffered one casualty under his leadership. Returned to HE in October 1918. Post war he became a harbour engineer in South Africa.

	1918			DH9				
1	3 May	Albatros DV	(a)	B7596	206	S Merville	1855	DES(F)
2	7 Jun	EA	(b)	„	„	Bac St Maur	1150	OOC
3	1 Jul	Pfalz DIII	(c)	„	„	Houthem	2015	DES(F)
4	29 Jul	Pfalz DIII	(c)	„	„	Roulers	0840	OOC
5	„	Pfalz DIII	(c)	„	„	N Menin	1920	DES(F)
6	„	Pfalz DIII	(c)	„	„	N Menin	1922	DES(F)
7	1 Aug	Pfalz DIII	(c)	„	„	Menin-Wervicq	0830	OOC
8	„	Pfalz DIII	(c)	„	„	„	0830	DES

Total: 5 destroyed, 2 & 1 shared out of control = 8.
Obs: (a) Pte J T O'Brien; (b) 2/Lt Penny, and shared with 2/Lt C M Hyslop/ Cpl J W Pacey B5590; (c) Lt L A Christian.

WILTON Frederick Charles   2nd Lieutenant   98 SQN

Born 29 May 1892 he came from Durban, Natal, South Africa. Saw service with the Special Service Troop Engineers in German West Africa between 4 October 1914 and 19 July 1915. Coming to England, he joined the RFC on 9 November 1916 and became a cadet on 16 September to 1 January 1917. Joined 98 Squadron on 6 June 1918. Awarded the DFC during the summer. Saw considerable action, once being reported missing after a combat east of the Bois de Biez on 12 June (DH9 C1208) but he and his observer, Sgt Reed, got back. On 11 July he and 2/Lt E V Austin (in D1724) were forced down after a combat with Jasta 43 and their aircraft shelled on the ground, followed on the 18th by being shot up by a Pfalz Scout (in C2221). On 23 October his observer was wounded during a fight while bombing Hirson railway station (D7346), while on the 30th he was shot up again (D692) during a raid on Mons railway station.

	1918			DH9				
1	16 Jul	Fokker DrI	(a)	C2221	98	Forêt de Ris	1720	DES(F)
2	„	Fokker DrI	(a)	„	„	„	1725	DES
3	18 Jul	Pfalz DIII	(a)	„	„	Forêt de Fère	0800	DES
4	8 Aug	Fokker DrI	(b)	„	„	Barleux	1815	DES(F)
5	30 Oct	Fokker DVII	(b)	D692	„	W Mons	1130	DES(F)
6	„	Fokker DVII	(b)	„	„	„	1130	DES(F)

Total: 6 destroyed = 6.
Obs: (a) Lt C P Harrison; (b) Capt G H Gillis.

CHAPTER THREE

Bomber and Corps Observer Aces

APPLEBY Percival Ewart   Lieutenant   104 SQN

A Canadian from Port-la-Tour, Nova Scotia, born 27 June 1894, Percy joined No.1 Field Ambulance in 1914, serving in France in February 1915 and later in Salonika. Back in England he was commissioned into the King's Royal Rifles on 26 April 1917, serving with them until 27 January 1918, on which date he was attached to the RFC and became an observer with No.10 Kite Balloon Section. Wishing to transfer to aircraft he was posted to 104 Squadron, Independent Force, on 17 May, operating with them until he returned to the UK on 21 October. After the war he became a farmer, then a small business man and a music teacher. Served as a Recruiting Officer with the RCAF in WW2. Died of a stroke, May 1968.

	1918			DH9				
1	1 Jul	Albatros DV	(a)	C6204	104	Metz	0720	OOC
2	1 Aug	Pfalz DIII	(a)		„	Boulay	co830	DES
3	11 Aug	Albatros DIII	(b)		„	Karlsruhe	0910	OOC
4	7 Sep	Fokker DVII	(a)	C6264	„	Saverne	1230	DES(F)
5	„	Fokker DVII	(a)	C6264	„	Saverne-Landau	1400	DES
6	15 Sep	Pfalz DIII	(a)	C6264	„	Metz	1105	DES

Total: 4 destroyed, 2 out of control = 6.
Pilot: (a) Capt R J Gammon; (b) Lt E Cartwright.

BELL Frank William   Sergeant   9 & 49 SQNS

Born Cheshire, 1 January 1895, he became an iron and brass moulder before the war. Enlisted on 31 January 1915 and became an observer with 9 Squadron between November 1916 and December 1917. In July 1918 he was assigned to 49 Squadron with the rank of sergeant (102018). Won the DFM for taking part in 18 bomb raids, gazetted 2 November 1918 for an action fought on 23 August in which he and his pilot claimed five victories. Was forced down with his pilot, Lt A R Spurling, after being shot up on 24 August (in D3056) but survived.

	1918			DH9				
1	25 Jul	Fokker DVII	(a)	D3056	49	Mont Notre Dame	1900	OOC
2	23 Aug	Fokker DVII	(a)	„	„	Lens	1915	DES(F)
3	„	Fokker DVII	(a)	„	„	Lens	1915	DES
4	„	Fokker DVII	(a)	„	„	Lens	1915	OOC
5	„	Fokker DVII	(a)	„	„	Lens	1916	DES(F)
6	„	Fokker DVII	(a)	„	„	Lens	1916	DES

Total: 4 destroyed, 2 out of control = 6.
Pilot: (a) Lt A R Spurling.

BETTS Eric Bourne Coulter   Captain   2N/202 SQN

Born 24 January 1897, the family coming from Dalkey, Dublin. Joined the RNVR as a signalman aboard HM Trawler *Ugiebank* and HMS *Royal Arthur* in 1915 before he joined the RNAS on 31 January 1916, and by 13 March was an observer. Was with 1 Wing at Dunkirk in May and became a full lieutenant on 1 April 1917. The following month he was an observer instructor at Eastchurch, between flying DH4s with 2 Naval, later 202 Squadron RAF. Betts was awarded the DSC on 12 March 1917, for a successful recce mission to Bruges (1 February 1917), the Croix de Guerre with Palme on 16 April and the DFC in September 1918, the citation for the latter recording involvement with eight enemy aircraft shot down. He usually flew with Captain N Keeble DSC DFC. In between his tours with the Squadron he also had a period with the

Grain Test Flight in March 1918. Received a permanent commission in August 1919 and remained in the RAF. Served in South Russia in 1920-21, on the carrier HMS *Pegasus* operating off Novorossick, Kertch and on the Black Sea. Attended the Andover Staff College in October 1922. Commanded 101 Squadron 1934-35 and by 1939 he was a Group Captain; promoted to Air Commodore in 1941. Received the CBE and was an acting Air Vice-Marshal from 14 March 1943, but retired from the service soon after the end of hostilities. Died 30 October 1971.

	1917			1½ St				
1	1 Feb	Albatros DII	(a)	9417	2N	Wendyne	1420	OOC
	1918			DH4				
2	5 Jun	Pfalz DIII	(b)	A7446	202	N Eassen	1200	DES
3	9 Jun	Albatros D	(b)	„	„	Maria Aalter		DES
4	10 Aug	Fokker DVII	(b)	„	„	Bruges	1425	OOC
5	16 Sep	Pfalz DXII	(b)	„	„	Benkemaere	1105	DES
6	„	Fokker DVII	(b)	„	„	Dudzeele	1125	DES(F)

Total: 4 destroyed, 2 out of control = 6 (possibly 8).
Pilot: (a) FL Holden; (b) FL N Keeble.

BLACKETT Basil John   Lieutenant   25 & 18 SQNS

Born at Potters Bar on 23 June 1886, Blackett was a civil engineer before becoming a tea and rubber planter, and was living in Australia pre-war. In August 1914 he was a second lieutenant in the Australian Military, transferring to the AIF in May 1915. In February he joined the 16th Battn. serving in France until February 1917, when he joined the 18th Battn. On 23 April Blackett transferred for observer training to No.1 Observer School at Reading, graduating on 2 June. Joined the AFC as an observer a week later and posted to 25 Squadron on 18 June. Transferred to 18 Squadron on 8 October. Between 10 and 22 February he was with 102 Bomber Squadron, then returned to 18. Posted to England on 7 July 1918 and was awarded the Belgian Croix de Guerre on 12 July. From then until October 1918 he was at No.1 School for Navigation and Bomb Dropping, transferring to the RAF until he left in April 1919. In 1923 he was living in southern India.

	1917			DH4				
1	5 Aug	Albatros DV	(a)	A7477	25	Perenchies	1730	DES
2	3 Sep	Albatros DV	(a)	„	„	Quesnoy	0940	OOC
3	„	Albatros DV	(a)	„	„	Douai	1930	OOC
	1918							
4	30 May	Fokker DVII	(b)	A8018	18	Bac St Maur	2030	DES(F)
5	„	Fokker DVII	(b)	„	„	Bac St Maur	2050	OOC

Total: 2 destroyed, 3 out of control = 5.
Pilot: (a) Lt C T Lally; (b) Capt A G Waller.

BLENNERHASSET Giles Noble   2nd Lieutenant   18 SQN

From Leoville, Sligo, Northern Ireland, born 16 April 1895, he attended Sligo Grammar School between 1907-14. A married man, he joined the 4th Royal Irish Rifles (SR) on 1 June 1916 and later attended the Inns of Court OTC. Seconded to the RFC on 24 March 1917 and became an observer and temporary second lieutenant on 1 July. Flew FEs and DH4s with 18 Squadron from 31 December 1916 and received the MC, gazetted on 26 July 1917. Posted to Home Establishment on 19 July, Blennerhasset later became a pilot and in December 1917 served with 78 HD Squadron. He later flew with 112, 153 and 39 HD Squadrons. Posted to India at the end of 1919 he was with 48 Squadron (which became 5 Squadron) at Quetta, returning home in October 1920. Resigned his commission and left the RAF on 22 January 1921.

	1917			FE2b				
1	4 Feb	Albatros DII	(a)	A5460	18	N Le Sars	1600	OOC
2	5 Apr	Albatros DII	(b)	4969	„	Inchy	1200	OOC

3	„	Albatros DII	(b)	„	„	Inchy	1200	OOC
4	6 Apr	Albatros DII	(c)	A5468	„	Beaumetz-Beugny	1000	DES
5	16 Apr	Albatros DII	(d)	A5461	„	Cagnicourt	0830	OOC
6	3 May	Albatros DIII	(e)	A5506	„	Bourlon Wood	1830	OOC
7	23 May	Albatros DIII	(f)	7003	„	E Eswars	1325	DES
8	„	Albatros DIII	(f)	„	„	E Eswars	1325	OOC

Total: 1 & 1 shared destroyed, 6 out of control = 8.
Pilots: (a) 2/Lt R W Farquhar; (b) 2/Lt V H Huston; (c) 2/Lt Reid and shared with 2/Lts C Parkinson and Power;
(d) 2/Lt S J Young; (e) Capt W H Tolhurst; (f) 2/Lt D Marshall.

BLIZARD Charles Cecil   Second Lieutenant   104 SQN

From Putney, south-west London, he was born on 21 November 1897. A student at Mill Hill
School between 1910-15 he joined the 20th Battn. of the Middlesex Regiment and attended the
4th Army Signals School in 1917. Becoming an RFC observer, he flew in DH9 bombers with
the Independent Air Force in 1918, joining 104 Squadron on 7 April. Left the RAF on 19 June
1919 and was still living in Putney at the start of WW2.

	1918			DH9				
1	30 Jun	Albatros D	(a)		104	Landau	0740	DES
2	6 Jul	EA	(a)	C2960	„	Metz	0845	OOC
3	12 Aug	Fokker DVII	(a)		„	Saverne	0715	DES
4	„	Albatros DV	(a)		„	Saverne	0715	OOC
5	6 Nov	Fokker DVII	(b)	D847	„	Buhl A/F	1400	OOC

Total: 2 destroyed, 3 out of control = 5.
Pilot: (a) Capt J B Home-Hay; (b) 2/Lt P Hopkins.

BOTTRILL William Eric   2nd Lieutenant   104 SQN

From Hamilton, Ontario, Canada, but born in Burton-on-Trent, England, on 26 September
1892. Moved to Canada with his family as a youngster, and pre-war Bottrill was a salesman for
the International Silver Combine of America between 1911-14, and a stockbroker. Enlisted into
the 36th Battn. CEF as a sergeant, then commissioned. Joined the 41st Canadian Infantry
Regiment, serving in France with the 4th Battn. then transferred to the RFC as an observer.
Flew in DH9s with 104 Squadron of the Independent Air Force in 1918, claiming five victories
with his pilots. Mentioned in Despatches (LG 3 June 1919) he was then awarded the DFC,
gazetted 10 October 1919. Left the RAF on 13 January 1919. During WW2 served with the
Canadian Army and rose to colonel in the local Dundas Regiment. Died in Dundas, Ontario,
6 October 1971.

	1918			DH9				
1	12 Aug	EA	(a)		104	Saverne	0715	OOC
2	22 Aug	Pfalz DIII	(a)		„	Mannheim	0805	DES
3	14 Sep	Pfalz DIII	(b)	D3035	„	S Metz	0840	DES
4	23 Oct	Pfalz DIII	(b)		„	Metz-Sablon	1210	OOC
5	29 Oct	Pfalz DIII	(b)		„	Jametz	1245	OOC

Total: 2 destroyed, 3 out of control = 5.
Pilot: (a) Lt D P Pogson; (b) Capt E J Garland.

BRITTON Arthur Frederick   Lieutenant   57 SQN

Britton came from Streatham, and following service with the Machine Gun Corps, transferred
to the RFC in May 1917 and was assigned to 57 Squadron. He was wounded on 27 July, flying
with Captain L Minot (DH4 B3963) in combat with an Albatros Scout, and again on 20 August
while engaged on a photo op. For his services he received the MC, gazetted on 1 January 1918,
and the French Croix de Guerre, gazetted on 18 April. By June 1918 he had become an
administrative lieutenant. However, he resigned his commission due to ill-health on 28
September 1918, with the rank of Honorary Lieutenant.

	1917			DH4				
1	3 Jul	Albatros DIII	(a)	A7487	57	Zonnebeke	1225	OOC
2	„	Albatros DIII	(a)	„	„	Zonnebeke	1225	DES(F)
3	7 Jul	Albatros DIII	(b)	A7449	„	NE Ypres	0830	OOC
4	27 Jul	Albatros DV	(a)	B3963	„	Houthulst	1730	OOC
5	„	Albatros DV	(a)	„	„	Houthulst	1730	OOC
6	„	Albatros DV	(a)	„	„	Houthulst	1730	OOC

Total: 1 destroyed, 5 out of control = 6.
Pilot: (a) Capt L Minot; (b) Lt A D Pryor.

BURGESS David Luther   Lieutenant   25 SQN

Born in Kleinburg, Ontario, Canada, 28 January 1891. Joined the 188th Battn. CEF in June 1916, going overseas in October and serving with the 15th Reserve Battn. and then the 52nd Battn. CEF, the Prince Albert Volunteers. Seconded to the RFC and served with 25 Squadron from 30 May to 20 October 1917. Received the MC, gazetted 5 September and all his victories were whilst flying with Captain J F Morris MC. Later learnt to fly at Amria, Egypt and in 1918 was with No. 34 TDS at Scampton, Lincs. After the war he became a civil servant and was active with the Canadian Legion, being President 1959-60. Died in Ottawa, 30 November 1960.

	1917		DH4				
1	7 Jul	Albatros DV	A7505	25	Dorignies	1300	OOC
2	11 Jul	Albatros DV	„	„	W Douai	0940	OOC
3	22 Jul	Albatros DV	„	„	Lille	1430	DES(F)
4	5 Aug	Albatros DV	„	„	Perenchies	1720	DES(F)
5	14 Aug	Albatros DIII	„	„	NE Dourgies	1300	DES
6	„	Albatros DIII	„	„	NE Dourgies	1300	OOC
7	15 Aug	Albatros DV	„	„	La Bassée	1015	DES(F)

Total: 4 destroyed, 3 out of control = 7.

CHRISTIAN Leo Arthur   Lieutenant   206 SQN

Born on a farm near Armstrong in British Columbia, Canada, 9 October 1892 and bred horses pre-war before being accepted as a probationary flying officer in the RNAS in April 1917. He graduated as a pilot but was unable to take heights, so volunteered to be an observer! Operated with 6 Naval Squadron which he joined on 19 January 1918, later 206 Squadron RAF, winning the DFC in 1918, for 47 bomb raids and four combat victories. Post war he returned to British Columbia and bred racehorses. Served with the RCAF in WW2 but died shortly after that war ended.

	1918			DH9				
1	19 May	Albatros DV	(a)	C6240	206	Gheluwe	1940	OOC
2	7 Jun	Fokker DrI	(a)	C1181	„	Bac St Maur	1200	DES(F)
3	12 Jun	Pfalz DIII	(a)	C6240	„	Zonnebeke	1232	DES
4	1 Jul	Pfalz DIII	(b)	B7596	„	Houthem	2015	DES(F)
5	29 Jul	Fokker DVII	(c)	„	„	N Menin	1920	DES(F)
6	„	Fokker DVII	(c)	„	„	N Menin	1922	DES(F)
7	„	Fokker DVII	(c)	„	„	W Courtrai	1930	DES
8	1 Aug	Fokker DVII	(c)	B7598	„	Menin-Wervicq	0830	OOC
9	„	Fokker DVII	(c)	„	„	Menin-Wervicq	0830	DES

Total: 6 & 1 shared destroyed, 2 out of control = 9.
Pilot: (a) Capt G L E Stevens; (b) Capt Stevens and shared another crew; (c) Lt L N Warren; (d) Capt L N Warren.

COLLINS Lewis Isaac   Captain   18 SQN

Collins, from Dundee, Scotland, was born 7 November 1894. Assistant Manager in the family business in Dundee pre-war. Joined the 19th Battn. of the Yorkshire Regiment and served with them from 27 September 1915 until 22 May 1917, being commissioned on 27 March 1917, becoming a temporary captain. Seconded to the RFC and flew with 18 Squadron, often as observer to D A Stewart, with whom he shared all his victories. Awarded the MC in May 1918, gazetted 16 September, the citation recording 12 raids, 15 low bombing and recce flights, ten photo sorties and at least two aircraft shot down. Returned to Home Establishment on 13 July and left the service on 25 February 1919.

	1918		DH4				
1	25 Mar	2-seater	A8038	18	Loupart Wood	1715	DES
2	27 Mar	Fokker DrI	A7800	,,	SW Albert	1130	DES
3	28 May	Albatros DV	A8038	,,	W Douai	1140	DES
4	17 Jun	Pfalz DIII		,,	Hulloch	0845	DES
5	,,	Pfalz DIII		,,	Loos	0850	OOC

Total: 4 destroyed, 1 out of control = 5.

COREY Irving Benfield   2nd Lieutenant   103 SQN

A Canadian serving with 103 Squadron in 1918 was involved in six out of control victories whilst flying with Lieutenant, later Captain, R E Dodds, and was awarded the DFC, gazetted 3 December 1918.

	1918		DH9				
1	10 Aug	Fokker DVII	C2877	103	Péronne	1815	OOC
2	,,	Fokker DVII	,,	,,	Péronne	1815	OOC
3	11 Aug	Fokker DVII	,,	,,	Estaires	1900	OOC
4	,,	Fokker DVII	,,	,,	Estaires	1900	OOC
5	25 Aug	Fokker DVII	,,	,,	Pernes	0900	OOC
6	30 Oct	Fokker DVII	E8884	,,	Mainvault	0955	OOC

Total: 6 out of control = 6.

COURT Leslie Simpson   Sergeant   25 SQN

Firstly as a 1AM, served with 25 Squadron in 1916. On 20 July, in FE2b 6932, with 2/Lt L L Richardson as pilot, they were shot-up in combat, Richardson being wounded. When Tom Mottershead arrived in July 1916 (he would win the VC in January 1917 with 20 Squadron), Court was his observer on his first practise flights and initial war sorties. On 5 August, Court and 2/Lt W H Rilett (4922) were brought down behind the front lines where their FE was shelled. On 27 September he and 2/Lt V W Harrison were in combat with a two-seater of FA22, crewed by the ace team Ltn Albert Dossenbach and Oblt Hans Schilling. Both machines were brought down in this action although all four men survived. Court received the French Medaille Militaire, gazetted on 1 May 1917, having been promoted to corporal and then sergeant (10060) prior to his fight with Dossenbach.

	1916			FE2b				
1	26 Jun	Fokker E	(a)	4283	25	Lens	0800	DES
2	15 Jul	Fokker E	(b)	6932	,,	Fromelles	0825	DES
3	20 Jul	Fokker E	(a)	,,	,,	E Lens	1830	DES
4	,,	Fokker E	(a)	,,	,,	E Lens	1830	OOC
5	9 Sep	2-seater	(c)	6993	,,	Harnes	1600	OOC
6	27 Sep	LVG C	(d)	4839	,,	Tourmignies		DES
7	22 Oct	Scout	(e)	7693	,,	Seclin	0855	DES
8	9 Nov	Fokker D	(e)	,,	,,	Hénin-Liétard	0830	OOC

Total: 5 destroyed, 3 out of control = 8.

Pilots: (a) 2/Lt L L Richardson; (b) Capt M C B Copeman; (c) 2/Lt N W W Webb; (d) 2/Lt V W Harrison; (e) 2/Lt J L Leith.

CRAIG Fergus Gray   2nd Lieutenant   57 SQN

From Carmarnock, Scotland, born 10 October 1899. An apprentice machine grinder/engineer for most of 1917 while waiting to enlist, he became a signaller with the 5th Scottish Rifles. Transferred to the RAF in 1918 and flew in DH4 bombers with 57 Squadron, being credited with five victories. In 1919 he served with 25 Squadron briefly and then 18 Squadron but was released from duty on 24 September. On 8 May 1939 he enlisted in the Auxiliary Air Force as an AC2 and by August 1942 had become a Leading Aircraftman.

	1918			DH4				
1	8 Aug	Fokker DVII	(a)	D8382	57	Moislains A/F	0805	OOC
2	16 Aug	Fokker DVII	(b)	„	„	Abscon-Douai	1100	OOC
3	1 Sep	Fokker DVII	(c)	D8425	„	Cambrai	1345	DES(F)
4	5 Sep	Fokker DVII	(c)	„	„	W Marcoing	1125	OOC
5	27 Sep	Fokker DVII	(d)	A8017	„	Cambrai	1800	OOC

Total: 1 destroyed, 3 and 1 shared out of control = 5.
Pilots: (a) Sgt D E Edgley; (b) Lt L K Devitt; (c) Lt F O Thornton; (d) Lt F O Thornton, and shared with Lt F C Harding and 2/Lt I Woodhouse.

DANCE Charles Cannon   2nd Lieutenant   103 SQN

Born 25 February 1899, he lived in Forest Hill, south-east London. Joined the London Scottish Regiment and served overseas with them from June to November 1916. Seconded to the RFC on 29 August 1917 and on 10 April 1918 he was flying with 103 Squadron. He and his pilot, Captain J S Stubbs, with whom all his victories were achieved, were shot down during a balloon attack on 20 May (DH9 C6186) but survived. He was injured in a crash on 11 July but returned on 29 August, continuing service until the war's end.

	1918			DH9				
1	20 May	Balloon		C6179	103	Seclin	1100	DES
2	6 Jun	Fokker DVII	(a)	„	„	Fretoy, SW Ham	1620	DES(F)
3	„	Fokker DVII	(a)	„	„	Fretoy	1620	OOC
4	4 Jul	Pfalz DIII		C6150	„	La Bassée	2030	OOC
5	30 Aug	Fokker DVII		D3162	„	E Bac St Maur	1100	OOC
6	6 Sep	Fokker DVII		„	„	W St André	1130	DES

Total: 2 and 1 shared destroyed, 2 and 1 shared out of control = 6.
(a) shared with 2/Lt I W Leiper/Pbr J Buffery (D1007) and 2/Lts C H Henderson and C E Eddy (D5569).

DARBY Edward   2nd Lieutenant   5N & 202 SQNS

Born Liverpool, 7 March 1888. Served as a gunlayer in 5 Wing RNAS and then 5 Naval Squadron, 26 April 1916 to October 1917. Joined 202 Squadron on 9 May, by which time he had 120 hours as an observer, but was taken prisoner of war on 28 September, he and Lt C R Moore becoming lost in a storm over Nieuport in A8066 at 0725 am.

	1917			DH4				
1	5 Aug	Albatros DIII	(a)	N5982	5N	Snelleghem	1800	OOC
	1918							
2	4 Jun	Pfalz DIII	(b)	N5993	202	Off Zeebrugge	1915	DES
3	27 Jun	Pfalz DIII	(c)	A8025	„	Ostende	1520	OOC
4	16 Jul	Pfalz DIII	(d)	A7632	„	S Ostende	1700	OOC
5	16 Sep	Pfalz DXII	(c)	„	„	Lisseweghe	1105	OOC
6	„	Fokker DVII	(c)	„	„	Dudzeele	1125	DES(F)

Total: 2 destroyed, 4 out of control = 6.
Pilots: (a) FC R Jope-Slade; (b) Lt A L Godfrey; (c) Lt L H Pearson; (d) Capt A V Bowater.

DYKE William Norman   Sergeant   8 SQN

Flew with 18 Squadron as a Corporal (No.204157) and then Sergeant (No. 121180). Received both the DCM and DFM, the latter gazetted on 21 September 1918 for 29 bomb raids, 14 recce sorties and ten photo ops. Wounded in combat on 28 July with 2/Lt A Pickin as pilot, in DH4 A7911.

	1918			DH4				
1	6 Mar	Albatros DV	(a)	A7833	18	Lens/Pont-à-Vendin	1115	OOC
2	„	2-seater	(a)	„	„	„	1115	OOC
3	17 Jun	Pfalz DIII	(b)	A7799	„	Hulloch	0850	OOC
4	19 Jun	Pfalz DIII	(b)	A8010	„	Lille	2000	OOC
5	20 Jul	Pfalz DIII	(c)	A7931	„	Douai	0830	DES

Total: 1 destroyed, 4 out of control = 5.
Pilots: (a) Sgt W McCleery; (b) 2/Lt A Pickin; (c) Lt R Minors.

EDDY Charles Ewart   Lieutenant   103 SQN

Eddy was from Wynberg, Cape Town, born 15 July 1892. Pre-war he worked as a builder in Eddy Brothers, Cape Town, but joined up in August 1914. Served as an officer with the 1st South African Infantry before secondment to the RFC in November 1917. Served with 103 Squadron between May and August 1918. Survived being shot-up on 18 June with Captain K T Dowding as pilot (DH9 D7226) but was wounded on 30 August during a photographic sortie, and left the unit; he received a Mention in Despatches. In 1919 he was with 14 and then 11 TDS, before leaving the service on 5 August.

	1918			DH9				
1	6 Jun	Fokker DVII	(a)	D5569	103	Fretoy, SW Ham	1620	DES(F)
2	„	Fokker DVII	(a)	„	„	„	1620	OOC
3	2 Jul	DFW C	(b)	C2213	„	Steenwerck	2025	OOC
4	30 Aug	Fokker DrI	(c)	C2204	„	Laventie	1750	OOC
5	„	Fokker DrI	(c)	„	„	Laventie	1750	OOC

Total: 1 shared destroyed, 4 out of control = 5.
Pilots: (a) 2/Lt C H Henderson and shared with Capt J S Stubbs/2/Lt C C Dance (C6179) and 2/Lt C H Heebner/Pbr J Buffery (D1007); (b) Capt K T Dowding; (c) Lt G B Hett.

EMSDEN Leonard H   Sergeant   25 SQN

Joined the RFC as an Air Mechanic (No.65935), but rose to corporal (No.P7259) and finally sergeant. Flew with 25 Squadron in 1917, being wounded in the hand on 1 May. He had already been recommended for the DCM which was awarded and gazetted on 18 June, his citation stating that he was ". . . continually bringing down his opponents with great skill and daring."

	1917			FE2b				
1	4 Mar	LVG C	(a)	7693	25	Courrières	1115	DES
2	17 Mar	Albatros DIII	(b)	6940	„	Oppy-Beaumont	1115	DES(F)
3	„	Albatros DIII	(c)	7683	„	Arras	1725	OOC
4	6 Apr	Halberstadt D	(d)	4847	„	E Vimy	1045	DES
5	13 Apr	Albatros DIII	(e)	A6383	„	Hénin-Liétard	1930	DES
6	1 May	Albatros DIII	(e)	7672	„	Izel	0620	DES
7	„	Albatros DIII	(e)	„	„	W Lens	0645	CAPT
8	„	Albatros DIII	(e)	„	„	Bois Bernard	1800	DES(F)

Total: 5 & 1 shared destroyed, 1 captured and 1 out of control = 8.
Pilots: (a) 2/Lt R G Malcolm, and shared with Lt A E Boultbee/Sgt J Brown (A5439), 2/Lt W D Matheson/Lt W A Barnes (7025), 2/Lt R N L Munro/Lt G Goodburn (A780); (b) Lt H E Davis; (c) Capt J L Leith; (d) 2/Lt B King; (e) 2/Lt R G Malcolm.

GOMPERTZ Harry Christopher Travers   Lieutenant   55 SQN

From Ilfracombe, South Devon, born 25 May 1898, his father was the Honourable Mr Justice
Gompertz at the Supreme Court in Hong Kong. Gompertz had attended Winchester College
and been an outstanding student in 1916. Commissioned as a second lieutenant in the Royal
Field Artillery (SR) on 23 June 1917 he was seconded to the RFC in August, and confirmed as
an observer officer on 26 June 1918. Served with 55 Squadron, Independent Force, being
wounded in the shoulder on 30 August, during a raid on Thionville (DH4 A8069); he also had
several bullets pass through his Sidcot suit. Survived the war, but only just, for on 10 November,
he and his flight commander pilot, Captain D R G Mackay DFC, were shot down by AA fire.
Mackay died of his wounds but Gompertz survived as a prisoner (DH4 F5725). Repatriated on
29 November, he left the RAF on 28 January 1919.

	1918			DH4				
1	12 Aug	Pfalz DIII	(a)		55	Vosges	0730	OOC
2	14 Aug	Albatros DV	(a)		„	Offenburg	1500	OOC
3	30 Aug	Fokker DVII	(b)		„	Metz	1030	OOC
4	„	Fokker DVII	(b)		„	Metz	1030	OOC
5	3 Nov	Fokker DVII	(a)		„			OOC

Total: 5 out of control = 5.
Pilots: (a) Capt D R G Mackay; (b) Lt S L Dowdeswell.

GRANT James   Sergeant   57 SQN

From Sandbank, Argyllshire, Sergeant Grant (No.100425) flew with 57 Squadron in 1918 and
received the DFM, gazetted on 3 December 1918. His citation mentioned the combat he had
on 1 September, shooting down one enemy fighter from a force of 15 Fokker DVIIs and five
Fokker DrIs that attacked them. He often flew with Captain A MacGregor, and on 5 September
they were shot up by a Fokker DVII but force landed without serious injury.

	1918			DH4				
1	10 Jun	Fokker DrI	(a)	D9248	57	Grevillers-Vimy	2010	DES(F)
2	„	Fokker DrI	(a)	„	„	„	2025	DES
3	19 Jun	Pfalz DIII	(b)	A7821	„	Bapaume	1930	OOC
4	14 Aug	Fokker DVII	(c)	D8377	„	Roisel	1035	DES
5	1 Sep	Fokker DVII	(c)	D8419	„	Cambrai	1400	DES
6	4 Sep	Fokker DVII	(d)	„	„	Bourlon Wood	1000	OOC
7	5 Sep	Fokker DVII	(d)	„	„	W Marcoing	1125	DES
8	„	Fokker DVII	(d)	„	„	W Avesnes-le-Sec	1605	DES

Total: 6 destroyed, 2 out of control = 8.
Pilots: (a) Lt C W Peckham; (b) Lt J T Kirkland, and shared with Capt C H Stokes/Cpl J H Bowler (D8398);
(c) Lt E M Coles; (d) Capt A MacGregor.

HAMBLIN Stanley Herbert   2nd Lieutenant   205 SQN

From Hermitage, near Newbury, Berkshire, Hamblin was born on 3 November 1893. Became
a partner with his father in an architect and surveying company in Birmingham between 1910
and 1914. Joining the colours he flew with 205 Squadron until he returned to England on
22 August 1918. During his period of service he flew on over 60 bomb raids and 15 recce
missions. He began pilot training but the war ended prior to completing the course. Left the
RAF on 20 March 1919.

	1918			DH4				
1	3 May	Pfalz DIII	(a)	D8401	205	Chaulnes-Rosières	1545	DES(F)
2	„	Pfalz DIII	(a)	„	„	„	1545	OOC
3	17 May	Albatros DV	(b)	D9255	„	W Chaulnes	1605	DES(F)
4	20 May	Pfalz DIII	(b)	D9260	„	Rosières	0825	OOC
5	10 Aug	Pfalz DIII	(b)	A7587	„	Brie Bridge	1540	OOC
6	11 Aug	Pfalz DIII	(b)	„	„	W Péronne	0756	OOC

Total: 1 & 1 shared destroyed, 3 & 1 shared out of control = 6.
Pilot: (a) Lt R Chalmers and shared with several other crews; (b) Lt R Chalmers.

HARRISON Charles Philip   Lieutenant   98 SQN

Born in Wimbledon, south-west London, on 27 July 1888. Pre-war he was a mining engineer and mechanical draughtsman between 1910-14. Commissioned with the Royal Engineers on 15 November 1915 and served in France and nine months in German West Africa. Seconded to the RFC on 1 November 1917, he was an observer with 98 Squadron from 17 March 1918 and won the MC. Returned to Home Establishment on 31 July. Put up for the Legion d'Honneur but only received the Croix de Guerre, in August 1918. However, he received the Croix de Chevalier in November. His MC was gazetted on 16 September 1918, recording the occasion his pilot was wounded and passed out. Harrison shot down their attacker, then took control of the aeroplane despite having little knowledge of piloting, and got them back to their airfield, saving the life of his pilot and preventing their machine falling into the hands of the enemy. Sent to the Armament School in South Africa in May 1919, he left the service the following month and then worked in Salisbury, Rhodesia.

	1918			DH9				
1	21 Apr	Fokker DrI	(a)	C6108	98	Bailleul	0700	OOC
2	8 May	Albatros DV	(b)	,,	,,	Menin-Wervicq	1920	DES(F)
3	16 Jul	Fokker DrI	(c)	C2221	,,	Forêt de Ris	1920	DES(F)
4	,,	Fokker DrI	(c)	,,	,,	,,	1920	DES
5	18 Jul	Pfalz DIII	(c)	,,	,,	Forêt de fère	0800	DES

Total: 4 destroyed, 1 out of control = 5.
Pilot: (a) Lt A M Phillips; (b) Lt N C MacDonald; (c) Lt F C Wilton.

HARROP W   Sergeant   104 SQN

Won the Military Medal while serving with the 95th Field Company, Royal Engineers as a Pioneer (No.49486), gazetted 14 December 1916. Joined the RAF and flew with 104 Squadron, Independent Force in 1918, observer to Lt G B H Smith. Both were taken prisoner on 22 August 1918 on a disastrous raid on Mannheim. On 12 August one of the German pilots lost was Vfw Heinrich Krüger of Jasta 70.

	1918			DH9				
1	1 Aug	Pfalz DIII	(a)		104	Boulay a/f	0830	OOC
2	12 Aug	Pfalz DIII	(a)		,,	Saverne	0715	DES
3	,,	Albatros DV	(b)		,,	Saverne	0715	DES
4	,,	Scout	(a)		,,	Saverne	0715	OOC
5	15 Aug	Pfalz DIII	(c)		,,	Pelm	1830	OOC

Total: 1 & 1 shared destroyed, 2 & 1 shared out of control = 5.
Pilot: (a) 2/Lt G B H Smith; (b) 2/Lt Smith and shared with Lt Pickup/2/Lt A B Rattray; (c) 2/Lt Smith and shared with Lt H P Wells/2/Lt J J Redfield.

HARTIGAN Edward Patrick   2nd Lieutenant   57 SQN

From Reens, County Limerick, Eire, he served with the Royal Munster Fusiliers, being commissioned on 1 October 1916. Seconded to the RFC he flew with 57 Squadron in 1917 but died of injuries sustained in a crash on 20 November, along with his pilot, Captain D S Hall, in A7568, on the first day of the Cambrai offensive. He was 22 years old. On 2 October they claimed four victories in a fight with Jasta 18, their Squadron losing three DH4s. All claims achieved with Hall.

	1917			DH4				
1	2 Oct	Albatros DV		A7568	57	Roulers	1335	OOC
2	,,	Albatros DV		,,	,,	Roulers	1336	DES(F)
3	,,	Albatros DV		,,	,,	Roulers	1337	OOC

4	„	Albatros DV		„	„	Houthulst	1340	DES
5	28 Oct	Albatros DV		„	„	W Roulers	1230	OOC

Total: 2 destroyed, 3 out of control = 5.

HOLLIGAN Philip Terence   Lieutenant   49 SQN

From Withington, Manchester, born 20 May 1898, he attended the University of Manchester School of Technology between 1915-16. Joining the 9th OCB, he transferred to the RFC and was commissioned on 29 August 1917. Holligan flew with 49 Squadron from 11 December 1917. Awarded the DFC, which was gazetted on 2 November 1918, the citation for which recorded he had participated in 50 bomb raids and photo recce sorties, with particular good work during the Battle of the Marne. Left the RAF on 1 February 1919.

	1918			DH9				
1	8 Mar	Rumpler C	(a)	A7705	49	Brebières	1315	OOC
2	10 Mar	LVG C	(a)	„	„	Marquion	1400	OOC
3	23 Apr	Albatros DV	(b)	C6114	„	E Nieuport	1550	OOC
4	8 Aug	Fokker DVII	(c)	D3052	„	Bethencourt	1820	OOC
5	9 Aug	Fokker DVII	(c)	„	„	Falvy	0630	OOC
6	„	Fokker DVII	(c)	„	„	Marchélepot	1700	OOC

Total: 6 out of control = 6.
Pilot: (a) 2/Lt G Fox-Rule; (b) Lt A H Curtiss; (c) Capt G Bowman.

JACKSON H S   Gunlayer   5N SQN

Flew DH4s with 5 Naval Squadron, often as observer to C P O Bartlett and T F Le Mesurier, sharing all victories with the latter pilot.

	1917			DH4				
1	5 Aug	Albatros DV		N5967	5N	Snelleghem A/F	1800	DES
2	„	Albatros DV		„	„	Dixmude	1800	OOC
3	19 Aug	Albatros DV		N6005	„	SW Ostende	0600	OOC
4	11 Sep	Albatros DV		N5968	„	Sparappelhoek	1100	OOC
5	15 Oct	Albatros DV		N5967	„	E Dixmude		OOC
6	21 Oct	Albatros DV		„	„	Houttave A/F		OOC

Total: 1 destroyed, 5 out of control = 6.

JONES William   Sergeant   205 SQN

Bill Jones was awarded the Distinguished Flying Medal, gazetted 21 September 1918, the citation noting 105 raids carried out, during which he had accounted for six German aircraft. He had earlier been a Gunlayer with the RNAS. However, only one victory can be found for him and his name may have become confused with Sergeant Jones of 22 Squadron.

KILROY M B   Sergeant   18 SQN

Kilroy was an NCO gunner with 18 Squadron in 1918, often flying with two of the unit's successful pilots, Atkey and Waller. Credited with five combat victories.

	1918			DH4				
1	6 Mar	Albatros DV	(a)	A7798	18	Carvin	1125	OOC
2	10 Mar	Albatros DV	(a)	A7790	„	Carvin-Fromelles	1215	OOC
3	16 Mar	Albatros DV	(b)	A7770	„	Fromelles	1520	OOC
4	12 Apr	Pfalz DIII	(c)		„	Estaires	1025	DES(F)
5	„	Pfalz DIII	(c)		„	EStaires	1025	OOC

Total: 1 shared destroyed, 3 & 1 shared out of control = 5.
Pilot: (a) Capt A G Waller; (b) Lt A C Atkey; (c) Lt F J Morgan, and shared with Lt A C Atkey/Sgt H Hammon (A7998), 2/Lt H R Gould/Capt M S E Archibald, Capt A G Waller/2/Lt J Waugh.

LANGSTONE S F   Sergeant   205 SQN

Joined 205 Squadron in March 1918, and remained until January 1919. During the last year of the war he flew on 96 bomb raids and 25 recce sorties. Became a flying cadet but when the war ended he transferred into the reserve on 19 March 1919.

	1918			DH4					
1	3 May	Pfalz DIII	(a)	D9238	205	Chaulnes-Rosières	1545	DES(F)
2	„	Pfalz DIII	(a)	„	„	„	1545	OOC
3	20 May	Pfalz DIII	(b)	„	„	Mericombe	0830	DES(F)
4	13 Aug	Fokker DVII	(c)	„	„	Péronne	1100	DES
5	15 Sep	Fokker DVII	(c)		„	Busigny	1520	OOC

Total: 1 & 2 shared destroyed, 1 & 1 shared out of control = 5.
Pilots: (a) Lt C J H Haywood, and shared with Capt E Dickson/AGL C V Robinson (D9237), Lt G E Siedle/AGL. Middleton (A8071), Lt W B Elliott/AGL. Whalley (N6009), Lt Wilson/AGL. Mackay (D9241), Lt W Grossart/AGL. Richards (A7811), Lt Fox/AGL. C F Ambler (D8412), Capt J Gamon/2/Lt Scott (N6004), Lt R Chalmers/2/Lt S H Hamblin (D8401), Lt Scott/AGL. Humphrey (D9243); (b) Lt C J H Heywood, and shared with Capt J Gamon/Sgt W Jones (N6006), Lt J M Mason/Sgt C V Robinson (A7739), Lt Wilson/AGL. Mackay (D9241), Lt D J T Mellor/AGL. Gillman (A8071), Lt W B Elliott/AGL. Richards (A7561), Lt Fox/AGL. Ferrie (D6412), Lt W Grossart/2/Lt A R Crosthwaite (A7811); (c) Lt C J H Heywood.

LEATHLEY Forde   Lieutenant   57 SQN

Born 17 February 1896, Trillick, Dunboyne, Ireland. Transferred to the RFC from the 1st Battn. Royal Inniskillen Fusiliers, into which he had been commissioned on 16 June 1915. Flew with 57 Squadron during 1917 and received the Military Cross, in September 1917, gazetted on 6 January 1918. The citation noted seven victories with his pilot in addition to flying successful recce and photo ops. He later took pilot training, being awarded his Royal Aero Club Certificate on 26 November 1917 (No.5455).

	1917			FE2d				
1	30 Apr	Albatros DIII	(a)	A1966	57	Buissy	0945	OOC
				DH4				
2	28 Jul	Albatros DV	(b)	A7537	„	Ingelmunster	1830	OOC
3	„	Albatros DV	(b)	„	„	„	1830	DES
4	16 Aug	Albatros DV	(b)	A7563	„	Houthulst	1745	OOC
5	17 Aug	Albatros DV	(b)	„	„	Menin	0730	OOC
6	„	Albatros DV	(b)	„	„	„	0730	OOC
7	„	Albatros DV	(b)	„	„	W Menin	0732	OOC
8	20 Aug	Albatros DV	(b)	A7564	„	E Ypres	1115	OOC

Total: 1 destroyed, 7 out of control = 8.
Pilot: (a) Lt C S Morice; (b) Maj E G Joy.

MACKAY Harry William Mackintosh   2nd Lieutenant   18 SQN

From Aberdeen, Mackay had served with the 6th Battn. of the Gordon Highlanders before transferring to the RFC. Flew with 18 Squadron but died of wounds following an action on 6 March 1918, against Pfalz Scouts between Lens and Pont-à-Vendin, although his pilot, 2/Lt D A Stewart, was not harmed. The controls of their DH4 — A7797 — were shot out and they had to make a crash-landing. Mackay was aged 20 and was buried at Aire.

	1918			DH4				
1	6 Jan	Albatros DV		A7653	18	Valenciènnes	1205	OOC
2	6 Mar	Pfalz DIII		A7797	„	Lens-Pont-à-Vendin	1115	OOC
3	„	Pfalz DIII		„	„	„	1115	DES
4	„	Albatros DV		„	„	„	1120	OOC
5	„	Albatros DV		„	„	„	1120	OOC

Total: 1 destroyed, 4 out of control = 5.

MENENDEZ Frank Tremar Silby   Lieutenant   57 SQN

From Midford, near Bath, born 26 January 1896, he was the nephew of Sir M R Menendez. Educated at Wycliffe School he went up to Cambridge in September 1914. He left to serve in the 11th Yorks and Lancs Regiment in March 1915, then the Gloucester Regiment from September, becoming a Captain in July 1916. Transferred to the RFC in May 1917, going to France in July. His usual pilot was Lt A T Drinkwater with whom he shared all his victories. He returned to England in January 1918 having received the MC on 27 October, gazetted on 18 March 1918. He was involved in a flying accident on 1 August being seriously injured. Relinquished his commission due to ill-health on 5 June 1919.

	1917			DH4				
1	18 Aug	Albatros DV		A2138	57	Courtrai	1920	OOC
2	20 Aug	Albatros DV		A2132	„	Houthulst Forest	1130	OOC
3	21 Sep	Albatros DV		A7581	„	Dadizeele	1050	DES
4	„	Albatros DV		„	„	„	1050	OOC
5	12 Nov	Albatros DV		A7424	„	SE Houthulst	1145	OOC
6	„	Albatros DV		„	„	„	1145	OOC

Total: 1 destroyed, 5 out of control = 6.

MIDDLETON William James   Sergeant   5N/205 SQN

From Woodford Green, Essex, Middleton flew as a lowly airman on joining 205 Squadron in early 1918 but rose to sergeant rank (No.216604) and won the DFM, gazetted on 21 September, recording that he had participated in 67 bombing raids plus 54 other operations. In addition he received the French Medaille d'Honneur avec Glaive en Argent. This was for an action fought on 10 August 1918 while gunner to Captain J M Mason. By this date he had participated in 121 raids and was the leading observer in the Squadron. During a recce sortie on 3 October 1918, his DH9a (F1024) was shot up and he was mortally wounded, dying the next day; he was aged 21.

	1918			DH4				
1	9 Mar	Albatros DV	(a)	N6095	5N	Mont d'Origny	1045	OOC
2	23 Apr	Fokker DrI	(a)	A8071	205	Chaulnes	1920	OOC
3	3 May	Pfalz DIII	(b)	„	„	Chaulnes-Rosières	1545	DES(F)
4	„	Pfalz DIII	(b)	„	„	„	1545	OOC
5	10 Aug	Pfalz DIII	(c)	D9255	„	Brie Bridge	1540	DES(F)
6	4 Sep	Fokker DVII	(d)	D9259	„	Roisel	1715	OOC

Total: 1 & 1 shared destroyed, 3 & 1 shared out of control = 6.
Pilot: (a) Lt G E Siedle; (b) Seidle and shared with Capt E Dickson/AGL. C V Robinson, D9237; Lt C J H Heywood/AGL F S Langstone, D9238; Lt W B Elliott/AGL. Whalley, N6009; Lt Wilson/AGL. Mackay, D9241; Lt W Grossart/AGL. Richards, A7811; Lt Fox/AGL. C F Ambler, D8412; Capt J Gamon/2/Lt Scott, N6004; Lt R Chalmers/2/Lt S H Hamblin, D8401; Scott/AGL. Humphrey, D9243; (c) Capt J M Mason; (d) Lt D J T Mellor.

MILLER William   Lieutenant   18 SQN

From Newcastle-on-Tyne, born 12 May 1892, he became a graduate of Durham University, where he studied between 1911 and 1914. Served with the 20th Battn. of the Northumberland Fusiliers before joining the RFC in 1918. Joined 18 Squadron on 4 April. Wounded in action on 6 September 1918 in combat with enemy aircraft over Monchy. He was flying with Captain G W F Darvill DFC, and with their controls shot up they were forced to land their DH4 (A7815) in a shell hole near the front lines. Invalided back to England, Bill Miller was awarded the DFC, gazetted 1 January 1919. At the beginning of August 1918 he was with the Northern Area Airship Section at East Fortune, but left the service on 10 October 1919. Made an Honorary Lieutenant and appointed to Territorial Forces in June 1921.

ABOVE THE BRITISH WAR FRONTS

Above: Capt R N G Atkinson MC DFC, 98 and 206 Squadrons.

Top right: Capt C P O Bartlett DSC, 5 Naval/205 Squadron.

(Bruce/Leslie collection)

Middle: Sgt Walter Beales DCM, observer, 48 Squadron.

Right: 2/Lt C C Blizard, observer, 104 Squadron 1918.

Top left: Lt C G Boothroyd DFC, observer 20
Squadron 1918.

Top right: 2/Lt W E Bottrill DFC, observer 104
Squadron 1918. *(via S K Taylor)*

Above left: Lt W C Cambray MC, 20 Squadron, with
Capt F D Stevens (left).

Above right: Capt D H M Carbery MC DFC,
59 Squadron.

Top left: Capt T L Purdom and his observer, Lt P V G Chambers, 62 Squadron.

Top right: Lts H G Crowe MC and D G Cooks MC, 20 Squadron. *(Bruce/Leslie collection)*

Above left: 206 Sqn group (l to r): Lt E A Burn,

Capt G L E Stephens, Lt L A Christian DFC ob. (9 victories), Capt L N C Clarke, Capt J M Beddall (AO) & Capt J S Wright DSC.

(E A Burn via S K Taylor)

Above right: Capt F R Cubbon MC & Bar, 20 Squadron observer 1917.

Top left: Capt G W F Darvill MC DFC, 18 Squadron pilot.

Top right: Capt Euan Dickson DSC DFC, 5N/205 Squadron 1917-18.

Bottom left: Sgt Ernest A Deighton DCM, observer, 20 Squadron.

Bottom right: 2/Lt H L Edwards DFC MM, observer, 20 Squadron 1918.

Top left: Capt W B Elliott DFC,
205 Squadron 1918.

(via S K Taylor)

Top right: Capt Alfred Atkey MC
and observer, Lt C G Gass MC,
22 Squadron.

Left: Capt W E Staton MC DFC
and Lt J R Gordon MC,
62 Squadron.

Above: Lt Ernest Hardcastle DFC,
observer 20 Squadron 1918.

Top left: Capt H R Harker MC, 57 Squadron pilot 1917.

Top right: Capt J B Home-Hay MC DFC, 53 and 104 Squadrons 1917-18.

Above left: Lt J Hills (far right), 20 Squadron. Others

l to r: Boothroyd (DFC), Hardcastle DFC, D E Smith and V E Groom DFC. Hills was taken prisoner two days after this picture was shot, on 14 August 1918.

Above right: Lt A N Jenks, 20 Squadron observer 1918

Top left: Major E G Joy DFC, pilot, 57 and 205 Squadrons. *(Mrs Joy via S K T)*

Top right: Lt S A W Knights MC and Capt G E Gibbons MC, 62 Squadron.

Above left: Lt C T Lally MC & Bar AFC, 25 Squadron 1917. *(S Jones via S K T)*

Above right: Capt T F Le Mesurier DSC & 2 Bars, 5 Naval Squadron. Killed in action with 211 Squadron, 26 May 1918. *(Bruce/Leslie*

Top left: Lt T A M S Lewis MC, observer, 20 Squadron.

Top right: Capt A MacGregor DFC, 57 Squadron 1918.

(Mrs I J MacGregor)

Above left: Lt F T S Menendez MC, observer 57 Squadron.

Above right: Lt A Mills DFC and Lt L M Price, 20 Squadron 1918.

Top left: Lt H F Moore, observer 22 Squadron 1917-18.

Top right: Capt Ross-Smith MC DFC and Lt E A Mustard DFC, 1 AFC Squadron, Palestine 1918.
(Bruce/Leslie collection)

Middle left: Lt L A Powell MC & Bar, observer 11 Squadron 1917.
(via Bob Lynes)

Middle right: Lt Walter Noble DFC, 20 Squadron observer, 2nd from left. Others are (l to r): Capt D Latimer MC DFC, Lt Paul Iaccaci DFC,-?-, and Capt T P Middleton DFC.

Far left: Capt J E Pugh MC DFC, pilot with 25 Squadron 1917-18.
(S Jones via S K Taylor)

Left: Lt Hervey Rhodes DFC & Bar, observer 12 Squadron 1918.
(Mrs H Sutcliffe)

Top left: Lt L M Thompson, observer 62 Squadron 1918. *(via S K Taylor)*

Top right: Lt George Thomson DFC, observer 22 Squadron 1918. *(S K Taylor)*

Above left: Lt Len Potts and Lt Jim Traill, 1 AFC Squadron Palestine 1918.

Above right: Lt A E Woodbridge, observer 20 Squadron 1917.

ABOVE FLANDERS FIELDS

Top left: Willy Coppens, 37 victories, of which 35 were balloons.

Top right: Edmond Thieffry, ten victories. Note comet insignia on his Nieuport Scout.

Middle left: Andre Demeulemeester, 11 victories; note thistle insignia on the Camel.

Above: Fernand Jacquet, 7 official victories, 9 unofficial.

Left: Jan Olieslagers, 6 official and at least 17 unofficial claims.

ABOVE THE ALPS

Top: The 91ª Squadriglia, the so-called "aces' squadron". From left to right, Serg D'Urso, Serg Aliperta, Ten Novelli (8 victories), Serg Magistrini, obscured, (6), Cap Costantini (6), Cap Ruffo di Calabria (20), T Col Piccio (24), Ten Keller, Magg Baracca (34), Ten Ranza (17), Ten De Bernardi, Ten Bacula, Serg Nardini (6), S Ten Olivero.

Bottom: These 10º Gruppo pilots at Gazzo Padovano airfield in September 1918 comprise three aces: Ten Eleuteri (sitting, with pipe, numbered 2), Ten Avet (sitting, 6) and Ten Resch (standing, centre, 13).

1 CAP. BERTOLETTI	4 TEN. CAMIRATO	7 SERG. IMALESI
2 TEN. MAZZINI	5 SERG. CERUTTI	8 SERG. REALI
3 S.TEN. MELLONI	6 SERG. NICELLI	9 SERG. CIOTTI

Top left: The 79ª Squadriglia at Nove di Bassano on 22 December 1917 with aces Serg Cerutti (numbered 5), Serg Imolesi (7) and Serg Reali (8).

Top right: "Giannino" Ancillotto, who in December 1917 flew through a flaming balloon, photographed in Peru in 1921.

Middle left: The semi-official poster of the Army aces published in March 1919 by the magazine *Nel Cielo*, the portraits of Bedendo and Riva were already unavailable.

Above: Antonio Amantea, fifth from the right, as tenente colonnello, taken shortly after the Italian armistice in 1943.

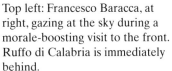

Top left: Francesco Baracca, at right, gazing at the sky during a morale-boosting visit to the front. Ruffo di Calabria is immediately behind.

Top right: Ernesto Cabruna (left) in front of his 77ª Sqn Spad. The heart denotes the unit, the badge his home town of Tortona (c. 1918).

Above: Umberto Calvello was credited with five victories in the official Navy list.

Right: Studio portrait of Flavio Torello Baracchini, the first fighter pilot awarded a Gold Medal. The wounded left jaw is evident.

1 CAP. BERTOLETTI   4 TEN. CAMIRATO   7 SERG. IMALESI
2 TEN. MAZZINI   5 SERG. CERUTTI   8 SERG. REALI
3 S.TEN. MELLONI   6 SERG. NICELLI   9 SERG. CIOTTI

Top left: The 79ª Squadriglia at Nove di Bassano on 22 December 1917 with aces Serg Cerutti (numbered 5), Serg Imolesi (7) and Serg Reali (8).

Top right: "Giannino" Ancillotto, who in December 1917 flew through a flaming balloon, photographed in Peru in 1921.

Middle left: The semi-official poster of the Army aces published in March 1919 by the magazine *Nel Cielo*, the portraits of Bedendo and Riva were already unavailable.

Above: Antonio Amantea, fifth from the right, as tenente colonnello, taken shortly after the Italian armistice in 1943.

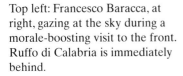

Top left: Francesco Baracca, at right, gazing at the sky during a morale-boosting visit to the front. Ruffo di Calabria is immediately behind.

Top right: Ernesto Cabruna (left) in front of his 77ª Sqn Spad. The heart denotes the unit, the badge his home town of Tortona (c. 1918).

Above: Umberto Calvello was credited with five victories in the official Navy list.

Right: Studio portrait of Flavio Torello Baracchini, the first fighter pilot awarded a Gold Medal. The wounded left jaw is evident.

Top left: Sottotenente Alvaro Leonardi scored 8 victories with the 80ª Squadriglia.

Top right: Federico Martinengo scored five victories, all shared, and died in action against the Germans in 1943.

Middle: Formerly of the 91ª Squadriglia, Cesare Magistrini (third from right) later became one of Italy's most successful airline pilots.

Left: Carlo Francesco ('Francis') Lombardi by his Spad 7, marked with the red heart insignia of the 77ª Squadriglia.

Top left: After the war Amedeo Mecozzi (at the table, speaking) became an advocate of tactical airpower.

Top right: Guido Nardini served with the 91ª Squadriglia from 1918 until his death in a flying accident in 1928.

Middle right: Giorgio Michetti was Scaroni's wingman in the 76ª Squadriglia.

Above: Formally an Austrian subject, Giorgio Pessi was forced to conceal his identity and became "Giuliano Parvis".

Left: Despite being a 5-victory ace, Guido Masiero is mostly remembered for his role in the 1920 Rome-Tokyo flight.

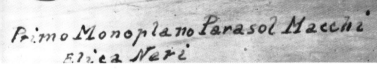

Ten.te Tacchini = Cap.no Piccio Ten.te Valdimiro
V.a Squad.a = Busto Arsizio = 1914

Primo Monoplano Parasol Macchi
Elica Neri

Top left: Pier Ruggiero Piccio, centre, was outstanding as both fighter pilot and commander.

Top right: Orazio Pierozzi, the leading naval ace.

Left: With 17 confirmed victories, Ferruccio Ranza, at left, was the sixth Italian ace.

Above: Antonio Reali of the 79ª Squadriglia scored 11 victories.

Top left: Cosimo Rizzotto aboard a 77ª Squadriglia Ni.17.

Top right: Fulco Ruffo di Calabria, at left, was Baracca's successor and Italy's fifth leading ace.

Above left: Born in Italy but raised in Ecuador, Cosimo Rennella is considered by some the only Latin American ace of the war.

Above centre: Silvio Scaroni, 26 victories, seen postwar with the insignia of ADC to the King.

Above right: After scoring 6 victories, Mario Stoppani transferred to Ansaldo to begin a 40-year career as test pilot.

Right: Romolo Ticconi scored many of his victories together with Scaroni.

ABOVE THE PIAVE

Top left: Julius Arigi, 32 victories, Flik 55J.

Top centre: Gottfried Fr von Banfield, Naval ace with 9 victories.

Top right: Godwin Brumowski, CO Flik 41J; 35 victories.

Above: Andreas Dombrowski, 6 victories (left) with Karl Seltner of Flik 29, Romania August 1917.

Top: Pilots of Flik 51J, August 1918 (l to r): Stefan Fejes (16), Oblt Michael Dorcic, Benno Fiala (28), Franz Rudorfer (11) and Eugen Bönsch (16).

Above: Friedrich Hefty seated in an Aviatik DI of Flik 42J. He achieved five victories with four more unconfirmed.

Right: Benno Fiala Ritter von Fernbrugg, 28 victories.

Far right: Franz Gräser with the Silver Bravery Medal; 18 victories.

Top left: Adolf Heyrowsky achieved 12 victories, mostly with Flik 19 which he commanded in 1917.

Top right: Josef Kiss scored 19 victories before his death in combat on 24 May 1918 in this aircraft, 422.10, a Phönix DIIa.

Above: Hptm Heinrich Kostrba, Flik 8, eight victories. Seen seated in a Fokker Eindekker in February 1916, while with Flik 4.

Top: Hptm Josef von Maier, CO of Flik 55J (centre) with some of his pilots at Pergine. Note the insignia on this Phönix Scout.

Middle: Friedrich Navratil, ten victories, seated in his Albatros DIII, summer 1918. The white arrow pierces a red heart; Flik 3J.

Right: Oblt Frank Linke-Crawford, Flik 60J, summer 1918. Killed in action 31 July 1918.

Far right: Oblt Bela Macourek CO of Flik 1 scored five victories.

op left: Franz Rudorfer, 11 victories, while with Flik 19 as an observer in 1917. Later flew with Flik 51J as a pilot.

op centre: Ernst Strohschneider of Fliks 42J and 61J ored 15 victories.

op right: Karl Teichmann, five victories, with Fliks 42J,)J and 14J.

Above: Pilots of Flik 41J (l to r): Beno Fiala, Ickovits, Heinrich Mayrbaurl, Italian observer PoW, Brumowski and Linke-Crawford; the captured Italian pilot is in the cockpit of Brumowski's Albatros DIII, the latter's 20th victory (23 August 1917).

ABOVE THE STEPPES

Top left: Captain A A Kazakov, Russia's top ace of WW1 with 20 victories.

Top right: Leaders of Russia's four fighter groups in 1917 (l to r): Kazakov (1st Group), Captain I J Zemitan (3rd Group), Captain Y N Kruten, seven victories (2nd Group) and Captain Kulvinkski (4th Group).

Middle right: Alexandr de Seversky, six victories.

Above: Captain Ivan Smirnov, 11 victories scored with 19 Squadron.

Left: Captain Smirnov, airline pilot post-WW2.

	1918			DH4					
1	30 May	Fokker DVII	(a)	A8038	18	Neuve Chapelle	1300	DES	
2	„	Fokker DVII	(a)	„	„	Richebourg	1305	OOC	
3	8 Jul	Fokker DVII	(b)	A7815	„	Hénin-Liétard	0830	DES	
4	28 Jul	Fokker DVII	(b)	„	„	Vitry	0735	OOC	
5	4 Sep	Fokker DVII	(b)	„	„	Cantin	0750	DES(F)	
6	„	Fokker DVII	(b)	„	„	Aubigny-au-Bac	0751	DES	

Total: 4 destroyed, 2 out of control = 6.
Pilot: (a) Capt A D Stewart; (b) Capt G W F Darvill.

NAYLOR Walter   Gunlayer   5N/205 SQN

Often flew with C P O Bartlett DSC during 1917-18, having joined the Squadron in August 1917. Received the DSM, gazetted on 17 April 1918 at which time he had flown on more than 20 bomb raids, although his total operations later reached at least 91.

	1917			DH4					
1	21 Oct	Albatros DV	(a)	N6008	5N	Houttave A/F		OOC	
2	4 Nov	Albatros DV	(a)	„	„	Engel A/F	1400	OOC	
3	18 Dec	Albatros DV	(b)	N6001	„	Engel A/F	1400	DES(F)	
4	„	Albatros DV	(b)	„	„	„	1400	OOC	
5	19 Dec	Albatros DV	(b)	„	„	off Ostende	1230	DES	
	1918								
6	30 Jan	Albatros DV	(c)	„	„	Engel A/F	1330	OOC	
7	17 Feb	Albatros DV	(d)	N6000	„	W Ostende	1210	OOC	
8	18 Feb	Albatros DV	(d)	„	„	Schoore	1300	OOC	
9	18 Mar	Albatros DV	(c)	N5961	„	Beaurevoir	1102	OOC	
10	21 Mar	Fokker DrI	(c)	N6000	„	Honnecourt	1804	OOC	
11	27 Mar	Albatros DV	(c)	„	„	Fontaine	1045	OOC	
12	28 Mar	Pfalz DIII	(c)	N6001	„	Raincourt	1000	DES	
13	„	Fokker DrI	(c)	„	„	„	1000	DES	
14	„	Fokker DrI	(c)	„	„	„	1000	DES	

Total: 5 destroyed, 9 out of control = 14.
Pilot: (a) FL A Shaw; (b) FC C D Sproatt; (c) FC C P O Bartlett; (d) FL E Dickson.

PULLEN H   2nd Lieutenant   25 SQN

Flew as an observer to several different pilots in DH4 bombers in 1918, being involved in five victories.

	1918			DH4					
1	29 Mar	2-seater	(a)	A8078	25	Foucaucourt	1045	DES	
2	8 Jun	Fokker DrI	(b)	A7626	„	Lille-Tournai	1615	OOC	
3	24 Jul	Pfalz DIII	(c)	D9271	„	SW Lille	1815	DES	
4	4 Aug	Pfalz DIII	(c)	„	„	Lille	1745	OOC	
5	22 Aug	Pfalz DIII	(d)	A7637	„	Douai	1730	OOC	

Total: 2 destroyed, 3 out of control = 5.
Pilot: (a) 2/Lt S Jones; (b) Lt W H G Milnes; (c) Lt L Young; (d) Lt J H Latchford.

RATTRAY A B   2nd Lieutenant   104 SQN

Flew as an observer to several different pilots while operating with the Independent Force on raids on Germany and German airfields.

	1918			DH9					
1	12 Aug	Pfalz DIII	(a)		104	Saverne	0715	DES	
2	„	Pfalz DIII	(b)		„	„	0715	OOC	
3	22 Aug	Albatros DV	(c)		„	Mannheim	0805	DES	
4	23 Oct	EA	(d)	D3100	„	Anney	1210	DES	
5	29 Oct	Fokker DVII	(d)		„	Jametz	1245	DES	

Total: 4 destroyed, 1 shared out of control = 5.
Pilot: (a) Lt Pickup; (b) Pickup and shared with 2/Lt G B H Smith/Sgt W Harrop; (c) Lt Pope; (d) 2/Lt J H Cuthbertson.

RHODES Hervey   Lieutenant   12 SQN

Born 12 August 1895, he worked in the woollen industry pre-war. When war came he served with the King's Own Royal Lancashire Regiment from 1914 and later the Yorkshire Regiment; in 1915 he was with the 7th Battn. KORL's Signals Platoon. Seconded to the RFC he flew as observer to C R Pithey with whom he won the DFC and Bar, gazetted on 3 August and 3 December 1918 respectively. Wounded in action on 27 September he saw no further combat and in fact it was not until 1921 that he fully recovered. He became a woollen manufacturer and was MP for Ashton-under-Lyne between 1945-64. Four years later he was made Lord Lieutenant of Lancashire. While an MP he was Parliamentary Secretary to the Board of Trade in 1950-51 and 1964-67. He became a Baron in 1964 and a PC in 1969. He lived in Oldham, Lancashire and died on 11 September 1987.

	1918			RE8			
1	7 May	Balloon		12			DES
2	8 May	EA		"			OOC
3	4 Jun	Balloon	B7715	"	Sheet 57c B8	0920	DES
4	7 Jun	Pfalz DIII	"	"	"	0920	DES
5	"	Pfalz DIII	"	"	"	0920	OOC
6	"	Pfalz DIII	"	"	"	0920	OOC
7	21 Aug	Fokker DVII	E47	"	Behaignies	1130	OOC
8	23 Aug	LVG C		"	Boyelles	1740	DES(F)
9	28 Aug	DFW C	F6097	"	E St Leger	0945	DES
10	30 Aug	Fokker DVII	"	"	Bullecourt	0650	DES(F)
11	3 Sep	LVG C	"	"	Lagnicourt	1715	DES

Total: 5 destroyed, 2 balloons, 4 out of control = 11.
Pilot: all scored with Lt Pithey except No.2, with 2/Lt N Garland.

ROBINSON Charles Victor   Sergeant   5N/205 SQN

Served initially as a RNAS Gunlayer, then RAF Sergeant (207177), having joined 5 Naval Squadron in August 1917. He remained with 205 until August 1918, having won the DSM (noted in the communiqué on 2 June 1918) and DFM, the latter gazetted on 18 November 1919. He had flown on well over 100 bomb raids.

	1918			DH4				
1	30 Jan	Albatros DV	(a)	A7744	5N	Engel A/F	1330	OOC
2	22 Apr	Fokker DrI	(b)	A7739	205	Chaulnes	1615	OOC
3	23 Apr	Fokker DrI	(b)	"	"	"	1940	OOC
4	3 May	Pfalz DIII	(c)	D9237	"	Chaulnes-Rosières	1545	DES(F)
5	"	Pfalz DIII	(c)	"	"	"	1545	OOC
6	18 May	Albatros DV	(b)	D9238	"	W Chaulnes	1130	DES(F)
7	20 May	Pfalz DIII	(d)	A7739	"	Mericombe	0830	DES(F)

Total: 1 & 2 shared destroyed, 3 & 1 shared out of control = 7.
Pilot: (a) FSL J M Mason; (b) Capt E Dickson; (c) Dickson, and shared with Lt C E Siedle/AGL. Middleton, A8071; Lt C J H Heywood/AGL F S Langstone, D9238; Lt W B Elliott/AGL. Whalley, N6009; Lt Wilson/AGL. Mackay, D9241; Lt W Grossart/AGL. Richards, A7811; Lt Fox/AGL. C F Ambler, D8412; Capt J Gamon/ 2/Lt Scott, N6004; Lt R Chalmers/2/Lt S H Hamblin, D8401; Lt Scott/AGL. Humphrey, D9243; (d) Mason, and shared with Capt J Gamon/Sgt W Jones, N6006; Lt C J H Heywood/Sgt F S Langstone, D9238; Lt Wilson/AGL. Mackay, D9241; Lt D J T Mellor/AGL. Gillman, A8071; Lt W B Elliott/AGL. Richards, A7561; Lt Fox/AGL. Ferrie, D6412; Lt W Grossart/2/Lt A R Crosthwaite, A7811.

SCOTT Walter Henry Lieutenant 5N/205 SQN

From Lockerbie, Scotland, born 9 December 1898. Joined the RNAS 20 May 1917 and began training as a pilot but then decided to become an observer. At this time he requested a commission in the RFC but the RNAS refused permission for him to transfer. Posted to 5 Naval Squadron and often flew as observer to E Dickson DSC. By the time he left on 28 May 1918 he had participated in over 50 bombing raids. He was then at No.4 Aircraft Park.

	1918			DH4				
1	9 Mar	Albatros DV	(a)	N6001	5N	Mont d'Origny	1045	OOC
2	16 Mar	Albatros DV	(b)	A7739	,,	Bohain-Le Catelet	1100	DES
3	18 Mar	Albatros DV	(b)	A7620	,,	Beaurevoir	1054	OOC
4	6 Apr	Pfalz DIII	(b)	A7739	205	Abancourt	1550	OOC
5	23 Apr	Fokker DrI	(c)	D9237	,,	Chaulnes	1950	DES(F)
6	,,	Pfalz DIII	(c)	,,	,,	,,	1950	DES
7	3 May	Pfalz DIII	(d)	N6004	,,	Chaulnes-Rosières	1545	DES(F)
8	,,	Pfalz DIII	(d)	,,	,,	,,	1545	OOC

Total: 3 & 1 shared destroyed, 3 & 1 shared out of control = 8.
Pilot: (a) FL T Watkins; (b) Capt E Dickson; (c) Capt J Gamon; (d) Gamon, and shared with other crews (see list for C V Robinson, page 92).

SIMPSON Edward Arthur 2nd Lieutenant 49 SQN

Born 24 May 1892 he lived with his wife in London (N17) and joined the Royal Irish Fusiliers. Commissioned 2/Lt 5 August 1917. With the RAF he joined 49 Squadron on 7 June 1918, flying with Lt J A Keating, an American pilot. Won the DFC for five victories in two days in August although they were themselves forced to land after the 9 August combat.

	1918		DH9				
1	22 Jul	Fokker DVII	C2202	49	Sergy	1820	OOC
2	8 Aug	Pfalz DIII	,,	,,	Bethencourt	1835	DES(F)
3	9 Aug	Fokker DVII	,,	,,	Marchélepot	c0630	DES(F)
4	,,	Fokker DVII	,,	,,	Ablaincourt	,,	DES(F)
5	,,	Fokker DVII	,,	,,	Soyecourt	,,	OOC
6	,,	Fokker DVII	,,	,,	,,	,,	OOC

Total: 3 destroyed, 3 out of control = 6.

SLOOT Lambert Louis Theodore 2nd Lieutenant 57 SQN

From Hampton on Thames, Middlesex, he joined the General List of the RFC from the HAC in September 1917 and was commissioned temporary second lieutenant on 15 January 1918 with seniority from 20 November 1917, having been on probation since August. Joined 57 Squadron in France. Back in England he was at Reading in June and then with 28 TDS. He left the service on 6 June 1919.

	1918			DH4				
1	6 Jan	Albatros DV	(a)	A7637	57	NE Courtrai	1200	OOC
2	19 Jan	Albatros DV	(a)	A7901	,,	Roulers	1445	OOC
3	26 Feb	Albatros DV	(a)	A7637	,,	Dadizeele	1115	DES(F)
4	16 Mar	Albatros DV	(b)	A2174	,,	SW Roulers	1215	OOC
5	,,	Albatros DV	(b)	,,	,,	,,	1215	OOC

Total: 1 destroyed, 4 out of control = 5.
Pilot: (a) Sgt E R Clayton; (b) Sgt C W Noel.

SMITH James Robert 2nd Lieutenant 18 SQN

From the Isles of Orkney, Scotland, born 8 May 1891, he went to Canada as an electrical and mechanical engineer in the city of Prince Albert, Saskatchewan between 1910-12. Became self-employed 1913-14 in Regina. Coming back to Britain when war began, he was a Probationary second lieutenant in the RFC General List from 21 March 1917, seniority from 25 November 1916. Serving with 18 Squadron he was wounded in the stomach on 11 April 1917. On 14 July he was awarded the French Croix de Guerre with Palme. Back in England he was with 33 and then 51 (HD) Squadrons in 1918, being injured in the left eye on 6 August. Served with 78 (HD) Squadron from May 1919 prior to being repatriated to Canada at the end of that year.

	1916			FE2b				
1	26 Dec	Albatros DII	(a)	A5458	18	Velu	0950	OOC
	1917							
2	11 Mar	Albatros DII	(b)	4984	„	Velu-Bapaume	1145	DEC
3	„	Albatros DII	(b)	„	„	„	1200	OOC
4	5 Apr	Albatros DII	(c)	A5464	„	Inchy	1200	OOC
5	6 Apr	Albatros DII	(c)	„	„	Ecoust St Mein	1000	CAPT

Total: 1 destroyed, 1 captured, 3 out of control = 5.
Pilots: (a) 2/Lt W F MacDonald; (b) Lt H A R Boustead; (c) Capt R H Hood.

SMITH William Thomas   Flight Sergeant   45 & 104 SQNS

Born in 1897, he came from Maida Vale, north London. Served with the Royal Engineers in France for 2 years, winning the Military Medal. He was then seconded to the RFC, serving with 45 Squadron in 1917, with his rank of pioneer, where he won the DCM for an action on 11 August. His pilot was wounded and fainted but Smith climbed out onto the wing, took control of the machine and managed to get the pilot back to consciousness, to fly them back over the lines to a crash landing. In 1918 he joined 104 Squadron of the Independent Force, as a sergeant (No.48027), often flying with Captain J B Home-Hay MC. They led a raid on Mannheim on 22 August but were shot down to become prisoners of war. Smith emigrated to Australia after the war and in WW2 was an instructor in the RAAF. He died in Australia in 1994.

	1917			1½ St				
1	11 Aug	Albatros DV	(a)	A5244	45	Deulemont	1845	DES(F)
	1918			DH4				
2	11 Aug	Albatros DV	(b)		104	Karlsruhe	0910	OOC
3	13 Aug	Albatros DV	(b)	„	„	Corny	1545	DES
4	„	Albatros DV	(b)		„	S Corny	1547	DES
5	15 Aug	Albatros DV	(b)		„	Château Salins	1830	OOC

Total: 3 destroyed, 2 out of control = 5.
Pilot: (a) Capt J McA Pender; (b) Capt J B Home-Hay.

WALKER Eric   Lieutenant   18 SQN

From Mirfields, Yorkshire, born 10 July 1896. Between 1913-15 he worked for a clock manufacturer in Batley. Served with the 1st West Riding Light Infantry, and the 1st Army Signals School as an instructor. Flew with 18 Squadron and received the DFC, which was gazetted on 2 November 1918. The citation for this award recorded that he had been on 35 bomb raids, 21 recce sorties, many at low level, and ten photo ops, as well as accounting for four enemy planes. Returned to Home Establishment in October and left the service on 13 March 1919.

	1918			DH4				
1	31 May	Fokker DrI	(a)	A7990	18	S Armentières	1200	OOC
2	„	Fokker DrI	(a)	„	„	„	1200	OOC
3	20 Jul	2-seater	(b)	A7907	„	Esquerchin	0720	DES
4	„	Fokker DVII	(b)	„	„	„	0730	DES
5	31 Jul	Fokker DVII	(b)	„	„	Brebières	1050	DES
6	„	Fokker DVII	(b)	„	„	„	1050	OOC

Total: 3 destroyed, 3 out of control = 6.
Pilot: (a) 2/Lt J Waugh; (b) Lt J Gillanders.

WHITHAM Charles Myers   2nd Lieutenant   205 SQN

From Halifax, Yorkshire, born 24 November 1898. An articled clerk with a firm of chartered accountants between 1914-17 he was then a private with the 7th TR Battn. Joined the RFC in August 1917 and flew with 205 Squadron from May 1918 and remained with them until the end of the war. By that time he had participated in more than 50 bombing raids and 30 recce sorties and shared five victories with his pilot Lt W H Clarke. Left the service on 23 January 1919.

	1918		DH4				
1	10 Aug	Fokker DVII	A7573	205	Brie Bridge	1540	OOC
2	11 Aug	Pfalz DIII	D8387	„	Péronne	0800	OOC
3	„	Fokker DVII	„	„	Biaches	1910	OOC
4	13 Aug	Pfalz DIII	D9265	„	Péronne	1110	OOC
5	21 Aug	Fokker DVII	D9277	„	NE Bethencourt	1505	DES

Total: 1 destroyed, 3 & 1 shared out of control = 5.
(a) shared with Lt E Johnson/Lt Taylor, A8029.

PART TWO
ABOVE FLANDERS FIELDS

I   The Belgian Air Service

When the war began the Belgian Air Service had one air depot, two Escadrilles equipped with Henri Farmans with two more Escadrilles in the course of formation. In all the Service — the Compagnie des Aviateurs — had 37 qualified pilots together with eight civilian pilots who volunteered their services, one of whom was Jan Olieslagers.

The two operational units had already been sent to their war landing grounds, near Liege and Namur, in order to co-operate with the forts there. As the Belgian army fell back in front of the German land assault, the Air Service reformed at Calais and St Pol and in April 1915 was renamed Aviation Militaire, moving to airfields at Houthem and Coxyde.

There were now five Escadrilles equipped with Voisin, Henri and Maurice Farmans to support the five Belgian divisions, a sixth division being held in reserve. A sixth Escadrille, with BE2s, was established in 1916 (6me). However, it was the 1ere Escadrille with Farmans and a lone Nieuport, which really became the first Belgian fighter unit when it equipped with Nieuport Bebé scouts, joined at De Moeren by 5me Escadrille, which also changed its role to Chasse. The decision to form a fighter unit came on 18 January 1916 and 1ere Escadrille was transformed to fighters on 22 February.

The Belgian Aviation Militaire was never very large, being commensurate with its country's size, half of which was in any event under German occupation. However, the pilots and observers were as brave and resourceful as their contemporaries in either the British or French air forces, and helped hold the northern end of the line. In so doing, its airmen were often pitted against the German Marinefeld Jastas along the north-sea coast.

The fighters were grouped together in a Groupe de Chasse during February/March 1918, 1me and 5me becoming 9me and 10me, being joined by a third fighter Escadrille, 11me. Commanded by Fernand Jacquet, by the express wishes of King Albert of Belgium, these three Escadrilles de Chasse were all based at De Moeren. It is reported that between March and November the Groupe had 587 air fights which resulted in 68 official air combat victories.

The Belgian Chasse Escadrille

1me/9me Escadrille

Escadrille I became 1me Escadrille de Chasse in February 1916, flying Nieuport Bebé fighters, with its base at De Panne. By August it was receiving Nieuport 11s. In December 1916 it moved to De Moeren (Les Moeres in French). Its first CO was Kapitan Arsene Demanet, who was succeeded by Kapitan Fernand Jacquet in June. By the summer of 1917 it was operating with Nieuport 17s and these carried the unit's insignia, the thistle ('le chardon'), on fuselage sides. During August and September it began to equip with Hanriot HD1 scouts together with a few British Sopwith Camels, but the latter were not preferred by the pilots. Kapitan Walter Gallez took over command on 12 December 1917, a post he retained until the Armistice. When the Belgian Groupe de Chasse was formed in March 1918, 1me was renumbered 9me Escadrille. By the end of the war the Escadrille had achieved 73 victories (16 as 1eme, 57 as 9me) including 41 balloons. As 1er Escadrille it had lost six pilots killed, and as 9me lost three pilots taken prisoner or severely wounded.

Lt W Coppens 37	Lt A Demeulemeester 11	Lt J Olieslagers 5(6)

5me/10me Escadrille

Formed in August 1916 equipped with Nieuport 11s, under the command of Kapitan Jules Dony and by the early summer of 1917 was based at De Moeren, and re-equipped with Nieuport 17s and Spad VIIs. Its insignia was a red comet. A total of 35 Spads were delivered and this was the only Belgian unit to operate with them. In March 1918 the updated Spad XIIIs began to arrive. Dony was killed following a flying accident on 1 October 1918, the new CO being Lieutenant Frederic de Woelmont, a former observer who had received his wings in 1918. Four days later Lt L Robin took command. When the Belgian Groupe de Chasse was formed in March 1918, the Escadrille was renumbered 10me. Spad XIIIs began to replace the Spad VIIs in 1918 although the latter were still used. As 5me it had claimed 17 victories with seven more probables, and a further 9 confirmed and 12 probables as 10me. Two pilots had been killed before the change, three more plus two taken prisoner and one wounded after the change.

S/Lt E Thieffry   10

11me Escadrille

In March 1918, the Belgian Groupe de Chasse was formed under the command of Fernand Jacquet and the 1me and 5me Escadrille were renumbered 9me and 10me. At this time a third Escadrille de Chasse was formed, numbered 11me. It was equipped with British Sopwith Camels which the 1/9me had rejected and commanded by Kapitan Paul Hiernaux. It also had a few Hanriots. The insignia of the unit was a 'cocotte' — marked as a folded piece of paper in the shape of a chicken. This unit too was based at De Moeren. The unit was credited with just six victories with five more probables for the loss of two pilots killed and one wounded.

II   The Belgian Aces

COPPENS Willy Omer Francois Jean   Lieutenant   6,4,1 & 9 ESC

Born in Watermaal-Bosvoorde, near Brussels, 6 July 1892. His passion before the war was designing and building land-yachts (and flying kites) on the beaches of La Panne. Between 1907-13 he built seven, and after the war he built others. He joined the 1st Grenadier Regiment when war came and was attached to the Belgian Motor Machine Gun Corps but in September 1915 was accepted for flight training. Learnt to fly in England where he obtained Royal Aero Club Certificate No.2140 on 9 December at Hendon, then went to France and the Belgian Aviation School at Etampes. It took Coppens almost a year to get to the front, going to 6eme Escadrille d'Observation in April 1917 to fly BE2c two-seaters. He had his first air fight on 1 May for which he received his first citation. He was transferred to the 4eme Escadrille on 17 June, now flying Sopwith 1½ Strutters but on 14 July moved again to the 1ere Escadrille de Chasse (which later became 9me), to become a fighter pilot as he had wanted. He had his first combat on 21 July, flying a Nieuport 11. Promoted to Adjutant on 19 August, he was commissioned in June 1918, by which time he had begun his scoring run against the Germans and in particular against German kite balloons, flying the Hanriot. With his victories came awards: the Croix de Guerre; the Ordre de la Couronne in May 1918, the l'Ordre de Léopold, then being made an Officer of the Ordre de la Couronne in July and a Chevalier de l'Ordre de Léopold at the same time; The French Légion d'Honneur and Croix de Guerre; then the British presented him with the Military Cross after his second triple on 22 July 1918 as they were made over the British front within five minutes of each other. On 22 August he became a flight commander (Belgian units only had three machines in a flight). His almost insatiable desire to destroy balloons made him the war's leading victor over these dangerous targets, 35 of his 37 confirmed being 'drachens'. It brought him other awards, including the British DSO and the Serbian Order of the White Eagle together with others from Portugal, Italy and Poland. His last combat occurred on 14 October. At 0540 hrs he started out with Sgt Etienne Hage for what was to become both pilots' last flight. They had set out to destroy the balloon over Praatbos, near Dixmude, Coppens making it his 36th victory at 0600, then they went for the next balloon above Torhout. At 500m distance from the balloon, Coppens got a direct hit from a flak-unit which smashed the tibia of his left leg, severing the artery as well. He continued with the attack and destroyed the 'gas-bag', although it was not officially confirmed until the late 1930's. Meantime, Hage shot down a balloon over Roulers, also being wounded, in the arm. Coppens crashlanded in a field to the east of Dixmude and was soon in hospital, where his leg was amputated. The next day the King of Belgium visited him, investing him with the Rosette of Officer of the Ordre de Léopold. Coppens became Baron Willy Coppens de Houthulst after the war and remained in the army despite the loss of his left leg, being persuaded to stay in the service by King Albert himself, although he was to regret the move in later life. He finally left the service in 1940 having only attained the rank of Major in that time, having spent much of his time as a military attaché in Italy, Switzerland, France and England. During WW2 he resided in Switzerland organising some resistance work and marrying. In the late 1960's he returned to Belgium and lived his last five years with Jan Olieslagers' only daughter until his sudden death on 21 December 1986. Author of the well known book *Jours Envoles*, translated into English as *Days on the Wing* (Hamilton, 1932).

	1917							
–	7 Jul	2-seater		1½ St	4me	Middlekerke	1555	u/c
–	30 Sep	2-seater		,,	1er	Roulers	1040	FTL
–	1 Oct	2-seater		Hanriot	1me	nr Beerst		u/c
	1918							
–	12 Mar	2-seater		Hanriot	9me	St Joris	0910	DES
1	25 Apr	Scout	(a)	,,	,,	St Joris	1220	DES
2	8 May	Balloon		,,	,,	Zarren	0710	DES
3	,,	Balloon		,,	,,	Houthulst	0955	DES
4	15 May	Balloon	(b)	,,	,,	Houthulst	0807	DES
5	19 May	Balloon		,,	,,	Houthulst	0945	DES
6	5 Jun	Balloon		,,	,,	Houthulst	0640	DES
7	9 Jun	Balloon		,,	,,	Zonnebeke	0922	DES
8	10 Jun	Balloon		,,	,,	Ploegsteert	0747	DES
9	24 Jun	Balloon		,,	,,	Warneton	0645	DES
10	,,	Hannover CL		,,	,,	Ploegsteert	0646	DES
11	30 Jun	Balloon		,,	,,	Bovekerke	0630	DES
12	,,	Balloon		,,	,,	Gheluvelt	0830	DES
13	,,	Balloon		,,	,,	Passchendaele	0834	DES
14	14 Jul	Balloon		,,	,,	Passchendaele	0930	DES
15	16 Jul	Balloon		,,	,,	Bovekerke	1855	DES
16	19 Jul	Balloon		,,	,,	Ruyterhoek	1920	DES
17	20 Jul	Balloon		,,	,,	Houthulst	0557	DES
18	22 Jul	Balloon		,,	,,	Gheluwe	0730	DES
19	,,	Balloon		,,	,,	Wervicq	0731	DES
20	,,	Balloon		,,	,,	Comines	0734	DES
21	24 Jul	Balloon		,,	,,	Ruyterhoek	1920	DES
22	3 Aug	Balloon		,,	,,	Reutel	0750	DES
23	10 Aug	Balloon		,,	,,	Leffinge	0605	DES
24	,,	Balloon		,,	,,	Ruyterhoek	0625	DES
25	,,	Balloon		,,	,,	Leffinge	0745	DES
26	24 Aug	Balloon		,,	,,	Ploegsteert	1455	DES
27	,,	Balloon		,,	,,	Warneton	1457	DES
28	3 Sep	Balloon		,,	,,	Tenbrielen	1102	DES
29	4 Sep	Balloon		,,	,,	Wercken	0923	DES
30	27 Sep	Balloon		,,	,,	Leffinge	1105	DES
31	,,	Balloon		,,	,,	Leffinge	1106	DES
32	29 Sep	Balloon		,,	,,	Leffinge	1005	DES
–	2 Oct	2-seater	(c)	,,	,,	Menin	1245	OOC
33	3 Oct	Balloon		,,	,,	Leffinge	1520	DES
34	5 Oct	Balloon		,,	,,	Lendeleede	0814	DES
35	,,	Balloon		,,	,,	Cruypenaerde	0820	DES
36	14 Oct	Balloon		,,	,,	Praatbos	0600	DES

| 37 | „ | Balloon | | „ | „ | Torhout | 0605 | DES |

Total: 1 and 1 shared aircraft and 35 balloons destroyed = 37.
(a) shared with Kapt Walter Gallez (1); (b) rammed by Coppens when his ammo was expended; (c) shared with Sgt Etienne Hage but not found in official papers of the Groupe de Chasse, only noted in Coppens' book.

DEMEULEMEESTER Andre Emile Alfons   Lieutenant   1 & 9 ESC

Born in Bruges, 28 December 1894, he volunteered for the Flying Corps on 26 January 1915 and was officially assigned to the 1ere Escadrille de Chasse on 8 April 1917, although he had been with it since October 1916 as a sergeant. He was soon nicknamed 'The Eagle of Flanders' by his compatriots. He was severely wounded following his fifth victory, on 21 August 1917, by the two-seater's observer, and was more than a month in hospital. He returned later in the year and in the spring of 1918, his unit was renumbered 9me Escadrille. By May he had ten official victories and was commissioned on the 21st, but was wounded again on 11 July. In the crash-landing he suffered facial injuries and lost several teeth, but again returned to duty. In all he flew over 200 patrols with the 9eme Escadrille, had more than 55 air fights and gained four official kills and five probables. Nearly all his victims fell to pieces in the air and twice he was attacked by British aeroplanes. The first time was on 29 June, by a DH4 crew, and again on 7 July, by a DH4 and some Dolphins, one of his flight (Gusto de Mevius) having to force land through damage. Demeulemeester was awarded the Belgian Croix de Guerre with Palme, made a Chévalier de l'Ordre Léopold II with Palme, Chévalier de l'Ordre Léopold I, the French Croix de Guerre with Palme and the Italian Medaglia d'Argento al Valore Militare. Five citations from the Belgian and French armies and six 'chevrons de front' and one 'chevron blesse'. Disgusted with being made a Lieutenant de Reserve on 21 November 1918, Demeulemeester left the army on 17 July 1919 and never flew again. He went into the family brewery company and died in his home town on 7 March 1973.

	1917							
–	1 Feb	Rumpler C		Nieuport	1ere	Lombardzijde	1515	FTL
1	30 Apr	2-seater	(a)	„	„	Leke	am	DES
–	2 May	2-seater		„	„	Schoore	0710	FTL
2	12 Jun	2-seater	(b)	„	„	Vladso	1540	DES
–	15 Jun	Scout	(c)	„	„	Keiem	1115	DES
3	10 Jul	2-seater		„	„	Ramskapelle	2000	DES
4	20 Jul	2-seater		„	„	Yser River	0620	DES
–	23 Jul	Scout		„	„	Kortewilde	1550	OOC
5	21 Aug	Albatros C		„	„	Yser front	–	DES
–	30 Sep	2-seater		„	„	Roulers	1040	FTL
–	1 Oct	2-seater		„	„	Beerst	1545	OOC
–	18 Oct	Albatros		„	„	Tervaete	0915	OOC
–	28 Oct	Scout		„	„	S Keyem	1545	OOC
6	4 Nov	Albatros DIII	(d)	„	„	Kloosterhoek	0750	DES
–	17 Nov	Albatros		„	„	Leke	1133	OOC
	1918							
–	16 Feb	2-seater		„	„	Pervyse	1104	OOC
–	21 Feb	2-seater		„	„	Clercken	0850	OOC
7	„	Albatros DV	(e)	„	„	Dixmude	1450	DES
8	17 Mar	2-seater	(f)	Hanriot	9ere	Dixmude	1100	DES
–	26 Mar	Pfalz DIII	(g)	„	„	Dixmude	1700	DES
–	11 Apr	2-seater		„	„	Schoore	1815	OOC
9	3 May	Scout	(h)	„	„	Schoorbakke	1135	DES
–	9 May	2-seater	(i)	„	„	Hondeghem(?)	1315	OOC
10	17 May	2-seater	(j)	„	„	Houthulst	1030	DES
–	25 Aug	2-seater	(k)	„	„	Houthulst	0930	FTL
–	2 Oct	Halberstadt CL		„	„	Beveren/Leie	1825	OOC
11	5 Oct	Balloon		„	„	Torhout	0705	DES

Total: 7 and 3 shared destroyed, one balloon destroyed = 11.

(a) shared with British Sopwith; (b) shared with Kervyn de Lettenhove, FA3 machine; (c) credited to Olieslagers; (d) shared with Sgt G Kervyn de Lettenhove, although he did not receive credit for an official victory; (e) shared with Capt H Symons, 65 Sqn RFC; (f) FA13; (g) shared with de Mervius, not credited (Flgmt Hans Groth MFJ II); (h) shared with Sgt G Kervyn de Lettenhove; (i) with 2/Lt Gusto de Mevius; (j) FA288; (k) with de Mevius and de Lettenhove.

JACQUET Fernand Maximillian Leon   Capitaine-Commandant

1ESC & GROUPE DE CHASSE

Born 2 November 1888, in Petit Chapelle, in the province of Namur, into a wealthy landowning family. Went to the Military Academy as a cadet in October 1907 and became an infantry officer on 25 June 1910, joining the 4th Line Regiment at Bruges. He received his brevet (No.68) on 25 February 1913 and flew with 2me Escadrille. By the outbreak of war he was with Escadrille Demanet (I) in Liege, and later Namur, and in the early days of the war, often operated at the front in a car equipped with a Lewis gun, driven by Prince de Caraman-Chimay. Once he began flying regularly he was the first Belgian pilot to score an official victory, on 17 April 1915. He continued flying recce sorties but sought combat whenever he could and was always asking for 'les missions speciales.' On 18 March 1917 he was the first pilot to fly King Albert to the front line, and also became the first Belgian ace. Jacquet replaced Commandant Demanet of the 1me Escadrille de Chasse in December 1916 and when the Belgian Groupe de Chasse was formed in March 1918, Jacquet assumed command, insisted upon by the King himself. He never flew single-seaters, always two-seaters, flying to allow accurate fire from his observers, which proved extremely successful. Thus he gained his victories on Farman 80s and 130s, Sopwith 1½ Strutters, and Spad XIs. He himself wanted a Bristol Fighter but it was refused as it was not a machine used by the Belgian Air Force. Promoted to Capitaine-Commandant on December 1917, he was made a Chévalier de l'Ordre Léopold I, received the Croix de Guerre with six citations, eight chevrons de front, Croix Civil 3rd Class, Medaille de Victoire, Medaille de Commemorations 1914-18, made an Officer de l'Ordre de la Couronne, then Chévalier of this Ordre with Palme, Chévalier de la Légion d'Honneur, French Croix de Guerre, the Russian St Anna Order, and was the only Belgian pilot to receive the British DFC. In 1920 he left the army and formed a flying school at Gosselies, near Charleroi, in 1921. During WW2 he was an active member of the resistance, and taken into custody in 1942 and imprisoned at Huy Fortress, in the Ardennes. He died in Beaumont, 12 October 1947.

	1915							
1	17 Apr	Aviatik C	(a)	Farman	1ere	Beerst	–	DES
–	20 Jun	EA	(b)	,,	,,	–	–	OOC
–	26 Jul	Aviatik C	(b)	,,	,,	Westende	1820	FTL
	1916							
2	20 May	Seaplane	(c)	,,	,,	Nieuport	2030	DES
–	26 May	Aviatik C	(c)	,,	,,	Torhout	1820	OOC
–	27 May	Aviatik C	(c)	,,	,,	Koekelare	1925	FTL
–	22 Jun	LVG C	(c)	,,	,,	Staden	0830	DES
3	23 Jun	Fokker	(c)	,,	,,	Koekelare	0800	DES
–	30 Jun	Aviatik C	(c)	,,	,,	Handzame	1900	FTL
–	8 Jul	LVG C	(c)	,,	,,	Middlekerke	1650	OOC
–	30 Jul	LVG C	(d)	,,	,,	Houthulst Forest	1200	DES
4	,,	LVG C		,,	,,	Houthulst	1630	DES
	1917							
5	1 Feb	Rumpler C	(c)	Sop 1½	,,	Lombartszijde	–	DES
	1918							
–	5 Jun	Fokker DrI	(e)	Spad XI	GdC	Houthulst	0642	OOC
6	4 Oct	Rumpler C	(e)	Spad XI	,,	Gits	0800	FTL
7	6 Nov	2-seater	(e)	Spad XI	,,	Ghent	0900	FTL

Total: 7 destroyed.

Obs: (a) Lt Vindevoghel; (b) Lt Leon Colignon; (c) Lt Louis Robin; (d) Lt Robin and shared with Sgt Barthes & Mech Baudoin, French Esc MF36; (e) Lt Marcel de Crombrugghe de Looringhe.

OLIESLAGERS Jan   Lieutenant   5,2,1 & 9 ESC

The 'Antwerp Devil' was born on 14 May 1883 at Antwerp. His father died in 1894 so at age of 11 Jan worked in the shipyards, and the next year worked for a cycle maker. Fascinated by speed, he left his bicycle for a motorcycle and in 1902 became a world champion and the first man on earth to reach over 100 kph on a motorbike. He raced in all the major tournaments in western Europe, London and Turin, and lived in Paris. In 1909 he bought a Blériot and in October gained his flying brevet, No.5. Seven world records are on his list of achievements between 1910-13. In 1910 he won the Meeting d'Aviation de Rheims and in June 1914 he had an ex-aequo with Roland Garros, the French aviator, in an aerobatic game. He even took his machine to North Africa to fly demonstration flights. When the German army invaded Belgium in 1914, Olieslagers received a letter from the German Government asking him to help them in observation duties, but immediately presented himself, with his two brothers, Max, also a pilot, and Jules, a mechanic, together with their three Blériots, to the Belgian Army. He soon became a sergeant and before 1914 was out he had been commissioned. He was the first Belgian single-seater fighter pilot to claim a victory, on 12 September 1915. He could have had many more victories but he never took claiming very seriously and hardly claimed anything. He also had many fights far over the German lines. On 30 March 1916 he downed a German over Praatbos, and soldiers of the 3rd Division confirmed the fight and the aeroplane falling out of control but as no officer was around to uphold confirmation, it was never made official. Olieslagers was an excellent pilot who looked after his new pilots, and hardly took any leave. He occasionally made visits to London, but otherwise would mostly be found on his airfield, working on his machines or in the hangars or garden. He was decorated with the Croix de Guerre, made a Chévalier de l'Ordre Léopold, French Légion d'Honneur and Croix de Guerre, Russian St Stanislaus Order and Serbian Golden Medal. In all he made some 491 war flights and had 97 combats. After the war he returned to his home town and opened a garage. In 1923 he was the man behind the opening of the Antwerp Airport at Deurne, and at its entrance today is a statue of him, in his honour. He died of cancer in March 1942. The Hanriot on display in the Brussels Air Museum is painted in the colours of Olieslagers' machine.

	1915							
1	12 Sep	Aviatik C		Nieup 10	2me	Oudstuivekenskerke	1011	DES
–	22 Sep	2-seater		„	5me	Avekapelle		OOC
–	30 Nov	2-seater	(a)	„	„	Furnes	1115	OOC
	1916							
–	14 Mar	EA		„	1me	Dixmude	1530	OOC
–	30 Mar	EA		„	„	Praatbos	0930	OOC
2	17 Jun	Fokker DII		Nieup 11	„	Pijpegale	1515	DES
–	25 Jun	LVG C		„	„	Nieuport	1715	OOC
–	„	Fokker		„	„	Dixmude	1720	OOC
–	28 Jul	LVG C		„	„	Handzame	1545	FTL
–	30 Jul	LVG C		„	„	Houthulst Forest	am	FTL
–	31 Jul	LVG C		„	„	Houthulst Forest		OOC
–	3 Aug	EA		„	„	Ghisteles	1000	FTL
–	28 Sep	Albatros C		„	„	Ghisteles	1900	FTL
	1917							
–	7 Feb	LVG C	(b)		„	Klerken	pm	FTL
–	8 Feb	LVG C	(c)		„	St Jacques	am	OOC
3	14 Jun	2-seater			„	Schoore	1800	DES
4	15 Jun	Fokker DII			„	Keyem	1115	DES
–	4 Sep	Albatros C		Hanriot	„	Woumen	am	OOC
–	1 Oct	2-seater		„	„	Beerst	1545	OOC
	1918							
–	3 May	Scout		„	9me	Eesen	0940	OOC
5	3 May	Fokker DVII	(d)	„	„	Westende	1750	DES
6	19 May	Albatros DV	(e)	„	„	Woumen	1740	DES
–	8 Oct	2-seater	(f)	„	„	Gits	1200	FTL

Total: 5 and 1 shared destroyed = 6.

(a) shared with three others; (b) FA19, Obs Ltn Erich Ziemke, DoW; (c) believed to have collided slightly with one of three LVGs and it went down; (d) Ltn Walter Lippold?; (e) Vzfw Andreas Treibswetter of Jasta 16b, killed, also claimed by Lt W E Gray and Capt J W Pinder, 213 Sqn RAF. Attacked first by Olieslagers. (f) shared with four other pilots.

THIEFFRY Edmond Sous Lieutenant 4 & 5 ESC

Born in Etterbeek, near Brussels, on 28 September 1892. Was studying law at Louvain University before conscription in 1912 sent him to the 14th Line Regiment until January 1914. Back at University he completed his law studies a few days before war started. Sent to the 10th Line Regiment at once he was taken into captivity by the advancing Germans but managed to escape through Holland on an old motorbike, was interned but managed to get himself released back into Belgium to rejoin his unit on the Yser front. Joined the Air Service and received his military brevet at Etampes on 21 September 1915. Went to the front to fly Farman and Voisin machines on observation duties. A fearless pilot, he broke nearly every aircraft he flew so his commander persuaded him to transfer to single-seaters. Posted to 5me Escadrille de Chasse on 11 December 1916 and on 24 January 1917 flew over occupied Brussels, throwing some leaflets for his family, fiancée and his old school. His 5th and 6th victories on 3 July were the first double scored by a Belgian fighter pilot, and for this action he was commissioned and decorated as a Chévalier de l'Ordre Léopold and the Belgian Croix de Guerre. He was also decorated personally by the King of Italy in September 1917. Thieffry scored ten official victories and was the only ace of 5me Escadrille, which carried the comet marking on its machines. He was shot down on 23 February 1918, waiting too long to open fire on an adversary, whose own fire struck his Spad, which was seen to spin down over Woumen. His Spad was credited to Gfr Lunecke and Ltn Sanbold of FA227, following a disputed claim by Uffz Donnabauer and Vfw Mann of SS26, south-east of Dixmude at 1307 hours. It was some weeks before it was learned that he had survived, although wounded, but he escaped on 13 April only to be recaptured in the Black Forest ten days later, being interned at Bad Aibling. From there he was sent to Ingolstadt, Fort Orft, Fort X and Fort 8, arriving back in Brussels on 6 December. On the 18th he returned to his lawyer duties and later became a politician in his home town. He was still in love with flying and on 12 February 1925 he started out with Léopold Roger and a mechanic, Jef De Bruycker, for the first flight to the Belgian Congo. It took them 51 days to reach Léopoldville. After further flights to try and create an air route he took a boat to the Congo and undertook some liaison flights in the country. Working as an advisor to help start an airline, he met his end on 11 April 1929. His aircraft, a single-engined Avimeta, was caught in a tropical storm and sent into the ground 150 km from Alberville, Thieffry being killed instantly, along with the pilot, Gaston Julien, although their mechanic, Eugene Gastuche, survived. For his work in the Congo he was made an Officer de l'Ordre Léopold I. He left a wife and five children.

	1917								
1	15 Mar	2-seater		Nieuport	5me			eve	DES
2	23 Mar	2-seater		,,	,,	Ghisteles		pm	DES
–	24 Apr	2-seater		,,	,,	Nieuport		am	OOC
–	26 Apr	Albatros DIII		,,	,,	Houthulst Forest		pm	OOC
3	12 May	2-seater	(a)	,,	,,	Houthulst Forest	0700	DES
4	14 Jun	Albatros DIII	(b)	,,	,,	Westende	2030	DES
5	3 Jul	Albatros DIII	(b)	,,	,,	N Dixmude	1330	DES
6	,,	Albatros DIII	(b)	,,	,,	,,	1332	DES
–	10 Jul	Gotha G		,,	,,	Houthulst Forest	1955	OOC
7	16 Aug	Albatros C		Spad	,,	Houthulst Forest	0915	DES
–	18 Aug	2-seater		,,	,,	Westende	1050	DES
8	22 Aug	Scout	(b)	,,	,,	Beerst	1015	DES
9	26 Aug	Scout	(c)	,,	,,	Slype	1940	DES
10	16 Oct	Scout		,,	,,	Merckem	1140	DES
–	9 Nov	2-seater		,,	,,	Oostkerke	0930	OOC

Total: 10 destroyed.
(a) Seefrontstaffel a/c; (b) MFJ I a/c; (c) Uffz C Conradt, Jasta 17.

These five then were the official Belgian aces. It will be noted that like the other Allied air forces, shared victories were also credited to an individual's total. However, unlike the British and French, only aircraft actually deemed destroyed were credited, out of control claims being recorded but not credited, as were unconfirmed claims for victories.

Had the Belgians noted out of control victories there might have been one or two more aces. In order to record here some of the more successful Belgian fighter pilots, the following information is presented:

KERVYN DE LETTENHOVE　　　Sous Lieutenant　　　1, 9 ESC
Baron Georges Maria Ghislain Gerard Bruno

Born Wakken, 11 February 1897, in 1915 he volunteered and assigned to the 1ere Regiment de Guide but followed his brother into aviation with the 4me Escadrille d'Observation, going to the front in late May 1917. Promoted to adjutant on 21 October and should have shared in a third victory on 4 November but for reasons unknown he does not appear to have done so. On this occasion, he and Demeulemeester attacked five Albatros Scouts and one was shot down by the latter, while Kervyn attacked another which went down rapidly to 800 metres then suddenly fell like a stone into the floods of the Yser while continually under attack by him. On 1 August 1918 he was lucky to survive an attack by Camels of 204 Squadron. Kervyn was commissioned on 16 September and by the end of the war had flown 209 sorties since March 1918, fought 55 air battles and had been decorated as a Chévalier de l'Ordre de la Couronne and Croix de Guerre, and Médaille de la Victoire. After the war he remained in the army becoming CO of an Escadrille de Reconnaissance, and then commanding a Groupe de Chasse in 1933. In WW2 he was a liaison officer to General Gort of the BEF and was taken prisoner. After WW2 he rose to General and CO of the Belgian Air Force. Retiring in 1950, he died in Ixelles, Brussels on 17 November 1979.

	1917							
1	12 Jun	2-seater		Nieuport	1me	Vladslo	1540	DES
–	14 Jun	Scout		,,	,,	Schoore	1800	DES
–	5 Aug	Scout		,,	,,	Tervate	1615	OOC
2	21 Aug	EA		,,	,,			DES
–	24 Sep	2-seater		,,	,,	Bien Acquis	1330	OOC
–	4 Nov	Albatros DIII	(a)	Hanriot	,,	Kloosterhoek	0750	DES
	1918							
–	21 Feb	2-seater		,,	,,	Clercken	0850	OOC
–	,,	Albatros	(b)	,,	,,	E Dixmude	1500	DES
–	26 Mar	Pfalz DIIIa	(c)	,,	9me	Dixmude	1700	DES
3	25 Apr	Pfalz DIIIa	(d)	,,	,,	Booitshoeke	1115	DES
4	3 May	2-seater	(a)	,,	,,	Schoorbakke	1135	DES
–	9 Jul	2-seater	(e)	,,	,,	Menin	1045	OOC
–	25 Aug	2-seater	(c)	,,	,,	Houthulst	0930	OOC

Official total — 4.

(a) shared with Demeulemeester; (b) shared with Demeulemeester and 65 Sqn RFC, who were given credit; (c) shared with Demeulemeester and de Mevius: Flgmt Hans Groth, PoW, of MFJ II (5923/17); (d) shared with de Mevius; Flgobmt Bruno Fietzmann, KIA, MFJ II (5942/17); (e) shared with de Mevius.

ROBIN Louis Marie Omer August　　　Lieutenant　　　1,2,4,3,10 ESC

Born Ixelles, Brussels, 1 June 1893 he attended the Military School in 1911, commissioned in December 1913 with the 5me Regiment de Lanciers before transferring to aviation in March 1915. While at cavalry school had been under Fernand Jacquet's brother so was soon with Jacquet's unit. On 29 September 1915 he and his pilot, S/Lt Castiau, flew over Brussels to bomb the Zeppelin sheds. Again with Castiau they dropped newspapers and a Belgian flag over Ghent and Antwerp. In 1916 he was Jacquet's usual observer and carried out 113 flights and had 70 fights, during which Robin was credited with three victories. He later flew with 4me and then

3me Escadrille. In 1917 he became a pilot and joined 10me but only in time to fly 18 sorties and have 11 fights, forcing one German down into Holland. Awarded the Chévalier de l'Ordre de Léopold, Officier de l'Ordre de la Couronne, Croix de Guerre with 8 Palmes and 4 Lions, became a Chévalier de la Légion d'Honneur and the French Croix de Guerre with two Palmes. A team manager in the 1920 Olympics he later helped Fernand Jacquet with his flying school and in 1922 was again with his old Lancers Regiment. Promoted to major in 1930. He commanded an armoured car unit in WW2 and was taken prisoner until June 1945. Retired from the service as a colonel in June 1946. Died at Etterbeek, 9 August 1976.

	1916								
1	20 May	Seaplane	(a)	Farman	1ere	Nieuport	2030	DES
–	26 May	Aviatik C	(a)	„	„	Torhout	1830	OOC
–	27 May	Aviatik C	(a)	„	„	Koekelare	1920	FTL
–	22 Jun	LVG C	(a)	„	„	Staden	0830	DES
2	23 Jun	Fokker DII	(a)	„	„	Koekelare	0800	DES
–	30 Jun	Aviatik C	(a)	„	„	Handzame	2100	FTL
–	8 Jul	LVG C	(a)	„	„	Middlekerke	1650	OOC
–	30 Jul	LVG C	(b)	„	„	Houthulst Forest	1200	DES
3	„	LVG C	(b)	„	„	Houthulst	1630	DES
	1917								
4	1 Feb	Rumpler C	(c)	Strutter	„	Lombardszijde		DES
	1918								
–	3 Nov	2-seater		Spad 13	10me	Zelzate	1200	FTL

Official total — 4.

(a) as Obs to F Jacquet; (b) Obs to Lt Ciselet and shared with de Roest and d'Henecourt; (c) with Jacquet and shared with Sgt Barthes and Mech Baudoin, French MF36.

HAGE Etienne Eduard Antoine Marie Joseph   Sergeant   9 ESC

Born Courtrai, 7 June 1896. Volunteered when war began and was an observer with the artillery. Transferred to the flying service in early 1917 and qualified as a pilot in February 1918. Assigned to 9me Escadrille in September 1918, flying his first patrol on the 16th. Flew with Coppens' White Flight and although he shared two two-seaters with Coppens in October, neither pilot received credit due to a lack of communication between the first line troops and HQ. In all Hage flew 31 sorties, had six air fights and claimed six victories. He was brought down by anti-aircraft fire on 14 October after gaining his third 'official' victory, crash-landing in Belgian lines with a smashed arm. He was made a Chévalier de l'Ordre Léopold and received the French and Belgian Croix de Guerre and French Médaille Militaire. Was commissioned in the army post war but then went into motor racing until 1933. Worked in a notary office in the late 1930s and in WW2 served as a liaison officer with the airforce. Not taken prisoner he began sending wireless messages to England. Retired from the military in 1954 as an Honorary Major, he handed over his notary office to his son in 1962 and retired from professional life. After Coppens' death in 1986, Hage was the only living Belgian fighter pilot from WW1. Died in Hasselt on 18 February 1988.

	1918								
1	29 Sep	Balloon		Hanriot	9me	Armentières	0700	DES
2	2 Oct	Balloon		„	„	Quesnoy	0725	DES
–	„	2-seater	(a)	„	„	Handzame		OOC
–	3 Oct	2-seater	(a)	„	„	Menin	0710	DES
–	8 Oct	2-seater	(b)	„	„	Gits	1200	FTL
3	14 Oct	Balloon		„	„	Houthulst	0615	DES

Official total — 3.

(a) shared with Lt W Coppens; (b) shared with Capt W Gallez, Lt J Olieslagers, Adj G Kervyn de Merendre and Sgt J Lemaire.

PART THREE
ABOVE THE ALPS

CHAPTER ONE

Air War on the Italian Front

Introduction

'You mustn't, therefore, imagine daily clashes in the air and aeroplanes falling as in France; because, whereas there aviation has an 800 km-long front and hundreds of aircraft, here the front, over which we can fly, is no more than 30 km and the Austrians have no more than some twenty aircraft', the future ace Francesco Baracca wrote his mother on 10 October 1915. Even taking into account the desire to reassure her about his safety, the description can still be taken as a valid summary of air war on the Italian front.

A number of factors conspired to give this campaign a flavour markedly different from that on the Western Front. In the first place, the war on the Italian front was about a year shorter. This was the direct consequence of the difficulties encountered by Italy in freeing itself from the alliance with Germany and Austria-Hungary (the 'Triple Alliance'), which it had signed in 1882 and renewed at five-year intervals, despite the uneasiness caused by the widespread popular identification of Austria with the traditional oppressor and occupying power of several ethnically Italian provinces. (It should not be forgotten that from 1797 to 1859 Austria controlled northern Italy all the way to Milan, while Venice was only returned to Italy in 1866 after the third war of independence).

Italian activists claimed that Austrians referred to their country as the 'Erbfeind', the hereditary enemy. Indeed, Austria still held the provinces of Trento, on the alpine Tyrolean border, and Trieste, on the eastern Adriatic border, both of which contained sizable Italian nationalist elements aspiring to be reunited with their motherland. When Austria declared war on Serbia (28 July 1914) it asked Italy to send troops in assistance, but three days later the Italian government proclaimed its neutrality. The following eight months saw a debate between those who favoured attacking Austria to seize the contested cities and the majority preferring neutrality. The Army used the interval to build up, but the Austrians also shored up their defences.

On 26 April 1915, Italy signed the secret Pact of London, under which it undertook to attack Austria within a month. On 3 May there followed the denunciation of the Triple Alliance and on 24 May it finally declared war on Austria. Germany, the third partner, immediately broke off diplomatic relations but Italy only declared war against it on 28 August 1916. By then, Germany could spare few resources to help Austria.

This long premise explains why the Italo-Austrian war was shorter than the Franco-British-German struggle. Because both Italy and Austria were the least industrialized of the major European powers, the scale of their war was smaller than that on the Western Front. The final element was geography. In the East the border ran at the foot of the Carso, a rough and broken plateau, while to the North ran the Alps — virtually impassable to infantry but prohibitive for early warplanes as well.

Early operations

The fact that, traditionally, both Italian and Austrian historians have considered their country's aviation assets at the outbreak of war as inferior to those of the enemy says much about the overall conditions. In May 1915 the Italian army fielded 14 operational squadrons, none of which were of fighters, for a total 86 aircraft and 70 pilots, whereas the Austrian army, which had some 89 pilots in August 1914, by the end of the year had risen to 147 serviceable aircraft in 14 Fliegerkompanie (Flik). These resources, however, were in part deployed to the Russian front.

While Italian aviation assets were divided amongst the Army and Navy aviation services, in the complex dual national arrangement of Austria-Hungary they came under the common k.u.k. Armee and common k.u.k. Navy. Although Austria and Hungary also had individual, separate national armies, these did not however have a separate national aviation.

Making an initially cautious advance, the Italian Army forsook the possibility of swift and decisive gains and soon found itself bogged down along the course of the Isonzo river. Over the next 30 months, this became the site of twelve bloody offensives. The first eleven of these were Italian and the last one was Austro-German.

As elsewhere, the first period was characterised by the numerically limited presence of aircraft and their modest capabilities. This was true of either side, both of which fielded obsolete and unarmed reconnaissance machines. What was lacking, in part due to the primitive technological evolution, was a realistic appreciation of what aircraft could achieve. Scaroni enjoyed telling the story of a high-ranking officer denying that anything of value could be seen from above — 'Why, you go too fast. And we all know how difficult it is to see accurately from a running train!'

With his sharp intuition, as early as June 1911 air war theoretician Giulio Douhet had written that 'aircraft will find their most formidable opponent in the air, in enemy aircraft, and even in these new forms of fighting the lighter than air shall be much more vulnerable than the heavier than air'. Two years later, in September 1913, Douhet specifically foresaw the need for a single seat aeroplane equipped with a forward-firing gun 'for fighting in the air'. Despite this, no such aircraft existed in May 1915.

Fighter doctrine also developed slowly. Despite the lack of a proper sighting and alarm network, the Supreme Command insisted upon using scramble tactics rather than mounting standing patrols. Poor climbing performance therefore ensured that any intruders escaped unhurt, while pilots complained about long periods of inactivity and inadequate performance. Although born in 1915 with the forming of the 1st Nieuport Biplanes Squadron, the Italian fighter arm was initially hampered by the inadequacy of its Nieuport 10 two-seaters. This is shown by the total number of combats in the air reported by the Italians in that year — a mere seven — while Austrian figures report two victories in the air on the Italian front against 85 losses to all causes on all fronts.

In an attempt to improve performance, the Ni.10 were operated as single-seaters but it was only the delivery of the first French-built Ni.11 that brought about a radical change and eventually allowed the first victories to be scored, on 7 April 1916. (Two Austrian losses in November 1915 and February 1916 were recorded but not claimed or confirmed by the Italians). In essence, air war on the Italian front was a year and a half behind that on the Western front.

Bombs over the cities

A unique feature of the Italian front was the use of the large trimotor Caproni bombers which had been developed in 1913-14 through the collaboration of Maggiore Giulio Douhet and designer Gianni Caproni, much against the will of the army hierarchy. The mighty aircraft flew their first sortie on 20 August 1915 against the Austrian airfield at Aisovizza. On 18 February 1916 the Capronis attacked Lubljana, deep inside enemy territory, in an epic action which led to the award of a Gold Medal to Capitano Oreste Salomone — the first airman to receive the highest Italian decoration. The award came for his bravery and skill in nursing his badly damaged bomber home despite the death of his two companions. The action showed the need to install a rear gun turret to protect the machine from rear quarter attacks.

The development of the bomber brought about two developments which were to become commonplace during WW2 — interceptors and escorts. The damage wrought upon the Capronis by Austrian fighters, evidenced by the number of bombers present in many aces' victory lists, led to the use of fighter escorts as early as August 1916.   Although Austria failed to develop the equivalent of the mighty Capronis, it carried out the first raids against cities inside Italy: on 24 February 1916, Austro-Hungarian Lohner B.VIIs and four Lloyds bombed Milan; on the following 11 July, La Spezia, on the coast of Liguria, was attacked by a single Brandenburg C.I flown by Feldwebel Joseph Siegel. While causing only slight damage, these attacks prompted the Italians to plan and establish a territorial air defence network to protect a number of important population centres and industrial areas from possible enemy attacks. By the end of the war this organization had expanded considerably and, despite the lack of further attacks, absorbed considerable resources.

The larger number of bombing raids therefore included population centres on either side of the front — not only major cities such as Venice or Trieste but even small towns such as Piazzola sul Brenta or Dottagliano. Unlike WW2, no attempt at 'area bombing' was made, but while specific military targets were usually sought, the rudimentary sights and lightweight bombs ensured that much 'collateral damage' was caused. Coastal towns such as Ancona, Bari and Durazzo were also quite open to threats, with raids continuing until the final days of war and clear pattern of retaliation whereby each side responded in kind to attacks. The last Italian raid was possibly that on Pola of 22 October 1918, to which the Austrians replied by hitting Venice the following day.

1916 and the Strafexpedition

On 14 May 1916, the Austrian army launched its Strafexpedition (Punitive expedition), designed to thrust down the Trento valley to break into the Veneto plains behind Italian defensive lines. Initially it was planned to comprise eight Austrian and eight German divisions, but when the proposal was turned down by the German Army Chief of Staff, the Strafexpedition was carried out with just 14 Austrian divisions. When the Austrians ran out of steam in late June, the Italians counterattacked.

This bloody episode achieved no major Austrian gain, except to place a permanent threat to the rear of the Isonzo front. Although in 1916 air activity in this area had been limited largely to reconnaissance, over the next two years the Austrian presence caused Italians to deploy fighter units here and the skies above places such as Asiago, Arsiero, the Altipiano dei Sette Comuni (Plateau of the Seven Communes); the Frenzela and Astico valleys became frequent fighting grounds and their names appear frequently in the victory lists of both sides.

Here, as well as on the Isonzo front, the Italian supreme command resorted to brutal frontal assaults in an attempt to break the line. More often than not, this only resulted in horrendous losses — just as in France. The same did not occur in the air, however, where neither side adopted an offensive policy similar to that of the RFC. Consequently, opportunities for encountering the enemy were much fewer and again this is reflected in the number of victories. At this time, fighter patrols tended to be flown in twos or threes at most, mainly inside friendly lines, dashing across only in hot pursuit of the occasional intruder.

The Austrian 1916 programme had foreseen assigning each corps a Flik and each army a Flik and two heavy combat companies, for a total of 48 Fliks but at the end of the year only 37 had been actually activated. New flying schools were formed, but it is worth noting that — in marked contrast to other major belligerents — observers could upgrade their training in the field to achieve pilot status. This route was followed, among others, by Franz Gräser at Flik 32. Another not uncommon Austrian practice was for single-seat fighters to be an integral part of two-seater units for escort purposes. One such unit was Flik 12D, a divisional reconnaissance unit with several KD fighters on strength.

Always adhering to a largely French model, Italian army aviation was also greatly expanded in 1916, eventually reaching in September a 'mobilised' (i.e., operational) strength of 42 squadrons with 328 aircraft, with 369 pilots (140 officers), 162 observers and 123 gunners. Training was greatly accelerated and took place only in proper schools with a 20-24 week course, some 568 pilots being licenced in the first five months of the year. According to official data, Italians achieved a total of 56 confirmed victories in aerial combat whereas the Austrians claimed 35 victories on the Italian front and suffered 176 losses from all causes on all fronts.

Aircraft and industry

Production totals afford a valid measure of the different scale of the air war on the Italian front. Whereas Germany produced slightly less than 48,000 aircraft, Italy built approximately 12,000 and Austria-Hungary only completed 5,180, including 413 seaplanes. Despite considerable wartime progress — Italian output peaked at 541 aircraft per month in 1918 — both countries suffered from the failure of various ambitious production programmes. In Italy, for instance, the structural weakness of the SIA 7 biplanes resulted in the waste of several hundred airframes, whereas it was only Giulio Macchi's stubborn refusal to join the bomber programme that allowed Nieuport-Macchi to deliver over 1,200 fighters in the last war year. Indeed, with the exception of limited numbers of Spad 7 and 13s and a couple of hundred Ni.27s, virtually every Italian fighter was built by Nieuport-Macchi.

The two opponents shared a largely agricultural economy, which experienced not only considerable difficulty in improving output but also in advancing technology. The main novelty was represented by the Caproni bombers, which were an early feature of the campaign, but in essence both belligerents relied on fighter technology transferred by their respective allies.

Both the Italians and the Austrians seemed to do better with reconnaissance machines, developing upgraded variants of the basic designs. In this case, the Austrians found the Hansa-Brandenburg Br. C.I family extremely well suited to gradual evolution. On the Italian side, the SIA 7 failure meant that the twin-boom Farman types outlived their usefulness. Indeed, a single Voisin unit, the 25ª Squadriglia, soldiered on until Caporetto, its hopelessly outdated aircraft taking horrendous losses in its final weeks of service.

Naval air war

Adriatic coastline was in essence a continuous border, with many population centres and harbours open to attack and difficult to defend. In its central area, the width of the Adriatic proved too much of a challenge for early seaplanes, especially their engines. The situation was very different in the south, where the narrow channel between Puglia and Albania was easily crossed, and in the north, where aircraft plying the route between Venice and Trieste could always seek haven along the Venetian coast. Although both sides would devote considerable resources to patrol and defend the entire Adriatic coastline, operational realities soon dictated that these areas became the fulcrum of activity.

The evolution of naval aviation followed the same pattern as its land-based equivalent, with an initial period of forced multitasking until specific types could be developed for specific tasks. Interestingly, various permutations of the Lohner flying boat equipped both sides in large numbers. This was a direct result of the forced landing of the Austrian Navy's L40 near Ravenna on 27 May 1915, for the Italians recognised the design as superior to their own and ordered Nieuport-Macchi to copy it — a feat accomplished in a mere 33 days. Repeatedly improved with upgraded engines, Italian and Austrian Lohners were still in service at the end of the war. The types were so similar that the Italians often pressed captured Lohners into service through-out the war, sometimes without so much as changing the engine.

The K series heavy flying boats remained unique to the Austrian navy. The mainstay of the naval bomber offensive, the K boats, proved a very difficult threat to counter and very few were lost in aerial combat. Their presence was largely responsible for the development of the Macchi seaplane fighters. The first of these, the M.5, basically consisted of Nieuport 17 sesqui-plane wings fitted to a single-seat hull — a pattern followed by the Austrians with their CC 'boats, which used the star-strutted wing of the KD landplane fighter. The final Italian seaplane fighter, the M.7, was an entirely new design with a performance equal or superior to landplanes. Very few were in service at the end of the war.

From an organizational point of view, the two opposing navies used 'stations' with a mixed complement of types. The fighter section led by Austrian naval ace Gottfried Banfield, for instance, was never a squadron. In 1917 the Italian navy adopted a squadron model which led to separate fighter and reconnaissance units, but because these shared the same bases pilots were frequently swapped between squadrons; also, unsuccessful pilots were occasionally demoted to observers.

1917 and Caporetto

Under an expansion programme calling for a total 68 Fliks by the end of the year, some 31 new Fliks were formed, all destined for the Italian front. A greater degree of specialisation was also introduced, with each Flik being identified according to its duties as either Divisional (adding suffix D to its number) or Corps (K), Fighter (J), Photographic (P or RB, depending on equipment), Long-range Reconnaissance (F), Heavy (G) and Ground Attack (S, mostly upgraded D units). There were 14 flying schools, with a total of 1,134 student pilots. In addition, a different command structure resulted in a greater degree of independence for aviation, belatedly following the experience of the other belligerents.

Despite this, the tide had turned and the Italian output, although still largely comprised of archaic types, was beginning to translate into a generalised superiority. During the 10th battle of the Isonzo (12 May-7 June), Austro-Hungarian air activity saw 64 aircraft fly 711 sorties, which resulted in 210 engagements and 22 victory claims against seven admitted losses. A total of ten tons of bombs were dropped.

The battle coincided with the forming, on the Italian side, of the 91ª Squadriglia which incorporated the best pilots of the 70ª and proceeded to earn an enviable reputation as the 'Aces' Squadron'. The Italians made a similar tactical use of aviation in June, during the bloody offensive around the Ortigara. At its peak, on 19 June, Austrian positions were struck by 5.5 tons of bombs, dropped from 61 bombers accompanied by 84 other aircraft, opposed by just three fighters and 23 two-seaters. The effort increased again in the summer, during the last Italian attack on the Isonzo: August saw over 200 aircraft available every day and the Austrians immediately began attributing the pressure to foreign reinforcements which in reality only came in reduced scale after Caporetto.

Known to the Central Powers as Operation Waffentreue, this attack is usually known as the 'Battle of Caporetto' and is probably remembered by most through the vivid — albeit embellished — narration of Ernest Hemingway's *Farewell to Arms*. To avoid the stigma attached to the name, Italians sometimes call it the 12th battle of the Isonzo. In any case, the Austro-German attack began in the early morning of 24 October and, through massive recourse to gas, broke through the Italian lines at Plezzo and fell upon the 19th Division at Tolmino. When it gave way, the Germans were able to march up the valley to Caporetto, cutting off the 4th Corps and part of the 7th. Within two weeks, the Italian army was rolled back to the Piave, where for another month it faced the 'halting battle'. The Piave line became both a material and a symbolic rallying point for the entire nation.

Once again, the intensity of the ground fighting was mirrored in the air, the Central Powers throwing aircraft into the battle to consolidate and exploit their success and the Italians in a desperate attempt to stem the tide. Fighters flew several sorties per day, while even the mighty Capronis were used in the tactical role against the advancing infantry columns. Even naval aircraft were called to operate over land. In consequence, losses and victories in this period were high on both sides.

The accelerated pace allowed new pilots to build up their scores with much greater speed than had been possible to some of their colleagues who had been in the line for months.

The aftermath of Caporetto left the Italian army air service badly depleted, with only 378 aircraft distributed amongst 59 squadrons and two flights, with 497 pilots, 284 observers and 152 gunners. Slightly more than 100 aircraft were fighters, almost evenly divided between obsolete Ni.11s and the new Spad 7s and Hd.1s. Although the Italian Supreme Command officially confirmed some 170 victories for the year (versus 247 Austrian claims), the Austro-German offensive had wiped out an entire year of Italian buildup — two years in terms of airfields (22 of which were lost), depots and other infrastructures. Only limited consolation was derived from the evident qualitative superiority, evidenced on 26 December in the famous air battle of Istrana, and the much reduced front.

Allies: the French, British and German presence

In the early phases of the war, the lack of Italian fighter units had prompted the French to deploy fighters to defend Venice. Later, reconnaissance units were added. But it was the aftermath of Caporetto which led to a far greater Allied presence. Although made conditional upon the removal of General Cadorna, the Italian Supreme Commander, Britain and France despatched several divisions to Italy, where they were initially deployed along the river Mincio to form a secondary line of defence behind the Piave. With the Army came the Royal Flying Corps, with four squadrons.

The aid was undoubtedly appreciated, especially in helping to buttress the shaken Italian morale, but relations were to some extent uneasy. The Italians found British claims to be out of proportion — 550 victories in a few months, against 633 Italian claims for the entire war — and could seldom find corroboration in the form of wrecks or aircrew.

This was especially evident during the lean winter of 1917, during which Italians often complained, in both private accounts and official documents, about the lack of aerial opposition. This was often explained with the myth of Austrian unwillingness to fight. In reality, the Austrian war machine was hampered by growing shortages of almost everything. In the last two winters of the war, a lack of coal often stopped production, with dire consequences upon supplies. Almost everything became 'Ersatz', replacement or makeshift.

Despite these major shortages, the German presence was limited in scope. The troops which spearheaded the Caporetto breakthrough, for instance, had been sent to the Italian front to *rest* from the Western one.

News of the presence of foreign units spread quickly on both sides and led to an interesting development: whenever an aggressive foe was encountered, it was attributed not to the main enemy but to its ally. Thus every Hanriot became a British Sopwith in Austrian eyes, and every Albatros D.III a German D.V. Only occasionally were these identifications correct: the famous air battle of Istrana of 26 December 1917 was started by a German attack on one of the main air bases on the Piave front. But by and large, the war remained an Italian-Austrian affair. According to Italian statistics, the year closed having witnessed some 700 dogfights in which 170 victories were claimed.

June 1918: the last Austrian attack

While the Austrians, surprised and exhausted by the sheer size of their unexpected success, caught their breath, the Italians rebuilt their Army under the new supreme commander Armando Diaz. To prevent shocked veterans from demoralizing the new recruits (the so-called 'boys of '99'), these were formed into separate regiments. More attention was devoted to internal propaganda and morale building, which included a greater generosity in awards and decorations. On the aeronautical side, a 'fighter mass' and a 'bomber mass' were created which allowed more powerful and concentrated strikes.

The Austrians envisioned 100 Fliks and 1,000 pilots by the end of the year, but despite completing 2,378 aircraft in 1918 this goal was only partially attained. By mid-June there were available 77 Fliks, 16 of which were fighters, and four Bombenfluggeschwader.

Diaz resisted calls for a Spring offensive, anticipating the need to counter the expected Summer Austrian attack which came on 15 June but ran out of steam in just over a week. The Austrians crossed the Piave near the Montello, but after heavy fighting were forced to retreat.

Once again, the full scale ground offensive led to increased air activity, more encounters and climbing losses: the Austrians claimed 43 aircraft and two balloons while admitting 31 aircraft and a balloon lost; the Italians claimed 72 aircraft and five balloons, but their losses included the ace of aces Francesco Baracca (lost on a strafing attack against the Montello on 19 June) and Flavio Torello Baracchini, who on 25 June suffered abdominal wounds which kept him out of combat until the armistice. Further grievous losses came in July, when Scaroni was severely wounded and Linke-Crawford was killed in combat.

On 9 August the 87ª Squadriglia flew a daring leaflet raid over Vienna, covering some 600 miles in six hours and 40 minutes. Conceived by the poet Gabriele D'Annunzio, who despite being 55 years old took part in a specially-modified SVA two-seater, the mission was virtually unopposed by Austrian defences and became a resounding propaganda success.

The Vittorio Veneto offensive

Despite Allied pressure for a Summer counterattack and internal fears of a sudden peace which would find the Austrians still occupying large parts of the Veneto, Diaz held out until late October. Eventually, news of peace rallies in Berlin and Vienna and the announced 'federalist' reform of the Dual Monarchy forced Diaz to attack on 26 October. After three days, the Austrians were already asking for an armistice, which the Italians delayed until 3 November in order to secure territorial gains and — above all — the lasting impression of a field victory.

Once again, the pace of the air war quickened. As part of an air force which counted some 400 serviceable aircraft, including British and French units, the Italian fighter mass was again unleashed. Victory claims were high, but the enthusiasm and diminished opposition also resulted in a large amount of overclaiming.

In the final war year, the Austrians suffered 525 losses to all causes on all fronts against 227 victory claims, while Italian claims for the year ran to 647 including Franco-British successes. As on every other front, and in every other war, the vast discrepancies in these figures would only be slowly cleared up over the years by enthusiasts, researchers and historians.

CHAPTER TWO

General Observations

The Italian Aces

In 1911, Italy became the first country to use aeroplanes in war and in WWI it produced over 12,000 aircraft. Despite this, its aviation history is largely unknown, and its WWI history even more so − the standard books of Italy's air war are fast approaching sixty years of age. In addition, a 1991 survey of WWI research carried out over the previous 30 years showed the Italian presence to have been limited to 11.2% of general stories but, more significantly, to 1.5% of biographies, 0.88% of heraldic studies and a flat 0% of unit histories.

This is in sharp contrast with the recent explosion of interest in Austria-Hungary, Italy's main opponent during the war, whose pilots and equipment have since the mid-1980s enjoyed a steady stream of articles and books.

While the reasons for this situation remain unexplained, it is therefore hardly surprising that this book represents the first attempt to compile and publish complete lists for all of the Italian aces of WWI which were officially recognized by Italian authorities at the end of the war – a total of 45 pilots, including 42 Army flyers and three Navy ones.

The numbers' war on the Piave

Among the first consequences of the lack of comparative studies on the Italian front is the wild oscillation in the number of victories and losses on either side. For instance, official Italian sources put Italian losses between 104 and 206 (variously said to comprise, with little respect for either consistency or mathematics, up to 127-128 landplanes, 37 seaplanes, 12-19 airships, 30 balloons) against 423 victories (including some 70 Allied) claimed by Austro-Hungarian aces and over 80 by German Jastas on the Italian front. Conversely, on the Allied side, the Italian Army pilots claimed 633 aircraft and balloons, the four British squadrons over 550 (420 of which were claimed by 43 aces), the sole French squadron adding another 16. Clearly, even taking into account double counting on all sides and OOCs on the part of the British, something is amiss.

Part of the problem arises from uncertainty on the criteria followed in assembling the data. Even without thorough cross-verification, it is easy to spot a discrepancy between the 128 landplanes lost and the over 1,000 Italian fliers deceased on operations (plus 750 in training). Even allowing for the greater incidence of multicrew aircraft on personnel losses, the average of six crewmen per aircraft seems on the high side.

Scoring systems

Possibly because of the heavy French influence on the development of the Italian fighter branch, the Italian scoring system does not appear to have differed much from the French system. Provided the destruction of an enemy aircraft could be confirmed, the same victim could be attributed in full to each participant in a given combat. Sharing was not automatic, however, and squadron records often attributed a victory only to some of the pilots involved in the action. In other words, it would appear that some kind of judgement was made at squadron level as to who had decisively contributed to the combat. Partial credit or half victories were not used, nor were aircraft strafed on the ground counted. 'Probable' and 'out of control' victories were not counted in any way.

Observation balloons (universally known as 'draken' in Italian) only counted if set on fire or in any other way seen positively destroyed. Balloons lowered to the ground did not count, even when the crew bailed out, nor did punctured envelopes which might be repaired and reflown.

Although no formal rules have been found regarding victory credit for the crews of multi-seat aircraft, individual cases would appear to indicate that the gunner and pilot in command each received credit. The entire question is to a large extent academic, as no gunner or bomber pilot has been discovered to have achieved ace status.

Whatever the system, the Italians appear to have applied it strictly. This is borne out clearly in the scores of major aces such as Baracca, Ruffo and Scaroni, which stand up very well to present scrutiny. The disallowed claims of Ranza and Baracchini testify to an admirable scruple and, taking into consideration the relative paucity of aircraft on either side of the front, speaks highly of the aces' skills.

The Records

In compiling the individual victory lists, we have drawn almost exclusively on Italian archival sources. This was dictated as much by necessity as by choice – the former stemmed from the utter lack of a reliable modern bibliography on Italian airpower in the Great War, the latter from a desire to cut through layers of oft-repeated myths and get back to what was originally put down.

Four main types of records were used in compiling the lists. The biographies and framework of each individual's service and score were first drawn up based on the personal records held by the Italian Air Force's Historical Office. The material in these files – only recently recovered and not available to previous researchers – can range from a basic card detailing transfers and administrative matters to a full flight log – combat reports, correspondence with the postwar review commission, even training records and examination transcripts. For a number of reasons, no such files were available for naval personnel, but luckily biographical details were found elsewhere.

Details were fleshed out from squadron records, also held by the Air Force, and again quite varying in content depending on luck, thoroughness of the squadron clerk, dedication of the office staff and other such bureaucratic variables. Some files abound in combat reports; others lack even the 'Diario Storico' (Historical Diary, equivalent to a British Operations Record Book – ORB), this being the case with the élite 91ª Squadriglia until 1993, when Prince Antonello Ruffo di Calabria presented the Air Force with a copy transcribed for his father in the 1920s. Sometimes, material lacking at squadron level could be found with the parent organization, the Gruppo, or, further up the organizational ladder, with the Comando Aeronautica di Armata (HQ of aviation units attached to a given army), but some gaps persisted despite our best efforts.

A third group of sources were citations for decorations and the Bollettini di Guerra del Comando Supremo (War Bulletins of the Supreme Command, not unlike the British communiqués). Citations are available in a convenient, if long out of print, book called the *Albo d'Oro*. Translating roughly as Roll of Honour, the Albo lists every decorated serviceman, often with a photo, with award details and full citations for major decorations – excluding, in other words, war crosses and foreign awards. Unfortunately, there are many typographical errors and the citations are not themselves without flaw. War Bulletins take the usual form of describing specific actions of military significance or morale value – such as an air victory – but do not usually provide the key elements of time, confirmation, victim. Unlike the famed Nachrichtenblatt, they do not contain a systematic running total of an individual's victories – although notable achievements such as a 25th or 30th victory were obviously noted.

A further reference came from the lists and announcements which appeared during the war in the Italian press, and particularly the aviation magazine *Nel Cielo* and its predecessors. Although often very quick to report from the front, and profusely illustrated with useful portraits, *Nel Cielo* must be used with some caution, as the news it carried does not always withstand close examination – it is at best a claim or a suggestion – but never proof. One of the reasons for this inaccuracy is that the journal relied on semi-official reports which it printed hurriedly, without the benefit of cross verification, intelligence or follow-up. Much to their credit, the editorial staff seemed to realize this and in March 1919 complained that "a greater accuracy in the compilation of these statistics would have been much better." Unfortunately it seems that some enthusiasts stopped reading *Nel Cielo* before reaching this crucial passage.

Finally, and exercising all the care necessary with words put on paper many years after the events, we have occasionally resorted to memoirs or other autobiographical material which might help understand why a certain victory was not accepted or claimed, or why a pilot known to have taken part was not considered as having shared in the victory.

Make up of the victory lists

Setting out to compile an Italian victory list has meant venturing into an uncharted land, without the benefit of the extensive and exhaustive network of fact-finding and research which has been devoted to other countries. In this respect, the Italian aces are unlike those who were on the Western front and rather closer to those of the Eastern front – although of course with the marked difference that archives exist and are easily accessed.

The lack of individual aces' lists is rather disconcerting, considering that the Army released its official score on 1 February 1919, after the Comando Generale di Aeronautica's 5ᵃ Sezione, the Informazione (Intelligence) office, had reviewed each pilot's claims. This document, the so-called Bongiovanni list, reproduced in its entirety in Appendix IV, is unfortunately not without errors, as it excludes at least one confirmed ace, Chiri. Furthermore, the 5ᵃ Sezione's stated aim to eliminate dubious claims created much ill feeling amongst those who saw their score cut, or those who thought that it had not followed consistent criteria. Baracchini, for instance, never overcame the idea that Piccio had deliberately reduced his victories, and almost half a century later his brother was still resentful. More diplomatically, Scaroni said that he had never found out which of his claims had been disallowed to produce his official score of 26. In the lower scores, soldier Panero and sergeant Arrigoni (credited with 5 victories each in February 1918) and sergeant Poli (6) were among the names dropped from the list.

In any case, in January 1919 the 5ᵃ Sezione sent individual ace-candidates lists of both allowed and disallowed victories, compiled from its records, and asked pilots to submit any further evidence. Certainly the short time allowed for this revision (Parvis was contacted on 11 January and asked to submit comments by 20 January) militated against its accuracy and explains in part the ill feelings it raised.

But Italy did not follow up on its good start and – with the exception of the national hero Baracca, whose score was carved in the stone of many monuments – individual lists were never made public. Worse yet, the review commission's papers have seemingly gone astray, making it very difficult to understand why a particular claim was allowed or not. Tenente Guido Masiero's score is a case in point. In his personal file, preserved in the archives of the Italian Air Force Historical Office, the commission's final report can still be read – one of the few cases in which this vital document has survived. It consists of a single, mimeographed sheet with typed details, stating that five victories (identified merely by date, with no reference to location, type, time, or sources) were allowed and four (again only cursorily recalled) disallowed. Everything quite clear and straightforward – until, having begun the cross-verification procedure, the researcher discovers that Masiero had claimed 11 victories (two of which have vanished without trace) and that among those that disappeared in the night is the one which, in 1916, had led to Masiero being awarded his first Silver Medal. Again, something is amiss.

The basic decision was, in keeping with the criteria followed in the previous three volumes, to let the record stand: it is virtually impossible today to understand why the review board chose to acknowledge a certain claim rather than another. Therefore, Masiero is listed as a five-victory ace. His other claims (we have traced a total of 10, one short of the 11 mentioned in the personal file) are listed as a possible starting point for further research. We have taken a similar attitude in the case of pilots such as Resch, whom the review committee put at four victories but was carried as an ace by Bongiovanni: it is entirely possible that the pilot forwarded detail of the missing victory without the letter having been preserved. Thus, the hasty demotion of Resch would have been unjustified.

Because victories could take a long time to confirm, the 14th victory (in chronological order) might be recognized after the 16th (in the official procedure). Again, following the precedent set with the previous volumes for clarity, victories are listed in strict numerical order. Unnumbered entries represent claims which were not officially sanctioned: any details available are keyed at the bottom.

Confirmations

The 'Provisional Norms on the Employment of Fighter Squadrons', issued on 20 June 1918 by the Fighter Squadrons Inspectorate (i.e. by Piccio, who had assumed the new post a few months earlier), set out clear instructions regarding victory claims. Upon landing, a pilot was expected to compile his combat report before discussing the sortie with anyone: "It is absolutely forbidden for a pilot to go personally begging for testimonies the majority of which cannot be considered valid, whether because of the incompetence of the witnesses or because of their provenance." For a victory to be confirmed, the document continued, it was necessary to have at least two confirmations from observers — whether artillery or balloon or front line — who could state beyond doubt that the victim had fallen with a fire on board or that it had crashed within their line-of-sight. In this case, a precise location was to be supplied.

Victories could also be confirmed by other irrefutable evidence such as POW interrogation, matching declarations by several other pilots who had witnessed the fight, or undoubted vertical plunge witnessed by several observers.

The norms added that "aviation commands have available within the Armies [to whom they are attached] the necessary means of information and that it is their duty to request such should they not be provided immediately." This rather cryptic sentence is thought to refer to the 'Informazione' (Intelligence) detachments which among other things collated the aviation units' reports with those of ground observers and other sources. Given the rather limited extension of the Italian front and the low frequency of aerial combat, the intelligence source often provided valuable insight.

Although on paper this system seems fair and effective, a measure of caution should be exercised: there is no way of knowing to what extent these instructions were actually followed or whether the pressures of war conspired to make them remain wishful thinking.

Naval Aces

In Italy and abroad, Tenente di Vascello Orazio Pierozzi is generally considered the sole Italian naval ace, a truism repeated even in the recent history published by the Italian Navy Historical Office. Research for this book, however, unearthed a document entitled; 'Official list of confirmed aerial victories of Navy pilots during the 1915-1918 War', which included two further pilots with five victories. Both were therefore included, while another, credited with four official victories, was deleted.

Fleshing out the victory lists was made somewhat complex by the fact that the Navy organized its air service along 'station' lines. Accordingly, the copious surviving papers are not divided by squadron but by station, with combat reports entwined with administrative, logistic and sundry other matters of a much larger organization. Sadly, although the archive is a treasure trove of naval aviation material, in many respects it seems that the operational side lost out.

The Navy appears not to have developed its own scoring criteria. Rather, it seems to have shared the Army's French-inspired system, allowing widespread double counting (or sharing) but banning OOCs. Because much fighting happened within a short distance of the coast, seaplanes forced down were often recovered by naval vessels, while the Italians developed a daring technique to recover their aircrew even with single-seat flying boats. In any case, seaplanes forced down and recovered were counted as full victories.

Since the main seaplane duels took place between Venezia and Trieste, it was our good fortune to have available an excellent recent history of the Austro-Hungarian Naval Air Service, organized chronologically by seaplane station and offering a detailed reconstruction of losses to match Italian claims. Despite this, we were unable to eliminate some minor gaps.

Locations

As on any other front, providing the exact location can be the key to matching claims and losses, or, indeed, disallowing them. It is therefore only natural that intelligence officers required pilots to provide an exact location. It is however just as obvious that a pilot engaged in combat might not be able to pinpoint a grid reference or, for that matter, even a precise time for a combat. Thus it is often the case that a combat report, an ORB and a confirming message all bear different locations. Sometimes even pilots sharing in a given victory give different locations. On some occasions this difference is merely a matter of degree of accuracy — 'Villa Ancillotto' indicates a very specific building but is of little use unless one already knows that the Ancillotto family, whose son was himself an ace, lived in San Donà di Piave. The same is true for most 'Casa' and 'Cascina', which mean 'House' or 'Farm' and are almost meaningless without reference to a town. Outside urban centres, locations can often be expressed in terms of a 'Mont' or 'Col' (mountain or hill), but also in terms of the valley below them, or as a 'Cima 12' (Hill 12). Again, it is possible for participants, especially if from different squadrons, to use different names for what is essentially the same place. A typical example is the Maserada sul Piave, Cimadolmo and Grave di Papadopoli, which refer to places within a two mile radius — i.e. towns on either side of the Piave and an island between them. We have wherever possible tried to give either the most accurate or the most explanatory name, occasionally adding details in the notes, and have in all cases exercised our best judgement when faced with conflicting names.

Aircraft types

Although aircraft identification tables and posters were widely available and distributed, Italian pilots do not seem to have honed their recognition skills too finely. This conclusion, no matter how unflattering to national pride, is inescapable after poring over reams upon reams of papers in which victims are described in the most cursory manner with the catch-all names 'Albatros' (by far the prevalent definition and usually referring to two-seaters rather than fighters), 'Aviatik' (often DFW C.Vs) or, rather infrequently, 'Brandenburg'; similarly, flying boats other than Lohner or K-types, easily identified by the large serial numbers obligingly painted on their hulls, would often be labelled 'Ago' or 'Abwehr' — although in fairness it should be added that the former name appeared even in Jane's All the World's Aircraft!

Some limited progress is evident towards the end of the war, and occasionally crews provided additional clues such as 'big', 'small' or the like. Still, participants in a given fight would often identify their victim in different ways. Further problems arose in late 1917 with the arrival of foreign units, i.e. German and British: suddenly all Allied aircraft became Sopwiths and Bristols, while the enemy consisted solely of German types. Obviously this does not help the researcher very much.

Still, in order not to compromise the written record, where no reliable alternative existed these vague terms have been retained. Where the documents allowed, however, we have endeavoured to specify whether the victim was a fighter or reconnaissance machine (which the Italians often called simply 'biposto', or '2-seater', a definition we have adopted). On a few occasions recovery crews or infantry were able to verify serial numbers, which is a great help in both confirming the victory (for it proves there was a wreck on the ground) and its unit, crew and other details. Again, a drawback is that numbers could be miswritten or misinterpreted, or the wrong number (e.g., a component number) noted. Despite these hurdles, in several instances photographic or documentary evidence have allowed us to specify the type, serial and even crew name.

Who got whom?

A source we have decided not to use are the lists privately produced in Italy in the 1960s and thence distributed via the enthusiasts' grapevine. Because of the general scarcity of archival resources available at the time, these documents tended to rely mostly on citations and wartime journalistic accounts. Often, in a desperate attempt to reconcile otherwise incomplete data, these lists ended up matching victors and victims who had in reality operated at the opposite end of the front, or on aircraft completely different from those claimed, or even — in some extreme cases — with pilots deceased in training accidents hundreds of miles away from the fighting.

Rather than mismatch, then, we have preferred to let the record stand as it was originally put down day by day. Where a fact is controversial, brief details are supplied in the notes; where it is unknown (as is often the case with hours), it is shown as such or simply left blank.

CHAPTER THREE

Unit Histories

The Italian Squadron numbering system

The early history of Italian aviation units is made rather confusing by the Italian Army adopting three different numbering systems in quick succession in the first year of the war. A brief explanation will thus be in order.

Initially, units were numbered according to type, with new numbers being assigned at every re-equipping. The potential for chaos was realised when, in the summer of 1915, many Blériot XI or Nieuport monoplane units were upgraded with new equipment and took up new identities.

On 29 November 1915 the Comando Supremo therefore decided to simplify things by adopting a system based on roles. From 1 December 1915, the 8ª Squadriglia Biplani Nieuport became for instance the 1ª Squadriglia Caccia (Fighters), co-existing with a Caproni-equipped 1ª Squadriglia Offesa (Offence, meaning Bombing) and so on.

This second system was short lived, as on 15 April 1916 it was decided to consolidate unit numbers in a single sequence and drop the role suffix in favour of a generic 'Aeroplani'. Although requiring some minor changes, such as moving a batch of SAML reconnaissance squadrons from the 70s to the 120s range, this method proved satisfactory and was retained until the end of the war. Some fine tuning was introduced in September 1917 by reserving numerical ranges for specific types, e.g. 1 through 20 for Caproni bombers, 21 to 40 for Savoia-Pomilio SP.3s.

In practice, the final twist made little difference for fighter units, most of which already fell within the 70-85 range reserved for Nieuport and Hanriot squadriglie. Production problems also conspired to produce gaps, thwarting plans to establish squadrons in the 86-100 range. Initially reserved for SVA and Spad fighters, the series saw only the 87ª and 91ª in front line service. Similarly, the failure of the mass-production programme planned around the SIA 7b biplane meant that the 41-60 range was eventually used for SVA reconnaissance units. Many others, although planned and put through the initial steps of activation, remained on paper.

To avoid unnecessary confusion, unit histories have been arranged according to the definitive system. Older designations, where applicable, have been inserted merely as references pointing to the final number. Also for the sake of clarity, it has been decided to omit the numerous territorial defence flights formed from 1916 onwards, none of which ever engaged a single enemy aircraft — largely because major cities such as Rome, Naples and Florence were well beyond the range of Austro-Hungarian aircraft.

A similar simplification has been made with regard to naval aviation, whose organization relied more on 'stations' than squadrons. Although these existed, being numbered from 240 upwards in the September 1917 system, their structure was quite flexible and in practice each station tended to pool its manpower and resources. Furthermore, few of the many naval squadrons were actually used in the fighter role, a fact which is reflected in their low scores. Only the two Venezia squadrons, which actively and continuously engaged the enemy throughout the conflict, are thus included here.

At the end of each unit history the reader will see a list of aces who served wholly or in part with the particular Squadriglia. Where a pilot flew with more than one unit, the figure in brackets gives his overall score. For ease of reference and completeness, aces or future aces who served with the unit without scoring any victories with it are also included. The listing is by number of victories with the squadriglia, then by total victories and, in case of further parity, in alphabetical order.

Sezione Difesa Albania
see 85ª Squadriglia

1ª Squadriglia Caccia
see 70ª Squadriglia

2ª Squadriglia Caccia
see 71ª Squadriglia

8ª Squadriglia Nieuport Biplani
see 70ª Squadriglia

70ª Squadriglia

The first Italian fighter unit, it was formed in Torino on 26 July 1915 as the 8ª Squadriglia Biplani Nieuport with Macchi-built Ni.10s. Intended to replace the Parasol-equipped 8ª Squadriglia Monoplani Nieuport, it was commanded by Capitano Guido Tacchini and was despatched to Aviano the following day. Its first flight was flown by Tacchini on 30 July. On 21 August two aircraft were detached to Campoformido to protect Udine and a first scramble was flown on 25 August. On 8 September the entire unit moved to Santa Caterina, where on 1 December it became the 1ª Squadriglia Caccia. During that month it belonged to the short-lived Udine Defence Group. In February 1916 it began re-equipping with the Ni.11, which on 7 April allowed Baracca to score a victory which was the first for him, for the squadron and for Italian aviation. On 15 April a new change in name gave birth to the 70ª, whose pilots quickly built up their score with great success. Olivari was soon proclaimed the first Italian ace, although many of his early victories would later be disallowed. In March 1917 the 70ª joined the 10° Gruppo, led by Maggiore Piccio, who was attached to the squadriglia. In April, shortly after receiving its first Ni.17s, the 70ª was split up to create the new 91ª Squadriglia, commanded by Maggiore Tacchini and comprising Baracca, Ruffo, Olivari and Piccio. With its personnel almost completely renewed, and Tenente Cesare Buzzi Grodenigo as CO, the 70ª went through a lean period. The aftermath of Caporetto took it to La Comina (28 October), Arcade and finally Istrana (9 November), where Tenente Rino Corso Fougier assumed command and saw it through a re-equipment with the Hanriot Hd.1. Although scrambled during the famous 26 December air battle, the 70ª failed to score any victories. A few days later it moved to San Pietro in Gu. Capitano Ferdinando Martinengo became CO, but soon fell ill, with Tenente Flaminio Avet temporarily replacing him until the arrival of Maggiore Vincenzo Lombard on 1 February 1918. Two days later the 70ª attacked the Austrian airfield at San Fior. On 14 March the 70ª returned to Istrana, detaching individual aircraft for the defence of Padova. Its strength was 19 aircraft and 15 pilots. On 26 April, Lombard became CO of 6° Gruppo, Avet taking over the 70ª again until the arrival of Capitano Ernesto Segni on 15 April. Two days later, six Hanriots intercepted six Austrians, claiming a two seater and two fighters. On 21 May the 70ª moved to Gazzo Padovano and on 17 June, following Segni's wounding by flak, Avet again took over as CO until the arrival of Capitano Giulio Cesare Paldaoff on 24 July. A single Ansaldo A.1 Balilla arrived on 10 August, followed by two Spad VIIs in August. By September there were 17 pilots, including 9 officers, with 16 Hanriots (two of which equipped for night flying), two Balillas and three Spads. The end of the war found Avet again at the helm, while the squadriglia had totalled 3,164 sorties, 188 combats and 24 victories, against four losses of its own.

Francesco Baracca	8(34)	Alessandro Resch	5(5)
Flaminio Avet	8(8)	Fulco Ruffo di Calabria	4(20)
Leopoldo Eleuteri	7(7)	Luigi Olivari	4(8)
Aldo Bocchese	6(6)	Pier Ruggero Piccio	0(24)

71ª Squadriglia

Formed in Torino on 30 January 1916 as the 2ª Squadriglia Caccia, initially under Capitano Giorgio Chiaperotti. Equipped with Ni.10 and Ni.11s, it deployed to La Comina but lacking machine guns it flew its first sortie only on 18 February. Because of adverse weather, a move to Cascina Farello, begun on 2 March, took almost a month to complete. On 2 April a Ni.10 flown by Sergente Maggiore Barattini with Soldato Moretto as gunner scrambled to intercept an EA gliding overhead with an engine failure: although the aircraft landed at Cascina Bianca and was destroyed on the ground by its crew, no victory was awarded. On 15 April the 2ª was renamed 71ª Squadriglia and on 23 May moved to Villaverla, joining the 3° Gruppo on 8 July. In September-October the 71ª was tasked with protecting the Asiago plateau and supporting the 45ª Divisione. The first Ni.17 was received in December, and on 17 January 1917 Capitano Amerigo Notari became CO, with Chiaperotti taking over 3° Gruppo. On 10 May the squadriglia came under the new 9° Gruppo. Late May saw the arrival of the first Spad VII, a photo variant used for long range reconnaissance. Following the Caporetto disaster, on 26 October the 71ª seconded four pilots to the 82ª at Campoformido, simultaneously receiving a SAML section and being temporarily attached to the 3° Gruppo. When the front reached the Piave, Villaverla came within enemy gunnery range, and on 23 November the 71ª moved to Sovizzo. On 16 December it passed to the new 16° Gruppo. Shortly thereafter, Tenente Palli and Sergente Arrigoni of the 5ª Sezione were attached to it with their SVA, carrying out some daring bombing raids on Innsbruck. On 30 December Sergente Pierino Camperi was KIA. When Notari left the unit on 5 January 1918, Palli, freshly promoted to Capitano, temporarily took over as CO, relinquishing the post in March to Tenente Aldo Anepini. On 28 May he was replaced by Capitano Ettore Croce, who three days later crashed to his death at Castelgomberto, where the 71ª had moved in mid May. Command reverted to Anepini until 16 July, when it passed to Capitano Salvatore Breglia. On 28 August a Hanriot Hd.1 section was received from the 75ª.

On 20 October the 71ª was split up: while the 2ª Sezione remained at Castelgomberto, the 1ª Sezione moved its six Spad VII to Quinto di Treviso to form a mixed squadriglia, with a section from the 75ª, and fly in support of ground operations. On 23 October the 71ª was incorporated in the 17° Gruppo, in turn assigned to the Massa da Caccia. On 29 October it lost Sergente Francesco Bellino, shot down while strafing enemy troops. Despite being wounded in action on 31 October, Breglia stayed at the helm until 6 November.

Since its inception, the 71ª flew 2,994 sorties, engaging in 203 combats and claiming 17 victories against its two combat losses. Another four were lost in accidents (in 1916, Soldato Silvio Amico, 22 March, and Sergente Roberto Ghelfi, 7 June; in 1917, Sergente Dino Menegoni, 21 January, and Croce).

Antonio Amantea	5(5)	Antonio Riva	0(7)
Sebastiano Bedendo	5(5)	Giovanni Sabelli	0(5)

72ª Squadriglia

On 21 October 1917, two sections of the 75ª Squadriglia were detached to form a new unit which assumed the identity of 72ª, previously used by a SAML squadron which had just been renumbered 120ª. Based at Castenedolo and equipped with Nieuport 17 fighters, it was initially assigned to the 3° Gruppo with CO Tenente Giuseppe Rigoni, who started his operational flying on 26 October. A third section was added on 16 November. On 1 December the 72ª transferred to the 9° Gruppo, re-equipping with Hanriot Hd.1s and receiving Capitano Mario Omizzolo as CO. Tasked with the defence of Brescia, it soon had 18 aircraft and pilots on strength. It also added a Farman section (transferred to the 37ª on 1 April 1918) and between 19 January-19 February 1918 detached a flight at Sovizzo.

In June, the 72ª served with the Massa da Caccia from Busiaco, returning to Castenedolo in July and transferring to the newly-formed 24° Gruppo. On 7 September, Omizzolo left to take over the 79ª and command passed to Capitano Renato Tasselli. In that month the 72ª came under the 20° Gruppo and then the 17°, moving to Quinto di Treviso. On 23 October it was again assigned to the Massa da Caccia. It was disbanded on 10 December 1918.

The 72ᵃ flew 1,358 sorties, scoring four victories in 61 combats. The losses consisted of five pilots, all in 1918, of which two in combat (13 May, Sergente Ezio Franzi, POW; 19 June, Tenente Camillo Sommariva, died following WIA) and three in accidents (4 August, Tenente Arrigo Archibugi; 23 October, Caporal Maggiore Alfredo Gardenghi; 4 November, Tenente Gino Suali). Its insignia was a red Lion of St. Mark.

Sebastiano Bedendo	0(5)

73ᵃ Squadriglia

On 10 December 1917 the needs of the Macedonian front brought about the forming of the 73ᵃ Squadriglia, achieved by upgrading the 1ᵃ Sezione of the 83ᵃ Squadriglia. The sezione had been formed on 1 May 1917 specifically for Macedonia, sailing from Taranto on 16 May and landing at Saloniki a week later. The first flight from the chosen base at Dudular was made on 1 June. The CO was Sottotenente Giovanni Righi and the entire strength comprised three pilots and a single Nieuport Ni.11, with more arriving over the next few weeks. On 1 August Tenente Ernesto Bonavoglia replaced Righi as CO. It later received Ni.17 fighters and was based at Hill 619, 20 km south of Monastir, in support of the Italian 35ᵃ Divisione. Following the wounding of Bonavoglia (20 January 1918) and Righi (30 January), Tenente Vittorino De Biase assumed command. From April 1918 the 73ᵃ re-equipped with Hanriot Hd.1s and on 24 May it joined the newly formed 21° Gruppo. A second sezione was formed in September 1918 and based at Uskub.

Before being renamed 73ᵃ, the sezione flew 189 sorties, engaging in 15 combats and claiming two victories. From then to the Armistice it added a further 384 sorties and 27 combats. Upon repatriating in August 1919 it was disbanded.

Antonio Riva	0(7)

74ᵃ Squadriglia

Formed at Castenedolo on 20 May 1918 from the 2ᵃ Sezione of the 83ᵃ Squadriglia, it was equipped with Ni.17s and Hanriot Hd.1s. Temporarily commanded first by Capitano Bruno Lodolo and later by Capitano Marinello Nelli, on 8 June it received Capitano Serafino Battaini as CO. Initially assigned to the 9° Gruppo, it passed to the 24° on 7 July, returning to the 9° on 25 September and finally settling with the 20° on 4 October. Three days earlier it had transferred to Ponte S. Marco, where it saw out the war. Tasked with protecting the Tonale mountain pass, it flew 800 sorties, engaging in 14 combats and claiming six victories. A sezione was detached to Cividate Camuno until the end of the war.

Although the 74ᵃ suffered no casualties, on 1 July 1918 Sergente Gino Romuzzi landed by error in Switzerland and was interned. On 19 July Sergente Giosuè Lombardi landed his Hd.1 on Mount Adamello. The squadron was disbanded on 9 February 1919.

75ᵃ Squadriglia

The squadron was formed with Nieuport 11s at Tombetto airfield on 1 May 1916, under Capitano Maffeo Scarpis. Tasked with the defence of Verona, it was assigned to the 3° Gruppo. Two days later it detached a section at Villaverla under Capitano Ettore Croce. A first inconclusive combat took place on 11 June, while on 27 June De Bernardi, Buzio and Nardini shared in the first victory. On 18 August Scarpis was transferred to the Direzione Tecnica in Torino and replaced by Capitano Mario Gordesco, succeeded in December by Capitano Salvatore Calori. Equipment now comprised both Ni.11 and 17s and the sezione was at Ghedi.

On 8 April 1917 Capitano Antonio Bosio assumed command and two days later the 75ᵃ was assigned to the 9° Gruppo. In November it was augmented with a Farman MF.14 night fighter section and Natale Palli's SVA section, soon transferred to the 71ᵃ. In December the squadriglia returned to the reformed 3° Gruppo.

It started receiving Hanriot Hd.1s from 25 March 1918, to which a week later it added the first Nieuport Ni.27. On 14 May it left Tombetta for Ganfardine, operating from Busiago between 15-29 June. With Bosio on leave, Capitano Raffaele Lione (4-20 July) became acting CO. On 20 July he was replaced by Capitano Arturo Oddo, who served until the Armistice. On 28 August 1918 a Hanriot Hd.1 section was detached to the 71ª.

The 75ª was disbanded in March 1919. Its war record came to 2,110 sorties, 89 combats and four victories, for a single loss.

Guido Nardini	1(6)	Alessandro Buzio	1(5)

76ª Squadriglia

One of the most successful Italian fighter units of the war, the 76ª was formed on 25 May 1916 at La Comina (Pordenone) under Capitano Ettore de Carolis, with four Ni.11 biplanes and five pilots. Two days later, the 76ª moved to S. Maria la Longa, joining the 1° Gruppo and flying its first mission on 30 May. On 18 July, Stoppani scored the first victory of the unit. On 24 February 1917 the squadron moved to Borgnano. When De Carolis was promoted Maggiore, Olivi became CO on 22 April but lost his life on 17 June. This initiated a series of short-serving COs (Capitano Salvatori Calori, from the 81ª, 1 July-11 August; Tenente Gastone Novelli 11-21 August, WIA; Tenente Francesco Di Rudinì, from the 91ª, 28 September-3 October KIA). The situation was only stabilised on 1 November 1917 with the appointing as CO of Capitano Alberto De Bernardi, who held the post for about a year. On 9 July the 76ª came under direct control of the Comando Aeronautica 2ª Armata, and for a brief period it was joined by Baracchini, who left it following his wounding on 9 August, but was still technically a squadron member when he was awarded the Gold Medal.

In November 1917 the Caporetto retreat brought about three successive changes of base, Aviano, Arcade and Istrana, where it came under the 6° Gruppo. Here, having converted to the Hanriot HD.1 and receiving new pilots, including Scaroni, who would soon become its top scorer, the squadron took part in the famous air battle, but repeated enemy night raids dictated a move to Isola di Carturo (2 February 1918) and finally Casoni (17 February). On 9 September 1918, Capitano Amerigo Notari assumed command.

The Armistice found the 76ª still at Casoni, with 19 pilots and 21 Hanriot Hd.1s, 17 of which were serviceable. In the course of the war it had flown a total of 5,088 sorties and engaged in combat 340 times, claiming 69 victories suffering just four losses, all in 1917 (14 May, Ten. Broili; 17 June, Ten. Olivi, CO; 3 October, Ten. Di Rudinì, CO; 25 October, Ten. Alessandro Veronesi, flying accident) and its pilots were awarded two Gold Medals, 34 Silvers, 9 Bronzes and 3 War Crosses. Eleven achieved ace status.

Silvio Scaroni	26(26)	Giorgio Michetti	5(5)
Flavio Torello Baracchini	6(21)	Alessandro Buzio	4(5)
Luigi Olivi	6(6)	Mario Fucini	3(7)
Mario Stoppani	6(6)	Gastone Novelli	0(8)
Romolo Ticconi	6(6)	Amedeo Mecozzi	0(5)
Giulio Lega	5(5)		

77ª Squadriglia

Known as the "red heart" squadron on account of its insignia, the 77ª was formed on 31 May 1916 at La Comina and in June moved to Fossalunga. Equipped with Ni.10 two-seaters and commanded by Capitano Pier Ruggero Piccio, it was assigned to the 3° Gruppo. Making its combat debut in July, in August it moved to Cascina Farello. The airfield was bombed on 14 November, killing a pilot and a mechanic. The 77ª soon began receiving Ni.17s and, on 26 January, Piccio was replaced as CO by Capitano Ettore Croce, in turn temporarily replaced for two months by Tenente Ferruccio Ranza. In March the 77ª received its first Spad VIIs and moved to Aiello, but in the summer it lost two pilots. The Caporetto events forced moves to La Comina, Arcade and finally Marcon, where it was placed under 13° Gruppo whose CO, Capitano Mario Gordesco, flew with it together with the temporary CO Tenente Alberto Marazzani. Sottotenente Giannino Ancillotto soon became the hero of those days, specialising in balloon busting and earning a Gold Medal. Unfortunately squadron records were lost in the retreat, preventing a detailed reconstruction of some of the other pilots' scores. On 24 July 1918, Ancillotto scored Italy's first night victory, and in August Capitano Filippo Serafini assumed command. Another pilot, Cabruna, earned a Gold Medal.

The fine wartime record of the squadriglia stood at over 5,000 sorties, with 250 combats and some 50 victories, against four losses.

Carlo Lombardi	8(8)	Ferruccio Ranza	4(17)
Giovanni Ancillotto	7(11)	Pier Ruggero Piccio	1(24)
Ernesto Cabruna	6(8)	Michele Allasia	0(5)
Cosimo Rizzotto	6(6)	Antonio Chiri	0(5)

78ª Squadriglia

Formed on 29 June 1916, it was ready on 16 August and deployed to Campoformido on 3 September. Equipped with seven Ni.11s and a single Ni.10, it was commanded by Capitano Domenico Bolognesi. It flew its first sortie on 9 September 1916 and remained independent until 10 April 1917, when it was attached to the 10° Gruppo. In August it moved briefly to Borgnano, while in October it moved to Aviano, leaving the 10° Gruppo to come directly under the fighter inspector Piccio. It then went to Aviano, where it remained until 8 November, eventually settling at Istrana. On 20 November, Bolognesi handed over his command to Capitano Antonio Riva, recently transferred from the 71ª, who would remain CO until the Armistice. In the same month it replaced the Nieuports with Hanriots. On 24 January 1918 it was assigned to the 15° Gruppo, moving to Nove di Bassano on 16 February. On 15 March it reached San Luca, where it would see the war out. On 18 July it transferred to the 23° Gruppo.

The overall war record came to 4,770 sorties, 443 combats and 88 victories against four losses.

Cosimo Rennella	7(7)	Mario Fucini	4(7)
Antonio Riva	6(7)	Guido Nardini	2(6)
Guglielmo Fornagiari	6(6)	Cesare Magistrini	1(6)
Antonio Chiri	5(5)	Bartolomeo Costantini	0(6)
Guido Masiero	5(5)	Giorgio Pessi	0(6)
Amedeo Mecozzi	5(5)		

79ª Squadriglia

Formed at the Arcade CFS in November 1916, the squadriglia was ready in January 1917 and on the 13th reached Istrana to operate over the Asiago plateau. Its first CO was Capitano Francesco Chimirri and it was initially equipped with Ni.11s, which it later replaced with Ni.17, Ni.27 and Hanriot Hd.1. Unattached to any group, it flew its first sortie on 20 January. On 28 March it detached the 3ª Sezione, including Caporale Cerutti, to defend Padova. On 10 April it was assigned to the 10° Gruppo, switching to the 7° Gruppo a month later. On 2 June 1917, Reali engaged in the first combat of the 79ª, scoring his and its first victory the next day. Together with Cerutti, Nicelli and Imolesi, Reali would be one of the four aces of the squadriglia — uniquely among all fighter squadrons, all NCOs. On 15 June, Chimirri was hospitalised following a take-off stall from Casoni, being replaced by Tenente (Capitano from 10 September) Cesare Bartoletti. On 2 November the 79ª moved to Nove di Bassano, Tenente Umberto Mazzini becoming temporary CO on 3 December while the squadriglia joined the 15° Gruppo. In March 1918 it moved to San Lucia and in June served with the Massa da Caccia, before transferring again to the 23° Gruppo. Upon being promoted capitano, Mazzini became full commander, relinquishing the position on 3 September 1918, Tenente Eugenio Mossi occupying the post until the arrival of Capitano Arturo Freddi Cavallotti on 3 October.

Adopting as its insignia a black she-wolf looking forward, the 79ª flew 4,411 sorties, engaging in 227 combats and claiming 47 victories against five losses.

Marziale Cerutti	17(17)	Giovanni Nicelli	8(8)
Antonio Reali	11(11)	Attilio Imolesi	6(6)

80ª Squadriglia

Formed at the Arcade CFS in February 1917, it was equipped with Ni.11s and commanded by Capitano Mario Gordesco. Assigned to the 1° Gruppo, on 28 February it was at Santa Maria La Longa with five aircraft and as many pilots. By 12 March it had 10 Ni.11s, enabling it to fly its first sortie on 15 March. The first enemy was met two days later by Allasia, but the first victory was scored by Tenente Guido Keller on 24 April. On 30 April the 80ª moved to Aiello, where it remained some six months.

After Caporetto, on 27 October it was ordered to withdraw to La Comina, burning five unserviceable aircraft to avoid their being captured. On 1 November it moved to Arcade, eventually reaching Marcon on 10 November. Gordesco, made CO of 13° Gruppo, handed over his command to Capitano Raoul Da Barberino. He was wounded in a flying accident a week later, being temporarily replaced by Tenente Guido Sambonet. Hanriot conversion was also carried out. The year 1918 saw a succession of commanders, Tenente Giorgio Zoli (6 February-30 April), Capitano Umberto Gelmetti (30 April-7 June) and finally Capitano Achille Pierro from 7 June.

Adopting early on an insignia consisting of a red star on a white circle with a black border (with some variations depending on the aircraft colour), during the course of the war the 80ª flew some 4,637 sorties, engaging in 167 combats with 21 victories for no losses of its own.

Giovanni Ancillotto	4(11)	Michele Allasia	3(5)
Alvaro Leonardi	8(8)	Ernesto Cabruna	2(8)

81ª Squadriglia

Formed at the Arcade CFS in March 1917, it deployed to Borgnano airfield in April under Capitano Salvatore Calori and was attached to the 2° Gruppo. Equipped with Ni.11s, it flew its first sorties on 23 April and engaged in combat the next day. The first victory was scored by Sergente Enrico Sorrentino on 1 May. On 24 June, Capitano Mario Zoboli replaced Calori, who took over the 76ª. In July its own Baracchini became the first fighter pilot to be awarded a Gold Medal.

The Caporetto retreat brought about a move to Aviano (27 October), followed by La Comina (29), Bassano (30) and Arcade (31). Following some confusion about its leadership — Zoboli was supposed to transfer to the 76ª on 1 November, to be replaced by Capitano Alberto De Bernardi of the 86ª, but the orders were rescinded and Zoboli returned on 6 November, while De Bernardi proceeded to the 76ª — on 9 November the 81ª moved to Istrana to join the 6° Gruppo. Here it took part in the 26 December air battle.

In February 1918 the Hanriot Hd.1 started replacing the Nieuport 17s, being later augmented by Ni.27s. On 2 February it moved to Isola di Carturo, but on 17 February it reached its final destination at Casoni. On 25 March, Zoboli was posted to Torino and replaced by Capitano Renato Mazzucco. Baracchini returned in March, but was again wounded on 25 June. On 26 October the 81ª was included in the Massa da Caccia.

At the Armistice it had 21 Hanriots and a Ni.27. Its war record included 4,118 sorties, 230 combats and 34 victories against four own losses.

Flavio Torello Baracchini	13(21)	Alessandro Buzio	1(5)
Gastone Novelli	3(8)	Giulio Lega	0(5)

82ª Squadriglia

Formed at the Arcade CFS in March 1917, it received its equipment before pilots. Although assigned to the 10° Gruppo on 11 April, it was therefore only on 25 May that it was able to despatch its 1ª Sezione to Santa Caterina. Its initial equipment comprised seven Ni.11s and its first CO was Tenente Giorgio Pessi, alias Giuliano Parvis, soon transferred to the 78ª and replaced by Tenente Antonio Fochessati on 9 June. In the first month of service the 82ª engaged in combat four times. On 2 July command passed to Capitano Pietro Cavadini, who held it until 8 September, when Fochessati took over provisionally.

On 28 October the squadriglia retreated to Pordenone, then to Arcade, finally settling at Istrana on 10 November. It then started turning in its Nieuports for new Hanriots, with which it took part in the air battle of 26 December. With Fochessati on leave, Tenente Flaminio Avet served as CO between 3-17 January 1918 and on 29 January Maggiore Ferruccio Coppini took over until the end of the war. In an effort to reduce the attractiveness of Istrana as a target, from 9 January the 82ª moved to San Pietro in Gu, returning to Istrana on 14 March. On 21 May it moved to Gazzo with 13 aircraft and 17 pilots, remaining there until the armistice.

At the end of the war the 82ª had 22 aircraft, including 15 Hanriot Hd.1, six Spad VII and a single Balilla. Its war record included 2,383 sorties, 99 air combats with five victories against one loss. Its aircraft were marked with large 82 numbers and individual code letters.

| Flaminio Avet | o(8) | Alessandro Resch | o(5) |
| Giorgio Pessi | o(6) | | |

83ª Squadriglia

The decision to form the unit was made on 31 March 1917 and two weeks later it was made known that its three sezioni would operate independently at Saloniki, S. Pietro al Campo (Belluno) and Cavazzo Carnico. The first deployed on 1 May and its history is narrated under the heading of 73ª Squadriglia, as it was renamed in December 1917.

The other two sezioni, 2ª and 3ª, both with Ni.11s, also deployed in May 1917. The 2ª, under Tenente Vittorio Bonomi (who would later also serve as CO for the entire squadriglia), scored its most famous victory on 1 September 1917, when Sergente Arturo Dell'Oro crashed his Nieuport into a Br. C.I, bringing it down near Monte Pelf but losing his life in the attempt, a heroic deed which led to the posthumous award of a Gold Medal. In October the 2ª Sezione was further split up between Feltre and Belluno, then retreating to Casoni (2 November), returning to Feltre four days later before finally settling at Marcon (11 November), where it was reunited with the 3ª. On 30 November it received a rocket-equipped Ni.11 for balloon busting and a month later it started re-equipping with the Ni.17.

On 30 January 1918 Capitano Giulio Moroni took over as CO, and on 17 March the two sezioni were again split, with the 1ª (formerly 3ª) going to San Pietro in Gu and the 2ª to Castenedolo. On 22 March Capitano Rino Corso Fougier became CO, with the 1ª Sezione being built up to squadriglia strength in anticipation of the 2ª Sezione becoming the 74ª Squadriglia, this taking place on 19 May.

The 83ª took part in the fierce battles of June 1918, being called upon to perform ground support duties, including dropping 422 bombs of 100-mm calibre. Although the unit served until the very end, its complex history makes it difficult to compile statistics, but it is known that some 2,500 operational flights were made in 1918. Its only loss in addition to Dell'Oro was Tenente Enrico Gadda, who crashed on 23 April 1918 during an escort mission.

84ª Squadriglia

Possibly the shortest lived Italian fighter unit, the 84ª Squadriglia started its existence on 15 May 1917 at the Arcade CFS. Equipped with Nieuports and commanded by Capitano Giuseppe Fancelli, it was declared ready on 1 July and transferred to Santa Maria la Longa on 3 July, assigned to the 1° Gruppo reporting to the 3ª Armata. On 13 July two of its pilots engaged the first enemy aircraft, and on 26 September the 84ª moved to Aiello. On 26 October it was transferred to the 10° Gruppo for unspecified special duties. The Caporetto retreat brought about a move to La Comina, where the 84ª was disbanded on 11 November 1917 without having scored any victories.

The forming of a new Hanriot-equipped unit bearing the same number started at the Ponte San Pietro CFS on 15 October 1918, but with the end of the war in sight the order was rescinded two weeks later.

Ernesto Cabruna	o(8)	Mario Fucini	o(7)

85ª Squadriglia

Although deprived of much military glory by its service on the Albanian front, where opposition was limited, the 85th had a complex origin. The original scheme to form it in July 1917 was shelved on account of the planned number of Nieuport squadriglie having been reached. The number was then assigned to the Sezione Difesa Nieuport which had been operating in Albania since September 1916, first from Durazzo and then from Tahiraga. Initially under Tenente Giovanni Sabelli and then Capitano Ernesto Pellegrino, it was soon assigned to the local 8° Gruppo. To bring the section up to full squadriglia strength, two new sections were formed in Torino on 31 August 1917 and embarked in Brindisi on 12 September, enabling the 85ª Squadriglia to be formed on 22 September.

In February 1918, under the temporary command of Capitano Mario Sarrocchi, the 85ª moved to Piskupi, in Macedonia, where in May it began re-equipping with Hanriot Hd.1s. From 15 June to the Armistice, command passed to Capitano Mario Ponis. While the lack of air opposition limited its victory score, in May-June and August 1918 the squadriglia flew many air support missions. Its overall war record was 925 sorties, losing a single pilot (17 April 1918, Sergente Lorenzo Cortesi, KIA).

Giovanni Sabelli	o(5)

91ª Squadriglia 'Baracca'

Formed at Santa Caterina on 1 May 1917, from resources drawn from the 70ª Squadriglia, it was initially led by Maggiore Guido Tacchini and had four Spad VIIs and three Nieuport Ni.11s. A black griffon was chosen as squadron insignia. The presence in its ranks of pilots like Baracca, Ruffo di Calabria, Ranza and Olivari allowed the new 91ª to claim 14 victories in its first month. On 6 June it moved to Istrana, in support of operations in the Trentino, returning to Santa Caterina on 29 June and being reinforced with other expert pilots, soon becoming known as the 'Squadriglia degli assi' — the aces' squadron, justified by the dozen aces which served with it. In September the 91ª was asked to evaluate the new SVA, the pilots uniformly remarking negatively about its handling as a fighter. On 13 October, Olivari died in a take-off stall, while Sabelli was shot down on 26 October. The Caporetto disaster forced the 91ª to retreat to La Comina, then Arcade and finally Padova, where it was rebuilt. When Baracca and Ruffo were called to Torino to evaluate new fighters, Costantini became temporary CO from 24 December 1917 to 24 January 1918, but the appalling weather prevented flying in this period.

On 11 April the 91ª moved to Quinto di Treviso, acquiring an additional ground support role which on 19 June would lead to the loss of Baracca over the Montello. Two days later, he was succeeded as CO by Ruffo. Shortly thereafter, in an unprecedented move, King Victor Emmanuel III decreed that the 91ª be officially named after Baracca. By 31 August the 91ª had 25 aircraft and 16 pilots. On 18 September Ranza became acting CO while Ruffo was on leave. When the latter was promoted to 10° Gruppo CO, in October, Ranza's new position was officially sanctioned.

Overall, the 91ª claimed 60 victories against six losses. Baracca, Piccio and Ruffo were decorated with Gold Medals.

Francesco Baracca	26(34)	Gastone Novelli	5(8)
Pier Ruggero Piccio	23(24)	Cesare Magistrini	5(6)
Fulco Ruffo di Calabria	16(20)	Giovanni Sabelli	5(5)
Ferruccio Ranza	13(17)	Luigi Olivari	4(8)
Bortolo Costantini	6(6)	Guido Nardini	3(6)
Giorgio Pessi	6(6)	Guido Masiero	o(5)

260ª Squadriglia

The first naval fighter squadron, 260ª was formed in Venezia in early November 1917 under Tenente di Vascello Luigi Bologna. It remained based at the local Sant'Andrea seaplane station throughout the war. Although it tested both the SVA and Hanriot Hd.1 seaplane variants, throughout the period the 260ª was equipped with Macchi M.5 flying boats, with a single M.7 on hand at the Armistice. Among its pilots was Giorgio Parodi, a wealthy Genova entrepreneur, who with his wartime mechanic, Carlo Guzzi, would later establish the Guzzi motorcycle company. In late December, Bologna became CO of the newly formed Venezia seaplane fighter group, his place in the 260ª being taken by Tenente di Vascello Federico Martinengo, who would later become an ace and in June was replaced by Tenente di Vascello Bortolozzo. From March 1918 the new group CO, Tenente di Vascello Orazio Pierozzi, often flew with the 260ª although he did not formally belong to it. During the final Vittorio Veneto offensive its flying boats operated over land in ground support missions. On 2 November, while flying aerobatics over Trieste, evacuated by the Austrians but still unoccupied by the Italians, Pagliacci could not resist the temptation to alight and became the first Italian to enter the city. The 260ª adopted as its insignia six black bands wrapped around the rear fuselage.

Orazio Pierozzi	6(7)	Federico Martinengo	5(5)
Umberto Calvello	5(5)		

261ª Squadriglia

The second fighter unit in the Venezia group, the 261ª was formed in early 1918. From 1 June 1918 to the Armistice it was commanded by Sottotenente di Vascello Domenico Arcidiacono. Although it took part in the same operations as the 260ª, none of its pilots achieved ace rank. At the end of the war, equipped with a mix of Macchi L.3, M.5 and M.8 flying boats, it moved to Trieste.

CHAPTER FOUR

The Aces — Biographical and Claim Notes

ALLASIA Michele   Sottotenente   SQ 37ᵃ, 80ᵃ, 77ᵃ, 5ᵃ SEZ SVA

Born in Ferrara on 24 June 1893, Allasia earned his wings at the Busto Arsizio flying school on 30 May 1916 and served initially with the 37ᵃ Squadriglia Farman, a reconnaissance squadron, totalling 42 hrs flying time. On 9 March 1917 he was posted to the 80ᵃ and was officially rated a Nieuport 11 pilot on 28 April — six weeks after his first dogfight. Wounded over Doberdò on 17 May 1917, Allasia was hospitalised until July, returned to the 80ᵃ, where he scored the first of four victories (in 368 hrs) on 13 July. Allasia had a brief stay with the 77ᵃ, in which he flew little (37 hrs, including, however, some night flying experiments) and was said to have engaged in combat only once. On 8 June 1918 he was transferred to the 5ᵃ Sezione SVA, where he claimed two victories but lost his life on 20 July in a flying accident. In addition to being commissioned sottotenente, Allasia was awarded three Silver Medals (the first was awarded in the field by HRH Emanuele Filiberto, Duke of Aosta on 1 September 1917; a second, also in the field, on 12 December; and a third for the 15-23 June 1918 period) and a Bronze Medal on 25 April 1917. He claimed six victories, five of which were confirmed by the postwar verification committee.

	1917				
–	13 Jul	seaplane	(a)	Trieste	80ᵃ
1	10 Aug	EA			80ᵃ
2	2 Nov	EA			80ᵃ
3	7 Nov	EA			80ᵃ
	1918				
4	15 Jun	EA		Fontigo	5ᵃ Sez
5	23 Jun	EA		Falzè	5ᵃ Sez

(a) no matching Austrian loss found.

AMANTEA Antonio   Sottotenente   SQ 43ᵃ, 71ᵃ

Born on 28 September 1894 in Lecce, he was called up in September 1914 and assigned to the 13th Field Artillery Regiment. On 30 September, ranked caporale, he was sent to the Battaglione Aviatori and on 30 October 1914 reached the Pisa school, gaining his wings on 1 September 1915 in a Blériot. On 31 October he was assigned to 43ᵃ Squadriglia, a reconnaissance unit with whose Caudron G.3 he flew 90 sorties on the Gorizia front. Converting to Nieuports in April 1917, on 12 May he was transferred to the 71ᵃ Squadriglia and allowed to receive reserve officer training there. Promoted aspirante in October and sottotenente in November. On 6 May 1918 he was posted to Busto Arsizio as an instructor. Tenente on 15 November 1918, Amantea was decorated with three Silver Medals and a Bronze Medal. The postwar review confirmed five victories. Amantea remained in the Army and in 1923 transferred to the new Regia Aeronautica, serving mainly in Italy's North African colonies. Between 1926-33 he fought in Tripolitania against Arab resistance, variously as CO with 89ᵃ and 104ᵃ Squadriglia and temporary AOC Tripolitania, earning a fourth Silver and a Bronze medal. He was promoted maggiore on 31 January 1931 and in 1933 he commanded the 10° Gruppo. Tenente colonnello in February 1935, he returned to Africa as CO of 44° Gruppo in Eritrea, earning two more Silver Medals and being knighted in the Military Order of Savoy. Returning to Italy, he was CO of the 50° Stormo (1938), the Foggia school (1939) and Lecce airbase (1942). Retired on 28 January 1946 and promoted generale in the honorary list, he resided in Lecce until his death 13 July 1983, the last surviving WWI Italian ace.

	1917				
1	2 Aug	EA		N Arsiero	71[a]
–	23 Aug	EA		Monte Pasubio	71[a]
2	24 Aug	Albatros D.III	(a)	Forte Luserna	71[a]
–	24 Sept	EA	(b)	Monte Verena	71[a]
3	18 Nov	EA		Monte Spitz	71[a]
–	,,	EA		Tonezzo	71[a]
	1918				
–	28 Jan	EA		Val Frenzela	71[a]
4	22 Mar	EA		Pasubio	71[a]
5	3 May	EA		M. Spitz/Tonezza	71[a]

(a) 53.33, Flik 24, Offizierstellvertreter Julius Kowalczik; shared with Riva and Tola; (b) quoted by American researchers; possibly date mistaken with 24 Aug.

ANCILLOTTO Giovanni   Tenente   SQ 114[a], 27[a], 30[a], 80[a], 77[a]

Born in San Donà di Piave, Venice province, on 15 November 1896, at the outbreak of war 'Giannino' (as he was universally known) was an engineering student at the Turin Polytechnic. On 4 November 1915 he was accepted as a volunteer pilot candidate with soldato rank. After a basic military drill course at Mirafiori, on 5 December 1915 he transferred to the Gabardini flying school at Cameri. He graduated in March 1916, among the first in the 80-cadet course, and in May attended the Busto Arsizio and Malpensa schools for advanced training. On 25 June 1916 Ancillotto was posted to the 114[a] Squadriglia, where on 31 August he became caporale, moving on to the 27[a] (1 October-20 December 1916) and becoming aspirante on 6 January 1917 before proceeding to the 30[a] (18 February-13 April). This reconnaissance work earned him a first Silver Medal. After converting to Nieuports and attending gunnery school in Pisa, on 14 June Ancillotto reached the 80[a] Squadriglia, where on 24 July he scored his two first victories. On 10 November 1917 he was assigned to the 77[a], where he earned another Silver Medal. After the Caporetto rout, Ancillotto specialized in balloon busting, shooting down three and forcing many others down in one week. In the celebrated action of 5 December 1917, 'Giannino' pressed his attack so close that his Nieuport 11 flew across the balloon's flaming debris, returning with large parts of its fabric draped around his badly damaged fighter. These successes earned him the Gold Medal, awarded in March 1918. In February Ancillotto began experimental night flying patrols with Allasia and Liut and in July 1918 he was able to shoot down two intruders, earning a third Silver. Between 6 September and 27 October he served with the Commissariato Generale d'Aeronautica, returning to the front for the final offensive. Credited with 11 victories in the postwar review, Ancillotto turned to sport flying and on 11 September 1919 flew non-stop from Rome to Warsaw. He followed this up in May 1921 with the crossing of the Andes in Peru. He died on 18 October 1924 in a car crash in Caravaggio (Bergamo province).

	1917					
1	26 Oct	seaplane	(a)	Doberdò		80[a]
2	,,	EA		Vallone Brestovica		80[a]
3	27 Oct	EA		Doberdò		80[a]
4	3 Nov	German a/c		Ravarè		80[a]
5	30 Nov	balloon		Fossalta		77[a]
6	3 Dec	balloon		S. Polo di Piave		77[a]
7	5 Dec	balloon		Rustignè		77[a]
	1918					
8	22 Jul	Brandenburg C.I	(b)	S. Elena	0105	77[a]
9	24 Jul	Brandenburg C.I	(b)	Trepalade	0055	77[a]
10	21 Aug	EA	(c)	Ponte di Piave		77[a]
11	27 Oct	Pfalz D.III	(d)	S. Fior		77[a]

(a) possibly K366, Gröger/Mericka; shared with Leonardi; (b) night victory; (c) shared with Conelli; (d) shared with Serafini and two RAF aircraft, by Austro-Hungarian airfield; date also quoted as 28 Sept.

AVET Flaminio   Tenente   SQ 73ª, 82ª, 70ª

Born in Nice, France, on 3 August 1890, Avet was an officer in the 9th 'Firenze' Lancers' Regiment. He transferred to the air service in early 1916, making his first flight in a Blériot trainer at the Venaria Reale school on 25 May, where he earned his wings on 9 September and his military pilot brevet on 15 November. Rated on the Aviatik on 1 January 1917, he joined the SAML-equipped 73ª Squadriglia on 3 February and flew his first sortie on 14 March 1917. On 31 August he travelled to Malpensa for Nieuport 17 conversion, followed by gunnery school at San Giusto but returned to Malpensa for SVA conversion. On 1 November 1917 he moved to the 82ª Squadriglia, serving as acting CO for two weeks and scoring his first success. January 1918 found him with the 70ª, until February as acting CO, a post he would hold again in June-July. Between May and October 1918 he flew 86 combat sorties, engaging in combat eight times and scoring two shared victories. Avet's eight victories all survived the postwar commission's scrutiny and he was awarded three Silver Medals. He returned to Nice, where he died on 21 August 1928.

	1917					
–	27 Nov	EA	(a)	Val d'Arsa		82ª
	1918					
1	17 Apr	2-seater	(b)	Valdobbiadene		70ª
–	„	fighter	(b)	Valdobbiadene		70ª
–	„	fighter	(b)	Valdobbiadene		70ª
2	25 Apr	fighter	(c)	Conegliano		70ª
3	„	fighter	(c)	Conegliano		70ª
4	3 May	fighter		Zenson		70ª
5	17 May	2-seater	(d)	Maserada	0958	70ª HD
6	15 Jul	EA	(e)	Montello		70ª
7	4 Oct	Albatros D.V	(f)	Grave di Papadopoli		70ª Spad VII
8	8 Oct	fighter	(g)	Oderzo		70ª
–	28 Oct	EA	(h)	Arcade		70ª

(a) not allowed; (b) all shared with Bocchese, Eleuteri, Resch; (c) shared; (d) two crew POW; shared with Fucini and Rennella; (e) shared with Bocchese and Eleuteri; some sources also mention a second victory; (f) date controversial — flight log has 3, citation 5! (g) shared with Eleuteri; (h) forced to land at Italian airfield; shared with Bocchese and Eleuteri.

BARACCA Francesco   Maggiore   SQ 1ª, 70ª, 91ª

Born in Lugo di Romagna, Ravenna province, on 9 May 1888, he studied at the 'Dante' lyceum in Florence. In October 1907, against his father's wish, he entered the Scuola Militare in Modena, emerging two years later as a sottotenente. After a year's training at the Pinerolo cavalry school, in 1910 he was posted to the 2nd 'Piemonte Reale' Cavalry Regiment. Volunteering for pilot training, Baracca earned his French licence in Reims on 9 July 1912, following up with the Italian civil and military licences on 26 September and 8 December. Promoted tenente, he was seconded to the Battaglione Aviatori and in 1914 served in the 5ª and 6ª Squadriglias. In May 1915 Baracca was sent to Paris to convert onto Nieuport biplanes, returning to Italy in August to join the new 1ª Squadriglia. The Nieuport 10 proved inadequate and it was only the Nieuport 11, which arrived in April 1916, that allowed Baracca to earn his first victory on 7 April which, recognized as the first official Italian victory of the war, earned him a Silver Medal. A second Silver came after his fourth victory and a third on 24 May 1917, the latter being upgraded to Gold on 5 May 1918. Promoted capitano on 9 September 1916, Baracca remained with the unit, even after its name change to 70ª Squadriglia, transferring to the new 91ª on 1 May 1917. The previous month he had adopted a black prancing horse as his personal insignia, applying it to Nieuport 17, Spad VII and Spad XIII. A dedicated fighter pilot, Baracca found life away from the front unbearable and strove to remain with the 91ª even after being promoted maggiore in November 1917. His 30th victory came on 7 December but was followed by five lean months. At 1815 hrs of 19 June 1918, Baracca took off with Osnago for his final flight, a strafing mission on the Montello. He never returned and his body was only found on the 23rd, his demise having been variously attributed to ground fire, an Austrian Phönix C.I and even suicide to avoid the consequences of an on-board fire. A few days later the King decreed that the 91ᵃ be named after Baracca. The postwar review confirmed 34 victories, making Baracca the Italian ace of aces of the war. In addition to the Gold Medal and three Silver Medals, he was made an Officer of the Military Order of Savoy and decorated with a French Croix de Guerre with Palms, a British Military Cross, a Serb Gold Star and was awarded the Officer's Cross of the Belgian Crown.

	1916					
1	7 Apr	Brandenburg C.I	(a)	Medeuzza	1720	1ᵃ
2	16 May	Lohner B.VII	(b)	Gorizia		1ᵃ
3	23 Aug	Brandenburg C.I	(c)	Gorizia/Carso		1ᵃ
4	16 Sep	Lloyd C.III	(d)	Staro Stelo	0930	70ᵃ
5	25 Nov	Brandenburg C.I	(e)	Chiarzò	1125	70ᵃ
	1917					
6	1 Jan	Brandenburg C.I	(f)	Castagnevizza	1600	70ᵃ
7	11 Feb	Brandenburg C.I	(g)	Selvis Ozzano	c 1200	70ᵃ
8	26 Apr	Brandenburg C.I	(h)	S. Martino del Carso	1100	70ᵃ
9	1 May	Brandenburg C.I	(i)	Nebresina		91ᵃ
10	10 May	Brandenburg D.I	(j)	Vertoiba		91ᵃ
11	13 May	Brandenburg C.I	(k)	Monte Corada	1015	91ᵃ
12	20 May	Brandenburg C.I	(l)	E Plava/Globua		91ᵃ
13	3 June	Brandenburg C.I	(m)	Plava/Monte Cucco	0930	91ᵃ
14	7 July	Brandenburg C.I	(n)	Castagnevizza	2030	91ᵃ
15	31 Jul	Brandenburg C.I	(o)	Oslavia/Peuma	0630	91ᵃ
16	3 Aug	Brandenburg C.I	(p)	Wochein Val di Sava	0950	91ᵃ
17	19 Aug	Brandenburg C.I	(q)	1 km NE Selo	0725	91ᵃ
18	1 Sept	Brandenburg C.I	(r)	Ternova	1940	91ᵃ
19	6 Sept	Brandenburg C.I	(s)	Monte Sabotino	1830	91ᵃ
20	22 Oct	DFW C.V		Ravne	pm	91ᵃ
21	„	DFW C.V		Chiapovano	pm	91ᵃ
22	25 Oct	Brandenburg C.I	(t)	Panovizza		91ᵃ
23	26 Oct	DFW C.V	(u)	Clabuzzano	1115	91ᵃ
24	„	DFW C.V	(v)	S.Pietro Natisone	1200	91ᵃ
25	6 Nov	Albatros D.III	(w)	Fossalta	1030	91ᵃ
26	„	DFW C.V	(x)	Godega S.Urbano	1100	91ᵃ
27	7 Nov	DFW C.V	(y)	nr Orsago	1145	91ᵃ
28	15 Nov	DFW C.V	(z)	Istrana	1230	91ᵃ
29	23 Nov	Albatros D.III	(aa)	Falzè di Piave	1500	91ᵃ
30	7 Dec	Brandenburg C.I	(bb)	Monte Kaberlaba		91ᵃ
	1918					
31	3 May	Brandenburg C.I	(cc)	Grave di Papadopoli	1100	91ᵃ
32	22 May	Albatros D.III	(dd)	Borgo Malanotte	0950	91ᵃ
33	15 June	Brandenburg C.I	(ee)	E Saletto	1230	91ᵃ
34	„	Albatros D.III	(ff)	S. Biagio di Collalto	1245	91ᵃ

(a) 61.57, Flik 19, FTL; later flown extensively; Zgf Ott/POW/Oblt Lenarcic DOW in hospital 31 May; (b) 17.42, Flik 12, Korp Knelly/Fhr Horvath-Tima; (c) 61.61, Flik 19, Zgsf Himmer; shared with Ruffo; (d) 43.74, Flik 16, Korp Franz Morozko, KIA, Ltn Anton von Czaby, DOW; shared with Ruffo and Olivari; (e) 68.03, Flik 16, Korp Fuchs, KIA/Ltn Kalman Sarkozy WIA; confirmed by 29ᵃ Sq; (f) Flik 12; Neuwith/Huber; (g) 27.74, Flik 35; Korp Ludwig Stech/Ltn Simienski; shared with Ruffo, Gorini, Poli; (h) 129.17, Flik 35, Zgf Majsai KIA/Ltn Treer POW; shared with Gorini; Imolesi and Olivari participated but not credited; (i) possibly 64.07, Flik 12, Ltn Frank Linke-Crawford/Ltn Herberstein; damaged and forced down, not counted until 31 July but counted after 3 August: confirmation probably arrived these days; (j) 28.57, Flik 41J, Stohr, WIA; (k) 129.20, Flik 14D, Fw Busa/Oblt Grossler, both KIA; (l) 229.10, Flik 12, Zgst Ferschel/Ltn Csutka; (m) 129.51, FlG 1, Zgf Rotter/Oblt Bednarzik; (n) 129.68, Flik 46; Fw Duschek/Ltn Bozö; (o) 69.93, Flik 46, Julius Klaus/Oblt Erich Boch, both KIA; (p) Flik 10; shared with Baracchini; (q) 229.23, Flik 35; Korp Gerlich/Ltn Wania; (r) 69.10, Flik 101G, Fw Nölscher WIA/Ltn von Khuepach KIA; (s) 129.50, Flik 34, Horth WIA, Gerey KIA; shared with Sabelli; (t) 29.63, Flik 19, Lambert/Pappius, both KIA; shared with Piccio; (u) FA.39, Schulze/Ltn d R Werner Schulze; shared with Parvis; (v) FA.17, Ltn Hans Schlüter/Vzfw Bruno Fuchs; shared with Parvis; Baracca took hits and force landed at Natisone; (w) 153.08, Flik 41J, Ltn Radames Iskra, POW; (x) possibly FA.219, Ltn d R Albrecht Binder DOW/Vzfw Werner Schröder KIA; shared with Parvis; (y) 3955/17;

possibly FA. 204, Gefr. Wilhelm Appelt/Ltn Paul Wilkening; set on fire on ground by Baracca; shared with Parvis; (z) possibly FA.14, Lts Müller/Peucer, KIA/KIA; Parvis present but did not participate; (aa) Ltn Karl Überscher, Jasta 39, two victories, KIA; Novelli present but share in kill uncertain; (bb) 29.20, Flik 45; Fw Schütze/Ltn Mehrfurt; Novelli present but not counted; (cc) 369.28, Flik 19D, Zgsf Josef Friedrich/Oblt Karl Rosenbaum, both KIA; shared with Nardini; (dd) 153.155, Flik 51J; Fhr d R Ernst von Pontalti; (ee) 369.116, Flik 32, Tomasik/Fellner, both KIA; (ff) 153.266, Flik 51J, Ltn Sigmund von Josipovich WIA/POW.

Notes

1. Antonio Foschini's 1939 Baracca biography lists a victory on 23 March 1917 which is unsupported in either flight log or squadron ORB.
2. Some researchers credit Baracca with two victories he did not claim, an Albatros B.I which crashed within Austrian lines (19 November 1915) and a Brandenburg C.I which crash landed at Prosecco (13 September 1916), in both cases following combat.

BARACCHINI Flavio Torello   Tenente   SQ 7ª, 26ª, 81ª, 76ª

Born in Villafranca Lunigiana, Massa province, on 28 July 1895, he attended technical schools in La Spezia. Nominally assigned to the 3rd Engineer Regiment, in Autumn 1915 he began pilot training at the SIT school in Torino, earning licences on 15 October and 1 December 1915. Converted to Voisin on 27 January 1916, on 28 February he was posted to the 7ª (later 26ª) Squadriglia, a Voisin unit with which he flew until 20 November. In December 1916 he was promoted sottotenente and sent to Cascina Costa to convert on Nieuports. In April 1917 he was posted to the 81ª Squadriglia which was being formed at Arcade and with which he would remain until July, scoring eight victories in a gruelling 39-day cycle in which he engaged in combat 35 times, a feat which led to the award of the Gold Medal, the first ever to a fighter pilot. On 14 July 1917 he transferred to the 76ª, but was wounded in the left jaw on 8 August and hospitalised in Udine. In March 1918 Baracchini rejoined the 81ª, fighting until 25 June, when a serious abdominal wound forced his second hospitalisation. He would never see combat again. Baracchini was credited with up to 33 victories in citations, and the war bulletin for 25 June 1918 announced his 30th success, a number matching the claims traced in the records. The postwar review reduced this to 21, leaving Baracchini and his family bitter forever despite a promotion to capitano. Badly burned in an explosion in his chemical lab on 29 July 1928, he died in Rome the following 18 August.

	1917					
–	15 May	Albatros	(a)	S. Marco		81ª Ni.11
1	20 May	EA		Vodice		81ª Ni.11
2	23 May	EA		Aisovizza		81ª Ni.11
3	25 May	EA		Ochroglyocha		81ª Ni.11
4	3 June	EA		nr Vertoiba		81ª Ni.11
5	6 June	EA		Vodice		81ª Ni.17
6	18 Jun	EA	(b)	nr Ochroglyocha		81ª Ni.17
7	19 Jun	EA	(c)	W Aisovizza		81ª Ni.17
8	22 Jun	Brandenburg C.I	(d)	Stara Gora		81ª Ni.17
9	17 Jul	EA		Lom		76ª Hd
10	29 Jul	EA		Tolmino		76ª Hd
11	3 Aug	Brandenburg C.I	(e)	Wochein/Val di Sava	0950	76ª Hd
–	7 Aug	round balloon	(f)			76ª Hd
12	8 Aug	Albatros		Tolmino		76ª Hd
	1918					
–	3 Apr	balloon	(g)	Premaor		81ª Hd
13	2 May	fighter		Cimadolmo		81ª Hd
–	3 May	EA	(h)	Sernaglia		81ª Hd
14	13 May	fighter		Arcade		81ª Hd
–	„	fighter	(i)	Montello/across Piave	0930	81ª Hd
–	18 May	balloon	(j)	Montello		81ª Hd
15	20 May	EA	(k)	NW Sernaglia	0910	81ª Hd
16	26 May	fighter		Cimadolmo		81ª Hd
–	2 Jun	2-seater		Susegana		81ª Hd

17	15 Jun	2-seater			Moriago	81ª Hd
18	„	fighter			Montello	81ª Hd
–	„	EA	(l)		Montello	81ª Hd
–	18 Jun	balloon	(m)		Collalbrigo	81ª Hd
19	21 Jun	balloon			S. Pietro	81ª Hd
20	22 Jun	EA	(n)		Falzè	81ª Hd
21	25 Jun	fighter	(o)		Montello	81ª Hd

(a) unconfirmed; (b) forced to land; (c) shared; (d) 229.05, Korp Hegedes/Oblt Mikosi, (e) Flik 10; shared with Baracca; (f) not counted for unknown reasons; (g) shared with Scaroni and Nannini; not claimed; (h) shared with Michetti; (i) forced to land on Austrian side of river, facing Montello; unconfirmed; (j) shared with Di Loreto; (k) shared with Di Loreto and Baggini; (l) unconfirmed; (m) shared; (n) shared with Ni.27 of 79ª; (o) shared with Corti.

BEDENDO Sebastiano   Sottotenente   SQ 48ª, 42ª, 72ª, 71ª

Born in Rovigo on 18 July 1895, he served initially with the 5° Fortress Artillery Regiment. He was accepted for flight training on 17 April 1916 and made his first flight in a Caudron G.3 on 20 April, earning his wings on 19 June in Busto Arsizio. In the course of the year he was rated on Caudron G.3 (1 July), Farman (1 September) and Caudron G.4 aircraft (3 October). On 7 October 1916 he was assigned to the 48ª Squadriglia, a G.4 reconnaissance unit, transferring to the 42ª on 17 February 1917. Accepted for fighter training, on 18 October he was sent to Malpensa for Nieuport conversion, reaching the 72ª Squadriglia on 27 November via the Arcade Squadriglia Formation Centre. On 18 January 1918 he was detached for a month to the 71ª Squadriglia's Hanriot flight, returning then to the 72ª for another month before permanently joining the 71ª on 11 March. The first of his eight claims, five of which were confirmed postwar, came on 19 March. In May, June and August he was thrice mentioned in the orders of the day of the 1ª Armata. Decorated with a Silver Medal and a Bronze Medal, after the war Bedendo left the Army, possibly to study engineering. On 1 October 1924 he rejoined the newly-formed Regia Aeronautica (Royal Italian Air Force) as a capitano in the engineering branch, specializing in electrics and w/t, achieving maggiore rank in December 1930. Despite his new career, he did not stop flying and on 6 March 1933 he carried out the maiden flight of the Nuvoli N.5 light touring monoplane, with which, between April and June, he established world records in the appropriate category for distance and speed over 100 and 500 km courses. Bedendo's association with Nuvoli's light planes bore several other records until, on 24 August 1935, disaster struck and Bedendo was killed when the N.5Cab he was scheduled to fly in the Littorio Air Rally crashed at Spinosa di Ottiglio.

	1918					
–	19 Mar	EA	(a)		Pergine	71ª
–	7 Jun	EA	(b)			71ª
1	29 Jul	fighter	(c)		Val Terragnolo	71ª
2	30 Jul	EA			Monte Cadria	71ª
–	6 Aug	2 EA	(d)		Lartebasso	71ª
3	10 Aug	fighter	(e)		Val Terragnolo	71ª
4	22 Aug	EA	(f)		Castel Santo/Vallarsa	71ª
5	16 Sept	EA	(g)			71ª

(a) glided into its own lines; (b) recorded as shared with English a/c but no matching claim found; (c) this is the only victory inscribed 'confirmed' in flight log; (d) 2-seater seen to go down OOC, fighter seen to fall trailing smoke; unconfirmed; with Vecco; (e) possibly from Flik 3J; (f) went down trailing smoke; shared with Breglia; (g) mentioned as 7th victory in squadron history.

BOCCHESE Aldo   Sergente Maggiore   SQ 70ª

Born in Milan on 23 December 1894, Bocchese served initially with the 49th Infantry Regiment and was sent to Cascina Costa for pilot training on 7 March 1917 as a sergente. He earned his initial licence on 20 August 1917, followed by a SAML (100 HP variant) rating on 16 September and the advanced licence on 4 November. On 8 November he was sent to Malpensa for Nieuport training, followed on 1 December by a SAML 200 HP rating (possibly a belated sanction of an earlier examination) and transfer to the Furbara gunnery school on 7 December. Assigned to the 70ᵃ Squadriglia, he flew 67 sorties and scored three victories until July, followed by 52 sorties and two shared victories until the Armistice, plus a final victory unidentified in documents. The postwar committee confirmed him an ace with six victories. He was discharged as a sergente maggiore in 1919 and was decorated with two Bronze Medals. In 1963 he moved from Milan to Signa, in Tuscany. Bocchese died in Florence on 19 March 1976.

	1918				
1	17 Apr	2-seater	(a)	Valdobbiadene	70ᵃ
2	„	fighter	(a)	Valdobbiadene	70ᵃ
3	„	fighter	(a)	Valdobbiadene	70ᵃ
4	15 Jul	EA	(b)	Montello	70ᵃ
5	28 Oct	EA	(c)	Arcade	70ᵃ
6		EA	(d)		70ᵃ

(a) shared with Avet, Eleuteri, Resch; (b) shared with Avet and Eleuteri; some sources also mention a second victory — if confirmed, this could be the missing victory; (c) forced to land at Italian airfield; shared with Avet and Eleuteri; (d) no details known — also see (b).

BUZIO Alessandro   Tenente   SQ 75ᵃ, 81ᵃ, 76ᵃ

Born in Pavia on 13 January 1893, he studied accounting before being called up on 13 December 1913 for reserve officer training in the Army's engineering branch. Initially assigned to the 1st Engineers Regiment, he was made caporale on 31 March 1914 and sergente on 31 July, becoming sottotenente with the 5th Engineers on 8 November 1914. Assigned to the Technical Aeronautics Directorate on 23 May 1915, by 9 June he had been chosen for flying training and was named a military pilot on 7 December 1915. In February 1916 he was flying Macchi Parasols. Assigned to the 75ᵃ Squadriglia on 24 April 1916, by June he had scored his first victory, which brought him a Bronze Medal. Buzio was promoted tenente in October and on 27 April 1917 reached the 81ᵃ Squadriglia, where he earned a first Silver Medal. On 1 November 1917 he was posted to the 76ᵃ, where he remained until sent to the Furbara gunnery school on 24 September 1918, earning a second Silver Medal. He put in claims for six victories, only five of which were accepted by the postwar committee. He remained in the Air Force reserve throughout the 1930s, transferring to non-flying duties in December 1940 with the rank of tenente colonnello. He died on 1 October 1972.

	1916				
1	27 Jun	EA	(a)	Verona	75ᵃ
	1917				
2	31 Jul	EA	(b)		81ᵃ
3	22 Sept	EA		Isonzo	76ᵃ
4	19 Dec	EA		Val Seren	76ᵃ
	1918				
5	3 May	EA	(b)	Piave/Brenta	76ᵃ
6	„	EA	(b)	Monte Asolone	76ᵃ

(a) shared with Consonni, De Bernardi and Nardini; (b): shared.

CABRUNA Ernesto   Sottotenente   SQ 28ᵃ, 84ᵃ, 80ᵃ, 77ᵃ

Born in Tortona, in Alessandria province, on 2 June 1889, Cabruna joined the Carabinieri Reali (Royal Carabiniers, an Army branch with both civil and military police duties) on 18 October 1907. Promoted vice brigadiere on 30 September 1911, he served in Tripolitania from April 1912 through May 1913 and later took part in the occupation of Rhodes. Promoted brigadiere on 31 January 1915, he served with the Turin and Allievi (Cadets) Legions and was posted to the 10ᵃ Compagnia in October 1915. On 15 May 1916, while serving in Asiago, Cabruna was awarded a Bronze Medal for rescuing victims of an Austrian bombing raid. Two months later he was in Torino for flying instruction, earning his licences on MF14s on 6 October and 16 November 1916. On 28 December he reached the 28ᵃ Squadriglia, flying his first sortie on

2 January 1917. On 31 May he was promoted maresciallo and, after converting to Nieuports, on 24 June he reached the 84ᵃ Squadriglia. On 21 September 1917 he was transferred to the 80ᵃ, with which he scored two victories and earned a first Silver Medal. On 26 January 1918 Cabruna reached the 77ᵃ Squadriglia, where on 4 April he was promoted sottotenente for war merit. He often engaged the enemy against impossible odds, including one against 11 on 29 March and against 30 aircraft on 15 June.

While flying Ansaldo A.1 No.6548, on 26 September 1918, Cabruna broke his collarbone in a landing accident but despite a still incomplete recovery on 28 October he returned to the front to take part in the final Vittorio Veneto offensive. Despite his handicap, on 2 November he destroyed two enemy aircraft on the ground at Aiello airfield. His indomitable spirit earned him a Gold Medal for the 1918 cycle. Cabruna marked his Spad VII with nine kill markings but only eight were confirmed postwar.

In April 1919 Cabruna was promoted tenente and assigned to the 39ᵃ Squadriglia, but soon found himself involved in D'Annunzio's Fiume adventure. In December 1923 he transferred from the Carabinieri to the Regia Aeronautica and served briefly in Tripolitania. Promoted capitano in 1925, he was ADC to the Chief of Staff but did not fit in with the peacetime organization and was finally discharged on 2 June 1932. He died in Rapallo on 9 January 1960 and is now buried in D'Annunzio's Vittoriale mansion. Cabruna's original Spad VII is on display in the Italian Air Force Museum, at Vigna di Valle, near Rome.

	1917					
1	26 Oct	EA		Grado		80ᵃ
2	5 Dec	EA				80ᵃ
	1918					
3	12 Mar	EA		S. Donà di Piave		77ᵃ
4	29 Mar	fighter	(a)	Ponte di Piave		77ᵃ
5	15 Jun	EA		Tezze		77ᵃ Spad
6	20 Jun	EA		Musetta		77ᵃ
7	21 Jun	balloon	(b)	Ceggia	0730	77ᵃ
8	25 Oct	EA	(c)			77ᵃ
–	25 Oct	EA	(c)			77ᵃ

(a) one of three "red" aircraft in group of 11; (b) shared with Molino; some accounts mention two balloons, but flight log has just one; (c) mentioned in Gold Medal citation but no details known.

CALVELLO Umberto   Sottotenente di Vascello   SQ 260ᵃ

Born in Pistoia on 28 May 1897, he served initially as an observer, then as a reconnaissance pilot. Transferring to fighters, he reached Venice in Spring 1918 and was posted to the 260ᵃ. He flew a variety of missions, including some behind the lines to supply informers with carrier pigeons. During a ground support mission on 31 October, he was forced to alight in a swamp near Caorle, but was rescued by Ravazzoni, who put down next to him and, perilously climbing in under the engine, offered him the controls. The pair thus returned to Venice. In 1919 Calvello was carried as a five-victory ace in the official postwar Navy list, against which a single individual victory and three shared ones have been found. Decorated with two Silver Medals and a Bronze, he died on 18 August 1919.

	1918				
1	22 April	Lohner TL	(a)	W of Gronghera	260ᵃ M.5
2	4 May	Hansa-B W.18	(b)	Trieste	260ᵃ M.5
3	„	Hansa-B W.18	(c)	Trieste	260ᵃ M.5
4	„	'Ago'	(d)	Trieste	260ᵃ M.5
5	no details known				

(a) R.1, FTL, von Herbetz/Bauer, recovered; shared with Rivieri and Pagliacci; (b) A.91, Niedermayer, captured by the Italians; (c) A.78, Boros, captured by the Italians; (d) coded A.IV according to Italian reports, unconfirmed in Austrian sources; (b-c-d) shared with Martinengo, Rivieri, Jannello and Pagliacci; tentative attribution.

CERUTTI Marziale   Sergente   SQ 79ª

Born in Brescia on 10 March 1895, Cerutti was drafted and served with the 25th Field Artillery Regiment when he volunteered for flight training. Admitted to the Pisa flying school on 30 November 1915, he was promoted caporale on 15 May 1916 and then sent for further training to Busto Arsizio (on Maurice Farmans, 26 June) and Malpensa (on Caproni 300s, 11 September). On 14 September Cerutti was sent to Cascina Costa for Nieuport training and two months later he was assigned to the 79ª Squadriglia, with which he would serve throughout the war with the rank of sergente. His first two victories, scored single-handed above Mt. Grappa, earned him his first Silver Medal, awarded in the field. An excellent and daring pilot with a flamboyant personality (the Nieuport 27, with which in the later stages of the war he replaced his earlier Nieuport 11 No. 2124, was marked simultaneously with the Ace of Clubs insignia and the letters MIR, which stood for 'Marziale Imperatore Romano', or 'Martial the Roman Emperor'), in June 1918 Cerutti was proposed for a commission for 'extraordinary merits', becoming sottotenente with effect from 23 March 1919. He was awarded three Silver Medals, including two in the field (the second on 28 January 1918, Asiago front) and the third on 7 November. In March 1918 he also received a French Croix de Guerre and a Serb Star of Karageorgevic with Swords. In February 1919 the victories committee confirmed 17 kills. In 1923 Cerutti transferred to the Regia Aeronautica and his postwar career saw him become CO of 6° Gruppo in 1931, of 15° Stormo in 1935 with colonnello rank, of 11° Stormo in 1936. Assigned to the HQ of the Italian Armed Forces in North Africa in June 1940, on 28 June he witnessed the accidental shooting down of Marshal Italo Balbo on Tobruk's T2 airfield. On 20 March 1941 he was promoted generale di Brigata Aerea and in August was appointed Chief of Staff of the 'Servizi Aerei Speciali', the Italian Transport Command. After the 8 September 1943 Armistice he briefly joined the Aeronautica Nazionale Repubblicana of Mussolini's Italian Social Republic, a fact which cost him a suspension from Regia Aeronautica service at the war's end. Before his case could be reviewed, on 26 May 1946 Cerutti died in a crash on a motorcycle he had built himself.

	1917					
–	14 Jun	EA				79ª
–	26 Oct	fighter		Volzano	c.1445	79ª
–	30 Oct	seaplane	(a)	Isonzo		79ª
1	24 Nov	fighter		Grappa	1200	79ª
2	24 Nov	2-seater		Grappa	1200	79ª
3	27 Nov	2-seater	(b)	Albaro di Piave	1200	79ª
	1918					
4	28 Jan	EA	(c)	Bertiaga/V. Vecchia	1345	79ª
5	„	EA	(c)	nr M. Melago	1410	79ª Ni.27
6	5 Feb	2-seater	(d)	Casa Grande	0830	79ª
7	11 Feb	black fighter		Asiago	0810	79ª
8	24 Feb	fighter		Crespano/BV del Covolo	0900	79ª
9	25 Mar		(e)	Moriago	1150	79ª
10	21 Jun	EA				79ª
11	21 Jun	EA	(f)	Susegana		79ª
12	24 Jun	Brandenburg C.I	(g)	NE Susegana	1945	79ª
13	31 Jun	balloon	(h)			79ª
14	10 Aug	EA		Montebelluna		79ª
15	11 Sept	EA		E of Ponte della Priula		79ª
16	26 Sept	EA		M. Malanotte		79ª
17	27 Oct	Albatros D.III	(i)	Vazzola	1445	79ª Ni.27
–	„	fighter		Cittadella di Piave		79ª Ni.27
–	„	2-seater		Monterano		79ª Ni 27

(a) forced to land in Isonzo; (b) forced to land; (c) both shared with Reali; (d) forced to land; shared with Nicelli; (e) shared with Ciotti; (f) victim landed at Susegana; (g) victim crash landed; (h) s/d in flames; (i) possibly 153.69, Flik 101G, Obltn Richard Koderle; shared with Chiri.

CHIRI Antonio   Sergente Maggiore   SQ 77ᵃ, 78ᵃ

Born in Locana, near Ivrea, on 26 August 1894, Chiri was drafted on 9 September 1914 in the 17th Field Artillery Regiment. Admitted to the Pisa flying school on 18 April 1915, he was soon suspended from training but stayed with the school as a sheet-metal fitter and eventually, in November, was allowed to resume the pilot's course. On 1 April 1916, still a pilot candidate, he was promoted to caporale. After this very long training period, Chiri was posted to the 77ᵃ Squadriglia on 8 June 1916, moving on to the 78ᵃ on 11 October. Shortly afterwards, on 31 October, he was promoted sergente. Chiri scored his first victory on 19 March 1917, for which he was awarded a Silver Medal in the field. A second one followed on 26 August 1917, and a third one, also in the field, at the war's end, together with a War Cross. Although credited by modern literature with shooting down the Austrian ace Franz Gräser on 17 May 1918, together with Reali and Lucentini, in fact none of them put in claims that day. On 15 September Chiri became sergente maggiore, but on the following 21 December he suffered a bad flying accident which caused him to be discharged as permanently unfit for military service. He had flown over 250 combat sorties. Chiri is one of the few pilots for whom the 1919 verification committee's report survives: curiously enough, it lists six confirmed victories, whereas the official published ranking only carries five. Despite the consequences of his accident, Chiri remained in the Regia Aeronautica reserve and eventually reached capitano rank on 8 June 1942. He died in Torino on 6 January 1971.

	1917					
1	19 Mar	Brandenburg C.I	(a)	Gallio Bassano		78ᵃ
2	26 Aug	EA		Loque		78ᵃ
–	13 Nov	EA	(b)	Arcade		78ᵃ
–	20 Nov	EA	(c)	Moriago		78ᵃ
–	10 Dec	EA				78ᵃ
3	26 Dec	DFW C.V		Istrana area		78ᵃ
	1918					
–	21 Feb	EA		Buso/Val Frenzela	1130	78ᵃ
–	4 Apr	EA	(d)	Montello		78ᵃ
4	17 May	Albatros D.III	(e)	Pero	1015	78ᵃ
5	31 Aug	EA	(f)	Mandre	1330	78ᵃ HD
6	27 Oct	Albatros D.III	(g)	Vazzola	1445	78ᵃ HD
–	„	fighter		Cittadella di Piave		78ᵃ Ni.27
–	„	2-seater		Monterano		78ᵃ Ni 27

(a) 27.55, Flik 21, two crew POW; (b) shared with Masiero; (c) shared with Masiero; (d) explicitly listed as disallowed; (e) 153.221, Ltn d R Franz Gräser, Flik 61J; adjudged to Nardini with Magistrini and Novelli, with several others taking part; this is possibly the victory not counted in order to produce official total of 5; (f) with Fucini and Rennella; (g) possibly 153.69, Flik 101G, Obltn Richard Koderle; shared with Cerutti.

COSTANTINI Bartolomeo   Capitano   3ᵃ, 13ᵃ, 14ᵃ, 78ᵃ, 43ᵃ, 91ᵃ

Born in Vittorio Veneto, Treviso province, on 14 February 1889, Bartolomeo (often shortened to 'Bortolo') Costantini was commissioned sottotenente on 21 January 1912 and assigned to the 5th Engineers Regiment. Volunteering for flight training, he was sent to the Aviano school where he earned his FAI licence (No. 177 in Italy) on 13 September 1912. Mobilized when the European war broke out, Costantini reported to the 3ᵃ Squadriglia at Cuneo on 12 August 1914, moving on in quick succession to the 13ᵃ (27 August), the 14ᵃ (September) and Turin's Technical Section (also in September). This frantic period came to an end in October, when he was released from duty. Called up following Italy's intervention, Costantini served in the 3rd Fortress Artillery Regiment until sent to the 3rd School Group at Pisa on 25 April 1916, from where in July he proceeded to Cascina Costa to convert onto Nieuports. On 12 August 1916 he was assigned to the 78ᵃ Squadriglia, where he served until transferring to the 43ᵃ, a reconnaissance unit, on 5 May 1917. A month later, on 6 June, he made his definitive return to fighter service with the newly established 91ᵃ. When Baracca and Ruffo went to Turin for fighter evaluation trials, Costantini served as temporary CO of this élite unit from 24 December 1917 to early

January 1918. Having engaged in 18 combats and put in claims for seven victories (of which six were recognized by the postwar committee), Costantini was discharged in 1919 with two Silver Medals and a War Cross. In 1940 he was called up as a tenente colonnello in the reserve, with non-flying duties in the Regia Aeronautica's support branch, but died through illness on 19 July 1941.

	1917					
1	25 Oct	Aviatik C	(a)	Tolmino		91ª
2	26 Oct	Aviatik 2-seater	(b)	Castelmonte		91ª
3	23 Nov	German 2-seater	(c)	Cornuda		91ª
4	30 Nov	German a/c	(d)	Crocetta Sevegliano/Rivasecca		91ª
	1918					
5	12 Aug	Albatros D.III		S. Lucia di Piave	2000	91ª
6	22 Aug	German 2-seater	(e)	Marano di Piave	1050	91ª

(a) shared with Ruffo; (b) two crew KIA; (c) shared with Magistrini; (d) shared with Olivero and Bacula; (e) aircraft s/d in flames, pilot KIA, observer jumped with parachute.

ELEUTERI Leopoldo   Tenente   SQ 73ª, 121ª, 70ª

Born on 17 December 1894 in Castel Ritaldi (Perugia province), he attended a technical school and when drafted in 1915 was sent first to the Terni Ordnance Factory, then to its Rome branch, and finally to the 3rd Infantry Regiment. Accepted for flying training, he gained his wings on 18 October 1916 at the Gabardini school in Cameri. He was rated a Caudron G.3 pilot on 4 December and on SAML on 28 April 1917. Initially assigned to the 73ª and 121ª Squadriglie, both SAML units, he attended the gunnery course at Furbara in January 1918 before being sent to the 70ª, which he reached on 22 February. After a number of patrols, on 3 April he attacked a balloon and two weeks later scored his first victory. During the war he flew a total of 151 sorties and engaged in 26 combats. The postwar committee confirmed seven victories — including the only one achieved by any pilot flying an Ansaldo A.1 Balilla — and he was decorated with three Silver Medals and a War Cross. Upon being discharged, he enrolled in the Milan Polytechnic to study engineering, graduating in 1922. A year later he rejoined the Regia Aeronautica, taking part in the first engineering officers' competition and being accepted as capitano in its construction department with seniority from 31 October 1923. Assigned to the Furbara Experimental Establishment as CO of the armament flight, he lost his life in an in-flight collision on 19 January 1926. The fighter school at Castiglione del Lago was named after him.

	1918				
1	17 Apr	2-seater	(a)	Valdobbiadene	70ª
2	„	fighter	(a)	Valdobbiadene	70ª
—	„	fighter	(a)	Valdobbiadene	70ª
3	15 Jul	EA	(b)	Montello	70ª
4	19 Jul	EA		Falzè	70ª
5	4 Oct	Albatros D.V	(c)	Moriago	70ª Spad
6	8 Oct	fighter	(d)	Oderzo	70ª A.1
7	28 Oct	EA	(e)	Arcade	70ª

(a) shared with Avet, Bocchese, Resch; (b) shared with Avet and Bocchese; (c) shared with Avet; (d) shared with Avet; (e) forced to land at Italian airfield; shared with Avet and Bocchese.

FORNAGIARI Guglielmo   Sergente Maggiore   SQ 78ª

Born in Lizzano in Belvedere, Bologna province, in 1892, he reached the 78ª Squadriglia on 3 September 1916, with which he remained throughout the war. On 27 June 1917 he suffered an engine failure on take-off from Fossalunga and crashed into a vineyard: although he escaped unhurt, two civilians were killed and two injured. He was awarded two Silver Medals (the first for the 22 August 1917 victory, the second for the October-December 1917 period) and a Bronze. His decorations also included the Serb Cross of Karageorgevic. The review committee confirmed six victories. Ranked aiutante di battaglia in May 1919, he remained in service with the 78ᵃ Squadriglia until May 1925. He died in Bologna on 3 February 1956.

	1917					
–	19 Jun	EA		Levico		78ᵃ Ni.11
1	22 Aug	EA		Tarnova/Bainsizza		78ᵃ
2	2 Oct	2-seater		Podmelec		78ᵃ
–	8 Oct	EA		Globokac		78ᵃ HD
3	26 Dec	EA	(a)	Musano		78ᵃ
4	„	EA	(b)	Falzè		78ᵃ
	1918					
5	27 Jan	fighter		S. Francesco/Liser/Cismon		78ᵃ
6	21 Feb	fighter		Gallio		78ᵃ
–	15 Jun	2-seater	(c)	Bigolino	0645	78ᵃ HD

(a) shared with Masiero; (b) shared with Cornandone; (c) shared with Gritti and Schiona.

FUCINI Mario   Tenente   SQ 5ᵃ, 25ᵃ, 84ᵃ, SEZ DIF GROTTAGLIE, 87ᵃ, 76ᵃ, 78ᵃ

Born in Empoli on 1 February 1891, he enlisted in the Engineering Corps and was named sottotenente on 9 March 1915. He earned his licence on 13 March 1916, followed by a Voisin rating in April. Assigned to the 5ᵃ Squadriglia Voisin (later 25ᵃ) on 12 April 1916. On 28 July he earned a Silver Medal for completing a bombing mission whilst under constant attack from two enemy fighters. On 16 February 1917 a Bronze recognized his ability in landing at Monfalcone with his Voisin ablaze. In March 1917 Fucini was selected for conversion to Pomilio PCs but late May found him attending the Pisa gunnery school as a freshly promoted tenente. Posted to the 84ᵃ on 1 June, two weeks later he was flying Nieuports as CO of the Grottaglie Defence Section. In September Fucini travelled to Malpensa for SVA conversion and on the 27th was assigned to the 87ᵃ Squadriglia, then being formed at Ponte San Pietro. Although he was officially posted to the 76ᵃ on 5 December 1917, he had possibly reached the unit a few weeks earlier. His final transfer to the 78ᵃ came on 11 February 1918 and on 15 August his fighter work was recognized with a second Silver. On 3 November he was hospitalised and a week later was posted to the Turin Technical Section. Claiming some 13 victories, he was credited with seven in the review. He enjoyed a long postwar career, serving as CO of 29ᵃ and 78ᵃ Squadriglia. Promoted tenente colonnello in 1931, two years later he was CO of the Castiglione fighter school. The nephew of writer Renato Fucini, Fucini published his wartime memoirs *Voli sul nemico* in 1932 and from December 1933 to August 1935 served as editor of the Regia Aeronautica's official journal, the *Rivista Aeronautica*. He retired on 15 September 1937, was promoted generale in the reserve in April 1953 and died in Rome on 1 September 1977.

	1917					
1	13 Nov	2-seater	(a)			76ᵃ
–	19 Nov	EA				76ᵃ
–	26 Dec	DFW C.V	(b)	Camalo	0920	76ᵃ HD
2	„	DFW C.V	(c)	Camalo		76ᵃ HD
	1918					
3	28 Jan	2-seater	(d)	Biadene		76ᵃ HD
4	17 May	EA	(e)	Maserada	c.0915	78ᵃ
–	„	2-seater	(f)	Maserada	0958	78ᵃ HD
5	16 Jun	Brandenburg C.I	(g)	Malborghetto/Fontigo	1030	78ᵃ HD
6	„	Brandenburg C.I		Moriago	1045	78ᵃ HD
–	„	Albatros D.III	(h)	Nervesa/Frati	1809	78ᵃ HD
–	25 Jul	Brandenburg C.I	(i)	Moriago	0945	78ᵃ HD
–	31 Aug	EA	(j)	Mandre	1330	78ᵃ HD
7	27 Oct	Pfalz D.III	(k)	Vazzola	1650	78ᵃ HD

(a) no details known — possibly same action as Chiri and Masiero victory of same day; (b) participated but victory credited to Scaroni, Michetti and RFC pilots of 28 Sqn; (c) shared with Cornandone; (d) shared with Scaroni; (e) shared with Rennella; (f) shared with Avet and Rennella — possibly same as previous?; (g) shared with Riva and Venier;

(h) clearly OOC; with Bocca, WIA; (i) clearly OOC; with Venier; (j) guns jammed, so possibly not counted; with Chiri and Rennella; (k) with Copparucci; date given as 28 Oct by Fucini.

IMOLESI Attilio   Sergente   SQ 79^a

Born in Cesena on 11 October 1890, Imolesi was accepted for flying training on 31 December 1915 and sent to the Malpensa school. He earned his wings on 1 May 1916 on MF12s, progressing to MF14s on 1 July. Assigned to the Rimini Defence Flight, not far from his home, he applied for fighter training and by 2 September 1916 was converting on Nieuport 11 at Cascina Costa. His rating came through on 25 November and five days later he was posted to the 79^a Squadriglia as caporale. He made his first operational flight on 21 January 1917. In May he was briefly seconded, with his Nieuport 17, to the 43^a Squadriglia on escort duty. On 26 August he was awarded a Bronze Medal in the field, followed on 26 September by a Silver, also in the field. Promoted sergente, Imolesi was badly wounded in a flying accident (variously reported as combat) and died in the Marostica field hospital on 11 March 1918. The postwar review confirmed six victories.

	1917					
–	2 Apr	2-seater	(a)	nr Asiago		79^a
–	26 Apr	Brandenburg C.I	(b)	S. Martino del Carso	1100	79^a
1	26 Aug	EA	(c)	Monte S. Michele		79^a
2	14 Sept	2-seater	(d)	Monte Cismone		79^a
3	26 Sept	Brandenburg C.I	(e)	Altopiano di Asiago		79^a
4	„	EA	(f)			79^a
5	13 Dec	2-seater	(g)	Bosco Cabele	1000	79^a
	1918					
6	14 Jan	2-seater	(h)	Val Stagna		79^a

(a) unconfirmed; (b) 129.17, Flik 35, Majsay/Treer, both KIA; victim of Baracca and Gorini, Imolesi participated but not credited; (c) shared; (d) confirmed; (e) 129.69; (f) no details; (g) confirmed by Bassano Defence HQ; (h) shared with Reali.

LEGA Giulio   Capitano   SQ 21^a, 76^a, 81^a

Born in Florence on 12 November 1892. He served with the 2nd Grenadiers Regiment as a reserve officer and took part in the ground fighting for the first year of war, earning a War Cross on 20 November 1915 and a Bronze Medal 'in the field' on 30 May 1916. He then volunteered for flying duties, earning his licence on 1 November with an MF14 rating earned on 1 September. Assigned to the 21^a Squadriglia on 30 January 1917, he was then rated on SP2s on 14 February, just as he achieved tenente rank. His reconnaissance work between May and November 1917 was sufficient to warrant a Silver Medal. On 16 November he transferred to Malpensa for Nieuport conversion (officially sanctioned on 6 April 1918), from whence he progressed to Furbara for gunnery school: he passed his test on 27 December 1917 with a 'mediocre' ranking. By early 1918 he was with the 76^a Squadriglia, where he flew 46 sorties (19 patrols, 15 free hunts and 12 escorts), engaging in five combats. He earned a Silver Medal for his work in the March-June 1918 period and the review credited him with five victories, all shared. He transferred to the 81st in mid July and served out the war with no further victories. In July 1920 Lega graduated from the University of Bologna's school of medicine but remained in the Air Force reserve, rising to tenente colonnello in May 1935. On 13 March 1931 he became the head of the medical service of the Chamber of Deputies, a position he held until 1957 despite being called up during WW2 to be assigned to the Servizi Aerei Speciali headquarters. He died on 11 July 1973.

	1918					
1	17 Mar	EA	(a)	Col d'Astiago		76^a
2	25 Mar	EA	(b)	Montello		76^a
3	24 Jun	EA	(c)	Passagno		76^a
4	25 Jun	fighter	(d)	Moreno di Piave	c. 1030	76^a
5	„	Albatros D.III	(e)	Moreno di Piave	c. 1030	76^a

(a) shared; (b) shared with Fanti and Retinò; (c) shared; (d) shared with Scaroni and Ticconi; (e) 153.202, Flik 42J, Oblt August Selinger shared with Scaroni and Ticconi.

LEONARDI Alvaro   Sottotenente   SQ 41ᵃ, 80ᵃ

Born in Terni on 16 November 1895, in September 1915 he was with the Technical Services Directorate and later the 6th Railroad Engineers' Regiment. By 29 April 1916 he had earned his wings at Mirafiori on Caudron G.3s, from where in May he was sent to the Centocelle Observation School. Serving with the 41ᵃ Squadriglia, he was promoted caporale on 31 July 1916 and sergente on 31 October. Soon he was selected for fighter training and by 3 November was at Cascina Costa for Nieuport conversion (the rating was officially sanctioned six months later, on 2 May 1917). On 25 January 1917 he was with Malpensa's Nieuport Defence Flight, but by February he was again at the front with the 80ᵃ Squadriglia. On 25 October 1918 he was transferred to the 122ᵃ Squadriglia and on 3 December 1918 was with the 301ᵃ Squadriglia, the former Foggia Defence Flight. Leonardi's wartime service comprised 700 flying hours, 140 escort flights and 21 combats, during which he claimed 11 victories, eight of which recognized by the postwar committee. Decorated with two Silver Medals, he was discharged on 6 November 1919 but later joined the Regia Aeronautica, rising to tenente colonnello in March 1938. Qualified as instructor in April 1934, he embarked on a new career serving at Cameri (1934-1936), Grottaglie (1936-1938, CO), Malpensa (1940-1941), Fano (1941-1942), Capua (1942-1943), and Venaria Reale (1943). Despite being in German-occupied territory, after the Armistice he did not join the ANR and in March 1944 started a limited co-operation with the Resistance. He retired in February 1946 and died in Cameri, near Novara, on 1 January 1955.

	1917				
1	24 May	seaplane	(a)	Grado	80ᵃ
2	27 Oct	seaplane	(b)	Doberdò	80ᵃ
3	6 Nov	Brandenburg C.I	(c)	S.Michele di Conegliano	80ᵃ
–	27 Nov	EA		Zenzon di Piave	80ᵃ
	1918				
4	5 Feb	Albatros D.III	(d)	Rai	80ᵃ
–	5 Mar	balloon	(e)	lower Piave	80ᵃ
5	24 Mar	EA		Vendrome	80ᵃ
6	23 May	EA		Quarto del Sile	80ᵃ
–	18 June	EA		Monastir	80ᵃ
7	15 Jul	EA		Treviso	80ᵃ
8	20 Aug	EA		Campo Bernardo	80ᵃ

(a) possibly L136 Plasil/Riesner, which were attacking the British monitors HMS *Earl of Peterborough* and HMS *Sir Thomas Picton*; (b) possibly K366, Gröger/Mericka; shared with Ancillotto; (c) 229.24, Flik 12D, Zgf Josef Feiler KIA/Ltn Othmar Schwarzenbach POW; shared with Rizzotto; (d) 153.126, Flik 51J, Fw Karl Semmelrock (3 victories), KIA; shared with Piermattei; (e) set on fire but not confirmed.

LOMBARDI Carlo Francesco   Tenente   SQ 77ᵃ

Born in Genoa on 21 January 1897 and initially assigned to the 22nd Infantry Regiment, Lombardi, universally known as 'Francis', trained as a reserve officer and was sent to the Venaria Reale school on 18 May 1916 to earn his wings on Blériots. Following an Aviatik rating on 31 August, he was declared a military pilot on 6 October 1916 and on 1 January 1917 posted to Cascina Costa to convert onto Savoia-Pomilio SP.2. On 14 February he got an instructor's rating and found himself posted to the same school. On 27 July 1917 he reached Malpensa for Nieuport training, proceeding to San Giusto for gunnery school and finally reached the 77ᵃ Squadriglia on 23 August, where he started scoring in October. His second and fourth victory were crowned by a Silver Medal. In December he flew reconnaissance missions 100 km into the enemy lines, earning a second Silver. The third and final Silver recognised his June 1918 victories. In August, Lombardi was posted to the Ufficio Squadriglie in Torino, returning to the front to take part in the final offensive. Although credited with eight victories in the official postwar review, only six claims have been traced in the records. After taking part in

D'Annunzio's Fiume adventure, Lombardi returned to civilian life to manage his family's rice refinery. He remained, however, quite active on the sport aviation scene, founding the Vercelli Gruppo Turismo Aereo in 1928. In 1930 he made, with an 85 HP Fiat AS.1 monoplane, three remarkable flights (Rome-Mogadishu, Vercelli-Tokyo and a round-flight of Africa), earning a Silver Medal for Aeronautical Valour for each of the first two. Lombardi's greatest claim to fame was possibly the forming of the Avia company in 1938 to manufacture the L.3 two-seater, 500 of which were built for military schools and flying clubs. After WW2 Avia sold the design rights to Meteor to concentrate on automobile production until forced to shut down in 1976. That same year the Italian Air Force recognized Lombardi's career with a Gold Medal for Aeronautical Valour. In November 1981 he attended the WW1 aces commemorative meeting held in Paris. He died in Vercelli on 5 March 1983.

	1917					
1	26 Oct	K-boat	(a)	lake Doberdò		77ª Ni.17
2	27 Oct	EA		Ranziano		77ª Ni.17
3	„	EA		Korita		77ª Ni.17
4	3 Nov	German a/c		Ravaré		77ª Ni.17
5	4 Nov	EA	(b)			77ª Ni.17
6	no details known					
	1918					
7	15 June	Albatros D.III	(c)	S. Biagio	1315	77ª Spad VII
8	16 June	Albatros D.III	(d)	Pezzon di Melma		77ª Spad VII

(a) K212, Kramer/Anasipoli, KIA/POW but escaped; (b) mentioned in biography but not in logbook; (c) red with white crosses and black hand insignia (Flik 41J); by Villa Cucca; described by Lombardi as 'my last victory' but see below; (d) 153.222, Flik 41J, Ltn d R Hans Wolfschütz; by Villa Fantini; listed as 16 June in logbook and as 17 June in citation.

Note
'Francis' Lombardi is not to be confused with two other flyers named Carlo Lombardi — a capitano in the 26th 'Vercelli' Cavalry Regiment (born in Dronero, Cuneo province, on 13 December 1887, he flew with 10ª, 12ª and 32ª Squadriglia earning a Silver Medal) and a pilot candidate (born in 1898, undergoing pilot training at Sesto Calende in May 1918).

MAGISTRINI Cesare   Sergente   SQ 78ª, 91ª

Born in Maggiora, Novara province, on 26 January 1895 and began his flying training in December 1915, earning his basic licence in March 1916. As caporale, he served briefly with 2ª Squadriglia Parasol. He was assigned to the 78ª Squadriglia on 28 August and promoted sergente on 1 March 1917. He was awarded a Silver Medal in the field on 10 May for not breaking off a dogfight over the Podgora despite being severely wounded. On 1 November 1917 he joined the 91ª, where on 7 December he earned a second Silver Medal in the field having engaged in 20 combats and shooting down four aircraft. On 18 February he was again wounded, this time lightly, in the right knee, and on 16 March was sent on leave. Magistrini also earned a Serb medal and was awarded a Bronze Medal for the June-November 1918 cycle. He claimed nine victories, six of which were confirmed by the committee. Postwar Magistrini left the Service and joined the Fascist Party in October 1922. He soon returned to the Regia Aeronautica, serving with the 91ª and 84ª, but left definitively in 1927 to become a commercial pilot with Transadriatica. Following the company through its successive mutations as SAM and Ala Littoria, by Summer 1935 he had flown over a million km. By then he had also received a knighthood in the Order of the Italian Crown. In July 1931 he had become a sottotenente in the reserve, so that when the airline industry was militarized during WW2 he saw action again with the Servizi Aerei Speciali and earned a further Bronze Medal for the May-August 1942 period. In the same year he was recognized with a Silver Medal for Aeronautical Valour for having flown two million km. He died on 26 October 1958.

	1917					
1	17 Jun	Albatros	(a)	Luserna/Val d'Assa	0725	78ª Ni.17
–	18 Jul	2-seater	(b)	Asiago	0655	78ª HD
–	16 Oct	EA		Monte Nero		78ª

2	23 Nov	German 2-seater	(c)	Cornuda		91ᵃ
3	30 Nov	German 2-seater	(d)	Moriago/Vidor		91ᵃ
4	7 Dec	Brandenburg C.I	(e)	San Pietro di Nove		91ᵃ
	1918					
–	11 May	2-seater	(f)	N of Quero	1015	91ᵃ
5	17 May	Albatros	(g)	Pero	1015	91ᵃ Spad
6	12 Jul	fighter	(h)	Monte Santo	0815	91ᵃ
–	23 Aug	Albatros C	(i)	Oderzo		91ᵃ

(a) forced to land; (b) participated in Nardini's victory but not credited; (c) shared with Costantini; Magistrini's 4th victory according to the ORB; (d) possibly FA.232, Uffz Kurt Hieling/Ltn d R Hugo Huck, both KIA; shared with Novelli and Ranza; Magistrini's 5th victory according to ORB; (e) 369.21, Haupt Frick/Oblt Knezevic KIA; shared with Ranza; Bacula present but did not participate; (f) listed as probable in ORB; shared; (g) 153.221, Ltn d R Franz Gräser, Flik 61J; adjudged to Nardini, with many others taking part including Magistrini and Novelli; (h) this is probably the combat in which Lts A Rice-Oxley and C E Howell, both 45 Sqn, claimed a total of seven EA; Magistrini mentioned as witness to fight in British accounts; (i) unconfirmed in ORB.

MARTINENGO Federico   Tenente di Vascello   SQ 260ᵃ

Born in Rome on 18 July 1897, he graduated from the Livorno naval academy and served on the battleship *Cavour* before transferring to the naval air service. Stationed in Venice, in December 1917 he became CO of 260ᵃ Squadriglia, relinquishing the post in June 1918. Martinengo earned two Silver Medals and a War Cross and is credited with five victories in the official Navy list, against which four shared victories have been found. Postwar he elected to remain in the Navy, holding a number of posts including CO of the Tien Tsin naval detachment in 1931-33. As CO of the cruiser *Muzio Attendolo* he took part in the first naval battles of WW2. He rose to rear admiral rank to become in 1943 the CO of an anti-submarine unit at La Spezia. He was killed on 9 September on board *VAS 234* when the formation he was leading engaged a larger German group. He was awarded a posthumous Gold Medal.

	1918				
1	4 May	Hansa-B. W.18	(a)	Trieste	260ᵃ M.5
2	„	Hansa-B. W.18	(b)	Trieste	260ᵃ M.5
3	„	'Ago'	(c)	Trieste	260ᵃ M.5
4	14 May	'Ago'	(d)	Pola	260ᵃ M.5
5	no known details				

(a) A.91, Niedermayer, captured by the Italians; (b) A.78, Boros, captured by the Italians; (c) coded A.IV according to Italian reports, unconfirmed in Austrian sources; (a-b-c) shared with Calvello, Rivieri, Jannello and Pagliacci; (d) shared with Pierozzi, Jannello, Balleri.

MASIERO Guido   Tenente   SQ 26ᵃ, 86ᵃ, 91ᵃ, 78ᵃ, 3ᵃ SEZ SVA

Born in Padova on 24 August 1895, Masiero volunteered for military service and joined the 5th 'Novara' Lancers Regiment on 4 December 1913. He was admitted to flying school on 1 February 1915 and achieved his MF pilot rating on 1 August. Assigned to the 26ᵃ Squadriglia, he reached the front on 15 October and earned a Voisin rating on 15 November. Ranked sergente, he earned a citation on 4 October 1916 and, by then a sottotenente, a Bronze Medal in February 1917. On 14 May 1917 he was sent to Malpensa for fighter training, where on 29 July he was promoted tenente, and on 10 September was assigned to the 86ᵃ Squadriglia, then being formed on SVA. The type's protracted development led to Masiero being sent briefly to the 91ᵃ (27 October) and finally to the 78ᵃ, on 3 November 1917. In less than five months Masiero flew 80 sorties for 102h 31min, putting in 11 claims (only five of which were confirmed) and earned a Silver Medal in the field (20 November 1917); he also received a Belgian Croix de Guerre. In March 1918 he was transferred to the 3ᵃ Sezione SVA where he saw out the rest of the war as a long range reconnaissance pilot. Lack of confirmation invalidated three claims put in during this period: in all, the postwar review allowed Masiero five victories and turned down four. Curiously, one of the two further Silver Medals awarded him shortly *after* the war refers explicitly to six victories plus a balloon!

In December 1918 Masiero joined the Experimental Directorate, and was discharged a year later. He was still wearing a uniform in 1920, however, when he made the famous Rome-Tokyo flight, together with mechanic Roberto Maretto. On 31 August 1928 he rejoined the Regia Aeronautica as tenente and was promoted capitano in December. On 16 July 1935 he was called up to serve with the 20° Stormo, eventually spending the period from 31 October 1935 to 18 November 1936 in Eritrea, where he earned another Silver Medal. Upon return from Africa, he served with the 5° and 50° Stormo, both ground-attack units, and between October 1937 and April 1938 saw service in Spain. He was finally discharged on 31 May 1938. Having joined the Breda company as test pilot, during WW2 Masiero was not called up. He lost his life on 24 November 1942 in a mid-air collision with his colleague capitano Francesco Agello, the former Schneider racer who on 23 October 1934 had set the world speed record flying the Macchi C.72 seaplane.

	1917					
–	7 Nov	EA			Aviano	78ª
1	13 Nov	EA	(a)		Arcade	78ª
2	19 Nov	EA			Arcade	78ª
–	19 Nov	EA				78ª
–	20 Nov	2-seater	(b)		Moriago	78ª
3	10 Dec	2-seater	(c)		San Donà di Piave	78ª
–	14 Dec	EA	(d)		Valle Seren	78ª
4	26 Dec	EA	(e)		Musano	78ª
5	„	EA	(f)		Falzè	78ª
	1918					
–	10 Jan	EA	(g)		M. Lisser	78ª
–	28 Jan	fighter	(h)		Asiago	78ª
–	„	fighter	(h)		E Asiago	78ª
–	18 Mar	balloon	(d)		Conegliano	78ª
–	20 May	EA	(d)		Trento	3ª Sez
–	1 July	EA	(d)		Feltre	3ª Sez

(a) shared with Chiri; (b) this claim, which in 1917 was listed as confirmed and indeed led to Masiero's first Silver Medal, is not mentioned at all in the postwar review (!); shared with Chiri; (c) nr Villa Ancillotto; shared with Scaroni; (d) disallowed postwar; (e) shared with Fornagiari and Panero; (f) shared; (g) mentioned in contemporary press reports but disallowed; (h) shared, disallowed postwar.

MECOZZI Amedeo   Tenente   SQ 46ª, 49ª, 48ª, 45ª, 50ª, 76ª, 78ª

Born in Rome on 17 January 1892, Mecozzi joined the Army engineering branch. Assigned to the air service in June 1915, he was sent to the Malpensa school on 2 September and earned his wings at Busto Arsizio in January 1916 in a Farman MF.12, progressing to the MF.14 for his military licence. By March he was with the 46ª Squadriglia, which he soon left for the 49ª and the 48ª. By August 1916 Mecozzi reached the 45ª Squadriglia. Promoted sottotenente on 1 January 1917, he moved on again to the 50ª, where his determination to carry out missions even with badly hit aircraft earned him two Bronze Medals (respectively on 8 January and 19 February 1917) and a War Cross (19 June 1917, Asiago). In September Mecozzi returned to Malpensa for fighter conversion and the following 4 October was promoted tenente for war merit. On 12 October he reached the 76ª Squadriglia, but November found him in the 78ª, with which he would remain through to February 1919 and earn a Silver Medal in the postwar honours list. In June 1918 his insignia was noted as 'two blue bands', replacing a previous white question mark on a black ball. The review committee confirmed five of his victories. Accepted for permanent service on 31 October 1919, Mecozzi enjoyed a long and successful postwar career, serving first with the Italian Aviation Mission in Paris and then with the Direzione Tecnica at Montecelio (where he flew many war booty types including Fokker D.VII and VIII, Pfalz, Phönix and Albatros types). Between 1926 and 1929 he served as chief of the Italian Air Ministry's Press Office. Promoted maggiore on 29 July 1927, on 10 October 1929 he became CO of the 7° Gruppo. Through successive promotions, which led him to become generale di

Brigata on 8 April 1937, Mecozzi developed the 7° Gruppo into a test centre for his 'assault' doctrines which, in sharp contrast with the prevailing strategic bombing theories, advocated the tactical use of aviation assets against purely military targets rather than population and industrial centres. Retired for health reasons, Mecozzi became president of the RUNA, the former Aero Club of Italy, and of the Editoriale Aeronautica, the Ministry's publishing branch. After WW2, in which he remained inactive, in 1945 Mecozzi reopened the *Rivista Aeronautica*, serving as editor for many years, and campaigned to establish a national air museum. He died in Rome on 2 November 1971.

	1917					
1	26 Dec	2-seater	(a)	Volpago/Selva	am	78ª HD
	1918					
2	26 May	2-seater	(b)	Maserada	0840	78ª HD
3	„	Albatros D.III	(c)	S. Michele	0840	78ª HD
4	15 Jun	Brandenburg C.I	(d)	Cimadolmo	1000	78ª HD
5	19 Jun	Brandenburg C.I	(e)	Susegana	1120	78ª HD
–	„	balloon	(e)	Barco		78ª HD
–	6 Oct	DFW C	(f)	Susegana	1550	78ª HD
–	„	Albatros D.V	(f)	Susegana	1550	78ª HD
–	27 Oct	DFW C		Susegana	0710	78ª HD

(a) shared with Benvenuto; hit a house and set it on fire; (b) Flik 57 Rb; Mecozzi in HD 11435; shared with Capparucci; (c) 153.230, Flik 42J, Zgsf Franz Hofstädter; KIA; Mecozzi in HD 11435; shared with Capparucci; (d) shared with Riva; (e) shared with Moresco; (f) unconfirmed; with Gandini and Riva.

MICHETTI Giorgio   Tenente   SQ 43ª, 76ª

Born in Francavilla a Mare (Chieti province) on 29 May 1888, the son of the painter Francesco Paolo Michetti, he served with the 27th Field Artillery Regiment. By 1 August 1915, ranked aspirante, he was with the Cameri flying school. Listed as having reached the front on 26 March 1916, in January 1917 he was with 43ª Squadriglia, where he struck up a friendship with Scaroni. Selected for fighter training, he went to Malpensa for Nieuport conversion on 20 June 1917 (the rating was sanctioned on 4 September) and to Pisa for the air gunnery course on 25 July. He reached the 76ª Squadriglia on 29 July, by now a sottotenente, where he was again joined by Scaroni. He scored his first victory on 26 December 1917 in the air battle of Istrana and was awarded a Silver Medal. A second Silver was awarded in the field in June 1918. On 1 February 1919, just as the review committee confirmed a five-victory score, Michetti was assigned to the 350ª Squadriglia, a special unit formed to promote Italian aviation industry in Argentina, and on 20 June 1919 he flew a remarkable Buenos Aires-Montevideo round trip in 3h 5min. Little is known about his postwar life, except that his marriage was dissolved in Austria in May 1935. In 1936 he took up residence in Rome and in December 1938 he was promoted a tenente colonnello in the reserve. He died in Rome on 4 February 1966.

	1917					
1	26 Dec	DFW C	(a)	Camalo	0920	76ª
	1918					
–	12 Jan	EA	(b)	Cismon		76ª
–	21 Mar	Albatros D.III	(c)	Cascina Zocchi/SE Asiago		76ª
2	3 May	fighter	(d)	Sernaglia		76ª
3	22 May	2-seater	(e)	Quero		76ª
4	15 June	EA	(f)	Moriago		76ª
5	24 June	2-seater	(g)	Possagno/Paverion		76ª
–	14 Aug	fighter	(h)	Rasai/Valle Stizzone		76ª

(a) shared with Scaroni, Riva, and Lts Jarvis, Mulholland and Frayne of 28 Sqn RFC; (b) 'presumed forced down', according to war bulletin; (c) 153.100, Flik 55J, Korp Gottlieb Muczar, POW; credited to Scaroni alone; (d) shared with Baracchini; (e, f, g) shared with Scaroni; (h) claimed with Ticconi but credited to Ticconi alone.

NARDINI Guido   Sergente   SQ 75ª, 78ª, 91ª

Born on 30 July 1881 in Florence, Nardini is said to have earned his licence on 3 August 1911 but — since his personal file is virtually empty — this cannot be confirmed. A volunteer, he was a private in the Battaglione Squadriglie Aviatori at the outbreak of war. Still a mere soldato, Nardini was assigned first to the 75ª Squadriglia in Verona, where on 27 June 1916 he scored his first victory by intercepting an EA over Verona and shooting it down after a 20 km chase: the feat earned him a Bronze Medal awarded in the field and confirmed in January 1917. By February 1917 he was a caporale in the 78ª, using Nieuport 11 No.2184 as his mount. In June another victory over Val d'Arsa earned him a Silver Medal, also in the field. In early 1918 Nardini reached the 91ª, where he often flew as Baracca's wingman. On 10 February he suffered an accident while test flying Nieuport 17 No.5807, freshly arrived at the 91ª. On 17 May he shot down the Austrian ace Gräser (16 victories). His score in the May-June 1918 period earned him a second Bronze but returning from S. Luca airfield by motorcycle, on 23 August 1918, he fell and had to be hospitalised. The postwar review credited him with six confirmed victories. Electing to remain in service, in 1923 Nardini transferred to the new Regia Aeronautica and eventually rose to Maresciallo rank. He was killed on 26 January 1928 in a flying accident at Ciampino airfield, near Rome.

	1916					
1	27 Jun	EA	(a)	Verona		75ª Ni.10
	1917					
–	14 Jun	EA		Val d'Arsa/Borgo	0820	78ª Ni.17
2	,,	EA	(b)	Valsugana	0840	78ª Ni.17
3	18 Jul	2-seater	(c)	Asiago	0655	78ª
–	6 Sept	EA	(d)	Gorizia		78ª
	1918					
4	3 May	Brandenburg C.I	(e)	Grave di Papadopoli	1100	91ª
5	17 May	Albatros D.III	(f)	Pero	1015	91ª
6	15 June	Albatros D.III		Moriago	0915	91ª

(a) shared with Buzio, Consonni, De Bernardi; (b) shared with Amantea; "confirmed because of pilot's precedents"! (c) Magistrini participated but credit explicitly granted to Nardini; (d) 129.50, Flik 34, Horth WIA, Gerey KIA; participated with Baracca and Sabelli but not credited; (e) 369.28, Flik 19D, Zgsf Josef Friedrich/Oblt Karl Rosenbaum, both KIA; shared with Baracca; (f) 153.221, Ltn d R Franz Gräser, Flik 61J; shared with Magistrini and Novelli, several others also taking part in the action.

Note

Some confusion exists in publications between Guido and *Giulio* Nardini, the latter being born in Florence on 13 March 1883 and earning his licence at Etampes, France, on 22 August 1911.

NICELLI Giovanni   Sergente   SQ 79ª

Born in Lugagnano Val d'Arda, Piacenza province, on 27 October 1893. Unfortunately his personal file is missing, limiting the amount of biographical information available. Ranked caporale, by April 1917 was flying Nieuport 17s with the 79ª Squadriglia, where he would remain throughout the war. His first Silver Medal was awarded for actions in the hectic Caporetto days, when he forced two enemy aircraft to land. His 30 January 1918 victory was followed by the award of a second Silver Medal, in the field. On 4 May Nicelli single-handedly engaged seven aircraft over the Montello, achieving his two final victories and earning another Silver Medal in the field. He died tragically the following day, his Nieuport 27 breaking up in the air. At the time of his death Nicelli was reported as having taken part in over 70 combats. He was credited with 12 victories, nine of which were confirmed, but only eight were upheld in the postwar review. The airfield at San Nicolò, on Venice's Lido island, is still named after him. His decorations included a Belgian Croix de Guerre.

	1917					
–	14 Jun	EA	(a)	M. Verena		79ª
1	25 Oct	EA	(b)	Marcesina	0800	79ª
2	7 Nov	EA	(c)	Fonzaso	c. 1615	79ª

3	7 Dec	EA		Val d'Assa	1130	79ᵃ
4	13 Dec	EA		Asiago	c. 1100	79ᵃ
	1918					
5	30 Jan	2-seater	(d)	Asiago/Col d'Echele	1000	79ᵃ
–	4 Feb	black fighter	(e)	Val Stagna	c. 1100	79ᵃ
6	5 Feb	2-seater	(f)	Case Girardi	c. 0830	79ᵃ
7	13 Feb	fighter		Marcesina	0915	79ᵃ
–	24 Feb	EA		M. Grappa		79ᵃ
8	4 May	EA	(g)	Montello	0850	79ᵃ
9	„	fighter	(g)	Montello	1025	79ᵃ

(a) later disallowed; (b) forced to land; (c) forced to land inside Italian lines; own aircraft also forced down by engine trouble; (d) mentioned as "seventh victory" in citation; (e) shared with Reali; not confirmed; (f) forced to land; shared with Cerutti, to whom alone possibly credited in review?; (g) Austrian losses in this area in the morning were Albatros D.III 153.182, 153.195 and 153.210, all of Flik 68J, whose details however also match British claims of Lt GD McLeod, 28 Sqn, one Albatros D.V OOC; Lt GA Birks, 66 Sqn, two Albatros D.III DES at 0945; Lt GJM Apps, 66 Sqn, two DES; Lts WC Hilborn and VS Parker, one DES each.

NOVELLI Gastone   Tenente   SQ 28ᵃ, 76ᵃ, 81ᵃ, 91ᵃ

The son of an army general, Gastone Novelli was born in Ancona on 13 June 1895. He attended first the Rome Collegio Militare and then the Scuola Militare in Modena. In February 1915 he was assigned as sottotenente to the 8th 'Montebello' Lancers' Regiment. After serving briefly as a scout with the 43rd Artillery Regiment, by August 1915 Novelli was flying as observer with the 28ᵃ Squadriglia. He soon applied for pilot training, gaining his first licence on Caudron G.3s in April 1916 and the second on Farmans at Busto Arsizio three months later. From 12 August 1916 to 20 January 1917 he flew Farmans with the 30ᵃ Squadriglia, earning a Silver Medal for his reconnaissance work. At this time he was promoted to full tenente and nominally transferred to the 5th 'Novara' Lancers' Regiment. Although Novelli's official conversion on Nieuports took place in May, by April he had joined the 81ᵃ Squadriglia, a fighter unit where he scored his first victories. On 1 August 1917 he transferred to the 76ᵃ Squadriglia, serving as temporary CO from August 11 through 21, but he was wounded in the left arm and hospitalised. For having successfully completed the mission despite the wound, he was awarded a Silver Medal. He was still recovering at the time of the Caporetto retreat, but returned to the front and on 3 November 1917 joined the 91ᵃ Squadriglia, where his service until the end of the war earned him a third Silver. His other decorations included a War Cross and a Serb Golden Merit Medal. The postwar review confirmed him as an eight-victory ace, but on 3 July 1919 Novelli died in a take-off accident in Padova.

	1917					
–	15 Apr	EA	(a)			81ᵃ Ni
1	3 Jun	EA	(b)			81ᵃ Ni
2	19 Jun	EA	(c)	nr Aisovizza		81ᵃ Ni
3	21 Jun	EA	(d)	nr Stara Gora		81ᵃ
4	23 Nov	Albatros D.III	(e)	Falzè di Piave	1500	91ᵃ
5	30 Nov	German 2-seater	(f)	Moriago		91ᵃ
	1918					
6	17 May	Albatros	(g)	Pero	1015	91ᵃ Spad
7	26 May	fighter	(h)	i Ronchi	0840	91ᵃ
8	11 Aug	'new fighter'	(i)	Maserada	1445	91ᵃ

(a) mentioned in modern US sources but unconfirmed in original documentation; (b) forced to land; (c) shared; (d) shared; (e) Ltn Karl Überscher, Jasta 39, two victories, KIA; shared with Baracca, Novelli's share uncertain; (f) possibly FA.232, Uffz Kurt Hieling/Ltn d R Hugo Huck, both KIA; shared with Magistrini and Ranza; (g) 153.221, Ltn d R Franz Gräser, Flik 61J; adjudged to Nardini with participation of Magistrini and Novelli; (h) shared with Keller and Piccio; unidentified but possibly 153.230 attributed to Mecozzi; (i) shared with Piccio.

OLIVARI Luigi   Tenente   SQ 1ª, 70ª, 91ª

Born in La Spezia on 29 December 1891, Olivari earned his Aero Club licence on 27 November 1914. Shortly before Italy joined the war, on 19 May 1915 Olivari volunteered for pilot training with the Battaglione Aviatori. He earned his first licence on 50 HP Blériots on 15 June and the second, on the more powerful 80 HP variant, on 26 August. On 28 January 1916 Olivari, ranked aspirante, joined the 1ª Squadriglia (later 70ª), where on 7 April he scored the second official Italian air-to-air victory in the war and was awarded a first Bronze Medal. On 25 August Olivari became the first official Italian ace but most of these claims were in fact unconfirmed and were eventually disallowed. A second Bronze followed the second real victory on 16 September, while the third and fourth were recognized with a Silver Medal each. On 1 September Olivari was promoted a sottotenente in the reserve, officially in the Engineers corps. In April 1917 he used Nieuport 17 No. 3127 as his personal aircraft but also flew a Spad VII, and in May, when he was decorated with a third Silver, he transferred to the newly-formed 91ª Squadriglia. Detached to 77ª Squadriglia from 7 May to early June 1917, after his third Silver Medal he was promoted to tenente and assigned to the Technical Directorate as SVA test pilot. On 21 August 1917 he returned with a SVA prototype for evaluation by 91ª Squadriglia pilots and seems to have remained there. At 0957 hrs on 13 October 1917, while taking off, Olivari stalled his Spad VII and was killed in the crash. A final Silver Medal was awarded in February 1918. Novelli's decorations also included a French Croix de Guerre and a Serb Cross of Karageorgevic. Of his 19 claims, some 12 were confirmed during the war but the 1919 review cut the figure to eight — a total matching the number of victories mentioned in his citations, although with a different make-up. The airport at Ghedi, currently home of the Italian Air Force's 6th Stormo, is named after him.

	1916						
–	2 Apr	EA	(a)	beyond Cormons			1ª
1	7 Apr	2-seater	(b)	Cortello			1ª
–	16 May	EA		Gorizia			1ª
–	9 July	EA	(c)	Aisovizza			70ª
–	18 Jul	EA	(d)	Plava			70ª
–	25 Aug	EA	(e)	enemy territory			70ª
–	10 Sept	EA	(f)	Creda, nr Caporetto			70ª
2	16 Sept	Lloyd C.III	(g)	Staro Stelo		0930	70ª
3	31 Oct	2-seater	(h)	Monte Nero		am	70ª
	1917						
4	18 Mar	Brandenburg C.I	(i)	San Canziano		0935	70ª Ni.11
–	5 May	EA	(j)	St Veitsberg			91ª
5	18 May	big Albatros		Selo/Voiscizza		1220	91ª
6	24 May	Lohner Tl	(k)	Grado		0610	91ª
7	3 June	Albatros		San Marco		0930	91ª
8	6 June	Brandenburg C.I	(l)	M.Santo/Gargaro		0915	91ª

(a) unconfirmed; reported postwar by maternal uncle; (b) pilot Zgf Josef Mach, KIA/Oblt Johann Österreicher POW, Flik 2; shared with Bolognesi and Tacchini; (c) shared with Stoppani and Venchiarutti; forced down and set alight on ground; (d) said to have been forced down; extremely doubtful; (e) attacked over Medea, said to have crashed in enemy territory; mentioned in Silver Medal citation but unconfirmed; (f) mentioned in Silver Medal citation but unconfirmed; (g) 43.74, Flik 16; Korp Franz Morozko, KIA, Ltn Anton von Czaby, DOW; shared with Baracca and Ruffo; (h) pilot Korp Fuchs; victory confirmed on 29 Nov 1916 by diary found on 68.03, Baracca's 5th victim; (i) 29.53, Flik 23, Korp Halopy/Ltn von Heintochl KIA; (j) unconfirmed; attacked over Vippacco and said to be 'seen to put down on St Veitsberg'; (k) L136, Plasil/Riesner, both WIA/POW; (l) 229.19, Korp Vészpremy/Ltn Pirnos KIA.

OLIVI Luigi   Tenente   SQ 2ª ART, 42ª, 76ª

Born in Campobasso on 18 November 1894, he grew up in Ancona. Joining as a reserve officer, he was promoted caporale on 31 March 1914, sergente on 31 July and sottotenente on 8 November 1914. Despatched to the Aviano school for Blériot training on 31 July 1914, he earned his licence on 16 June 1915. He was injured in a flying accident at Malpensa on 25 October while flying a Macchi Parasol but by 7 November was with the 2ª Squadriglia per

Artiglieria (later 42ª). In June 1916 he was sent to Cascina Costa to convert on Nieuports, following which, on 25 July, he was posted to the 76ª Squadriglia, serving as its CO from 22 April 1917 to his death. His victories in 1916 were recognized with a Silver Medal, with a second one following for the October 1916-June 1917 cycle. On 17 July 1917 he scored his final victory but later in the day was killed near Moraro when he returned around 1015 hrs to photograph the wreckage. He had amassed 217 flying hours in 180 sorties, engaging in 48 combats and claiming eight victories, six of which upheld in the postwar review.

	1916					
1	8 Oct	EA		Aisovizza		76ª Ni.11
2	11 Oct	EA	(a)	Aisovizza/Biglia		76ª Ni.11
–	30 Oct	EA		Aisovizza		76ª Ni.11
3	23 Nov	EA		Gorizia		76ª Ni.11
4	25 Nov	EA	(b)	Schönpass		76ª Ni.11
	1917					
5	28 May	EA	(c)	Schönpass/Paskonisce		76ª Ni.17
6	17 Jun	EA		Merna/Vertoiba	am	76ª Spad VII

(a) shared with Stoppani; (b) citation has 26 Oct., unsupported in flight log; (c) shared.

PARVIS Giuliano   Tenente   SQ 91ª
war pseudonym of Giorgio PESSI, see below:

PESSI Giorgio   Tenente   SQ 82ª, 78ª, 91ª

Born in Trieste on 17 November 1891, he attended the local technical high school and went on to study engineering in Vienna and architecture in Munich. In January 1915 he fled to Venice and when Italy joined the war volunteered as a reserve cavalry officer, becoming a sottotenente in the 2nd 'Piemonte Reale' Cavalry Regiment. Transferring to the Corpo Aeronautico, he earned his advanced licence on a Nieuport 10 on 10 October 1916 at the Malpensa school, where he remained as instructor until May. Because the Austro-Hungarians considered those born in the Empire but fighting on the Italian side as traitors (not unreasonably from their point of view), Pessi, like others in his situation, on 3 May 1917 adopted the 'war pseudonym' of 'Giuliano Parvis', whose birthplace was given as 'Rome'. After completing the San Giusto gunnery school, on 25 May 1917 he was sent to the 82ª as CO — remarkable given his lack of experience — but on 13 June proceeded to the 78ª. In July 1917 'Parvis' reached the 91ª, where he scored all his victories and in the Autumn earned two Silver Medals. He also earned a French Croix de Guerre and the Serb Gold Medal. On 6 November he shot down the Austrian ace Ltn Szepessy-Sokoll, who crashed unseen by the Italians within Austrian lines. Flying a Spad VII marked with a crescent moon insignia, 'Parvis' remained with the squadron until 16 March 1918, when he was transferred to the Commissariato generale d'Aeronautica. During the next months he presumably converted onto Caproni bombers, for on 20 August 1918 he arrived in the USA as pilot for the American Ca.5 program. In 1919 'Parvis' actually flew a bomber under the Brooklyn bridge. The postwar review committee confirmed only six of his eight claims, despite the fact that all were shared. In 1922 he set up a flying school in Anatolia with Guido Keller. By 1926 he had joined the Aero Espresso Italiana airline as manager of its Brindisi-Athens-Rhodes-Constantinople line. He was lost at sea on 18 July 1933 on board Dornier Wal I-AZEE en-route to Rhodes.

	1917					
1	2 Aug	Brandenburg C.I	(a)	Ovcia Draga	0830	91ª Spad VII
–	29 Sep	Brandenburg C.I	(b)	lako Pietra Rossa	1040	91ª Spad VII
2	26 Oct	DFW C.V	(c)	Clabuzzano	1115	91ª Spad VII
3	„	DFW C.V	(d)	S.Pietro Natisone	1200	91ª Spad VII
–	6 Nov	Albatros D.III	(e)	Fossalta	1030	91ª Spad VII
4	„	DFW C.V	(f)	Godega S.Urbano	1100	91ª Spad VII
5	7 Nov	DFW C.V	(g)	nr Orsago	1145	91ª Spad VII
6	23 Nov	German 2-seater	(h)	Mt. Franchin/Moncader		91ª Spad VII

(a) shared with Ranza; (b) credited to Sabelli; (c) FA.39, Schulze/Ltn d R Werner Schulze; shared with Baracca; (d) FA.17, Ltn Hans Schlüter/Vzfw Bruno Fuchs; shared with Baracca; (e) 153.54, Flik 41J; Ltn Rudolf Szepessy-Sokoll, KIA; victory not acknowledged at the time as a/c crashed within its own lines; (f) possibly FA.219, Ltn d R Albrecht Binder DOW/Vzfw Werner Schröder; shared with Baracca; (g) 3955/17; possibly FA. 204, Gefr. Wilhelm Appelt/Ltn Paul Wilkening; shared with Baracca, who set it on fire on ground; (h) shared with Keller.

Note
It has been written that Parvis shared an unconfirmed victory with Piccio on 10 August 1918, but careful reference to the 91ª Squadriglia ORB shows that Piccio scored on 11 August together with Novelli.

PESSI-PARVIS Giorgio
erroneous contraction of Giorgio PESSI (see above) and Giuliano PARVIS (war pseudonym of Pessi).

PICCIO Pier Ruggero   Tenente Colonnello   SQ. 3ª, 77ª, 70ª, 91ª

Born in Rome on 27 September 1880, he entered the Scuola Militare in Modena on 29 October 1898 and on 8 September 1900 was posted as sottotenente in the 43rd Infantry Regiment. After three years he was seconded to the Foreign Affairs Ministry, which sent him to Kalambari, in Africa, from 5 November 1903 to 17 February 1907. From 13 March 1908 to 31 July 1909, Piccio served again abroad, with the 2nd Mixed Company in Crete. During the Turkish-Italian war, he transferred to the 37th Infantry and served in Libya from 14 December 1911 to 2 December 1912. In February 1912 Piccio was awarded a Bronze Medal as CO of a machine gun section. Upon returning, he was posted to the 19th Infantry and promoted capitano on 31 March 1913. Having become attracted to flying, he earned a licence on Nieuport monoplanes on 25 July 1913 and a Caproni rating the following 25 October. Soon thereafter he was made CO of the 5ª Squadriglia Aeroplani and on 31 December 1914 he was made a Knight in the Order of the Crown of Italy. When Italy joined the war Piccio was transferred to the Corpo Aeronautico Militare, earning a Bronze Medal for his May-August 1915 reconnaissance missions, in which he was hit several times. Also in August he went to Malpensa to convert onto Caproni bombers, which led to his being posted as 3ª Squadriglia CO from October 1915 to February 1916. After Nieuport conversion in Paris during April-May 1916, he returned on 31 May as CO of the newly-formed 77ª Squadriglia. In October he was awarded a Silver Medal for shooting down a balloon, possibly with Le Prieur rockets. On 26 January 1917 he was promoted maggiore, soon leaving the 77ª to became CO of 10° Gruppo, splitting operational flying with the 70ª (15 April-10 June; 30 June-5 July, 20 July-5 December) and 91ª (10-30 June, 5-20 July, 5-31 December), building up a steady score which led to the award of the Gold Medal on 5 May 1918. Promoted tenente colonnello on 3 October 1917, Piccio became CO of the 'Fighter Mass' and later Inspector of Fighter Squadrons, his work being recognized with a further Silver Medal in June 1918 and an Officer's Cross in the Military Order of Savoy. The postwar review upheld all his 24 victories and in 1921 Piccio went to Paris as air attaché. In March 1923 he was made honorary ADC to the King and on 25 December 1923, a full generale, became AOC (later Chief of Staff) of the Regia Aeronautica. He held the post until February 1927 and returned to Paris as air attaché. In November 1933 he was appointed Senator. He lived mainly in France but died in Rome on 31 July 1965. His son and grandson both became fighter pilots in the Italian Air Force, the former rising to flag rank and the latter now a tenente colonnello.

	1916					
1	18 Oct	balloon		Selo		77ª
	1917					
2	20 May	Albatros		E Plava	0930	91ª
3	28 May	Albatros		San Marco		91ª
4	1 June	EA	(a)	Gorizia/E Stara Gora		91ª
5	29 Jun	fighter		San Marco		91ª
6	28 Jul	2-seater		Ajdussina	1940	91ª
7	?	?	(b)			
8	2 Aug	2-seater	(c)	Volzano		91ª
9	„	2-seater	(c)	Volzano		91ª

10	7 Sept	Brandenburg C.I	(c)	Zagorje/Voglarje	0635	91ᵃ
11	14 Sept	Brandenburg C.I	(d)	Monte Verli/Ovsch	0815	91ᵃ
12	23 Sept	EA	(e)	Kal		91ᵃ or 70ᵃ
13	29 Sept	EA	(e)	Ternova		91ᵃ or 70ᵃ
14	2 Oct	2-seater	(f)	Bainsizza		91ᵃ Spad
15	3 Oct	2-seater	(g)	Leupa, nr Auzza	1610	91ᵃ Spad
16	25 Oct	Brandenburg C.I	(h)	Panovizza		91ᵃ
17	„	Aviatik		Castelmonte	1300	91ᵃ
	1918					
18	26 May	fighter	(i)	i Ronchi	0840	91ᵃ
19	9 June	2-seater		Moriago	0735	91ᵃ
20	19 Jul	Brandenburg C.I	(j)	S.Michele/S.Polo	1045	91ᵃ
21	29 Jul	Albatros D.V	(k)	Motta di Livenza	1010	91ᵃ
22	1 Aug	fighter	(l)	S.Polo/Cimadolmo		91ᵃ
23	5 Aug	EA	(m)	Conegliano	0800	91ᵃ
24	11 Aug	'new fighter'	(n)	Maserada	1445	91ᵃ
–	29 Sept	Ufag C.I	(o)	Montebelluna		91ᵃ

(a) forced to land; (b) no details in ORB, citations or elsewhere; (c) one of these thought to have been flown as single seater by Frank Linke-Crawford; (d) 229.31, Oblt Bruno Krainz/Rittm Eugen Somssich de Saard, both KIA, Flik 2; (e) not in 91ᵃ ORB but mentioned in citation and press; (f) obs Ltn Georg Müche KIA; (g) landed within Italian lines, both crew POW: possibly Flik 53D, Korp Josef Czarip/Ltn Bruno Belohlarak; (h) 29.63, Flik 19, Lambert/Pappius, both KIA; shared with Baracca; (i) shared with Keller and Novelli; unidentified but possibly 153.230 attributed to Mecozzi; (j) forced to land; (k) engaged combat over Motta, unable to pinpoint location of fall; possibly one of two Flik 74J a/c lost that day; (l) shared with British pilot — possibly Lt C McEvoy, 66 Sqn; (m) shared with Bacula; (n) shared with Novelli; (o) 123.34, Fw Breier/Oblt Karikas WIA; unconfirmed in 1918 but supported by current research.

Note

Irrespective of Piccio's nominal unit affiliation, all victories listed here as 91ᵃ were recorded in that unit's ORB.

PIEROZZI Orazio   Tenente di vascello

255ᵃ, STAZ BRINDISI, GRUPPO IDROCACCIA VENEZIA

Born in San Casciano Val di Siena on 8 December 1884, Pierozzi entered the Naval Academy in Livorno on 8 November 1908. He was assigned to the Sesto Calende flying school on 15 June 1916 and was officially rated a pilot candidate on 14 October, transferring on 17 October to the Brindisi naval air station, which he eventually rose to command and where he scored his first victories. In mid-1917 he earned three Silver Medals and a Bronze in quick succession and in December was CO of the 255ᵃ Squadriglia. On 18 March 1918 Pierozzi was transferred to Venice as CO of the newly-formed seaplane fighter group, comprising two fighter squadrons equipped with Macchi M.5 flying boats. Here he introduced rigorous training and operational procedures. On 3 November 1918 he was transferred to the newly occupied Trieste, where he ended the war having logged some 700 flights including 346 escorts, 30 recces over Trieste and Pola and 160 fighter patrols. He claimed 16 victims (nine Agos, four K-boats and three Phönix), seven of which were confirmed and upheld. On 17 March 1919 Pierozzi took off in poor weather from Venice in a Macchi M.9 flying boat, headed for Trieste and carrying on board HRH tenente di Vascello Ajmone di Savoia, himself an accomplished naval fighter pilot. Half a mile from their destination, a gale threw the M.9 against the dam protecting the harbour's entrance. Although the steamer *Tergeste* rescued both aviators, Pierozzi died the next day. He was awarded a posthumous Silver for his brave attempt to control his M.9 and protect Ajmone.

	1917				
–	15 May	K-boat	(a)		Brindisi
1	7 June	K-boat	(b)	Brindisi	Brindisi
	1918				
2	1 May	Hansa-B. W18	(c)	Grado	260ᵃ
3	14 May	Hansa-B. W18	(d)	Pola	260ᵃ
4	„	Hansa-B. W18	(d)	Pola	260ᵃ
5	„	"Ago"	(d)	Pola	260ᵃ

6	22 May	Phönix D.I	(e)		W of Rovigno	260ª
7	2 July	K-boat	(f)		Caorle	260ª

(a) no matching Austrian loss found; (b) K154, Poljanec/Prauer KIA; (c) A.67, Niedermayer; (d) A.70, Gindl, forced to land; A.85, forced to land and set on fire by Tb.80, Pichl, WIA; and a third, unidentified, shared with Jannello, Martinengo, Balleri; (e) A.115, Fregattenleutnant Wolleman, put down at sea and never found; (f) K394, shot down in flames; Guglielmi, Modler, Niedoba POWs.

RANZA Ferruccio Tenente SQ 43ª, 77ª, 91ª

Born in Fiorenzuola d'Arda, Piacenza province, on 9 September 1892, he was commissioned on 8 November 1914 as sottotenente in the 1st Engineers Regiment. Posted to the 43ª Squadriglia on 14 October 1915, he engaged in reconnaissance duties until June 1916, earning a Bronze Medal for completing a mission under very heavy fire on 1 April 1916. Accepted as a regular on 1 May 1916, after converting to Nieuports, he was posted to the 77ª on 22 July 1916 and scored a first victory on 14 September, for which he received a second Bronze. Before transferring to the 91ª on 1 May 1917 he had served as temporary CO for two months and scored three more times, receiving a Silver Medal. He continued flying with the 77ª Squadriglia until early June, but his score started climbing when he finally reached the 91ª, as acknowledged by two further Silver Medals. In the final stages of the war he succeeded Ruffo as 91ª CO and was knighted in the Military Order of Savoy. His war record comprised 465 operational sorties with 20 victory claims, 17 of which were upheld by the postwar review. Promoted to capitano for war merits, Ranza was also decorated with four War Crosses (one for Valour, one for Merit, a French one with palms and a Belgian one with crossed swords), the Serb Star of Karageorgevich.

Ranza enjoyed a long and distinguished postwar career, rising to CO of 13° Gruppo on 12 February 1924 and 2° Stormo on 15 April 1927. As AOC in Tripolitania, he saw action again in 1928 and, after a period in Italy, returned to Africa as AOC of Italian East Africa (7 January to 1 September 1935) and in March 1935 was promoted generale di Brigata Aerea. In May 1939 he became AOC Albania and in December AOC 4ª Squadra Aerea, in southern Italy. He retired on 29 January 1945 as generale di Squadra Aerea and died in Bologna on 25 April 1973.

	1916					
1	27 Jul	Brandenburg C.I	(a)		Martel	77ª Ni.11
2	14 Sep	seaplane	(b)		P. Sdobba/Miramar	77ª Ni.11
–	1 Nov	Albatros	(c)		Prosecco	77ª Ni.11
3	25 Nov	2-seater	(d)		Hermada	0930	77ª Ni.11
4	„	2-seater	(e)		Schonpass/Ternova	1145	77ª Ni.11
	1917					
–	4 Apr	EA	(f)		Prosecco		77ª
5	23 June	2-seater	(g)		Valsugana/Barco	0720	91ª
6	2 Aug	Brandenburg C.I	(h)		Ovcia Draga	0830	91ª
–	10 Aug	2-seater	(i)		Castagnevizza		91ª
7	23 Sep	Brandenburg C.I	(j)		Cotici	0930	91ª
8	25 Oct	German 2-seater	(k)		Lom	0800	91ª
9	21 Nov	German 2-seater	(l)		Casoni		91ª
10	30 Nov	German 2-seater	(m)		Moriago/Vidor		91ª
11	7 Dec	Brandenburg C.I	(n)		San Pietro di Nove		91ª
12	30 Dec	Albatros			Fonzaso		91ª
–	31 Dec	Brandenburg C.I	(o)		La Comina		91ª
	1918					
13	12 Jan	DFW C	(p)		Campo San Piero		91ª
–	4 Feb	EA	(q)		Cima Mandriolo		91ª
14	10 Feb	Brandenburg C.I	(r)		Val dei Signori	1105	91ª
15	„	fighter	(s)		Val d'Astico	1110	91ª
16	15 Jun	Brandenburg C.I	(t)		Grave di Papadopoli	0910	91ª
17	17 Aug	2-seater			S. Polo	2000	91ª
–	29 Sept	Ufag C.I	(u)		Montebelluna		91ª
–	29 Oct	fighter			Ponte di Piave		91ª
–	„	EA	(v)		Oderzo		91ª

(a) 61.23, Flik 24, Fw Alois Jezek/Oblt Georg Kenzian, both WIA; shared with Savio; (b) shared with Savio and Tesei; another forced to alight but recovered by torpedo boat was apparently not counted; victory confirmed but no matching Austrian loss found; (c) forced to land; (d) possibly Flik 14, Zgf Adolf Goldberger/Ltn Kasimir Schmid, POWs; (e) fell within enemy lines; possibly Brandenburg C.I 68.19 Oblt Brumowski and Nadherny; (f) forced to land; (g) observer WIA, possibly KIA; (h) shared with Parvis; (i) Oblt Ebner KIA/Haupt Kochrer POW; (j) 129.48, Flik 35, Fw Josef Baier/Oblt Eduard Hafner, KIA; shared with Sabelli; (k) possibly DFW of FA.39, pilot Fritz Böttcher KIA; (l) FA.39, Fw Konrad Strelocke/Oblt Detlev Lamp KIA; (m) possibly FA.232, Uffz. Kurt Hieling/Ltn d R Hugo Huck, both KIA; shared with Magistrini and Novelli; (n) 369.21, Oblt Knezevic/Haupt Frick KIA; shared with Magistrini; Bacula present but did not participate; (o) 329.36, forced to land, Fw Friedam WIA/Oblt Szabo; shared with Magistrini; not counted; date given as 1 Jan 1918 in ORB; (p) Reihenbilzug 1, Fw Hichleim/Oblt Heinrich von Ahlefeld; (q) from ORB: 'uncertain fate. Was acknowledged forced to land damaged'; no further discussion or confirmation but next victory clearly labelled 15th; (r) 29.68, Flik 17D, Fhr Guido Prodam POW/Oblt Julius Marsalek KIA; shared with Bacula; (s) shared with Bacula; (t) possibly 369.23, Flik 44D, Haupt Aladar Kerschbaum/Oblt Franz Petzny KIA; shared with Olivero; (u) 123.34, Fw Breier/Oblt Karikas WIA; not acknowledged in 1918 but confirmed by current research; (v) forced to land.

REALI Antonio   Sergente   SQ 79^a

Born in Ozegna, Torino province, on 31 March 1891, Reali was called up as a private soldier in the Engineering branch. He undertook flying training at the Coltano school, earning his MF12 and MF15 ratings respectively on 1 July and 15 August 1916. After getting his advanced licence on 14 July, Reali proceeded to Cascina Costa for Nieuport conversion. He eventually reached the 79^a Squadriglia, with which he would stay throughout the war, on 20 January 1917. In his first year of service, Reali achieved no confirmed victories, but he more than made up for this in 1918, scoring his first one on 14 January and becoming an ace on 1 February. For this feat he was awarded a Silver Medal in the field. Although credited by modern literature with shooting down the Austrian ace Gräser on 17 May 1918, the victory was in fact adjudged to Nardini. According to the committee's review, during 1918 Reali put in some 29 claims, of which 11 were upheld and the others denied. Reali was demobilized in early 1919 but after 1923 joined the Regia Aeronautica reserve, reaching capitano rank on 31 December 1940. He died in Fano, near Pesaro, on 19 January 1975.

	1917					
–	3 June	EA		Cima 12/Borgo		79^a
–	20 Dec	EA		Val d'Assa/Serena		79^a Ni.17
	1918					
–	10 Jan	fighter		Primolano	1215	79^a
1	14 Jan	2-seater	(a)	Valstagna/M. Zebio		79^a
–	25 Jan	EA		M. Zebio	1045	79^a Ni
2	28 Jan	EA	(b)	Bertiaga/Valle Vecchia		79^a
3	„	EA	(b)	nr M. Melago		79^a
4	30 Jan	2-seater		Val Chiara (?)		79^a
5	1 Feb	EA		Val Stagna	1500	79^a
–	4 Feb	black fighter		Val Stagna	1100	79^a
–	„	fighter		Val Stagna	1600	79^a
–	11 Mar	fighter		M. Erio/M. Ciullo	1415	79^a
–	8 Apr	EA		S. Lucia di Piave		79^a
–	17 May	Albatros D.III	(c)	Pero	1015	79^a
–	31 May	EA		S. Salvatore		79^a Ni.27
–	15 Jun	2-seater		Fara di Soligo	1215	79^a
–	„	EA		Valdobbiadene		79^a
–	17 Jun	EA		Ponte della Priula		79^a
6	20 Jun	fighter		Susegana/Montello	1895	79^a
7	„	EA		Susegana/Montello	1835	79^a
8	21 Jun	EA	(d)	nr Ponte della Priula	1949	79^a
9	„	EA	(d)	nr Ponte della Priula	1949	79^a
–	22 Jun	EA		Nervesa		79^a
–	„	EA		Nervesa		79^a
–	1 Jul	EA		nr Collalbrigo		79^a

–	30 Jul	EA		nr Susegana		79ª
10	11 Sept	German		nr Susegana		79ª
–	20 Sept	EA		nr Falzè		79ª
–	23 Sept	EA		Susegana/Conegliano		79ª
11	4 Oct	Albatros D.III	(e)	S of Moriago	1035	79ª
–	5 Oct	EA		nr Conegliano		79ª
–	6 Oct	EA		nr Pare		79ª
–	„	EA		nr Pare		79ª

(a) shared with Imolesi; (b) shared with Cerutti; (c) 153.221, Ltn d R Franz Gräser, Flik 61J; victory adjudged to Nardini with Magistrini and Novelli; Reali log lists no flight, but an official confirmation of his participation in the action exists! (d) one possibly Albatros D.III 153.188, Flik 51J, Obltn d R Friedrich Dechant (two victories), shot down over Tempio, 14 km W of Ponte della Priula; a third aircraft was claimed forced down but is unconfirmed; (e) 253.51, Flik 56J, Korp Josef Berggold, KIA.

RENNELLA Cosimo   Sergente   SQ 31ª, 32ª, 48ª, 45ª, 78ª

Cosimo Rennella was born in Secondigliano, Naples province, on 15 February 1890. Two years later the family emigrated to Guayaquil, in Ecuador, where the boy grew up as 'Cosme' and in accordance with the Spanish custom added his mother's surname, Barbatto. An athlete since 1907, in 1909 he took part in military operations against Peru with the Patria I volunteer battalion raised in his school. In 1912 the local Flying and Shooting Club underwrote the cost of sending Rennella to Italy to earn his civil licence at the Chiribiri school in Turin. This he achieved on 24 August 1912, after which he accompanied two Nieuport-type monoplanes to Panama. Again sent to Italy to purchase a Chiribiri monoplane, Rennella seized the occasion to earn an Italian military ticket at Torino on 25 July 1913. By 29 September he was back home (where he appears to have briefy flown in the Esmeraldas war) then moving on to Peru, Chile and Mexico, contributing to set up its first flying school. Learning of Italy's entry into WW1, in July 1915 Rennella returned to Italy and after pleading his case with the War Ministry was allowed to volunteer for service. On 17 September 1915 he entered the Pisa flying school. Rated a Farman student on 1 February 1916, he was transferred to the Busto Arsizio school on 6 February and finally to Turin in April to convert onto the MF14. Caporale Rennella joined the 31ª Squadriglia on 14 April, flying his first sortie the next day. By 20 April he was with the 32ª, moving on to the 48ª on 1 May and the 45ª on 12 July. On 6 August 1916 his aircraft was attacked by enemy fighters and on 31 August he was promoted sergente. On 23 June 1917 Rennella passed the medical examination for fighter training and proceeded to the Malpensa school. He was rated on Nieuport 11s on 7 August and two days later reported to Pisa for gunnery instruction, finally reaching the 78ª Squadriglia on 24 August 1917. He would serve with the unit throughout his war, often sending descriptions of his experiences to the Ecuador press and flying first Ni.17s and later Hanriot HD.1s. The postwar review credited Rennella — who had earned two Silver medals and Belgian, French and Italian War Merit Crosses — with seven confirmed victories against 17 claims. Demobbed in March 1919, in early 1920 he returned to South America, having been engaged as a stunt pilot in Venezuela, where he eventually established the Maracay military aviation school. In 1924 Rennella returned to Ecuador, joining its budding military aviation service as a capitan and eventually flying its first operational sorties in August 1932. In August 1934 he was decorated with the Abdòn Calderòn medal, 2nd Class. Promoted major, in 1937 he attended a gathering of WW1 aces in Dayton, Ohio. Treated for pneumonia in the Quito military hospital, Rennella died on 3 May 1937 and was posthumously promoted teniente colonel.

	1917					
1	24 Sept	fighter		Zagorje		78ª
–	26 Sept	EA		Lhom		78ª
2	21 Nov	fighter		Mosniga		78ª
	1918					
3	14 Jan	EA		Monte Grappa		78ª
4	15 Jan	EA	(a)	Arsiè	1500	78ª
–	17 Mar	fighter		Val Seren		78ª

-	17 Apr	EA		Conegliano		78ª
-	„	EA		Valdobbiadene		78ª
-	1 May	EA		Cimadolmo		78ª
-	17 May	EA	(b)	Maserada	c.0915	78ª
5	„	2-seater	(c)	Maserada	c.0958	78ª
6	30 May	Albatros D.III	(d)	Lovadina		78ª
-	20 Jun	EA	(e)	Sorgente Frati	1045	78ª HD
-	„	EA	(e)	Camapagnole		78ª
-	„	EA	(e)	between Fontana Boera and Villa Iacur		78ª
-	23 Jun	Albatros D.III	(f)	Falzè di Piave/Barbisano	1120	78ª
7	31 Aug	EA	(g)	Mandre	1330	78ª HD
-	27 Oct	2-seater		N San Polo	1445	78ª HD

(a) fell within enemy lines; (b) shared with Fucini; (c) shared with Avet and Fucini but apparently not included in Rennella's score; (d) 153.219, Flik 41J, Offzstv Karl Gebhardt, KIA; (e) claimed with Gandini but none confirmed to either pilot; (f) clearly indicated as OOC; (g) shared with, and confirmed by, Chiri and Fucini.

RESCH Alessandro   Sottotenente   SQ 26ª, 70ª

Born in Avezzano, L'Aquila province, on 19 November 1892, Resch was initially assigned to the 7th Bersaglieri Cyclist Battalion. Accepted for flying training, he earned his first and second licences on Voisins respectively on 16 June and 1 July 1916 and was soon posted to the Voisin-equipped 26ª Squadriglia. He was awarded a Silver Medal for the 22 August 1916 sortie, which he completed despite having been wounded. On 21 June 1917 Resch converted onto Nieuports, but his progress to fighter units was slowed by a further conversion, this time onto SP.2, in September, and it was only on 12 December 1917 that he reached the 70ª Squadriglia. His service there was rewarded with a Bronze Medal and two war crosses. On 26 February he was given night-equipped HD.1 518 and on 17 April he shot down three enemies in a single action. On 10 January 1919 he transferred to the 91ª Squadriglia. Although the review committee credited Resch with five victories, its official letter to him listed only four! On 1 September 1928 he joined the Avio Linee Italiane airline as captain and chief pilot, flying some 500,000 miles over the next seven years. In 1935 a maggiore in the Air Force reserve, he rose to tenente colonnello in December 1939. He died in Avezzano on 8 January 1966. His son Arturo flew F-86E Sabres with the 2nd Stormo of the Italian Air Force and the 'Lancieri Neri' aerobatic team in the late 1950s.

	1917				
1	no details known		(a)		
	1918				
-	3 Apr	balloon	(b)	Conegliano	70ª
2	17 Apr	2-seater	(c)	Valdobbiadene	70ª
3	„	fighter	(c)	Valdobbiadene	70ª
4	„	fighter	(c)	Valdobbiadene	70ª
5	12 Jul	EA		Bottat/Col dell'Orso	70ª

(a) As early as 30 June 1917, Resch was listed with a victory in wartime publications; (b) hauled down; probably not counted; (c) shared with Avet, Bocchese, Eleuteri.

RIVA Antonio   Capitano   SQ 29ª, 73ª, 71ª, 78ª

Born in Shanghai, China, on 8 April 1896, Riva volunteered as reserve officer on 31 December 1914 and was commissioned sottotenente in the 70th Infantry Regiment on 11 July 1915. Wounded in action for the first time on 12 November 1915, he returned to the 70th on 16 March 1916, passing to the 201st on 15 June, only to be wounded again on the 30th. He returned to the front, with the 44th Infantry, on 22 August, but after summer leave in September found himself in the 49th Infantry. Accepted for pilot training, on 25 September 1916 he was at San Giusto school. He was promoted tenente on 25 February 1917 and completed his training in Foggia in April. After a short stay with the 29ª Squadriglia, a reconnaissance unit with which he flew just 12 sorties, in June 1917 he converted on Nieuports at Malpensa, following up with gunnery school at San Giusto in July. On 19 July, Riva was assigned to the 73ª Squadriglia, transferring to the 71ª at the end of the month. With this unit he scored his first victory, the shared downing of Austrian ace Kowalczik. On 12 November 1917 he joined the 78ª Squadriglia, where he was promoted capitano on 31 October and became CO in November. He remained with the 78ª until 10 September 1918, when he was posted as CO of the 90ª Squadriglia, a SVA 5 unit which started being formed at Ponte San Pietro on 15 September 1918. Riva's decorations included a Silver Medal and the Knight's Cross of the Military Order of Savoy. The postwar review confirmed seven victories, against 13 known claims. Before being discharged in January 1921, in 1920 Riva served as commander of the Chinese stops for the Rome-Tokyo flight. Very little is known about Riva's later years, except that in February 1935 he was listed as a capitano in the reserve. Still living in China, during the Mao years he was arrested for alleged counter-revolutionary activities, sentenced to death by a military tribunal, and shot in Peking on 17 August 1951.

	1917					
1	24 Aug	Albatros D.III	(a)	Forte Luserna		71ª Ni.11
2	26 Dec	DFW C	(b)	Signoressa		78ª HD
3	26 Dec	DFW C	(c)	Camalo	0920	78ª HD
	1918					
4	27 Jan	EA	(d)	S. Marino, nr Gallio/Cismon		78ª HD
–	1 May	EA	(e)	Cimadolmo		78ª HD
5	15 Jun	Brandenburg C.I	(f)	Montello/Nervesa	1000	78ª HD
–	16 Jun	Brandenburg C.I	(g)	Malborghetto/Fontigo	1030	78ª HD
–	„	EA	(h)	Pilonetto		78ª HD
–	12 Aug	DFW C	(i)	S. Lucia di Piave		78ª HD
–	6 Oct	DFW C	(j)	Susegana	1550	78ª HD
–	„	Albatros D.V	(j)	Susegana	1550	78ª HD
6	27 Oct	2-seater	(k)	Pieve di Soligo	1620	78ª HD
–	28 Oct	LVG	(l)	Pederobba/		
				Grave di Papadopoli		78ª HD
7	29 Oct	Brandenburg C.I	(m)	Oderzo	0729	78ª HD

(a) 53.33, Flik 24, Offzstv Julius Kowalczik; shared with Amantea and Tola; (b) wreck recovered by 34 Sqn RFC and serialled G128; not immediately acknowledged, leading to Riva's protest on 30 July 1918; (c) Fl Abt 2; Uffz Hedessinski/Ltn Pallach, POW; shared with Scaroni, Riva, and Lts Jarvis, Mulholland and Frayne of 28 Sqn RFC; (d) on this day, Riva and Fornagiari shot down one aircraft each, individually, whereas Riva asked they each be credited with two shared; (e) shared with Rennella; unconfirmed; (f) shared with Mecozzi; (g) shared with Fucini and Venier; possibly not counted; (h) unconfirmed; (i) unconfirmed; with Mecozzi and Gandini; (j) unconfirmed; shared with Mecozzi and Gandini; (k) shared with Morfino; (l) nr Cascina Gregoletti; shared with four Camels of 66 Sqn?; (m) 369.175, two crew WIA; nr Cascina Colussi; shared with Morfino.

Note

Capitano *Antonio* Riva's transfer to the 78ª coincided with sergente *Giovanni* Riva's move from the 78ª to the 77ª. Care must be exercised in correctly identifying the two men.

RIZZOTTO Cosimo   Sergente   SQ 77ª

Born in Colognola ai Colli, Verona province, on 26 June 1893. He served as a soldier in the Battaglione Aviatori from 23 September 1913 and was accepted for pilot training in May 1915. He earned his licence at the San Giusto school, proceeding to Malpensa for MF training on 19 December. In January 1916 he was promoted caporale and by March he was with the Nieuport flight at Cascina Costa. From 30 March through 30 May he was sent to Paris, and upon returning in July he was assigned to the 77ª Squadriglia. Rizzotto scored his first victory, which earned him a Silver Medal, on 28 February 1917. A second Silver came for the July-November 1917 period. Credited with six victories by the postwar committee, Rizzotto emigrated to South America, serving as flying instructor in Argentina and Paraguay. He died in Milan on 18 February 1963.

	1917					
1	28 Feb	EA	(a)	Monfalcone		77ᵃ
2	7 July	EA		Fait/Castagnevizza		77ᵃ
3	11 Jul	EA	(b)	Voiscizza	0550	77ᵃ
–	29 Jul	EA	(c)	San Daniele		77ᵃ
4	29 Sep	EA		nr Pietre Rosse		77ᵃ
5	6 Nov	Brandenburg C.I	(d)	S. Michele di Cogliano	1150	77ᵃ
	1918					
6	15 Jun	'small Brandenburg' (e)		Ponte di Piave	1320	77ᵃ Spad

(a) aircraft forced to land nr Adria S.Giovanni road and bridge, then destroyed by artillery fire; (b) wreck recovered; serial reported as T112.2'; (c) forced to land; (d) 229.24, Flik 12D, Zgsf Feiler KIA/Ltn Schwarzenbach POW; shared with Leonardi; (e) possibly shared with Ltn FS Bowles, 45 Sqn, who claimed a 2-seater OOC over Ponte di Piave at 1320 hrs.

RUFFO DI CALABRIA Fulco   Tenente   SQ 4ᵃ, 44ᵃ, 42ᵃ, 1ᵃ, 70ᵃ, 91ᵃ

Born in Napoli on 12 August 1884 from a family of strong military traditions, including Cardinal Fabrizio Ruffo who led 25,000 men against the French in Calabria in 1797, he volunteered in the 11th 'Foggia' Light Cavalry Regiment on 22 November 1904 for reserve officer training. Caporale on 31 May 1905 and sergente on 30 November, he was commissioned sottotenente on 18 February 1906. He then went to Africa as deputy director of the Wegimont navigation company of Antwerp and only returned to Italy at the outbreak of war. Assigned to the Battaglione Aviatori on 20 December 1914, he earned his licence and reached the 4ᵃ Squadriglia artiglieria (later 44ᵃ Squadriglia) on 28 September, transferring on 26 January 1916 to the 2ᵃ (later 42ᵃ), where he earned a Bronze Medal in February and April. As a personal insignia he adopted a black skull and bones, which he applied to his Ni.11 and 17 and Spad VII. Following Nieuport conversion at Cascina Costa in May, on 28 June 1916 he was posted to the 70ᵃ Squadriglia, where in August his first two victories earned him a Silver Medal, followed by a Bronze in September. In March 1917 he was promoted tenente and became a regular officer, while in May he followed Baracca in the newly-formed 91ᵃ, earning a Bronze and a Silver Medal in that very month. In August he became capitano. His rapidly mounting score was rewarded with the Gold Medal on 5 May 1918 and he became CO following Baracca's death, but relinquished it to Ranza following a nervous breakdown. Appointed 10th Gruppo CO on 23 October, he continued flying and six days later was brought down near Marano by artillery fire. He engaged in combat 53 times, scoring 20 victories, confirmed by the postwar review. Knighted in the Military Order of Savoy, although nominally remaining in the reserve (where he reached tenente colonnello rank in 1942), by 1925 he had effectively retired to manage his estate at Paliano, near Frosinone. He died in Ronchi di Apuania on 23 August 1946. His daughter Paola, by virtue of having married Prince Albert on 2 July 1959, became Queen of Belgium on 9 September 1993.

	1916					
1	23 Aug	Brandenburg C.I	(a)	Gorizia/Carso		1ᵃ
–	„	EA		Stariski		1ᵃ
2	16 Sept	Lloyd C.III	(b)	Staro Stelo	0930	70ᵃ
–	29 Dec	Albatros	(c)	Velichidol	0935	70ᵃ
	1917					
–	1 Jan	Albatros	(d)	Monfalcone	1515	70ᵃ
3	11 Feb	Brandenburg C.I	(e)	Selvis Ozzano		70ᵃ
4	16 Feb	Albatros		Manzano/Medeuzza		70ᵃ
–	28 Feb	EA	(f)	Gradisca d'Isonzo	1015	70ᵃ
5	5 May	2-seater	(g)	Sagrado		91ᵃ
6	10 May	fighter	(h)	Biglia	1100	91ᵃ Ni.17
7	12 May	fighter		San Marco	1900	91ᵃ
8	13 May	Albatros		Jelenik	am	91ᵃ
9	26 May	Albatros		Britof	1145	91ᵃ
–	24 Jun	Albatros	(i)	Asiago/Cima 12	0630	91ᵃ

–	26 Jun	Albatros	(j)	Asiago	0830	91ª	Spad
10	14 Jul	Albatros 2-seater	(k)	Castagnevizza	0915	91ª	
11	17 Jul	fighter		Log, S S. *Lucia*		91ª	
12	20 Jul	2-seater	(l)	E Nova Vas	0920	91ª	
13	,,	fighter	(m)	E Castagnevizza	0920	91ª	
14	25 Oct	EA		Lom	0800	91ª	
15	,,	Aviatik	(n)	Tolmino		91ª	
16	,,	2-seater		S. Marco		91ª	
	1918						
17	number skipped in ORB						
18	20 May	fighter		Volpago/Nervesa	0915	91ª	
19	number skipped in ORB						
20	15 June	Albatros		Grave di Papadopoli	0710	91ª	

(a) 61.61, Flik 19, Zgsf Himmer; shared with Baracca; (b) 43.74, Flik 16; Korp Franz Morozko, KIA, Ltn Anton von Czaby, DOW; shared with Baracca and Olivari; (c) unconfirmed; (d) unconfirmed; (e) 27.74, Flik 35; Korp Ludwig Stech/Ltn Simienski; shared with Baracca, Gorini, Poli; (f) unconfirmed but seen to go down very steeply and losing its rudder: a possibility; (g) forced to land behind its lines; (h) put down at Biglia; (i) mentioned by some but no kill claimed in ORB; (j) a possibility: EA seen to go down 'most steeply, almost falling'; (k) crashed by village; Costantini saw observer fall out; (l) crew KIA; (m) fell within own lines; (n) shared with Costantini.

Note

In the running tally in the 91ª Squadriglia's ORB, no victory appears between the 16th (25 Oct 1917) and 18 (20 May 1918) nor between it and the 20th (15 June 1918). The discrepancy is possibly explained by the late confirmation of a previous claim and probable candidates are therefore clearly labelled.

A rudder from a Brandenburg CI was presented to 9° Stormo (Serial No. 209.32) by Ruffo after the war. Today it is in the Sqn HQ at Gazzanise, nr Naples.

SABELLI Giovanni   Tenente   SQ AVIATIK, 2ª, 71ª, SEZ DIF ALBANIA, 91ª

Born in Napoli on 23 September 1886, Sabelli earned his civil Royal Aero Club licence (No. 178) at Brooklands, in England, on 30 January 1912. He took part in a number of flying competitions in a Deperdussin and it is said that in 1912 he helped to organise the Bulgarian Air Service in the war against Turkey. When Italy entered the war, he volunteered for service, becoming a reserve sottotenente in the Engineering Corps and earned basic and advanced military licences on Aviatiks in August 1915. By 30 August Sabelli was with the Squadriglia Aviatik at Aviano, but on 19 October he was sent to Le Bourget to convert onto Nieuports. Upon returning, on 30 January 1916 he was assigned to the 2ª Squadriglia Nieuport, with which he served until September 1916, earning a first Silver Medal despite having engaged in combat inconclusively. Between 29 May and 2 July he was seconded to Malpensa as a Nieuport test pilot. Promoted tenente on 9 September, he was selected to command the Nieuport Defence Section in Albania (later to become the 85ª) and served there from October 1916 to February 1917. After a brief period with the 71ª, on 9 May 1917 Sabelli was assigned to the 91ª, the transfer becoming effective on 23 June. The August-September 1917 period earned him a second Silver Medal, but on 25 October 1917 he was shot down in flames over the Bainsizza by a two-seater. This had been originally attacked by Piccio, but when he was forced to break off by jammed guns, Sabelli then pressed on the attack from the rear quarter, falling to the observer's gun at about 0930 hrs. His five victories were all upheld by the postwar review board.

	1917					
1	10 Aug	Albatros	(a)	Monte Stol	2000	91ª
2	6 Sept	Brandenburg C.I	(b)	Monte Sabotino	1830	91ª
3	17 Sep	Albatros	(c)	S. Andrea Gorizia	1020	91ª
4	23 Sep	Albatros	(d)	Cotici	0930	91ª
5	29 Sep	Albatros	(e)	lake Pietra Rossa	1040	91ª

(a) seen to land; (b) 129.50, Flik 34, Horth WIA/Gerey KIA; shared with Baracca; (c) 'seen to land beyond the Vertoiba'; (d) shared with Ranza; (e) Parvis present but not credited.

SCARONI Silvio   Tenente   SQ 4ª, 44ª, 43ª, 86ª, 76ª

Born in Brescia on 12 May 1893, while serving as caporale in the 2nd Field Artillery Regiment he volunteered for pilot training in March 1915 and was sent to the San Giusto school, where he earned his basic licence on Blériots on 28 August and his advanced on Caudron G.3s on 29 September 1915. Initially assigned to the 4ª Squadriglia per l'artiglieria, (later 44ª), he flew his first operational sortie on 8 October and a month later earned a Bronze Medal for a dangerous mission. In January 1917, promoted sottotenente and nominally transferred to the Engineering Corps, he was posted to the 43ª Squadriglia, also a reconnaissance unit, where he first met Michetti. In June Scaroni was awarded a Silver Medal for his 20 months at the front and posted to Malpensa for Nieuport conversion, followed by gunnery school at San Giusto. Initially assigned to 86ª Squadriglia, a SVA unit being formed in Ponte San Pietro, because of the Caporetto retreat Scaroni found himself diverted to the 76ª, flying Nieuport 17s, and on 3 November he had his first dogfight, coming away with the impression of a victory but not submitting a claim. He scored three times that month, earning a second Silver. On 26 December, during the famous battle of Istrana, he brought down three aircraft. He was by then flying an HD.1 marked with concentric black and white squares on the rear fuselage. On 13 July 1918 the war bulletin mentioned his 30th victory, which brought him a Gold Medal. But Scaroni had been badly wounded and would not see further combat. The postwar review credited Scaroni with an official score of 26, although in later years he claimed not to know which were disallowed. After the war, Scaroni served with the Italian Aeronautical Mission to Argentina (the 350ª Squadriglia, from 25 February to 15 October 1919) and upon returning was discharged in January 1920. In the following December, however, he rejoined as a regular. He served frequently abroad, in Britain (as Air Attaché, from January 1924 to September 1925), the United States (Air Attaché, October 1925 to February 1930) and China (as head of the Italian Aviation Mission, from July 1935 to December 1937). In 1930 he was CO of 88° Gruppo, a seaplane fighter unit. From 15 October 1933 to 16 June 1935 he served as ADC to King Vittorio Emanuele III. Rising to generale di Squadra Aerea, in WW2 he was from December 1941 to January 1943 AOC of the Aeronautica della Sicilia. He left the military following the September 1943 armistice, retiring to Carzago Riviera, on lake Garda. He died in Milan on 16 February 1977. He published four books of memoirs, two on WW1 (*Ricordi e impressioni di guerra aerea*, 1922; *Battaglie nel cielo*, 1934, last reprinted in 1971) and one each about China and serving with the King.

	1917					
–	3 Nov	EA	(a)	Ponti della Priula		76ª Ni.17
1	14 Nov	2-seater		Colbertaldo		76ª Ni.17
2	18 Nov	fighter		San Donà		76ª
3	19 Nov	Albatros D.III		Vidor	am	76ª
4	5 Dec	2-seater		Onigo	pm	76ª
5	10 Dec	2-seater		Noventa di Piave		76ª
6	19 Dec	2-seater		Conegliano		76ª
7	26 Dec	EA		Musano	0900	76ª HD
8	26 Dec	DFW C.V	(b)	Camalo	0920	76ª HD
9	26 Dec	AEG G.IV	(c)	Montebelluna	1235	76ª HD
	1918					
–	12 Jan	Brandenburg D.I	(d)	Val Stizzone		76ª HD
10	14 Jan	Berg D.I	(e)	Busa Melagon	1100	76ª HD
11	28 Jan	DFW C.V	(f)	Biadene		76ª HD
12	1 Feb	2-seater		Vidor/Col S. Martino		76ª HD
13	11 Feb	fighter		Cismon		76ª HD
14	"	fighter		Fontana Secca		76ª HD
15	18 Feb	2-seater		Possagno	am	76ª HD
16	21 Mar	Albatros D.III	(g)	Cascina Zocchi	am	76ª HD
–	3 Apr	balloon	(h)	Premaor		76ª HD
17	22 May	2-seater		Uson		76ª HD
18	8 Jun	2-seater		M. Cismon	0600	76ª HD
19	15 Jun	EA		Montello	0620	76ª HD

20	21 Jun	fighter		Mandre	pm	76ª HD
21	24 Jun	2-seater	(i)	Possagno/Paverion	1200	76ª HD
22	25 Jun	fighter	(j)	Moreno di Piave	1030	76ª HD
23	„	Albatros D.III	(k)	Moreno di Piave	1030	76ª HD
24	7 Jul	Brandenburg C.I	(l)	Cima Eckar	0900	76ª HD
–	„	Brandenburg C.I	(m)	Valbella		76ª HD
25	„	Albatros D.III	(n)	Valbella	0900	76ª HD
–	„	Phönix D.I	(o)	Casoni	0900	76ª HD
26	12 Jul	Albatros D.III	(p)	Monte Tomatico	0810	76ª HD
–	„	Phönix D.I	(q)	Monte Tomatico	0810	76ª HD

(a) seen to crash within enemy lines; no claim submitted; (b) possibly G.128; shared with Michetti, Riva and Lts Jarvis, Mulholland and Frayne of 28 Sqn RFC; (c) G.126, BG.IV; Uffz Franz Hertling, Ltn Georg Ernst, Ltn d R Niesz; shared with Brenta and Lts Mitchell, Wilson, Mackereth and Jones, 28 Sqn RFC; (d) 28.26, Flik 16, Raoul Stojsavljevic WIA; credited to Razzi and, possibly, Ltn Montgomery/B4682 and Ltn Lingard/B5244, both 66 Sqn RFC; (e) Fw Karl Cislaghi, Flik 21D; aircraft captured and taken to Marostica; (f) FA.219, Ltn d R Dietrich Stapelfeld/Vfzw Max Schreiber, both KIA; shared with Fucini; (g) 153.100, Flik 55J, Korp Gottlieb Munczar, POW; (h) shared with Baracchini and Nannini; no victory claimed by participants; (i) shared with Michetti; (j) shared with Lega and Ticconi; (k) 153.202, Flik 42J, Oblt August Selinger; shared with Lega and Ticconi; (l) 169.68, Flik 45D; (m) shared with Ticconi; possibly disallowed; (n) 153.240, Flik 9J, Korp Oswald Bierlotter, KIA; (o) 128.19, Flik 14J; Zgsf Josef Laczko, POW; an odd case: in his 1922 book Scaroni marked it as his own victory in the map while crediting Di Loreto in the text!; (p, q) shared with Capt Howell and Ltn Rice-Oxley of 45 Sqn, RAF who claimed two Albatros (one broken up, one OOC), a Pfalz D.III and a Berg; one possibly disallowed.

STOPPANI Mario   Sergente   SQ 3ª, 76ª

Born in Lovere, Bergamo province, on 24 May 1895, at age 15 Stoppani began his apprenticeship as an automobile mechanic in Fiorano al Serio. At 18 he volunteered for service in the Battaglione Aviatori and enlisted on 6 November 1913 but was only accepted for flying training in February 1915, when he was despatched to the Pisa school. In June, by now a sergente, Stoppani was assigned to 3ª Squadriglia, flying Macchi Parasols on reconnaissance duties from Medeuzza, earning a Silver Medal for his August-November work on the southern Isonzo front. From January 1916 Stoppani served as an instructor at the Malpensa school, but in May was assigned to the 76ª Squadriglia, a newly formed fighter unit at La Comina. Flying a Nieuport 11 (possibly No. 1650), he soon scored his first victories. By November 1916 Stoppani, already proposed for a second Silver Medal which was awarded in June 1917, was asked by Ltn Brezzi, a former field engineering officer who was setting up Ansaldo's aviation production, to become the firm's test pilot. This fixed his score at six victories, all confirmed in the postwar review. In January 1917 he received the Russian Cross of St. George, 3rd class, and in March took up his post in Genoa. The first aircraft tested were the SVA and A.1 Balilla. In 1922 Stoppani resumed instructing, first in Foggia and then in 1925 in Passignano, with SAI. The next move, in July 1927, took him to Trieste, where he would remain 16 years, first as chief pilot for the SISA airline and then as chief test pilot for Cant. His long association with designer Zappata led Stoppani to make 15 first flights and set 41 world records, for two of which he was awarded a Gold and Silver Medal for Aeronautical Valour. After WW2, Stoppani worked briefly for Breda before moving on to SIAI Marchetti. He died on 20 September 1959.

	1916				
1	9 July	EA	(a)	Aisovizza	76ª Ni.11
2	18 Jul	EA		Monte San Marco	76ª Ni.11
3	16 Aug	EA		Ranziano di Udine	76ª Ni.11
4	11 Oct	EA	(b)	Aisovizza/Biglia	76ª Ni.11
5	31 Oct	2-seater	(c)	Nad Logem	76ª Ni.11
6	1 Dec	EA		San Marco	76ª Ni.11

(a) shared with Luigi Olivari and Venchiarutti; (b) shared with Luigi Olivi; (c) pilot Ltn Franz Cik, Flik 12, KIA; shared with Caselli and Rossi.

TICCONI Romolo   Sergente   SQ 76ª, 81ª

Born on 25 March 1893 in Acuto, in the current Frosinone province, Ticconi was called up on 21 August 1914 and assigned to the 6th Company of the 81st Infantry Regiment three days later. He was promoted caporale on 16 December 1916. Assigned to flying duties very late, he was listed as sergente pilota with the Deposito Aeronautica Aviatori on 20 September 1917. Ticconi started flying with the 76ª Squadriglia on 27 January 1918 and during the first five months flew 111 hours in 74 sorties, earning a Silver Medal in July. He suffered three accidents, including an in-flight fire on 24 May 1918 which caused him first and second degree burns to the right leg. On 3 May Ticconi scored the first of seven victories, six of which were confirmed in the postwar review. The end of the war brought him a Bronze Medal for having, among other things, fought during the final offensive despite being ill. On 21 November 1918 he transferred to the 81ª Squadriglia. Also decorated with a War Cross, Ticconi was killed in a flying accident at Montecelio on 26 August 1919.

	1918					
1	3 May	2-seater	(a)	Monte Asolone		76ª
2	25 Jun	fighter	(b)	Moreno di Piave	1030	76ª
3	„	Albatros D.III	(c)	Moreno di Piave	1030	76ª
4	7 Jul	fighter	(d)	Valbella		76ª
–	„	fighter	(e)	M. Spitz		76ª
5	14 Aug	fighter	(f)	Rasai/Val Stizzone		76ª
6	15 Aug	EA		Colbertaldo, N Vidor		76ª

(a) shared; (b) shared with Lega and Scaroni; (c) 153.202, Flik 42J, Oblt August Selinger; shared with Scaroni and Lega; (d) shared; (e) possibly credited solely to Scaroni and thus not counted in Ticconi's score; (f) Michetti took part but not credited.

QUESTION MARKS

Past authors, especially in Italy, have occasionally labelled as aces certain names which were not only unrecognised as such by the postwar review but also seem to be unsupported by existing documentation. Although these pilots do not appear in the Italian chapter of this book, in order not to confuse the reader we are providing the following notes. As with similar cases in our previous books, we shall be delighted to learn of any information that proves us wrong, so that we may update them in any subsequent printing.

CARTA Egidio   Tenente Colonnello   SQ 2ª, 4ª, 5ª

Born in Cagliari on 4 August 1877, in a 1982 biography compiled by the Associazione Pionieri dell'Aeronautica this Caproni pilot was credited with five confirmed victories, which would make him notable as the only known non-fighter ace. However, squadron records and citations agree on the lower figure of three, comprising one probable near Adelsberg on 2 April and two over Ovcia Draga on 16 May 1916. Each of the incidents was honored with a Silver Medal.

DE BERNARDI Mario   Tenente   SQ 75ª, 91ª

One of the greatest Italian pilots of all times, he was born on 1 July 1893 in Venosa (Potenza province) and earned his licence at Aviano in 1914. On account of his many achievements, which included the 1926 Schneider Trophy in Norfolk, two world speed records and the aerobatics trophy at the 1931 National Air Races, he is often referred to as an 'ace', some publications crediting him with nine victories, but the postwar review only confirmed three. Posted to the 75ª Squadriglia in early 1916, he gained a confirmed victory on 27 June 1916 (shared with Nardini, Buzio and others) but did not score again before being assigned to Pomilio in Turin as test pilot. De Bernardi was able to return to the front in January 1918 and was posted to the 91ª Sqn, where he made three claims in September (1st, one probable nr Pordenone; 11th, nr Susegana, c. 0700 hrs; 17th, c. 1400 hrs) and one on 3 October (EA over Cascina) and earned a Silver Medal. In addition, he took part in the destruction of five aircraft on the ground at La Comina in late October. After an illustrious test flying career, he died in Rome on 8 April 1959. The airport at Pratica di Mare, home to the Italian Air Force's Experimental Flying Unit, is named after him. His daughter Fiorenza was the first Italian woman commercial pilot.

DE RISEIS Luigi   Sottotenente di Vascello
SQ 259ª, 261ª, 241ª, STAZ PORTO CORSINI

Born in Lerici on 23 July 1897, the son of Baron Arturo and Englishwoman Gladys Pearse (hence his nickname Billy), he volunteered for the navy in September 1915, serving first as observer and from October 1917 as pilot with the 259ª and 261ª Squadriglia. He has been mentioned in recent years as an ace in Italian naval journals, but the official Navy list of 1919 credits him with only four victories — possibly 1 May 1918 (Hansa-Brandenburg W.18 A.67, flown by Niedermayer, near Grado) and 14 May (three, including A.70 flown by Gindl and A.85, Pichl, KIA). Awarded a Silver Medal and a War Cross citation, he transferred to the Hanriot-equipped 241ª but with his perfect English was eventually assigned to assist the US Navy pilots at Porto Corsini. He died on 6 January 1926.

APPENDIX I

Rank Equivalents

Army

British rank	Italian	Abbr	Austrian	Abbr
Private	soldato	sold	Soldat	Sdt
Corporal	caporale	capor	Korporal	Korp
	caporal maggiore	capor m	Zugsführer	Zgsf
	brigadiere*	brig		
Sergeant	sergente	serg		
	sergente maggiore	serg m		
Warrant Officer I	maresciallo*	m.llo	Feldwebel	Fw
Warrant Officer II	aiutante di battaglia	aiut	Stabsfeldwebel	StFw
	aspirante	asp	Fahnrich	Fahnr
2nd Lieutenant	sottotenente	s.ten	Leutnant	Ltn
Lieutenant	tenente	ten	Oberleutnant	Oblt
Captain	capitano	cap	Hauptmann	Hptm
Major	maggiore	magg	Major	Maj
Lt Colonel	tenente colonnello	t col	Oberstleutnant	ObstLtn
Colonel	colonnello	col	Oberst	Obst

*Carabinieri rank

Navy

British rank	Italian	Abbr	Austrian	Abbr
Private	marinaio	marò	Matrose	FlMatr
Corporal	sottocapo	sc	Fliegerquartermeister	FlQuMa
			Fliegermaat	FlMaat
Sergeant	capo	C<	Fliegeruntermeister	Flugm
Petty Officer	2° capo	2° C	Fliegermeister	Flgm
			Seeaspirant	SAsp
			Seekadett	Skdt
Midshipman	Guardiamarina	gm	Seefähnrich	Sfähnr
Sub Lieutenant	sottotenente di vascello	stv	Korvettenleutnant	Kvltn
			Fregattenleutnant	Frgltn
Lieutenant	Tenente di Vascello	tv	Linienschiffsleutnant	Lschltn

No Italian naval aircrew achieved rank higher than tv.

APPENDIX II

Other abbreviations

CFS	Centro Formazione Squadriglie	Squadron Forming Centre
D	Divisions*	Divisional observation
F	Fernaufklärer*	Long-range recon
Flep	Fliegeretappenpark	Supply and repair depot
Flek	Fliegerersatzkompanie	Training units
Flik	Fliegerkompanie	Squadron
LFT	Luftfahrttruppen	Aviation Troops (A-H aviation service)
G	Grossflugzeug*	Bomber
J	Jagd*	Fighter
K	Korps*	Corps observation
kuk	Kaiserliche und Königliche	Imperial and Royal
P	Photoeinsitzer*	Single-seat photo recon
Rb	Rheinbildaufklärer*	Series photo recon
S	Schlacht*	Ground-attack
Sq	Squadriglia	Squadron
u/c	unconfirmed	
u/c FTL	unconfirmed — forced to land	

*as suffix

APPENDIX III

Place names

Because the WWI battle area has traditionally been disputed by many different governments or ethnic groups — the Austro-Hungarians, who might speak German or Hungarian, the Italians and various Slav states, with their Serbo-Croat language, plus minorities such as the Ladini with Romansch — geographical names in this region can take any number of different forms, causing much confusion amongst enthusiasts: the capital of Slovenia might be called Laibach, Lubiana or Ljubljana, just as the main city of the Carso region becomes respectively Görz, Gorizia and Gorica (sometimes rendered as Goritza to stress the phonetics of the Serbo-Croat language).

Original documents contain many spelling mistakes arising from approximate phonetic renderings by clerks or officers whose training did not, understandably, extend to linguistic subtleties. Adding to the potential confusion for the unwary researcher or amateur historian, both Italy under the Fascist régime and Yugoslavia under Communist rule engaged in a widespread "geographic cleansing" of recently acquired territories, which led first to a forced Italianization of Slavic names (for instance Kostanjevica became Castagnevizza) and later to the inverse process of Slavicization (with Fiume masquerading as a virtually unrecognizable Rijeka).

While it would be impractical to attempt to supply a comprehensive list of alternative names, a few of the most frequently encountered locations are detailed below.

Italian	German	Slavic
Adige	Etsch	–
Bolzano	Bozen	–
Bressanone	Brixen	–
Brunico	Bruneck	–
Canale	Kolowrat	–
Caporetto	–	Kobarid
Castagnevizza	–	Kostanjevica
Dobbiaco	Toblach	–
Fiume	–	Rijeka
Fortezza	Franzenfeste	–
Gorizia	Görz	Gorica
Lubiana	Laibach	Ljubljana
Monte Cucco	–	Kuk
Pola	Pola	Pula
Tarvisio	Tarvis	–
Tolmino	Tolmein	Tolmin
val (valle)	Tal	

APPENDIX IV

The Official List

The list which follows, issued in February 1919, is the official ranking of Italian army aces. Due to a typographical error, Sergente Chiri (5 victories), who appeared in the original typescript, was omitted in the first printed edition. Another obvious misprint, repeated in every edition, places the death of Baracca on June 18 rather than 19. The three naval aces Pierozzi (7), Calvello and Martinengo (5 each) were excluded as belonging to the Navy.

SUPREME COMMAND OF THE ROYAL ITALIAN ARMY
GENERAL AERONAUTICS COMMAND

OFFICIAL RANKING OF AERIAL VICTORIES
CONFIRMED SCORED BY ITALIAN LAND AVIATION PILOTS

between 24 May 1915 and 4 November 1918

The List includes only those victories for which all the prescribed confirming evidence were reached and which were officially certified, always granted following rigorous criteria. The present ranking therefore omits those victories which, although quite probable, could not be supported by full documentary evidence.

Position	Rank	Surname and name	Score	Notes
1	Maggiore	Baracca Francesco	34	+ 18 June 1918
2	Tenente	Scaroni Silvio	26	
3	Ten Col	Piccio Pier Ruggero	24	
4	Tenente	Baracchini Flavio	21	
5	Capitano	Ruffo di Calabria Fulco	20	
6	Tenente	Ranza Ferruccio	17	
,,	Sergente	Cerutti Marziale	17	
7	Tenente	Olivari Luigi	12	+ 13 Oct 1917
8	Tenente	Ancillotto Giovanni	11	
,,	Sergente	Reali Antonio	11	
9	Tenente	Novelli Gastone	8	
,,	Tenente	Avet Flaminio	8	
,,	Tenente	Lombardi Carlo	8	
,,	S Tenente	Leonardi Alvaro	8	
,,	S Tenente	Cabruna Ernesto	8	
,,	Sergente	Nicelli Giovanni	8	+ 5 May 1918
10	Capitano	Riva Antonio	7	
,,	Tenente	Fucini Mario	7	
,,	Tenente	Eleuteri Leopoldo	7	
,,	SergMagg	Fornagiari Guglielmo	7	
,,	Sergente	Rennella Cosimo	7	
11	Capitano	Costantini Bortolo	6	
,,	Tenente	Olivi Luigi	6	+ 17 July 1917
,,	Tenente	Parvis Giuliano	6	
,,	Sergente	Imolesi Attilio	6	+ 3 March 1918
,,	Sergente	Stoppani Mario	6	

Position	Rank	Surname and name	Score	Notes
,,	Sergente	Nardini Guido	6	
,,	Sergente	Bocchese Aldo	6	
,,	Sergente	Ticconi Romolo	6	
,,	Sergente	Magistrini Cesare	6	
,,	Sergente	Rizzotto Cosimo	6	
12	Capitano	Lega Giulio	5	
,,	Tenente	Sabelli Giovanni	5	+ 25 Oct 1917
,,	Tenente	Buzio Alessandro	5	
,,	Tenente	Masiero Guido	5	
,,	Tenente	Bedendo Sebastiano	5	
,,	Tenente	Mecozzi Amedeo	5	
,,	Tenente	Michetti Giorgio	5	
,,	S Tenente	Allasia Michele	5	+ 20 July 1918
,,	S Tenente	Amantea Antonio	5	
,,	S Tenente	Resch Alessandro	5	
,,	Sergente	Chiri Antonio	5	

There follow 200 other military aviators who have shot down between 4 and 1 aircraft each.

The total number of enemy aircraft shot down and draken balloons destroyed by Italian Pilots — of the landbased aviation — in the skies above our war theatre between 24 May 1915 and 4 November 1918, is 643.

Our losses, in the same period of time, due to enemy action, came to 128 aircraft.

War Zone, 1 February 1919   The General Aeronautics Commander
Bongiovanni

+ = Date of death in combat.

APPENDIX V

Italian Decorations

The main Italian military decorations and knightly orders are listed here in the official order of precedence. A translation and brief notes are included where necessary. Non-military decorations and orders are omitted, together with commemorative medals for specific campaigns. Although only introduced in 1927, decorations for Aeronautical Valour were awarded to certain WW1 aces in the course of their careers and are therefore included.

Ordine Supremo della SS. Annunziata

Supreme Order of the Most Holy Annunciation. Italy's highest award, which made the recipient a 'cousin of the King'.

No awards to WW1 pilots.

Ordine dei Santi Maurizio e Lazzaro

No awards to WW1 pilots.

Ordine Militare di Savoia

Military Order of Savoy ('of Italy' since 1947). It recognized heroism and achievement as military leader. Ranks: Officer, Commander, Great Officer, Knight of Great Cross.

Awarded to Piccio during the war and to others in their subsequent service.

Medaglia d'Oro al Valor Militare

Gold Medal for military valour.

Medaglia d'Argento al Valor Militare

Silver Medal for military valour.

Medaglia d'Oro al Valor Aeronautico

Gold Medal for aeronautical valour.

First proposed in 1913 to recognize airmen who died in the line of duty, it was introduced in 1927 for those who performed brave deeds or acts of philanthropy on aircraft in flight.

Several awarded to WW1 aces during their postwar careers.

Medaglia d'Argento al Valor Aeronautico

Silver Medal for aeronautical valour.

Ordine della Corona d'Italia

Order of the Crown of Italy.

Ranks: Officer, Commander, Great Officer, Knight of Great Cross.

Medaglia di Bronzo al Valor Militare

Bronze Medal for military valour.

Ordine Coloniale della Stella d'Italia

Colonial Order of the Italian Star. Ranks: Officer, Commander, Great Officer, Knight of Great Cross.

Croce al Merito di Guerra

War Merit Cross.

Croce al Valor Militare

Cross for Military Valour.

Medaglia di Bronzo al Valor Aeronautico

Bronze Medal for aeronautical valour.

PART FOUR

ABOVE THE PIAVE

I The Austrian–Hungarian Aces

ARIGI Julius   Offizierstellvertreter   FLIK 6, GI, 55J, IJ

Born in Tetschen, in what later became Czechoslovakia, on 3 October 1895 and for some years lived in Marienbad until he volunteered for Artillery Regiment No.1 in October 1913. The following March he transferred to the airship detachment of the Austro-Hungarian Army, followed by pilot training, passing his final tests on 23 November 1914 with the rank of sergeant (Zugsführer). He was assigned to Flik 6, in southern Dalmatia, Yugoslavia, where he operated against Serbian and Montenegran forces, in Lohner biplanes. Engine trouble in October 1915 forced him down to become a prisoner and he eventually escaped with some others, actually driving through the front lines in Prince Nikalous' car. Returning to his unit, Flik 6 later moved to Albania. On 22 August 1916 he took off without permission, as there were no officers available to be an observer, with another NCO in the rear cockpit of a Brandenburg CI, in order to engage a formation of six Italian Farmans heading for Durazzo. Engaging the Farmans, the two men shot down five, all crews being taken prisoner. However, the 34ᵃ Squadriglia, who despatched the five, only lost two! Transferred to Fluggeschwader No.1 in Northern Italy towards the end of the year, he flew Brandenburg DIs, bringing his score to 12, and was then transferred to Flik 41J, but he did not get on with his CO, Brumowski, so moved to Flik 55J, gaining his 13th victory in an Albatros DIII. Flik 55J moved to the southern Tyrol region in November 1917, Arigi adding twelve kills to his score flying Albatros DIIIs (Oef). In April 1918 he returned to Flik 6 in Albania, bringing his score to 28. Another move, this time to Flik 1J later in 1918, brought his score to 32. He received many decorations, becoming one of only two recipients of four Goldene Tapferkeitsmedailles (Gold Medal for Bravery), the highest award for an NCO, and he also received the Silver Bravery Medal, 1st Class, four times. Post war, Arigi began a flying organisation at Marienbad, but in 1935 moved to Wiener-Neustadt, and in company with Benno Fiala, founded the Wiener-Neustadt Airport Management Association. Just prior to WW2 he became a flying instructor for the Luftwaffe, becoming commander of a fighter pilot school at Schwecht once war began. It is understood that two of his star pupils were Walter Nowotny and Hans-Joachim Marseille, both top scoring aces of WW2. Arigi lived his last days in Attersee, the Austrian lake district, east of Salzburg, where he died on 1 August 1981.

	1916			Brand CI Flik			
1	22 Aug	Farman	(a)	61.64	6	Skumbi estuary	c 0745
2	„	Farman	(a)	„	„	„	„
3	„	Farman	(a)	„	„	„	„
4	„	Farman	(a)	„	„	„	
5	„	Farman	(a)	„	„		„
6	4 Sep	Farman	(b)	„	„	Fjeri (captured)	am
7	18 Sep	Caproni	(c)	„	„	Arta	am
	1917			Brand DI			
8	24 Apr	Voisin		28.06	GI	Farra	
9	3 May	Farman		„	„	Nogaredo	
10	4 May	Farman		„	„	N Podgora	1700
11	14 May	Farman		28.08	„	Gradiscutta	
12	15 May	Voisin		„	„	San Canziano	
				Alb DIII			
13	15 Sep	Spad 1		153.15	55J	SE Gorizia	
14	29 Sep	Nieuport Sct		153.36	„	Tolmein	
15	15 Nov	Caproni	(d)	„	„	Monte Cimano	
16	„	Caproni	(d)	„	„	„	
17	„	Caproni	(d)	„	„	„	
18	17 Nov	Savoia-Pomilio	(d)	„	„	SE Asiago	

19	„	SAML 2	(d)	„	„	„	
20	„	SAML 2	(d)	„	„	Cima Ecker	
21	18 Nov	Savoia-Pomilio	(d)	„	„	Monte Cengio	
22	„	EA	(d)	„	„	N Arsiero	
23	7 Dec	Pomilio PE 2	(d)	153.80	„	E Asiago	
24	„	SAML 2	(d)	„	„	Monte Sprung	
25	16 Dec	SAML 2	(e)	„	„	Arten, nr Feltre	1450
	1918			Aviatik DI			
26	17 Apr	Nieuport Sct		238.30	6	Singjerc	am
27	27 May	Br Seaplane		258.51	„	Sea, W Durazzo	1000
28	„	Br Seaplane		„	„	„	1000
29	24 Jul	DH4	(f)		1J	Adriatic	am
30	6 Aug	Seaplane		338.02	„	Skumbi estuary	am
31	„	Seaplane		„	„	„	am
32	23 Aug	DH4		338.01	„	SW Punta d'Ostro	0810

Total: 20 destroyed, 12 shared destroyed = 32.

Obs: (a) Fw Johann Lasi; however, only two Farmans of 34ª Sqn lost; (b) Ltn Fabian Lukas-Sluja; (c) Kdt Viktor Renvez; (d) shared with Hptm Josef v Maier & Stabs Josef Kiss; (e) shared with Kiss and Kpl Franz Lahner; (f) shared with FrgLtn Stefan v Grosschmid.

BANFIELD Gottfried Fr von   Leutnant   TRIESTE N.A.S.

Born in Castelnuovo on the Gulf of Cattaro (Yugoslavia) on 6 February 1890, the son of a naval officer. After attending a military secondary school in Austria he entered the Austro-Hungarian Naval Academy in 1905, graduating in June 1909 as a naval cadet, followed by a commission as Freggattenleutnant in May 1912. The following month he was accepted for pilot training at Wiener-Neustadt, completing his tests in August. Following a crash in 1913, that nearly cost him his right foot, by November 1914 Banfield was testing new aircraft at Pola. Shortly after Italy entered the war, Banfield established the Naval Air Station at Trieste, becoming its commander in February 1916. Before then, however, he was involved in much action from Trieste, scoring a number of victories, although several appear to be unconfirmed, or at least, no confirming documentation being available. He also flew bombing and recce missions as well as landing to rescue two brother flyers, and by May was promoted to Linienschiffsleutnant (Lieutenant Commander). Among his numerous combats in a flying boat, he was wounded by gunfire while attacking two Italian motorboats on the night of 16 May 1918. His left tibia was shattered but he just managed to get back to Trieste despite loss of blood and a badly damaged machine. He was back at his command a month later and was still in command at Trieste when the war ended, having flown over 400 sorties. He received the Knight's Cross of the Order of Léopold with War Decoration and Swords, the Order of the Iron Crown, 3rd Class with War Decoration and Swords and was the only airman to be awarded both the Gold and Silver Bravery Medals for officers. He was also presented with the Great Military Bravery Medal by Emperor Franz Josef himself, no other airman being awarded this. Finally he received the Empire's highest honour, the Knight's Cross of the Military Order of Maria Theresa, with which came the title of Freiherr. After the war he married and then took control of his father-in-law's shipping salvage company before he retired to Trieste. Died 23 September 1986.

	1915			Lohner T			
1	27 Jun	Balloon	(a)	L-47		Villa Vicentina	
–	1 Sep	Curtiss FB	(a)	„		E Grado	
–	„	Italian FB	(a)	„		Grado Harbour	
	1916			Lohner M			
–	17 Apr	Seaplane		L16		Golametto	1615
–	„	Seaplane		„		„	1715
2	23 Jun	FBA FB		„		Trieste	1900
3	24 Jun	Macchi L1		„		Gulf of Trieste	am
4	1 Aug	Caproni Ca.1		„		Volosca	0730
5	6 Aug	Caproni Ca.1		„		SE Sistiana	0800
6	15 Aug	FBA FB		„		Golametto	

7	„	FBA FB		„		nr Miramare	
				Albatros FB			
–	13 Sep	Nieuport Sct		K-150		Miramare	
				Brandenburg FB			
–	13 Oct	Farman		A-12		Sdobba estuary	
				Albatros Sct			
–	31 Oct	Caproni		A-3		„	1450
				Brandenburg FB			
8	3 Dec	Caproni Ca.1		A-12		E Mavhinje	
	1917			Oeffag H FB			
9	31 May	It Seaplane	(c)	A-11		Primero estuary	2230
–	4 Aug	Caproni		„		Salvore	0115
–	2 Sep	Seaplane	(d)	„		Gulf of Trieste	
–	21 Sep	Seaplane	(d)	„		Golametto	
–	23 Sep	Seaplane	(e)	„		SE Golametto	

Total: 9 destroyed; with 11 more driven down and/or unconfirmed.

(a) Obs: Seekdt H Strobl; (b) shared with G Brumowski Flik 12; (c) the first night victory by an Austrian; (d) shared with Seekdt Franz Pichl (A-24) and Ferrucio Maria Vio (A-46); (e) shared with Franz Puchl (A-24).

BÖNSCH, Eugen   Feldwebel   FLIK 51J

Born 1 May 1897, in Gross-Aupa, a village near Trautenau, in northern Bohemia, his parents came from the Sudetenland. Following a successful study period of mechanics and machine manufacturing at the State Trade School, he volunteered for the Army and soon afterwards requested a transfer to the Air Service. He began his career as a mechanical engineer with Fliegerersatzkompanie (Flek) 6 but in 1917 requested pilot training and trained at Flek 8, qualifying as a pilot in June and promoted to korporal. He was posted to Flik 51J in August in northern Italy, flying Oefflag-built Albatros Scouts. He gained his first kill over an Italian Nieuport scout on 1 September. For a courageous attack on a balloon on 28 September, despite stiff resistance by two Italian fighters, he received the Gold Medal for Bravery, the highest honour for an NCO. As well as air fighting, Bönsch was engaged in ground attack sorties. On 3 January 1918 he was brought down by Italian AA fire south of Motta in Albatros DIII 153.31, and during April attacked several Italian gun positions. In May he received a second Gold Bravery Medal. More low level attacks during the Battle of the Piave in June, plus attaining double-ace status, brought him a third Gold Medal in July, one of only six NCOs honoured in this way during the war. On 29 October he was shot down in flames but was saved by taking to his parachute. After the war he owned an inn in the northern Bohemian mountains. In WW2, by special decree due to his WW1 awards, he received a commission in the Luftwaffe, and with the rank of hauptmann, commanded the Oschatz aerodrome in Saxony. At the end of that conflict, he lived in his brother's hotel in Ehrwald, in the Tyrol, west of Innsbruck, where he died on 24 July 1951.

	1917			Alb DIII			
1	1 Sep	Nieuport Sct	(a)	53.57	F51J	Monte San Gabriele	
2	28 Sep	Balloon	(b)	153.35	„	N Plava	
3	29 Sep	Nieuport Sct	(c)	„	„	S Plava	
4	3 Dec	Balloon	(d)	„	„	Visnadello	am
	1918						
5	21 Feb	Camel	(e)	„	„	Casa Zonta	
6	16 Mar	Camel	(f)	153.140	„	Zenson	1140
7	3 Apr	Balloon		„	„	SW San Biaggio	
8	17 Apr	SAML 2	(g)	„	„	Monte Grappa	
–	3 May	Balloon		153.155	„	NW Monastier di Treviso	u/c
9	16 Jun	Balloon		153.140	„	Breda di Piave	
10	20 Jun	Scout		„	„	Montello	
11	8 Aug	Balloon		253.37	„	Vascon	2047
12	5 Oct	Balloon		„	„	W Ponti di Piave	
13	27 Oct	RE8	(h)	253.?	„	W Papadopoli	

14	„	Camel	(g)	„	„	Papadopoli island	
15	28 Oct	Hanriot HD1	(i)	„	„	„	
16	29 Oct	Hanriot HD1		„	„	„	

(a) shared with Rittm W v Floreich, Oblt J Hoffman and Fw L Neumann; (b) shared with Lt A Tahy; (c) shared with Tahy and Oblt G Kenzian; (d) shared with S Fejes; (e) shared with Oblt Tahy; (f) Shared with Oblt Benno Fiala; (g) shared with Lt F Rudorfer; (h) E235, 34 Sqn RAF; (i) 78ª Squadriglia.

BRUMOWSKI Godwin   Hauptmann   FLIK 1,12,41J

Born Wadowice, Galicia (now Poland), 26 July 1889, into a military family. Graduated from the Military Academy in Mödling, near Vienna, in August 1910 and became a leutnant in Field Artillery Regiment. Nr29. Became regimental adjutant to the 6th Artillery Division when war came, with the rank of oberleutnant, serving on the Russian Front until July 1915, where he received the Bronze and then the Silver Medals for bravery. He became an observer with Flik 1 in July 1915, operating on the Russian Front, and flying in Knoller-Albatros B.I machines, scored two victories during a bomb raid on Chotin during the Czar's visit there. Decided to become a pilot which he achieved in July 1916 and after returning to Flik 1, was later posted to Flik 12 on the Italian Front. In February 1917, with his score at five he was given command of Flik 41J, but before doing so he had himself attached to Jasta 24 on the Western Front to gain experience of combat tactics used by the Germans. He took command of Flik 41J in April and led the unit until late 1918, at which time he had raised his score to 35. He was then given command of the fighter squadrons of the Austro-Hungarian Army of the Isonzo, where he saw out the war. He received numerous awards including The Order of the Iron Crown, Knight's Cross of the Order of Léopold and the Gold Bravery Award to Officers. After the war he tried to farm the family estate but soon tired of this and returned to Vienna around 1930 to open a flying school at Aspern. However, on 3 June 1936 an aircraft in which he was the instructor crashed at Schiphol airport, Amsterdam, and he died of his injuries.

	1916			Albatros BI			
1	12 Apr	Morane P	(a)	22.23	F1	Iszkowcy	
2	„	Morane P	(a)	„	„	W Chotin	
3	2 May	Morane P	(b)	22.30	„	Lysskowcy	0945
				Brand D.I			
4	3 Dec	Caproni Ca.1	(c)	65.53	F12	E Mavhinje	pm
	1917			Brand C.I			
5	2 Jan	Farman	(d)	68.24	„	Nr Lake Doberdo	pm
				Brand D.I			
6	10 May	Voisin		28.10	F41J	Monfalcone	
–	12 May	Farman		„	„		u/c
7	„	Nieuport Sct		„	„		
–	13 May	Voisin		28.11	„		u/c
8	20 May	Spad 2	(e)	28.10	„	Monte Santo	1030
9	17 Jul	Voisin	(f)	28.57	„	Isonzo River	
10	10 Aug	Nieuport Sct		28.69	„	Chiapovano	
11	11 Aug	Caudron	(g)	28.57	„	Plava	
12	„	Caudron		28.69	„	W Plava	2000
13	14 Aug	Scout		„	„	Nr Grado	
–	„	Scout		„	„	„	u/c
–	18 Aug	Caudron		„	„	Monte Santo	u/c
14	„	Caudron		„	„	„	
–	19 Aug	Scout		„	„		u/c
–	„	Scout		„	„		u/c
				Alb DIII			
15	„	Caudron		153.06	„	Karbinje-Ivangrad	
16	20 Aug	Caudron	(h)	„	„	San Giovanni	
				Brand D.I			
17	„	Caudron	(g)	28.69	„	Nr Vertojba	
18	„	EA	(i)	„	„	Monte Santo	

19	22 Aug	Savoia-Pomilio	(i)	„	„	Gorizia	
20	23 Aug	Savoia-Pomilio	(j)	„	„	Bate	1040
–	25 Aug	Sopwith 2	(i)	„	„		u/c
21	26 Aug	Spad 1*	(i)	„	„	Monte San Gabriele	
–	28 Aug	Savoia-Pomilio		„	„		u/c
				Alb DIII			
22	9 Oct	Balloon	(k)	153.45	„	Shobba Estuary	1700
23	5 Nov	Macchi L3	(l)	„	„	W Latisana	
24	„	Macchi L3	(l)	„	„	„	
25	17 Nov	Balloon		„	„	Piave River Estuary	
26	23 Nov	Nieuport Sct	(i)	„	„	„	
27	„	Nieuport Sct	(i)	„	„	„	
28	28 Nov	Savoia-Pomilio	(e)	153.52	„	Casa Serpo	
29	13 Dec	Balloon	(m)	„	„	Nr Meolo	
	1918						
30	25 Mar	SIA 7b **		153.45	„	S Oderzo	
31	17 Apr	Camel	(n)	„	„	Arcade	
32	16 Jun	Balloon		153.209	„	Spresiano	
33	19 Jun	Balloon		„	„	Nr Passarella	1545
34	„	2-seater	(o)	„	„	S Candelu	
35	„	Ansaldo SVA.5		„	„	Montello	

Pilot: (a) Hptm O Jindra; Pilot: (b) Kurt Gruber; (c) shared with Lt G Banfield; (d) Obs: Oblt J G v Telekes; (e) shared with Karl Kaszala; (f) shared with F Jaschek and J Novak; (g) shared with F Jaschek; (h) shared with H Richter and H Mayrbäurl; (i) shared with Oblt F Linke-Crawford; (j) shared with Linke-Crawford and Mayrbäurl; (k) shared with Linke-Crawford and K Gruber; (l) shared with Linke-Crawford and Oblt R Szepessy-Sokoll; (m) shared with Linke-Crawford and Karl Kaszala; (n) shared with Oblt F Navratil; (o) shared with Oblt R Terk, CO Flik 63J.

* actually a SAML of 114 Sqn; ** probably a Pomilio PE, 131 Sqn.

BUSA Julius   Feldwebel   FLIK 14

Born 18 February 1891, in Budapest, and joined up when the war began, completing his pilot training in December 1915. Promoted to korporal he was assigned to Flik 14, a two-seater unit, operating on the Russian Front. In February 1916 he was promoted to sergeant and on more than one occasion brought his machine home following direct hits by AA fire. He flew a variety of two-seaters, Aviatik BII, Lloyd CII and the Hansa- Brandenburg CI. Awarded the Silver Bravery Medal, 2nd Class, and two 1st Class. This was followed by the Gold and promotion to Feldwebel. Moved to the Italian Front in October 1916 but on 13 May he and his pilot, Oblt Hermann Grössler, were shot down by the Italian ace Francesco Baracca, the Italian's 10th victory. Grössler jumped from the burning Brandenburg, without a parachute, Busa, presumably dead in his cockpit, fell to the ground near Plava. With his various observers, Busa had been credited with five victories.

	1916			Lloyd C.II				
1	23 Jun	Biplane	(a)	42.45	F14	Rudnia airfield	pm
2	„	Biplane	(a)	„	„	„	pm
				Brand C.I			
3	23 Nov	EA	(b)	26.60	„	Brody-Beresteczko	
4	„	EA	(b)	„	„	„	
5	„	EA	(b)	„	„	„	

Obs: (a) Hermann Klecker; (b) Ltn Johann Popelak.

DOMBROWSKI Andreas   Feldwebel   FLIK 29, 68J

Born of Sudeten-German parents, in Mahrisch-Ostrau (now Czech Republic), on 30 November 1894. Called to arms in 1915 he volunteered for the Air Service and soon showed himself a natural pilot. Completing his training in June 1916 he was assigned to Flik 29 as a korporal, on the Russian Front, flying Hansa-Brandenburg CIs. After gaining one victory, flew on the Romanian Front from September 1916, flying all manner of two-seater operations, and in air combat his various observers helped bring him to ace status. He received the Silver Bravery Medal 1st Class, the Prussian War Merit Medal, followed by the Gold Bravery Medal, the highest award for an NCO. Transferred to single-seaters in April 1918 and sent to Flik 68J in northern Italy, flying Albatros Scouts. He gained one victory but was slightly wounded, on 4 May, probably by the fire of Lt G F M Apps of 66 Squadron. After recovery he went to Flik 57Rb, again flying two–seater Brandenburg and Phönix C.Is on photo-recce sorties, where he saw out the war.

	1916			Brand C.I			
1	17 Aug	Voisin	(a)	26.37	F29	–	
	1917						
2	5 Feb	Nieuport Sct	(b)	26.44	„	W Comanestie	
3	13 Jun	Nieuport Sct	(c)	69.54	„	NW Onesti	0930
4	21 Jun	Nieuport Sct	(b)	69.61	„	N Borsani	
5	10 Jul	Bomber	(d)	„	„	Soveja	
				Alb DIII			
6	4 May	Camel		153.195	F68J	Montebelluna	am

Obs: (a) Franz Sycek; (b) Oblt Karl Patselt; (c) Rittm M K de Dercsika; (d) Ltn A Matisky.

FEJES Stefan   Feldwebel   FLIK 19, 51J

Born in Raab, Hungary, 30 August 1891, and served with Hungarian Infantry Regt. Nr.31 for his national service, in 1912. When war came he went to the front with his regiment but was severely wounded in September 1914. It took six months to recover, and he was then assigned to the Motor Service. Just over a year later he volunteered to become a pilot which he completed in early 1917. Assigned to Flik 19 as a sergeant, he flew two-seater Brandenburgs, gaining his initial victories on this type. In all he and his observers accounted for six enemy machines and he received the Silver Bravery Medal, 2nd Class, and two 1st Class awards of the same medal. In October 1917 Fejes was posted to Flik 51J, flying Albatros Scouts. In a drawn out dogfight on 30 March 1918, he claimed to have brought down his adversary but was slightly wounded in the heel. In all he claimed 20 victories, 16 being officially confirmed and he received the Gold Medal for Bravery three times, the highest award for an NCO, and one of only six to be thrice honoured. He was also promoted to staff sergeant. After the war he served in the 8th Squadron of the Red Air Corps, following the invasion of Hungary by Romanian, Czech and Serbian forces, flying Fokker DVIIs. However, in May 1919 he was forced down by a damaged engine and taken prisoner. In 1920 he flew at the Budapest Air Show and in 1928 was a flying instructor at the secret training school at Szombathely, where he was known by the students as 'Uncle Fejes'. He then became a commercial pilot, flying between Milan, Rome and Zurich during 1930-36, and then with the Hungarian Malert Company, until 1940. In WW2 he served as a transport and liaison pilot, after which he returned to Budapest.

	1917			Brand C.I			
1	17 Apr	Nieuport Sct	(a)	29.09	F19	Gorizia area	
2	14 May	Nieuport Sct	(b)		„	Merna	0730
3	20 May	Spad 1	(c)	29.63	„	Britof	0815
4	19 Jun	Nieuport Sct	(d)	„	„	Sober	
–	„	Nieuport Sct	(d)	„	„	„	u/c
5	26 Jun	Caudron	(b)	„	„	Sober	0920
				Alb DIII			
6	3 Dec	Balloon	(e)		F51J	Visnadello	am
7	9 Dec	SAML 2	(f)		„	Treviso	

8	10 Dec 1918	EA	(f)		„	Candelu	
9	18 Mar	Camel	(g)	153.132	„	W Salgareda	pm
10	22 Mar	RE8	(h)	153. ?	„	Susegana-Salleto	
11	30 Mar	Camel		153.142	„	Oderzo area	
12	17 Apr	Camel		153.128	„	Arcade	
13	1 May	Camel		153.142	„	Breda di Piave	
–	3 May	2-seater (Fr)		153.140	„	Arcade	u/c
–	„	Balloon		153.155	„	NW Monistier	u/c
14	22 May	Camel		153.142	„	E Spresiano	
15	15 Jun	Spad 1		153. ?	„	–	
16	1 Sep	Camel		253.54	„	Arcade	
–	12 Sep	EA		253. ?	„	Candelu	u/c

Obs: (a) Oblt O Zeisberger; (b) Ltn A Tahy; (c) Oblt K v Lang; (d) Ltn J Purer; (e) shared with Eugen Bönish; (f) shared with Eugen Ziegler; (g) shared with Franz Schwarzmann, possibly B6344, Capt J Mitchell, FTL at Istrana; (h) shared with Karl Balzareno.

FIALA, RITTER von FERNBRUGG, Benno   Oberleutnant   FLIK 1,19,12,56,51

Born Vienna, into a military family, on 16 June 1890, he served with the Hungarian Artillery Regiment Nr.1 as a volunteer in 1910. His brother Otto was a Naval flyer which helped influence him to fly too, transferring to the Air Service in late July 1914. He was then sent to Galicia on the Russian Front, first as a technical officer then an observer with Flik 1. Following an act of bravery when a train in which he was travelling was attacked by Russian troops, he was commissioned in the field. For service with Flik 1 he received the Silver Military Merit Medal, apparently for helping to down two Russian aircraft, on 6 and 13 June, although they remained unconfirmed. Later he was sent to Flik 19, in January 1916, on the Isonzo Front, Italy, where he scored his first official victory in April, and in May helped to destroy the Italian airship M4, but he was wounded during a bomb raid not long afterwards. Deciding to become a pilot he broke a collar bone in a training crash but following recovery and passing his flight programme, he was assigned to Flik 41J. Five weeks later he was sent to Flik 12D, a two-seater unit that had fighters for protection. Flying these, Fiala soon began to score, and was rewarded with the Order of the Iron Crown and then the Knight's Cross of the Order of Léopold. In November he was posted to Flik 56J, as second-in-command, but at the end of January 1918 was given command of Flik 51J, flying Albatros DIII (Oef) fighters. His score increased steadily, including the Camel of Alan Jerrard, who received the Victoria Cross following the report by his brother officers on the results of the fight. During a ground strafing sortie on 17 June 1918 he was wounded in the right hand but after treatment was quickly back in action. He was sent to Vienna in October to a staff assignment, having been awarded the Gold Bravery Medal for Officers. After the war he was at the Technical University in Vienna, receiving a degree in 1923 as a certified engineer, and while there founded the Officers Section of the Austrian Aero Club. In 1925 he became the personal assistant to Hugo Junkers in the latter's aircraft firm in Dessau, Germany, where he remained for eight years, even setting up an airline in Fürth. He also travelled to Japan and the US, setting up Junkers' subsidiaries. Although Fiala was a popular figure in Germany, he continually refused German citizenship; because of this he ran foul of both Hermann Göring and Junkers, and in 1933 he was expelled. Back in Austria he and Julius Arigi founded the Wiener-Neustadt Airport Management Association, in which Fiala was the director until 1936. In WW2 he was a Hauptmann in the Luftwaffe, commanding the airbase at Hörshing Linz, and post war he was chief designer for a Viennese company. He died on 29 October 1964, and four years later the Austrian Air Base at Aigen was named in his honour, 'Fiala-Fernbrugg'.

	1916			Brand C.I			
1	29 Apr	EA	(a)	26.08	F19	San Daniele	am
2	4 May	Airship M4	(b)	61.55	„	Merna	noon
	1917			Brand D.I			
3	9 Aug	Nieuport Sct	(c)	28.38	F12D	Auzza-Plava	0830
4	10 Aug	Caproni		„	„	„	1930

5	11 Aug	SAML 2			„	„	Plava	1930
–	12 Aug	Caudron			„	„	Selo	
6	14 Aug	Nieuport Sct		28.66	„	S Gorizia	0630
7	19 Aug	Caproni		28.38	„	N Fajtl Hrib	am
–	31 Aug	Nieuport Sct		„	„		ftl u/c
8	25 Oct	Spad 1		„ Alb DIII	„	S Monte San Gabriele	pm
9	30 Dec 1918	Caproni		153.77	F56J	Nr Vecchia	
10	21 Jan	Camel	(e)	153.128	F51J	San Andre di Treviso	
11	11 Mar	Camel		„	„	Spresiano	
12	13 Mar	SIA 7B	(f)	„	„	N Spresiano	
13	16 Mar	Camel	(g)	„	„	Zenson	1140
14	30 Mar	Camel	(h)	153.155	„	Gorgo del Molino	1150
15	1 May	Camel		153.128	„	San Biaggio	0910
16	„	SIA 7B		„	„	N Povegliano	0915
17	„	Balloon		„	„	Visnadello	1430
18	„	Balloon	(i)	„	„	San Biaggio	1435
19	3 May	Spad 1		153.141	„	SE Spresiano	
–	„	Camel		„	„	N Povegliano	
20	6 Jun	Spad 1		153.128	„	Salettuol	
21	„	Camel		„	„	Noventa di Piave	eve
22	15 Jun	Balloon		153.270	„	Breda di Piave	
23	19 Jun	2-seater		„	„	S San Biaggio	1830
24	20 Jun	Scout		„	„	Montello	
25	„	2-seater		„	„	„	
26	„	2-seater		„	„	Nr Susegana	
27	30 Jul	Scout		„	„	Passarella	
28	20 Aug	Ansaldo 2		„	„	Cessalto	

Pilot: (a) Ltn L Hautzmayer; Pilot: (b) Hptm A Heyrowsky; (c) shared with Johan Risztics, Flik 42J; (d) Ten. Enrico Ferreri, 91ª Sqn; (e) posssibly this date was 21 Feb; (f) shared with Oblt L Hautzmayer; (g) shared with Eugen Bönsch; (h) B5648, Lt A Jerrard, 66 Sqn, PoW; (i) shared with Ltn F Rudorfer.

FRIEDRICH Josef   Oberleutant   FLIK 16, 24

Another of those born of Sudenten-German parents, Friedrich came from the town of Zwiken, Bohemia, where he had arrived on 12 September 1893. An engineering student when war came, he joined the army, going to an infantry regiment, Kaiser-Schützen Nr.1. In November 1915 he volunteered for the Air Service, promoted to leutnant and became an observer. Posted to Flik 16 on the Carinthian Front, he undertook recce missions flying Hansa-Brandenburg C.Is. His usual pilot was Raoul Stojsavljevic, and together they scored four victories. He also undertook pilot instruction, and in January 1917 was deemed qualified as such and received his pilot's badge. His fifth victory was scored as a two-seat pilot, downed by his observer. In July 1917 Friedrich was assigned to Flik 24, another two-seater unit although it had a couple of Albatros DIIIs on charge for escort and protection. Flying one of these he began scoring as a fighter pilot, and although he spent a short time with Flik 51J, returned to Flik 24 until June 1918. He was promoted to oberleutnant der reserve, awarded the Silver Military Merit Medal and a second award of the Military Merit Cross, 3rd Class, with War Decoration and Swords. Leaving Flik 24 he went to the Jastaschule at Pergine, being appointed acting CO of the Jastaschule at Neumarkt, where he saw out the war. After the war he completed his engineering studies and settled in Reichenberg, Czechoslovakia.

	1916			Brand C.I				
1	4 Jul	Farman	(a)	64.14	F16	Malborghet	0825
2	25 Jul	Farman	(a)		„	Monte Paularo	
3	7 Aug	Farman	(a)	64.13	„	Val di Raccolana	
	1917						
4	17 Apr	Farman	(a)	68.11	„	Villach	
5	3 May	Farman	(b)	68.59	„	Seebach Valley	

				Alb DIII		
6	18 Aug	Spad 1		53.38	F24	Grigno
7	3 Nov	Balloon		53.29	„	Monte Peu

(a) Pilot: Hptm R Stojsavljevic: (b) Obs: Ltn Hans Rocker.

FRINT Johann   Hauptmann   FLIK 23

Born in Budapest, 6 May 1888, he was a natural military man and by the time war came he was already an oberleutnant and company commander with the Austro-Hungarian Infantry Regt. Nr.65, going with it to the Russian Front in 1914. Wounded in November, he was unable to continue his duties so transferred to the Air Service as an observer. He was assigned to Flik 23, flying both Lloyd and Brandenburg two-seaters, flying recce and photo sorties. Several sorties were flown with the unit's CO, Hauptmann Heinrich Kostrba, both scoring heavily together, three in one fight. Frint was awarded the Silver Military Merit Medal and the Order of the Iron Crown, 3rd Class with War Decoration. He applied for pilot training but he was not a natural or good pilot, although he did finally achieve his pilot's badge. He commanded several units, finally becoming CO of Flik 27 on the Russian Front and then to the southern Tyrol. He was killed on a test flight in an Albatros DIII on 25 February 1918, near Ora airfield, south-west of Bolzano. (It has been suggested that Frint only had four victories and none of them were officially confirmed.)

	1916			Lloyd C.III			
1	29 Apr	Farman	(a)	43.60	F23	W Monte Tomba	0750
				Brand C.I			
2	7 Jun	Farman	(b)	26.09	„	Corno d'Aquilo	0930
3	29 Jun	Farman	(b)	„	„	Val d'Leogra	0715
4	„	Farman	(b)	„	„	„	to
5	„	Farman	(b)	„	„	„	0820
6	8 Aug	Nieuport Sct	(c)	26.15	„	Val Grezzana	0830

Pilots: (a) Ernst Kerschischnig; (b) Hptm H Kostrba; (c) Ernst Franz.

GRÄSER Franz   Leutnant   FLIK 2,32,42J,61J

Born in Nyir-Mada, Hungary, on 26 October 1892, he attended a secondary school in science, then attended the Technical University in Budapest. War interrupted his studies and he joined the 72nd Infantry Regiment in October 1914, then attended the reserve officer's school in Esztergom in the first half of 1915. From August to July 1916 he commanded a machine-gun section on the Eastern Front, but was wounded. However, he received the Silver Bravery Medal for Officers, 2nd Class. Volunteering for the Air Service, he became an observer, serving with Fliegerkompanie Nr.2 on the Isonzo Front. Here he gained his first victory, although he and his pilot were also forced down, then Gräser was sent to Flik 32, where he gained a second victory. While with this unit he began informal flying lessons, and was found to be a natural pilot. Thus by September, he was flying reconnaissance sorties, without having attended a flight school, or even taking a flying licence. This did not stop him joining Flik 42J on 1 October, to become a fighter pilot, and he began scoring during the Battle of Caporetto in late October. For his work here he received the Order of the Iron Crown, 3rd Class. During January 1918 he was assigned to Flik 61J. On 17 May, while escorting a machine of Flik 12P over Treviso (in 153.221), he was attacked and shot down in flames by Sergentes Antonio Chiri of 78ª Squadriglia, Antonio Reali, Guido Nardini of 91ª, and Caporale Lucentini, of 79ª Squadriglia. Gräser was posthumously awarded the Knight's Cross of the Order of Leopold with War Decoration and Swords, the Empire's second highest award. He was 25 years old. In Flik 61J his Albatros Scout carried an owl insignia in a white circle on the fuselage sides.

	1917			Brand C.1			
1	10 Feb	Farman	(a)	29.58	F2	W Tolmein	am
2	20 May	Spad 1	(b)	229.20	F32	Monte Sabotino	0920

				Alb DIII			
3	25 Oct	Seaplane	(c)	153.13	F42J	Sdobba Estuary	
4	26 Oct	Balloon		„	„	–	
5	„	Nieuport Sct		„	„	Lake Doberdo	
6	27 Oct	Seaplane	(c)	„	„		
7	15 Nov	Camel	(c)	153.61	„	Meolo-Monistier	
8	23 Nov	Macchi L3	(d)	153.44	„	Agenzia	
9	27 Nov	SAML 2		„	„	San Dona di Piave	
10	29 Nov	SAML 2	(e)	153.61	„	Vianello	
11	5 Dec	Savoia-Pomilio		153.44	„	San Biaggio-LaFossa	
	1918						
12	26 Jan	Seaplane		153.106	F61J	Laguna Palude	1810
13	30 Jan	RE8	(c)	153.110	„	Cana Reggia	
14	24 Feb	Macchi M5	(f)	153.106	„	Marcello	
15	8 Mar	Balloon	(g)	„	„	Cenesa Canal	
16	12 Mar	Ansaldo SVA5		„	„	Monistier di Treviso	
–	„	Ansaldo SVA5		„	„	„	
17	16 Mar	Ansaldo SVA5	(c)	„	„	Casonetti	
18	23 Mar	SAML 2	(h)	153.111	„	Noventa di Piave	

Pilots: (a) Kpl S Wenczel; (b) Fw F Wognar; (c) shared with Oblt Ernst Strohschneider (13th victory 34 Sqn a/c); (d) shared with Paul Jelinek; (e) shared with Oblt Strohschneider and Oblt Karl Patzelt; (f) shared with Oblt Strohschneider, Ltn Otto Schrimpl and Ltn Edgar Mörath of Flik 63J; (g) shared with Otto Schrimpl; (h) Sgt Zardi/ Ten Busseti.

GRUBER Kurt   Offizierstellvertreter   FLIK 1,41J,61J

From Linz, in Austria, where he was born in 1896, the son of a teacher and future mayor, he was educated in Germany, studying to be an engineer. When the war began he joined the army and volunteered for the Airship Detachment, but was then assigned for pilot training. On completion he was posted to Flik 1 on the Russian Front, flying two-seaters, and promoted to sergeant in September 1915. Early in 1916 he was awarded the Silver Bravery Medal, 1st Class. Flying the Knoller-Albatros B.I, Gruber and his observers accounted for several Russian aircraft during the first half of 1916, to receive a second Silver Bravery Medal. At the end of the year he became a sort of test pilot but in May 1917 was assigned to Flik 41J on the Isonzo Front, under Godwin Brumowski, flying Brandenburg D.I fighters, but was injured in a crash before the month was out and was not returned to the squadron until September, by now flying the Albatros Scout. By the time he moved to Flik 61J in December he had achieved several more victories and been rewarded with the Gold Bravery Medal. Flik 61J operated to the north-west of Venice, and flew the Phönix D.I fighters. He was in constant action and by early 1918 had been awarded three Gold Medals for Bravery, one of only six NCOs to receive three, and promoted to Offizierstellvertreter. However, his luck ran out on 4 April. Attacked by two Sopwith Camels, he is thought to have shot down one (no RAF losses) but the other caught him and his fighter's wings collapsed. 66 Squadron made three claims at around 0915 this day, over Cismon. He was buried at Feltre and received a posthumous award of a fourth Gold Medal; only he and Julius Arigi were so honoured.

	1916			Albatros B.I			
1	14 Apr	Morane P	(a)	22.30	F1	Bojan	0630
2	2 May	Morane P	(b)	„	„	Lysskowcy	0945
3	6 Jun	Morane P	(c)	„	„	Dolcok	1800
	1917			Scout			
4	29 Sep	Nieuport Sct			F41J	Cormons	
5	9 Oct	Balloon	(d)		„	Nr Sdobba Estuary	1700
	1918			Phönix D.I			
6	10 Jan	SAML 2	(e)	228.24	F60J	Valstagna	
7	„	Nieuport Sct	(e)	„	„	„	
8	27 Jan	Nieuport Sct		„	„	„	
9	1 Feb	Nieuport Sct		„	„	Nr Vattaro	
10	26 Feb	Hanriot DI		„	„	N Monte Nuova	
11	4 Apr	Camel		„	„	Primolano	0915

Obs: (a) Hptm E H v Kirchberg; (b) Oblt G Brumowski; (c) Obs unknown; (d) shared with Brumowski and Oblt F Linke-Crawford; (e) shared with Linke-Crawford.

HAUTZMAYER Ludwig   Oberleutnant   FLIK 19,51J,61J

Born in Fürstenfeld, south of Vienna, Austria, on 25 April 1893, he studied at Graz and at the University there, in mechanical engineering. As a reserve officer he was with the 7th Infantry Regiment and when war came he was sent to the Russian Front, but was badly wounded in one leg in September. Recovering, he joined the Air Service as an observer and in March 1915 was assigned to Flik 15 as technical officer, again on the Russian Front. Flik 15 also saw action in Serbia, and flying Albatros B.Is, flew on more than 40 sorties with this unit. He was rewarded with the Silver Military Merit Medal and the Bronze Military Merit Medal. He applied for pilot training and was accepted in November, and by February 1916 had become a pilot and posted to Flik 19 on the Isonzo Front. He flew both fighter and two-seater machines, gaining some successes in a Fokker Eindekker, but then it was some months before he scored again, having now equipped with the Albatros Scout. He also received two awards of the Military Merit Cross, 3rd Class with War Decoration and Swords, the Order of the Iron Crown, 3rd Class, with War Decoration and Swords, and promotion to oberleutnant. In February 1918 he was posted to Flik 51J under Benno Fiala, and with this unit, Hautzmayer was awarded the Silver Bravery Medal, 1st Class (for officers). On 20 March he was given command of Flik 61J, leading this unit till the Armistice, being rewarded with the Knight's Cross of the Order of Léopold, with War Decoration and Swords. Post war he became a Hungarian citizen following his marriage to a Hungarian, his new name being Lajos Tatai in his new language, which he had to learn totally. He flew with the Hungarian Malert airline but was killed in a crash on 6 December 1936, trying to land in fog at Croydon airport, south of London. He is buried in Vienna.

	1916			Fokker E.III			
1	18 Feb	Caproni Ca1		03.52	F19	Merna, nr Gorizia	
				Brand C.I			
2	29 Apr	Bomber	(a)	26.08	„	San Daniele	
				Fokker E.III			
3	9 Aug	Caudron		03.42	„		pm
	1917			Alb DIII			
4	28 Aug	Caproni	(b)	53.62	„	Monfalcone	
	1918						
5	13 Mar	SIA 7B	(c)	153.142	F51J	N Spresiano	
6	7 Oct	Br a/c		253.26	F61J	W San Dona di Piave	
7	27 Oct	Ansaldo SVA		253. ?	„	Portobuffole AF	

Obs: (a) Oblt B Fiala; (b) shared with Oblt J Hoffmann; (c) shared with Oblt Fiala.

HEFTY Friedrich   Offizierstellvertreter   FLIK 12,44F,42J

Born in Pozsony, in what today would be known as Bratislava, Slovakia, on 13 December 1894, his father was a count, although he was never to use this title himself. He was called to military service in 1914, and having earlier watched Louis Blériot at an air show just outside Budapest, decided on the Air Service. In May 1915 he was sent to Flik 12 on the Isonzo Front, where he flew recce and bombing sorties on Lohner, Albatros and later Brandenburg two-seaters. He and his observer were both wounded by AA fire during a sortie on 7 October, but Hefty got them back over the front lines. He was also in hospital during December, having contracted typhus. He then flew as a test pilot from the autumn of 1916 but eventually returned to Flik 12. In April 1917 he was sent to Flik 44F (Fernaufklarerkompanie), which was employed on long-range reconnaissance sorties, and with this unit scored his first victory over Romania. Hefty became a pilot on posting to Flik 42J in October 1917, back on the Isonzo Front and saw action at Caporetto, and he often flew in company with Stabsfeldwebel Johann Risztics and Zugsführer Ferdinand Udvardy, and as all became recipients of the Gold Medal for Bravery, they became known as the 'Golden Triumvirate'. They even had sequential identifying numbers on their aircraft, Hefty with '6', Udvardy '7' and Risztics '8'. Hefty brought his score to an official five in June (but also had three unconfirmed claims), and was himself shot down on 22 August 1918, but was fortunate enough to be wearing a parachute and was thus able to bale out. It was the first time he had worn one, following an official order for pilots to do so! Hefty was a three times winner of the Golden Medal for Bravery, as well as a three-time winner of the Bronze Medal, and twice winner of both the 1st and 2nd Class of the Silver Medal. After WW1 Hefty flew with the Hungarians against the Romanian, Serb and Czech forces, and was imprisoned. Later he flew with the Nationalist Hungarian Air Force. He also received the newly established Order of Vitez. He remained in the aviation world for the next 20 years, flying for Malert Airline and for Air France, as well as starting his own flying and gliding clubs. In WW2 he was a lieutenant in the Hungarian Air Force, in the Correspondence Section, until his capture by advancing Allied troops. Upon release he went home to Hungary but later emigrated to America, being unable to agree with the communist régime. He set up home in Detroit, where he died on 20 January 1965.

	1917			Brand C.I			
1	23 Aug	Farman	(a)	69.79	F44F	Tirgul Ocna	
	1917			Berg D.I			
2	27 Oct	EA	(b)	38.10	F42J	Lake Doberdò	
	1918			Alb DIII			
–	4 Apr	EA			„	Montello	u/c
3	17 Apr	Camel	(c)	153.169	„	Montello	
–	16 Jun	Nieuport Sct		„	„	Montello	u/c
–	17 Jun	Caproni		„	„	Montello	u/c
4	20 Jun	Br 2-seater		„	„	Susegana	1045
5	„	2-seater		„	„	Montello	
–	„	Hanriot HD1		„	„	Spresiano	u/c
–	22 Jun	Nieuport Sct		153.265	„	Montello	eve u/c

Obs: (a) Ltn Prinzen; (b) shared with Zugs. Paul Jelinek; (c) shared with Stabs. F Takacs.

HEYROWSKY Adolf   Hauptmann   FLIK 2,9,12,19

Born in Murau, in the Styrian region of Austria, on 18 February 1882, he was the son of a gamekeeper. Graduated from the Military Academy in Prague in 1902, he joined the 90th Austro-Hungarian Infantry Regiment as an Offizierstellvertreter, and was commissioned in May 1904, then Oberleutnant six years later. In 1912 he volunteered for the Airship Section, and was assigned to pilot training. On the outbreak of war he was with Flik 2 on the Serbian Front, and flew numerous recce sorties and some bomb raids, for which he received the Bronze Military Merit Medal. In November he was given command of Flik 9, on the same Front, gaining his first victories in early 1915. Again he was decorated, this time with the Order of the Iron Crown, 3rd Class with War Decoration and Swords, and promoted to Hauptmann. He then took command of Flik 12 on the Isonzo Front, until January 1916, at which time he took command of Flik 19. Flying both Brandenburg and Albatros two-seaters, he led from the front, flying numerous sorties, and together with various observers, accounted for several enemy aircraft and assisted in the destruction of an Italian airship; he also downed one opponent flying a single-seat Eindekker monoplane. The Military Merit Cross, 3rd Class with War Decoration was added to his list of awards, for his part in the Battles of the Isonzo. This was followed in 1917 by the awards of the Knight's Cross of the Order of Léopold, with War Decoration and Swords. In October he was appointed a Staff Officer for Aviation, which he did not care for and in March 1918 became a liaison officer to General Ernst Wilhelm von Hoeppner, who commanded the German Army Air Service. As such he was able to participate in several bomb raids with the Germans, flying with both Bogohl 6 and 12, attacking French towns, and even made an attack on Dover with Riesenflugzeugabteilung (Rzb) 5. He returned to the Italian Front for the last battles on the Piave but was back in Germany when the war finished. Heyrowsky had been wounded at least twice during the war, and was the most successful two-seater pilot in terms of victories, just his one victory in a Fokker Eindekker not achieved from a two-seater machine. In WW2 Heyrowsky served as a colonel in the Luftwaffe, but died in 1945 at the age of 63.

	1915						
1	22 Feb	Balloon	(a)		F9	Belgrade	
2	3 Mar	Balloon	(a)		„	Belgrade	
	1916			Brand C.I			
3	4 May	Airship M4	(b)	61.55	F19	Merna	noon
4	10 Aug	Voisin	(c)	61.61	„	Nr Cormons	am
				Fokker E.III			
5	15 Aug	Voisin		03.42	„	Cormons	
				Brand C.I			
6	3 Dec	Caproni	(d)	29.61	„	Nr Gorizia	
7	28 Dec	Voisin	(e)	29.63	„	W San Marco	
	1917						
8	17 Apr	Nieuport Sct	(e)	29.64	„	Nr Gorizia	
9	15 May	Spad 1	(f)	29.64	„	Merna	
10	3 Jun	SAML *	(f)	„	„	Sober	0930
11	26 Jun	Nieuport Sct	(f)	„	„	Sober	0920
12	„	Caudron	(f)	„	„	Sober	0930

Obs: (a) Oblt O Safar; (b) Oblt B Fiala; (c) Oblt F Lerch; (d) S Wagner; (e) Oblt Ltn J Pürer; (f) Oblt L Hauser
* Previously noted as a Nieuport, this SAML was from 114 Sqn.

JÄGER Otto   Oberleutnant   FLIK 10,27,42J

With the perfect name for a fighter pilot, Otto Jäger was born in Asch, West Bohemia (today's Czech Republic) to Sudeten-German parents, on 6 April 1890. The year 1914 found him serving on the Russian Front with Hungarian Regiment Nr.67, being commissioned on 1 November following his first wound in August. During 1915 he was wounded twice more and rendered unfit for further duty. However, he was awarded the Bronze Military Merit Medal and the Silver Bravery Medal for Officers, 1st Class, while Germany presented him with the Prussian War Service Medal. Going to a training post he quickly volunteered for the Air Service and became an observer and technical officer, assigned to Flik 10 back on the Russian Front, in the Spring of 1916. Flying two-seaters he and his pilots scored several victories, and he received the Silver Military Merit Medal and the Military Merit Cross, 3rd Class, with War Decoration. Once again the Germans decorated him, this time with the Prussian Iron Cross, 2nd Class. Requesting pilot training in September 1916 he became a pilot by December and was posted to Flik 17 in March the following year, again flying two-seaters. However, his service here was short-lived, as he received leg injuries from a whirling propeller on 2 May. He was not back in action until July, but was assigned to Flik 27 in Russia, which also had Albatros Scouts in addition to two-seaters. He gained his first single-seat victory and was then sent to Flik 42J as a fully fledged fighter pilot. He brought down an Italian two-seater on the morning of 19 August 1917, but was himself shot down by a Nieuport, the wings of his machine collapsing. He was posthumously given the Order of the Iron Crown, 3rd Class, with War Decoration and Swords.

	1916			Alb B.I			
1	5 May	C-type	(a)	22.10	F10	Nr Koryto	0900
2	3 Jun	Farman	(b)	22.31	„	Stepan	0700
3	7 Jun	Farman	(a)	22.10	„	Chorlupy-Klewan	0730
4	„	Farman	(a)	„	„	„	0735
				Brand C.I			
5	2 Aug	Farman	(a)	64.15	„	E Szelwow	0700
	1917			Alb DIII			
6	20 Jul	2-seater		53.45	F27	N Brzezany	
7	19 Aug	Nieuport 2		153.14	F42J	Hermada	0840

Pilot: (a) Zugs. K Urban; (b) Zugs. Fritz Rottmann.

JINDRA Otto   Hauptmann   FLIK 1

Born near Wittingau, in the town of Chlumetz, Bohemia (now Czech Republic), of Czech parents, on 18 March 1986, he was destined to become the second highest scoring two-seat airman in the Austro-Hungarian Air Service. Deciding early on a military career, he entered the Artillery Academy in Vienna, graduating in 1905, going into the Mountain-Artillery Regiment Nr.14. Commissioned, he was an oberleutnant by late 1912 and when the war started he went to the Russian Front where he won the Bronze Military Merit Medal during the battles of Limberg. By September 1914, however, he had decided on a transfer to the Air Service, and became an observer in Flik 1. Almost at once he and his pilot were shot down, on 14 November, by ground fire and were lucky to make it back to their own lines. He became CO of the unit in January 1915, following the loss of Flik 1's CO, despite being only an observer officer. Obviously his talents had begun to shine through to the higher echelons. Flying Albatros B.I two-seaters, he and his pilots began to score victories over the Summer of 1915, Jindra being awarded the Military Merit Cross and the German Iron Cross, 2nd Class; he was also promoted to Hauptmann. Towards the end of the year, he began to take informal flying tuition and by December received his pilot's badge. However, on 5 January 1917, on one of his first jobs as a pilot, he received a slight head wound and was forced down to an emergency landing. Still flying the Knoller-Albatros B.I he gained his first pilot victory in March, and continued in action throughout the year, being himself brought down again on 13 September by AA fire, but he survived. He was now decorated with the Silver Military Merit Medal and the Order of the Iron Crown, 3rd Class, with War Decoration and Swords. In January 1918 he was appointed CO of Flek 11 (Fliegerersatzkompanie) but his wide experience of operations soon made him commander of a bomber group of five squadrons, known as Fliegergruppe G. But he was then injured in a night crash, which put him out of the war. In 1918 he received the Military Merit Cross, 3rd Class, for the second time. Post war he became a Czechoslovak citizen and helped establish the Czech Air Force, and later became its Commander-in-Chief. He died in 1942.

	1915			Alb B.I			
1	13 Jun	Morane P	(a)	22.29	F1	Dubowice	0610
2	„	Morane P	(a)	„	„	„	0620
3	27 Aug	Morane P	(b)	22.06	„	Tluste	
	1916						
4	29 Mar	Morane P	(c)	22.23	„	Sokal, E Chotin	
5	9 Apr	EA	(d)	„	„	SE Kamieniec	
6	12 Apr	Morane P	(e)	„	„	Iszkowsky	
7	„	Morane P	(e)	„	„	„	
				Brand C.I			
8	26 Sep	Nieuport	(f)	64.23	„	Solka	
9	18 Dec	Balloon	(g)	63.06	„	Mesticanestie	

Pilots: (a) Zugs. M Libano; (b) Fw J Mattl; Obs: (c) F Buchberger; (d) Ltn V Fiala; (e) G Brumowski; (f) Oblt E Strickel; (f) Obs unknown.

KASZA Alexander   Feldwebel   FLIK 55J

Born Tacskosuthfalva, Hungary, in 1896, he joined the 86th Infantry Regiment in 1915 prior to volunteering for the Air Service. Assigned to the balloon section near Vienna that September he began pilot training and was then retained as an instructor. Finally in August 1917 he managed to transfer to Flik 55J, as a fighter pilot, on the Isonzo Front, and claimed his first victory in November. His fourth victory was one shared with Kiss and Kenzian, an RE8 which they forced down, the crew and aircraft being captured. He had claimed six official victories by mid-1918 but was then assigned to Flik 15F, then to Flik 11F, to fly as a reconnaissance pilot. For his war service he received the Silver Bravery Medal, 1st and 2nd Class and the Karl Troop Cross. After the war he remained in the world of Hungarian aviation and was one of those who became a member of the Order of Vitez. During WW2 he lived with his family in Budapest, near Buda Castle which housed German soldiers. In a bombing raid on this part of the city in February 1945, his house received a direct hit, killing him and all his family.

	1917			Alb DIII		
1	15 Nov	Savoia-Pomilio	(a)	153.19	F55J	N Bassano
2	17 Nov	Nieuport Sct	(b)	„	„	N Valstagna

3	23 Nov 1918	Nieuport Sct		153.40	„		Bassano-Rubbio
4	12 Jan	RE8	(c)		„		Casa Rigoni
5	22 May	Camel			„		S Cima Maora
				Phönix D.II			
6	9 Jun	BF2b	(d)	422.14	„		E Acqua Viva

(a) shared with Fw A Lehmann; (b) shared with Ltn E Lupfer and OfStv E Stumpa; (c) shared with Oblt G Kenzian and OfStv J Kiss, RE8 A4445 of 42 Sqn, captured; (d) C4700, 139 Sqn, crew captured.

KASZALA Karl   Offizierstellvertreter   FLIK 1,41J

A Hungarian, born in 1892 in the city of Nyrita, in present day Slovakia. He joined the Austro-Hungarian army in 1914 but then volunteered for the Air Service and upon completion of his flight training was promoted to korporal, in October 1915. He was assigned to Flik 14 as a reconnaissance pilot, flying Aviatik B.IIIs, but he refused to fly them as he thought them dangerous, so was posted to Flik 1, lucky not to find himself in more serious trouble. From this unsteady start he soon became a proficient war pilot, and on several occasions his observer was Godwin Brumowski. Flying Brandenburg C.Is he scored three victories over the Winter of 1916-17, to receive the Silver Bravery Medal, 1st Class, and the German Iron Cross, 2nd Class — the only Austro-Hungarian NCO ever to be given this Prussian decoration. Then in February 1917, Kaszala was posted to Flik 21J to become a fighter pilot, but almost immediately went to Flik 41J, being formed by his comrade Brumowski. He flew both Brandenburg and Albatros Scouts on the Isonzo Front, scoring his first fighter kill on 12 May, and became an ace on the 20th. Kaszala was awarded a second Silver Medal, but he did not score again until November, downing three opponents in just over a fortnight. He had been promoted to Stabsfeldwebel in August, then to Offizierstellvertreter in October, and now came the award of a third Silver Bravery Medal, followed by the Gold. He left Flik 41J in April 1918 for a rest, becoming a test pilot at an aircraft supply depot, where he saw the end of the war. After the armistice he returned to his native Hungary and became active in aviation, serving initially as a pilot with the Hungarian Red Air Corps in 1919 against the Romanians, Serbs and Czechs. In 1927 he helped to found the Hungarian Technical University Aero Club and in 1930, when he left it, they presented him with a Hansa-Brandenburg B.I biplane. He and his wife used this to give demonstration flights at air shows, but at one show in 1932, the machine spun into the ground and the couple were killed.

	1916			Brand C.I			
1	13 Dec	EA	(a)		F1	Gurahumora	
	1917						
2	9 Jan	EA	(b)	63.23	„	Fundul-Moldovi	
3	23 Jan	EA	(c)	„	„	Kimpolung	
				Brand D.I			
4	12 May	Farman			F41J	Podsenica	
5	20 May	Farman	(d)	28.11	„	Monte Santo	1030
				Alb DIII			
6	28 Nov	Savoia-Pomilio	(d)		„	Casa Serpo	
7	10 Dec	Hanriot HDI	(e)		„	Monistier di Treviso	
8	13 Dec	Balloon	(f)		„	Meolo	

Obs: (a) Ltn N Feher; (b) Ltn W Varju; (c) Oblt J Baumgartner; (d) shared with Hptm G Brumowski; (e) shared with Oblt F Linke-Crawford; (f) shared with Brumowski and Linke-Crawford.

KENZIAN Edler von KENZIANSHAUSEN Georg   Oberleutnant   FLIK 24,55J

Born in Linz in 1894, the son of an army officer, George Kenzian always dreamed of following in his father's footsteps. In 1913 he entered the Austro-Hungarian army with the Engineer Battalion Nr.2, was later commissioned and in 1914 went to war on the Russian Front. Wounded in December, he returned to his unit and promoted to oberleutnant in September 1915. Not long afterwards he volunteered for the Air Service, trained as an observer and went to Flik 24 on the

Southern Tyrolean Front. Flying Brandenburg two-seaters he gained his first victory in June 1916 flying as back-seater to Josef Kiss. However, some weeks later, on 27 July, he himself was brought down by an Italian Nieuport and was wounded along with his pilot, Zugsführer Alois Jezek. Three months passed before he was able to return to Flik 24, although he was awarded the Order of the Iron Crown, 3rd Class, with War Decoration and Swords. In early 1917 Kenzian became an instructor at the officer's flight school at Wiener-Neustadt, and while so doing, trained as a pilot himself, becoming fully qualified in July. The following month he was posted to Flik 55J, as second-in-command. Flying on the Isonzo Front he gained his first single-seat victory in September and by the end of the year had raised his score to six. Along with Kiss and Alexander Kasza, Kenzian helped capture an RE8 and its crew on 12 January 1918, and by the end of March his score had risen to 9. He received the Military Merit Cross, 3rd Class, and the Gold Bravery Medal for Officers, one of only nine awarded. He was then given command of Flik 68J, operating north of Venice, and fought during the Piave battle in June, but achieved no further victories, but did receive the Silver Military Merit Medal with Swords. A month before hostilities ceased, he took command of Flik 42J. Immediately after the war he flew against the Slovenian forces in Carinthia while with the German-Austrian Republic forces, a conflict which ended in June 1919. Surprisingly, after this time almost nothing further is known of Kenzian.

	1916			Brand C.I			
1	16 Jun	Farman	(a)	61.18	F24	S Asiago	
2	20 Jun	Farman	(b)	61.23	„	Monte Cimone	noon
	1917			Alb DIII			
3	29 Sep	Nieuport Sct	(c)		F55J	S Plava	
4	18 Nov	Nieuport Sct	(d)	153.27	„	Arsiero-Villaverla	
5	27 Nov	SAML 2	(e)	„	„	S Asiago	
6	7 Dec	SAML 2	(f)		„	S Asiago	
	1918						
7	12 Jan	RE8	(g)		„	Casa Rigoni	
8	26 Jan	Sopwith		152.107	„	Cia Pralunga	
9	24 Mar	Sopwith			„	Val d'Assa	

Pilots: (a) Fw R Forst; (b) Zugs. J Kiss; (c) shared with Eugen Bönsch and Ltn A Tahy; (d) shared with Ltn E Lupfer, OffStv E Stumpa and Franz Lahner; (e) shared with Josef Kiss; (f) shared with E Stumpa and Gottlieb Munczar; (g) A4445, 42 Sqn, captured, shared with Kiss and Alexander Kasza.

KISS Josef   Leutnant   FLIK 24,55J

The son of a gardener who worked at the military cadet school in Pozsony (present day Bratislava, Slovakia), Josef Kiss was born on 26 January 1896. When war came he left school and enlisted in the army, but having terminated his schooling he fell short of the necessary qualifications to become an officer. Sent to the Russian Front with Infantry Regiment Nr.72, he was wounded in action late in the year, and when recovered, decided to join the Air Service. By late April 1916, he was assigned to Flik 24, in the southern part of the Austrian Tyrol, to fly reconnaissance missions. His first victory was scored with Georg Kenzian as his observer, forcing a Farman to land. His second victory was over a large Caproni bomber which he forced down near Pergine airfield, with a dead pilot and wounded co-pilot and gunner. His third victory came down beyond the front lines but was shelled to destruction by Austro-Hungarian artillery fire. By 1917, Kiss was flying the single-seat Brandenburg D.Is which Flik 24 used for protection sorties for their two-seater work. With these machines he increased his score and showed his aptitude for fighting patrols. In all he flew 112 sorties with Flik 24 and had received the Silver Bravery Medal, 1st Class on three occasions, the Gold Bravery Medal twice and had raised his score to seven. He was shot down on 14 September flying a camera-equipped KD, but survived. November 1917 saw him become a fully fledged fighter pilot with the posting to Flik 55J also based at Pergine, where he usually flew with Julius Arigi and the unit CO, Hauptmann Josef von Maier. With Flik 55J he added a further 12 victories to his score, which brought him a fourth Silver Medal and a third Gold. With a score of 19 he became the highest scoring

Hungarian pilot, but he was badly wounded in combat with three fighters on 27 January 1918. Indeed, his life was probably saved by his friend Arigi, who, upon discovering him unattended in hospital, dragged a doctor to tend him, the man having his dinner. In the event, Kiss lost part of his bowel but recuperated and returned to the front two months later, although he should not have been allowed to do so. He was shot down in combat with 66 Squadron at 1100 hours near Lamon, on 24 May 1918, credited to Lt G A Birks, in Camel B6424, although sometimes recorded as Captain W G Barker. He was flying a Phönix DIIa 422.10. Kiss' girlfriend, Enrica Bonecker, lived near the airfield at Pergine. She never married but is said to have visited his grave every day for the next 52 years of her life. His death was not lost on the RAF either, for they dropped a wreath onto the airfield on May 27, the date of his funeral. Because of the strict officer status of the Empire, Kiss was unable to receive a commission due to his below par education. His one wish was that he might receive a field commission, the only way he would be able to achieve officer status, although that was difficult enough. Twenty-four hours after his death he became the only NCO pilot ever to be promoted to commissioned rank.

	1916			Brand C.I			
1	20 Jun	Farman	(a)	61.23	F24	Monte Cimone	noon
2	25 Aug	Caproni	(b)	61.29	„	Fort Lusern	am
3	17 Sep	Caproni	(c)		„	Chizzola	
	1917			Berg D.I			
4	10 Jun	Nieuport Sct		28.37	„	Asiago	
5	14 Jun	SAML 2	(d)	„	„	Roana	
6	13 Jul	Savoia-Pomilio	(e)	„	„	Levico	
7	11 Sep	SAML 2			„	Asiago	
				Alb DIII			
8	15 Nov	Caproni	(f)	153.17	F55J	Nr Asiago	
9	„	Caproni	(f)	„	„	„	
10	17 Nov	SAML 2	(f)	153.47	„	SE Asiago	
11	18 Nov	Savoia-Pomilio	(f)	„	„	Monte Cengio	
12	„	EA	(f)	„	„	N Arsiero	
13	27 Nov	SAML 2	(g)	153.87	„	N Asiago	
14	„	SAML 2	(h)	„	„	Roana	
15	7 Dec	Pomilio PE	(f)		„	E Asiago	
16	„	SAML 2			„	Monte Sprung	
17	16 Dec	SAML 2	(h)		„	Nr Feltre	
	1918						
18	12 Jan	RE8	(i)		„	Casa Rigoni	
19	26 Jan	SAML 2		153.47	„	Monte Magna	

Obs: (a) Oblt G Kenzian; (b) Ltn K Fiedler; (c) Oblt K Keizar; (d) 5 Sqn, captured, and shared with Flik 17; (e) shared with Flik 17; (f) shared with Hptm J v Maier and Julius Arigi; (g) shared with Ltn E Lupfer and Korp. Franz Lahner; (h) shared with Arigi and Lahner; (i) A4445, 42 Sqn, captured, shared with G Kenzian and A Kasza.

KOSTRBA Heinrich   Hauptmann   FLIK 4,23

This air fighter gained early victories flying a Fokker Eindekker, the A.III, the Austro-Hungarian designation given to Fokker's E.I variant. Born in Prague, in 1883, his family had its origins in south Bohemia and in the pre-Hapsburg era, their family name amongst the nobility, if minor nobility, was Kostrba ze Skalice. He joined the army in 1903 being commissioned into the 73rd Infantry Regiment, making oberleutnant in May 1911. Interested in aviation he had become an observer prior to WW1 and when the war started went to Flik 8, to Russia, and was an early recipient of the Military Merit Cross, 3rd Class, as well as the German Iron Cross 2nd Class. The rank of hauptmann followed in May 1915. Moving to the Isonzo Front in July he joined Flik 6 to train as a pilot, which he achieved in October. Second-in-command of Flik 4 followed where he flew two-seaters and the Fokker monoplanes, and gained three victories on the Eindekker. In March 1916 he was made CO of Flik 23 on the southern Tyrolean Front, scoring five more kills on the Brandenburg two-seater and in November he took command of Fliegerersatzkompanie 2, where he seems to have served for most of the rest of the war. However, in late 1918 he was appointed commander of the Prague Military Police, and was therefore ideally placed to assist in the overthrow of the Austro-Hungarian government by the Czechs in their quest for independence. He then took command of the newly established Czech Army Air Corps, but was removed from office a year later. He returned to the Air Corps in 1921 as a squadron commander and was engaged in several undertakings. In 1926 he resigned in order to go to a job with the Czech State Airline, but before he did so, in September he led a group of Yugoslavian airmen on their journey from Prague to Warsaw. During the take-off run, his aircraft was hit by the lead Yugoslav machine and they crashed from about 30 feet, but Kostrba and two Yugoslavs were killed. He was given a State funeral on September 28th, in Prague, his coffin placed on the fuselage of an aeroplane and paraded through the streets.

	1916			Fokker E.I			
1	18 Feb	Caproni Ca.1	(a)	03.51	F4	Palmanova	0845
2	,,	Caudron		,,	,,	Nr Monfalcone	0925
3	,,	Caproni Ca.1	(b)	,,	,,	Merna	0950
				Brand C.1			
4	7 Jun	Farman	(c)	26.09	F23	SE Borghetto	0930
5	29 Jun	Farman	(c)	,,	,,	Leogra Valley	0715
6	,,	Farman	(c)	,,	,,	Val Ronchi	to
7	,,	Farman	(c)	,,	,,	E Vignola	0820
8	20 Aug	Farman	(d)	,,	,,	Arsiero	

(a) shared with Hptm M Bernath; (b) shared with two other Fokkers and two two-seater crews; (c) Obs. Oblt J Frint; (d) no observer carried.

KOWALCZIK Julius   Offizierstellvertreter   F24

Yet another whose parents were of Sudeten-German stock, Kowalczik was born in Mahrisch-Ostrau (present day Czech Republic), in 1885. Joined the army in 1914 and decided to transfer to the Air Service the following year, completing his pilot training in February 1916 with the rank of Korporal. Assigned to Flik 15 in March on the south Tyrolean Front, equipped with various two-seater types. A few single-seaters were also on hand for protection flights. Kowalczik flew whatever was available and on whatever sortie was scheduled, and was soon promoted to sergeant. A month later, in June, he was awarded the Silver Bravery Medal, 2nd Class. He achieved his first victory in October, flying with Oberstleutnant Leo Nadherny, and in co-operation with another crew. The following month he received the Gold Bravery Medal, an NCO's highest decoration. Flying continued into the new year and with it came further awards. March saw the second Silver Bravery Medal, 2nd Class, plus the 1st Class. He then trained as a fighter pilot at Wiener-Neustadt and returned to his unit, able to fly the Berg D.I scout, as well as the Albatros Scouts. In June he received the Gold Bravery Medal, followed in July by promotion to stabsfeldwebel and later to offizierstellvertreter. He was also recommended for a commission but this was virtually unknown within the Hapsburg Monarchy. On 24 August 1917 he was shot down over Monte Campolon, force landing his Albatros DIII 53.33 in Val D'Astico. His victors were Antonio Amantea, 71ª Squadriglia, and Anatonio Riva, 78ª Squadriglia, who would both become aces. Kowalczik was finally rested from operational flying in January 1918, and survived the war.

	1916			Brand C.I			
1	14 Oct	Farman	(a)	61.18	F24	Nr Pergine AF	1700
	1917						
2	18 Mar	Farman	(b)	29.71	,,	Asiago-Canove	1000
3	,,	Voisin	(b)	,,	,,	Nr Grigno	1015
4	10 Jun	Caproni	(c)	?	,,	Val d'Astico	
				Alb DII			
5	19 Jun	Caudron	(d)	53.02	,,	Cima Maora	

Obs: (a) Oberst L Nadherny and shared with another crew; (b) V Breitenfelder; (c) flying unknown single-seater and shared with a Flik 17 crew and a Flik 21 crew; (d) first confirmed victory by the Austro-Hungarian Air Service by a pilot flying an Albatros Scout.

LAHNER Franz   Feldwebel   FLIK 55J

Born in 1893, in the town of Bad Goisern, Austria, he joined the army soon after war came and in 1915 joined the 2nd Imperial Rifle Regiment. He served with this unit in action for 11 months, then volunteered for the Air Service, obtaining his Pilot's Certificate, No.734, on 26 July 1917. The following month he was assigned to Flik 55J on the Isonzo Front, saw action during the Caporetto Battle, then moved with his unit to the southern Tyrol, flying both Albatros and Phönix fighters, but scored his five victories in an Albatros. He became an ace on 21 March 1918 although he was shot up in this combat by the two-seater's escort and forced down near Radighieri. Oddly, he did not score again, despite staying in action till the end of the war. He was awarded two Silver Bravery Medals, 1st Class, and the Gold Medal. Post-war he served with the Police Squadron in Linz, Austria, then became a timber merchant. In WW2 he served in the Luftwaffe on ground duties, being commissioned on the edict of Hitler that all holders of the Gold Medal from WW1 should hold commissioned rank. Following WW2 he returned to his timber business. He suffered a stroke which left him severely handicapped and brought on an illness which led to his death, in Linz, on 19 July 1966. He was known by his comrades in Flik 55J as 'Papa Franz'.

	1917			Alb DIII		
1	18 Nov	Nieuport Sct	(a)	153.19	F55J	Arsiero-Villaverla
2	27 Nov	SAML 2	(b)	„		N Asiago
3	16 Dec	SAML 2	(a)	„		Fonzaso-Arten
	1918					
4	25 Jan	Nieuport Sct		153.70	„	Monte Alessi
5	21 Feb	Savoia-Pomilio		153.158	„	Asiago

(a) shared with Oblt G Kenzian, Ltn E Lupfer and OffStv E Stumpa; (b) shared with Ltn Lupfer and OffStv J Kiss; (c) shared with OffStv J Arigi and OffStv Kiss.

LANG Friedrich   Fregattenleutnant   DURAZZO & POLO AIR STATIONS

Lang was the only other Naval ace along with Gottfried Banfield, as well as one of the highest decorated Naval officers of the Austro-Hungarian Empire. Born an Austrian he joined the Navy in 1912 and attaining the rank of Naval Cadet, serving at sea after Cadet School. He became an ensign in 1915 and was decorated with the Silver Bravery Medal, 2nd Class, while serving on the destroyer *Balaton*. Transferred to the Naval Air Service in March 1916 and commissioned on 1 May. The following month he achieved Naval Pilot Certificate No.60 and later was assigned to the Naval Air Station at Kumbor (later Kotor, Yugoslavia). He was then sent to the air station at Durazzo, Albania, flying Lohner flying boats. On 22 August he and his observer were in the fight with Farmans of the Italian 34ª Squadriglia, in which Julius Arigi was much in evidence. Lang's machine was severely shot about but he shared in the loss of two of the Italians. In January 1917 he moved again, this time to Pola and from here won the Military Merit Cross, 3rd Class, with War Decoration and Swords, in addition to the Silver Military Merit Medal with Swords. When, in September, it was decided to form a fighter section at Pola, flying Phönix scouts, Lang was among the first assigned. He raised his personal score to five by the summer of 1918, receiving a second award of the Military Merit Cross, 3rd Class, as well as the Order of the Iron Crown, 3rd Class, with War Decoration and Swords. He left the Navy in 1919.

	1916			Lohner		
1	22 Aug	Farman	(a)	L.131	Albanian coast	0800
2	„	Farman	(a)	„	Skumbi estuary	0805
	1918					
				Phönix D1		
3	19 May	Macchi M.5		A.115	E of Po Estuary	1545
4	„	Macchi M.5		„	„	1550
5	12 Aug	Macchi L.3		A.117	W of Peneda	1555

(a) 34ª Squadriglia despatched five Farmans and lost two; see also Arigi and Lasi biographies who shared victories.

LASI Johann   Stabfeldwebel   FLIK 6

Lasi was the son of a Croatian family, born in the city of Katy, in 1890, which was the district capital of Bacs-Bodrog. By trade a cartwright he joined the army in 1911, later transferring to the Airship Service. Shortly after the war began he was assigned to Flik 6 as chief mechanic on the Balken Front, and later in Albania. Volunteering to fly as an observer, Lasi flew on more than a dozen raids and received the Silver Merit Cross with Crown. On 22 August 1916 he was flying with Arigi during the combat in which both men claimed five of the Farmans shot down. However, only two Farmans of 34ª Squadriglia were actually lost which reduces his status as an ace. Lasi received the Silver Bravery Medal, 1st Class. He then requested pilot training in the summer of 1916 and in June the following year was posted to Flek 1 as an instructor, seeing out the war with this unit.

	1916			Brand C.I			
1	22 Aug	Farman	(a)	61.64	F6	Skumbi Estuary	All
2	„	Farman	(a)	„	„	„	between
3	„	Farman	(a)	„	„	SW Skumbi Estuary	0730
4	„	Farman	(a)	„	„	Nr Skumbi Estuary	and
5	„	Farman	(a)	„	„	„	0800

(a) Pilot was Ltn Julius Arigi; aircraft of the 34th Italian Squadriglia, and two shared with Durazzo Naval Air Station aircraft flown by Friedrich Lang.

LINKE-CRAWFORD Frank   Oberleutnant   FLIK 41J, 60J

Born Cracow (Poland) the son of an army Major, married to an English woman by the name of Lucy Crawford, on 18 August 1893. He entered the Wiener-Neustadt Military Academy in 1910, graduating as a leutnant in 1913, posted to the 6th Dragoon Regiment. In 1914 he entered the war with the 1st Cavalry Troop and saw action on the Eastern Front, and took command of the Infantry Troop of his Regiment in November. For his actions during the Battle of Tymowa he received the Bronze Military Merit Medal. Despite a period away from the front due to dysentery and malaria, he continued brave actions but finally decided to transfer to the air service to become an observer. By March 1916 he was with Flik 22 and soon received the Military Merit Cross, 3rd Class. In September he requested pilot training, and completing this he was posted to Flik 12 on the Isonzo Front, at the beginning of 1917 as Deputy Commander. Here he flew both two-seaters on recce and bombing sorties and single-seaters on protection sorties. Flying a two-seater without an observer on 2 August, he was shot down inside the Austrian lines but survived. It is thought his victor was the Italian ace Pier Ruggero Piccio. Soon he received the Order of the Iron Crown, 3rd Class with War Decoration and Swords. He transferred to Flik 41J in August, commanded by Brumowski and had scored his first success before the month was out. With 13 victories he went to Flik 60J as commanding officer, bringing his score to 27 by late July 1918, but on 30 July he was shot down near Valstagna, in Berg D.I No.115.32. Evidence seems to point to his machine being damaged by Camels of 45 Squadron and he spun down, then recovered. With damage to his wings he had to fly straight and level, and was engaged by two Italian pilots. Although he endeavoured to fight them off he was handicapped by his severely damaged machine and eventually fell to Corporal Aldo Astolfi of the 81ª Squadriglia, his first and only confirmed victory.

	1917			Brand DI			
1	21 Aug	Nieuport Sct	(a)	28.40	F41J	Monte Santo	
2	22 Aug	Savoia-Pomilio	(a)	„	„	Gorizia	
3	23 Aug	Savoia-Pomilio	(b)	„	„	Bate	
–	25 Aug	Sopwith 2	(a)	„	„		u/c
4	26 Aug	Spad 1	(a)	„	„	Monte San Gabriele	
				Alb DIII			
5	23 Sep	Seaplane		153.04	„	Gulf of Trieste	pm
6	9 Oct	Balloon	(c)	153.11	„	Shobba Estuary	1700
7	23 Oct	Savoia-Pomilio		„	„	Hermada	1630
8	5 Nov	Macchi L.3	(d)	„	„	W Latisana	

9	„	Macchi L.3	(d)	„	„	„	
10	23 Nov	Nieuport Sct	(a)	„	„	Cortellazzo	
11	„	Nieuport Sct	(a)	„	„	„	
12	10 Dec	Sopwith Sct	(e)	153.16	„	Monastier di Treviso	
13	13 Dec	Balloon	(f)	„	„	Meolo	
	1918			Phönix DI			
14	10 Jan	SAML 2	(g)	228.16	F6oJ	Valstagna	
15	„	Nieuport Sct	(g)	„	„	„	
16	29 Jan	SIA-7B		228.14	„	Monte Lambara	
17	2 Feb	2-seater		228.06	„	Campolongo	
18	3 Feb	Nieuport Sct		„	„	S Monte Pertica	
19	24 Feb	Savoia-Pomilio		228.14	„	E Cismon	
20	11 Mar	Sopwith Sct		„	„	S Monte di Val Bella	
				Berg DI			
21	10 May	BF2b	(h)	115.32	„	Levico	0640
22	„	Scout		„	„	Barcarola	
23	11 May	Camel	(i)	„	„	Feltre	1015
24	1 Jun	Camel	(j)	„	„	Visone	
25	15 Jun	Sopwith Sct		„	„	Rocca	
26	21 Jun	Camel	(k)	„	„	Val Stizzone	am
27	29 Jul	BF2b	(l)	„	„	Valstagna	

(a) shared with Godwin Brumowski; (b) shared with Brumowski and H Maybäurl; (c) shared with Brumowski and Kurt Gruber; (d) shared with Brumowski and Oblt R Szepessy-Sokoll; (e) shared with Stabs K Kaszala; (f) shared with Brumowski and Kaszala; (g) shared with Kurt Gruber; (h) C4755, Z Flt; (i) B2455, 28 Sqn; (j) B6423, 45 Sqn, Lt E McN Hand, PoW; (k) possibly B5180, Lt C McEvoy, FTL at Istrana; (l) C990, 139 Sqn.

MACOUREK Bela   Oberleutnant   FLIK 23, 6F, 1J

The son of a Hungarian couple, he was born in Nebojsza, Pozsony, on 4 November 1889, today's Bratislava. Commissioned into the Royal Hungarian Mounted Artillery Division Nr.1 when war came, he saw considerable action and received the Bronze Military Merit Medal. In mid-1916 he volunteered for the Air Service and after training was assigned as an observer with Flik 23 in north-east Italy. As such he scored one victory and for his service with this unit was a recipient of the Silver Military Merit Medal with Swords and the 3rd Class of the Military Merit Cross with War Decoration and Swords. Desiring to be a pilot he was trained and then posted to Flik 6 on the Albanian Front, being deputy commander from mid-October 1917. He flew with this unit for several months but it was not until July 1918 that he had the chance to score again, downing two French recce machines. Not long after this event he was given command of Flik 1J, part of the defence system to the Cattaro naval base. Here he claimed two more victories to become an ace. He served with the Red Air Corps in 1919, became a Hungarian citizen post-war, his name being spelt Maklary, and then became a civil servant. In 1921 he was made a member of the Order of the Brave, and finally, in 1931, his wartime achievements were recognised by the award of the Gold Bravery Medal for Officers.

	1917			Brand CI			
1	21 May	Spad VII		129.46	F23	Selo	1030
	1918			Berg DI			
2	6 Jul	DH9		238.51	F6F	SE Fjeri	am
3	„	Caproni Ca3		„	„	Mi Foli	am
4	23 Aug	DH4	(b)	338.02	F1J	SW Punta d'Ostro	0810
5	6 Sep	DH4		„	„	W Punta d'Ostro	0945

Pilot: Zugs Franz Stalina; (b) shared with Julius Arigi; (c) N6418.

MAIER Josef von   Hauptmann   FLIK 55J

Von Maier was born in Poszony, in 1899, which today is Bratislava, (Slovakia), of Hungarian parents. He joined the army before the war and had risen to oberleutnant rank by 1914, while serving with an Engineer Battalion (No.5). Joining the Airship Company when war came he was assigned to Flik 14 in Russia as an observer, flying in Lohner machines. Within days of the war starting, he and his pilot were forced down inside enemy lines due to engine trouble, burnt their machine and were lucky enough to get back on foot. By the Spring of 1915, Maier had put in for pilot training, which he achieved in September. He was posted to Flik 13 as deputy commander, operating in Russia and then in Romania in the Summer of 1916 with Brandenburg CIs. He received both the Bronze and Silver Military Merit Medals, and the following year, the Order of the Iron Crown, 3rd Class, with War Decoration and Swords. Requesting a posting to a fighter unit in April 1917, he went to Flik 55J as CO, flying on the Isonzo Front and later on the Southern Tyrolean sector. He was to score seven victories, all downed in one brief three-week period between November and December 1917, while flying Albatros DIIIs. He was promoted to Hauptmann and received the Knight's Cross of the Order of Léopold with War Decoration and Swords. However, he made no more claims and left the squadron in September 1918, taking over command of the Fighter School where he saw out the war. He became a Hungarian citizen post-war and changed his name to the more Hungarian Joszef Modory. He served in the Red Air Corps in 1919 and was later associated with sport flying in Budapest and also served as a pilot in the Hungarian Air Transport Company, Malert. By 1935 he was commanding the Combat School in Szombathely followed three years later by an appointment as supervisor to the Air Force Academy. He retired in 1944 with the rank of colonel.

	1917			Alb DIII		
1	15 Nov	Caproni		153.64	F55J	Asiago
2	,,	Caproni	(a)	,,	,,	,,
3	17 Nov	Savoia-Pomilio	(a)	,,	,,	S Asiago-Arsiero
4	,,	SAML	(a)	,,	,,	,,
5	18 Nov	Savoia-Pomilio	(a)	,,	,,	Monte Cengio
6	7 Dec	Pomilio PE2	(a)		,,	E Asiago
7	,,	SAML	(a)		,,	Monte Sprung

(a) all shared with Julius Arigi and Josef Kiss.

NACHOD Kurt   Oberleutnant   FLIK 20

Kurt Nachod was born in Brünn (now Brno, Czech Republic) on 8 March 1890 and was an exceptional language student. His pre-war military service was spent in the infantry, and his well-off family provided him with a car with which he gained some fame as a driver and mechanic. Thus when war came he joined the Motor Corps Volunteers, and in Serbia chauffeured high-ranking officers about in his own car. Later he even commanded an armoured railway train in Northern Italy. Tiring of these activities he joined the Air Service in September 1915, became an observer and was assigned to Flik 10 in October. He flew on the Russian Front but in February 1916 moved to nearby Flik 20, helping to down a Russian aircraft while flying a Knoller-Albatros BI. He was to gain four more victories as an observer and he was rewarded with the Military Merit Cross, 3rd Class, with War Decoration, the German Iron Cross, 2nd Class, and the Silver Military Merit Medal with Swords. In July 1917 he moved again, this time to Fluggeschwader I on the Isonzo Front, and with them took unofficial flying lessons, eventually qualifying for his pilot's badge. He was badly injured in a flying crash on the night of 9 May 1918, practising night landings in a Hansa-Brandenburg CI, and died two days later. He received the posthumous award of the Order of the Iron Crown, 3rd Class, with War Decoration and Swords.

	1916			Alb BI	
1	31 May	Farman	(a)	22.18	Klewan
2	3 Jul	Farman	(b)	22.18	N Luck
				Brand CI	
3	20 Sep	EA	(c)	26.64	Russian lines
	1917				
4	7 Jan	Nieuport	(d)	26.54	nr Luck
5	,,	Farman	(d)	,,	nr Luck

(a) pilot unknown, shared with Zugs. Franz Zuzmann/Ltn Mathias Thaller; Pilot: (b) Franz Zusmann; (c) Zugs. Julius Minar; (d) Korp Friedrich Camoch.

NAVRATIL Friedrich   Oberleutnant   FLIK 41J, 3J

A soldier and airman who served throughout WW1, Navratil was born of Croatian parents on 19 July, 1893 in Sarajevo, entering the Infantry Cadet School after leaving school. When war came he was a leutnant with the Bosnian-Herzegovinan Infantry Regiment Nr.1, and fought in Serbia. He was wounded on 21 August 1914, but returned later in the year, only to be wounded again on 8 December. By June 1915 he was back on duty, now being based on the Italian Front, fighting in the Second Battle of Isonzo during July and August. He received the Military Merit Cross, 3rd Class, with War Decoration and Swords, also the Bronze Military Merit Medal with Swords, then promoted to oberleutnant in the field. He continued fighting with his Regiment in both Italy, the Tyrol and then Romania but was severely wounded again on 30 December 1916. He now received the Order of the Iron Crown, 3rd Class, with War Decoration and Swords, plus two awards of the Silver Military Merit Medal with Swords. Another field promotion came, almost unheard of in the Austro-Hungarian hierarchy, to hauptmannn. Transferring to the Air Service he became an observer with Flik 13 in Galicia (Russian Front), then went to Flik 11 in October 1917, but was soon requesting pilot training. A pilot by the new year he was assigned to Flik 41J on the Isonzo Front, where he gained one shared victory, but then was given command of Flik 3J in the southern Tyrol. He brought his score to ten during the summer, but when four of his pilots were shot down on the last day of August, he felt so bad about it that he hardly flew again. On 21 October, during a test flight, his seat broke and in making an emergency landing he wrecked his Albatros and was severely injured. He was still in hospital when the war ended. Post-war, Navratil joined the Yugoslav Air Force and as a career officer, rose to general by 1941, and following the German occupation was the Minister of Defence in Croatia, but disagreed with the régime and was replaced. Nevertheless he was tried by a 'people's court' under the Tito government for war crimes and was sentenced to death in 1946.

	1918			Alb DIII			
1	14 Apr	Camel	(a)	153.157	F41J	Arcade	am
2	28 Jun	Spad		153.198	F3J	Zugna	
3	16 Jul	Hanriot	(b)	253.06	,,	Val del Concei	
4	,,	Hanriot		(b)	,,	,,	,,	
5	23 Jul	BF2b	(c)	,,	,,	Mattarello	am
6	5 Aug	SIA-7b		,,	,,	nr Romagnano	
7	10 Aug	Scout		,,	,,	Monte Pasubio	
8	16 Aug	BF2b	(c)	,,	,,	Trento	am
9	23 Aug	BF2b	(c)	,,	,,	Gardolo airfield	am
10	31 Aug	EA	(d)	,,	,,	E Monte Pasubio	

(a) 28 Sqn B6342, shared with Godwin Brumowski; (b) shared with Oblt Stefan Stec and Oblt Franz Peter; (c) 139 Sqn, C4759, D8069, D7966; (d) claimed as a two-seater, but probably Camel of 45 Squadron.

NIKITSCH Karl   Hauptmann   FLIK 39

Older than most of his contemporaries, Karl Nikitsch was born on 17 January 1885, in Gross-Czakowitz, outside Prague, so was 29 when the war began. He was an army cadet pre-war and commissioned into the 35th Austro-Hungarian Infantry Regiment. He was also a well-known sportsman. Recruited into the Air Service soon after war was declared, by May 1915 he was at the Front as deputy commander with Flik 16 but in July was given command of Flik 14 on the Russian Front, flying with the 2nd Army. Flying mainly artillery observation sorties he was awarded the Bronze Military Merit Medal with Swords. In November he was with HQ of the Air Service, helping to form, train and equip new squadrons for the Front, although he was injured in a crash on 3 July 1916 flying a Fokker BI. Requesting a return to active duty he was given the task of forming Flik 39, and took it to the Romanian Front in March 1917. Although a two-seater unit, Nikitsch modified one two-seater into a single-seater for escort duties, often flying this machine himself. Eventually he was put in charge of four squadrons (Flik 29, 31, 33 and 39) known as Flieger-Detachments Nikitsch, providing escort and protection for the region's two-seaters. In these operations he downed six hostile aircraft, now flying an Albatros DIII and Brandenburg DIs. Flik 39 was transferred to the Isonzo Front for the Battle of Caporetto in late 1917 and Nikitsch was also nominated as Fliegergruppenkommandant of the Austro-Hungarian 1st Korps, encompassing both Austro-Hungarian and German squadrons. During his time with Flik 39 he received the German Iron Cross 1st and 2nd Class, the Order of the Iron Crown, 3rd Class, with War Decoration and Swords. In January 1918 he was given command of Flik 63J but before he took up this appointment he was badly injured in a crash which ended his wartime activities. Later in the year he commanded a training unit. After the war he was with the Air Police and studied law at the University of Graz where he received a doctorate. He was killed in a flying accident on 7 September 1927, aged 42.

	1917			Alb DIII			
1	19 Jul	Farman		53.24	F39	Fitonesti	
2	23 Jul	Spad Scout		53.41	,,	Zabrau Valley	0630
				KD DI			
3	9 Aug	Nieuport Sct		28.29	,,	Grosesci	1800
4	11 Aug	Nieuport Sct	(a)	,,	,,	Onesti	1130
5	30 Aug	Farman		,,	,,	Grosesci	1100
				Alb DIII			
6	27 Nov	Savoia-Pomilio		153.71	,,	Monte Grappa	

(a) shared with Zugs. Johann Hraman.

NOVAK Augustin Feldwebel FLIK 13, 39

Born of Czech parents in Batenwald, Novak was initially an artilleryman, enlisting in 1911. When war began he was with the 3rd Battery of the Horse Artillery Division Nr.7, and went to the Russian Front and won the Silver Bravery Medal, 2nd Class, during the Battle of Krasnik. In January 1916 he volunteered for the Air Service, trained as a pilot and then assigned to Flik 30 back on the Russian Front. He had hardly been with the unit when he crashed in a Lloyd CIII and was badly injured along with his observer. Upon his return, he discovered no observer wanted to fly with him, and soon he was moved to Flik 13 on the Romanian Front. Flying Hansa-Brandenburg CIs he flew bombing raids and in short order shot down aircraft that opposed him, receiving the Silver Bravery Medal, 1st Class. In December he was posted to Flik 39, north of Vienna, and he and his observers claimed another victory, although he was shot down and wounded in July and his observer killed. In August 1917 his work brought him a second Silver Bravery Medal 1st Class. Moving to the Isonzo Front for the Battle of Caporetto, he gained his fifth victory. Towards the end of January 1918 he became an instructor and did not return to operational duties.

	1916			Brand CI			
1	27 Dec	Farman	(a)	27.01	F13	Batesti	1120
2	,,	Farman	(b)	,,	E Onesti		1515
3	,,	Farman	(b)	,,	,,		1520
	1917						
–	1 Jun	Farman	(c)	67.38	F39	Comanestie area	u/c
4	21 Jun	Farman	(d)	69.53	,,	Comanestie A/F	0640
5	11 Nov	SAML		129.47	,,	Monte Grappa	

Obs: (a) Ltn A Souhrada; (b) Ltn A Kosutic; (c) obs not known, a/c FTL, unconfirmed; (d) Rittm Karl Lukats; (e) Ltn H Happack.

PATZELT Karl Oberleutnant FLIK 29, 42J, 68J

Born in Crajova, Bohemia, in 1893, he became an orphan while still a youngster and chose a military career before WW1. In 1914 he saw action with the 22nd Schützen Regiment on the Russian Front as a leutnant. Severely wounded in November, he returned the following month and continued in action into the Spring of 1915, receiving the Bronze Military Medal and the

Military Merit Cross, 3rd Class, with War Decoration and Swords. He was also promoted to oberleutnant in March. He then became training officer for the regiment's reserve unit, but returned to active duty in early 1916, to be wounded yet again in June. He now decided enough was enough and transferred to the Air Service and after training was assigned as technical officer to Flik 29 in Romania. He began flying as an observer, and scored two victories. In 1917 he took informal flight instruction from his pilot, meantime winning the Silver Military Merit Medal and the German Iron Cross 1st and 2nd Class. Still an observer, Patzelt then went to Flik 34, while continuing his unofficial flight training. Finally a fully-fledged pilot he went to Flik 42J in November 1917, scored more victories and received the Order of the Iron Crown, 3rd Class, with War Decoration and Swords. He was then given command of Flik 68J in February 1918 but was shot down and killed flying Albatros DIII 153.182 on 4 May, over Vidor, by Lieutenant G A Birks of 66 Squadron RAF.

	1917			Brand CI		
1	5 Feb	Nieuport Sct	(a)	26.44	F29	W Comanestie
2	21 Jun	Nieuport Sct	(a)	69.61	„	nr Cotofanestie
				(fighter)		
3	23 Nov	Sopwith	(b)		F42J	San Dona di Piave
4	29 Nov	SAML	(c)		„	Casa Tagli
5	29 Dec	Seaplane			„	Piave Vecchia

Pilot: (a) Zugs. A Dombrowski; (b) shared with Zugs. Karl Teichmann; (c) shared with Oblt E Strohschneider and Ltn Franz Gräser.

PETER Franz   Oberleutnant   FLIK 3J

Born in Vienna, on 8 October 1896, Peter was with Austro-Hungarian Infantry Division Nr.1 on the Eastern Front when war came, where he saw action for a year but then decided to transfer to the Air Service. He returned to Russia in January 1916 as an observer with Flik 14, carrying out his assigned tasks for almost two years, during which time he was awarded the Silver Bravery Medal for Officers, 2nd Class, two Silver Bravery Medals, 1st Class, and the Military Merit Cross, 3rd Class, with War Decoration and Swords. In 1917 he added the Bronze and Silver Military Merit Medals and the Order of the Iron Crown, 3rd Class, with War Decoration and Swords. He was promoted to oberleutnant in November. Peter was then transferred to Flik 47F on the Italian Front but then requested pilot training in March 1918. Once trained, he was posted to Flik 3J in the Southern Tyrol, near Trento, being deputy commander under Friedrich Navratil. He scored six victories but surprisingly received no further decorations. After the war he joined the Polish Air Force, saw active duty, was wounded, and also took command of No.6 Squadron. In the late 1920s, Peter went into the aircraft engine field, and the 'Peterlot' and 'Petersen' were two of his designs. As WW2 came he was moved to Romania and then to France, but when France fell he was compelled to return to Warsaw, with the choice of working for the Germans in a prison camp or in a factory. Choosing the latter, he saw out the war without making enemies which enabled him to live in Warsaw after the war, where he still lived in the 1960s.

	1918			Alb DIII		
1	16 Jul	Hanriot	(a)		F3J	Val del Concei
2	„	Hanriot	(a)		„	„
3	4 Aug	SVA-5		253.05	„	Etsch Valley
4	20 Aug	Pomilio	(b)	253.04	„	Vignola
5	17 Sep	Pomilio	(c)		„	Monte Pasubio
6	7 Oct	Camel	(d)	253.04	„	nr Trento

(a) shared with Friedrich Navratil; (b) a/c 7702 of 134 Sqn; (c) a/c No.6886; (d) shared with Zugs. Kurt Steidl, E1498 66 Sqn.

PÜRER Josef   Oberleutnant   FLIK 19

Born in Schönau, Austria, on 20 October 1894, Pürer volunteered for war service and fought with the 2nd Regiment of the Austro-Hungarian Field Howitzer Division. His two years of duty were rewarded with the Bronze Military Merit Medal and a commission. In 1916 he requested to join the Air Service and became an observer, then went to Flik 19 on the Isonzo Front. By mid-1917 he had achieved six victories and received the Military Merit Cross, 3rd Class, with War Decoration and Swords. In August he was sent to Flik 29 in Romania but became ill. After a period of recuperation he went to Flik 57F, where he received a second Military Merit Cross, one of only 18 men so honoured in the Air Service. In 1918 he decided to become a pilot which he achieved by July and was sent to Flik 3J, but he was killed in action on 31 August (Alb DIII 153.233) in a fight with Camels of 45 Squadron, downed by Lt Jack Cottle, his tenth of 13 victories.

	1916			Brand CI			
1	18 Nov	Voisin	(a)		F19	San Marco	
2	28 Dec	Voisin	(b)	29.63	„	W San Marco	
	1917						
3	28 Feb	Farman	(c)	68.32	„	enemy lines	
4	17 Apr	Nieuport Sct	(b)	29.64	„	nr Gorizia	
5	3 Jun	Nieuport Sct	(d)		„	Sober	0930
6	19 Jun	Nieuport Sct	(e)	29.63	„	Sober	
–	„	Nieuport Sct		„	„	„	u/c

Pilots: (a) unknown; (b) Hptm A Heyrowsky; (c) Zugs. E Heinz; (d) Zugs. K Reithofer; (e) Zugs. Stefan Fejes: they were then shot-up and forced to land near Schonpass.

RISZTICS Johann   Stabsfeldwebel   FLIK 42J

From Budapest, born in 1895, Risztics joined Hungarian Infantry Regiment Nr.44 in 1914, seeing action on the Russian Front. Wounded on 23 November, he recovered, joining the Air Service as a ground mechanic early in 1915 but then decided to fly, being granted permission to train as a pilot. As Gefreiter Risztics, he was posted to Flik 22 in March 1916 in Russia, and for his work received the Silver Bravery Medal, 2nd Class, and later the Silver Medal, 1st Class, also being promoted to korporal and then Feldwebel. He became a fighter pilot with a transfer to Flik 42J in April 1917 on the Isonzo Front, downing his first opponent in June. He took part in all the heavy fighting until mid-1918 when he was rested, and became an instructor. He had scored seven confirmed victories, all fighters, and had received the Silver Bravery Medal, 1st Class, followed by the Gold. In 1918 he received a second Gold Bravery Medal. Seeing out the war in the training role he became a Hungarian citizen post-war and served with the Red Air Force's 8th Fighter Squadron. He later became chief test pilot for the Junkers company in Germany, also setting up two world flying records in a Junkers G.4 machine.

	1917			KD DI			
1	30 Jun	Nieuport Sct		28.23	F42J	Podgora	1000
2	10 Jul	Nieuport Sct	(a)		„	Monte Sabotino	1745
3	9 Aug	Nieuport Sct	(b)		„	nr Rücken	0830
4	11 Aug	Spad Sct			„	Hermada	1800
5	?	Scout			„		
	1918			Alb DIII			
6	17 Apr	Scout			„	Montello	
7	4 May	Sopwith			„	N Cornuda	

(a) shared with Zugs. Ferdinand Udvardy, a/c shelled on the ground after being forced down; (b) shared with Oblt B Fiala, Flik 12.

RODLAUER Alois   Leutnant   FLIK 60J, 9J

Born on 15 July 1897, in the town of Urfahr, on the outskirts of Linz, Austria, Rodlauer was a science student but joined the army in 1915, being commissioned into the 12th Infantry Regiment. For his services he was rewarded with the Silver Bravery Medal, 1st Class, the Bronze Military Medal and the German War Merit Medal. He transferred into the Air Service early in 1917 although it seems he did not become qualified until December. Assigned to Flik 60J in March 1918 in Northern Italy but was injured in a crash shortly afterwards which put him in hospital until May. He was awarded the Military Merit Cross, 3rd Class, with War Decoration and Swords while with Flik 60J, sharing three victories. In early July he moved to Flik 9J and gained two more kills in October but was shot down towards the end of that month and injured in a forced landing. He was still in hospital when the war ended. He was awarded the Order of the Iron Crown, 3rd Class, with War Decoration and Swords. Rodlauer worked in Linz after the war in the electrical business. In WW2 he rose to major in the Luftwaffe being a liaison officer in Yugoslavia. He died on 26 April 1975. Due to the sparcity of Flik 9F records and the fact that shared victories while he was with Flik 60J were for a time not allowed, it was not until the 1980s that his ace status was recognised.

| | 1918 | | | Phönix DI | |
				Berg DI	
1			(a)		F60J
2			(a)		,,
3			(a)		,,
4	Oct				F9J
5	Oct				,,

(a) shared.

RUDORFER Franz   Oberleutnant   FLIK 19D, 51J

One of the top aces, he is famous for not having taken any formal pilot training. Born in Vienna, on 29 July 1897, he joined-up when war came and, assigned to Austro-Hungarian Infantry Regiment Nr.59, was commissioned in the field in August 1916 and awarded the Silver Bravery Medal, 1st Class, the following month. Volunteering for the Air Service in May 1917, he became an observer and posted to Flik 19D, reported in that July. Credited with one victory, a balloon, and while carrying out his duties as an observer, he began to take flight instruction from his pilots. Without going to flight school, he was posted to Flik 51J to fly fighters, in April 1918, and had downed his second victory before the month was out. In all he scored 11 confirmed plus two unconfirmed victories and received the Military Merit Cross, 3rd Class, with War Decoration and Swords as well as the Order of the Iron Cross, 3rd Class. He was also promoted to oberleutnant just before the war ended, by which time he had taken over command of his squadron. He survived the war by just over a year, dying of unknown causes on 19 November 1919, perhaps in the influenza epidemic that was sweeping Europe.

	1917			Brand CI			
1	15 Nov	Balloon	(a)		F19D	SE Treviso	
	1918			Alb DIII			
2	17 Apr	SAML	(b)	153.141	F51J	Monte Grappa	
3	1 May	Sopwith		,,	,,	nr Cimadolmo	
4	,,	Balloon		,,	,,	San Biagio	
5	6 Jun	Spad Scout		,,	,,	Salettuol	1220
–	,,	Sopwith		,,	,,		1900 u/c
6	21 Jun	Sopwith		,,	,,	Piave River	
7	30 Jul	Scout		,,	,,	Spresiano	
–	11 Sep	2-seater		253.	,,	E Maserada	1930 u/c
8	7 Oct	Camel	(c)	253.122	,,	Ceggia	
9	24 Oct	Balloon		253.124	,,	Breda di Piave	
10	27 Oct	Sopwith		253.	,,	Papadopoli Island	
11	,,	Sopwith	(d)	253.	,,	,,	

(a) Pilot: Zugs. J Schantl; (b) shared with Zugs Eugen Bönsch; (c) D8215, 66 Squadron RAF, shared with Fw E Bönsch; (d) 28 Squadron, one FTL.

SCHMIDT Roman   Oberleutnant   FLIK 7, 13, 30J, 74J

Schmidt was born in Warasadin, Croatia, on 1 November 1893, completing his education at the Technical University, although this was interrupted in 1913 due to his military call-up. Assigned to the 36th Artillery Regiment, he was a fähnrich by the time war came, and he was sent to the

Russian Front, where he stayed until the autumn of 1916, except for one small period of hospitalisation in 1915. He received the Bronze Military Merit Medal and later the Silver Military Merit Medal. He was commissioned in September 1915, then oberleutnant in the regular army in late 1916. He volunteered to fly with Flik 26 as an artillery observer but after a brief return to his regiment, he was posted to Flik 7 full time and in April the following year, he downed his first enemy aircraft, but his pilot was mortally wounded in the action and died some weeks later. For this action, Schmidt received the Military Merit Cross, 3rd Class, with War Decoration and Swords. Assigned to Flik 13 he gained a second victory in September. For this and a third victory he received the Order of the Iron Crown, 3rd Class. In January he moved to Flik 26 but the Russian Front was now inactive so he requested pilot training, which he completed in May 1918 and assigned to Flik 30J as deputy commander. He shot down two more aircraft and in September was given command of Flik 74J, with whom he downed his last victory. Not much is known of his post-war life, but his death was reported on 5 April 1959.

	1917			Brand CI			
1	13 Apr	Nieuport Sct	(a)	67.03	F7	Bohorodzany	am
				Oefflag CII			
2	8 Sep	Nieuport Sct	(b)	52.58	F13	Razbita	
				Lloyd CV			
3	4 Oct	Scout	(c)	46.01	„	Juridica	
	1918			Phönix DI			
4	12 Jul	SAML		128.12	F30J	Monte Tomba	
5	23 Jul	BF2b	(d)	„	„	San Godego	am
				Berg DI			
6	27 Oct	Caproni Ca3	(e)	138.	F74J	Vittorio-Belluno	1230

Pilots: (a) Fw Paul Hablitschek, DoW; (b) Korp W Oppelt; (c) Zugs. A Wiltsch; (d) C4762, 139 Sqn; (e) 6ª Squadriglia.

STOJSAVILJEVIC Raoul   Hauptmann   FLIK 34, 16

Known as the 'Iron Stoj', he was born in the capital of the Austrian Tyrol, Innsbruck, on 28 July 1887, of a Croatian father and Austrian mother. A graduate of the Maria Theresa Military Academy in 1908, he was commissioned into the Feldjäger Bataillon Nr.21, part of his duties being a ski instructor. He transferred to the flying services in 1913, and became a pilot in July having been promoted to oberleutnant. In that October he was a passenger in an aeroplane which made the first Austro-Hungarian flight over the Alps. When war came he was with Flik 1 on the Galician Front and for his recce work received the Bronze Military Merit Medal. Assigned to Flik 13 as deputy commander in November 1914, but he and his observer were forced down behind the Russian lines by a snow storm in February 1915 and although they destroyed their machine were taken prisoner. Six days later they managed to escape, followed by four months on the run, but finally their area of evasion was over-run by Austro-Hungarian forces and they were free. There followed the award of the Military Merit Cross, 3rd Class, with War Decoration, in addition to the German Iron Cross 2nd Class. Assigned to Flik 17 he was promoted to hauptmann in September 1915 and assigned to Flik 16 and later he took command of this unit. Teaming up with Leutnant Josef Friedrich as his observer, they soon began scoring victories. Stojsaviljevic then began to fly as a fighter pilot and after some success was attached to Jasta 6 on the Western Front in May 1917 to gain experience of German Jasta methods and tactics. Returning to southern Austria he continued his scoring run and by November had achieved ten victories. On 12 January 1918, in a two-seater Brandenburg CI (68.07) he was badly wounded with a shattered thigh bone by a bullet from an Italian fighter and forced down. Despite the severity of his wound he recovered sufficiently to command a training school in October. By this time other awards had been made; the Order of the Iron Crown, 3rd Class, with War Decoration, the Knight's Cross of the Order of Léopold with War Decoration and Swords, the Gold Bravery Medal for Officers and the German Iron Cross 1st Class. Taking full Austrian citizenship after the war he joined the Austrian Fliegertruppe, serving in the Flug-Polizei, but retired in 1921. A few years later he was again involved with the Austrian Air Force but his old war wound forced him again into retirement in 1925. He continued flying and was injured in a crash in 1927 but the following year he was with ÖLAG, Austria's largest airline. However, flying alone between Innsbruck and Zürich on 2 September 1930, his Junkers F-13 crashed into a mountain in fog, just outside Partenkirchen, Bavaria, and he was killed.

	1916			Brand CI			
1	4 Jul	Farman	(a)	64.14	F16	Malborghetto	0825
2	25 Jul	Farman	(a)	„		Monte Paularo	
3	7 Aug	Farman	(a)	64.13	„	Val di Raccolana	
4	1 Sep	Farman	(b)		„	Val Bogna	
	1917			KD DI			
5	13 Feb	Farman		65.68	F34	S Kostanjevica	1700
				Brand CI			
6	17 Apr	Farman	(c)	68.11	F16	Villach airfield	
				KD DI			
7	14 Jul	Farman		28.30	„	Mont Cullar	1130
8	23 Jul	Farman			„	Carnia	
9	7 Sep	SAML			„	Monte Skarnitz	
				Alb DIII			
10	21 Nov	SAML		153.66	„	nr Feltre	

Obs: (a) Lt J Friedrich; (b) not known; (c) J Friedrich, a/c forced down on the airfield and captured.

STROHSCHNEIDER Ernst   Oberleutnant   FLIK 23, FL.GI. FLIK 42J

Strohschneider was born in Aussig an der Elbe, (Czechoslovakia) on 6 September 1886, of Sudeten-German parents. A pre-war infantryman he was commissioned in early 1913 and when war came he was with the 28th Infantry Regiment on the Serbian Front. Wounded in the leg on 28 August 1914 he returned to the 42nd Regiment on the Russian Front, but again was wounded, this time in the knee, on 9 February 1915. Once more he returned to duty, still with the 42nd, in command of a machine gun section. He received his third wound on 19 September 1915 and was taken prisoner but he effected an escape and returned to his side of the lines. Now declared unfit for front-line service, he joined the Air Service, completed observer training in March 1916, and was sent to Flik 23 on the Southern Tyrolean Front. His first victory was not confirmed due to lack of witnesses. He then went to Flik 28 on the Isonzo Front but then decided to train as a pilot. Qualifying in December 1916, Strohschneider was posted to Flugegeschwader I, which later became Flik 101G, again on the Isonzo Front, and flying escort to the unit's two-seaters scored his first victories. He received the Silver Military Merit Medal with Swords and a second Military Merit Medal, 3rd Class. Made deputy commander of Flik 42J in August 1917 he brought his score to 15, winning the Order of the Iron Crown, 3rd Class, with War Decoration and Swords, and was also given command of Flik 61J and as Flik 63J was without a CO (Hptm Nikitsch injured) he led this unit too. Strohschneider was killed in a night landing crash on the night of 20/21 March 1918 following a raid on Italian positions near Zenson, in Phönix DI 228.36. He received a posthumous Knight's Cross of the Order of Léopold with War Decoration and Swords.

	1916			Lloyd CIII			
–	15 Jun	Seaplane	(a)	43.61	F23	Sarca Valley	0730
	1917			Not known			
1	3 Jun	Farman			FlGI	Monte Korada	1030
2	21 Jun	Farman			„	Cormons	
3	23 Sep	Spad Scout	(b)		F42J	nr Kostanjevica	
4	„	Savoia-Pomilio	(b)		„	Kostanjevica	
5	26 Sep	Spad Scout	(c)		„	Ronchi	
				Alb DIII			
6	3 Oct	Spad 2			„	Gradisca	
7	25 Oct	Seaplane	(d)		„	Grado	
8	26 Oct	Seaplane			„	Grado	
9	27 Oct	Seaplane	(d)		„		
10	15 Nov	Sopwith	(d)		„	Meolo	
11	29 Nov	SAML	(e)		„	Casa Tagli	

	1918						
12	26 Jan	Seaplane	(d)		F61J	'swamp area'	1810
13	30 Jan	Sopwith 2	(d)	153.111	„	Cana Reggio	
14	24 Feb	Macchi M-5	(f)	153.119	„	Marcello	
15	16 Mar	Ansaldo SVA	(d)	„	„	Casonetti	

(a) Pilot: Oblt F Schorn; (b) shared with Zugs F Udvardy; (c) shared with Udvardy, Fw V Magerl and Korp K Teichmann; (d) shared with Ltn Franz Gräser; (e) shared with Gräser and Oblt K Patzelt; (f) shared with Gräser, Ltns O Schrimpl and E Mörath.

SZEPESSY-SOKOLL Fr von NEGYES ET REMO Rudolf   Oberleutnant

FLIK 17, 3, 41J

Born in Hungary in 1891, Szepessy-Sokoll served with the Austro-Hungarian Hussar Regiment Nr.1 when war was declared, seeing action on the Russian Front. He was awarded the Silver Bravery Medal, 1st Class, in December 1914 and commissioned the following month. In March came the award of the Bronze Military Merit Medal. He volunteered for the Air Service in the summer of 1915, became an observer and assigned to Flik 17. For his work with this unit he won the Silver Military Merit Medal in June 1916. Requesting pilot training, he achieved his flying badge in March 1917 and was posted to Flik 10 on the Russian Front, then transferred to Flik 27 in August, detached to Flik 3 in September where he flew single-seaters. After gaining two victories he was sent to Flik 41J, east of Trieste, commanded by Brumowski. Here he brought his score to five before falling in combat on 6 November 1917. Wounded in the back from fire from the Italian ace, Giorgio Pessi, he crash-landed his Albatros DIII in his own lines near Latisana, at 1030 but died as he was taken from his cockpit. He received a posthumous Knight's Cross of the Order of Léopold with War Decoration and Swords.

	1916			Lohner BVII			
1	14 Feb	Caudron	(a)	17.36	F17	Milano	0900
	1917			Alb DIII			
2	20 Sep	Nieuport 2		53.11	F3	S Boratin	am
3	4 Oct	Balloon		53.45	„	Iwanczony	0815
4	5 Nov	Macchi L-3	(b)		F41J	W Latisana	
5	„	Macchi L-3	(b)		„	W Latisana	

Pilots: (a) Zugs. P Postl and shared with three other crews; (b) shared with Hptm G Brumowski and Oblt F Linke-Crawford. NB. Present research favours Pessi and not Baracca for Sokoll's loss.

TAHY Alexander   Oberleutnant   FLIK 19, 51J

A Hungarian, born in 1896 in the town of Nyregyhaza, he volunteered when war came and joined the Hungarian Heavy Howitzer Division Nr.6, with the rank of fahnrich, which later became the Heavy Field Artillery Regiment Nr.15. He was awarded the Silver Bravery Medal, 1st Class, in May 1915 and in early 1916 he decided to transfer to the Air Service. As an observer he went to Flik 12, but due to a disagreement with his CO went almost at once to Flik 19, often flying with Stefen Fejes. With a total of five victories, Tahy received the Silver and Bronze Military Merit Medals, and the Military Merit Cross, 3rd Class, with War Decoration and Swords. Training unofficially as a pilot, Tahy moved to Flik 51J and downed two more Italian aircraft, but his technique did not find favour with his CO, and he was sent away for formal flight training. Upon his return to Flik 51J in January 1918, he was promoted to oberleutnant, and gained one more victory. He was then killed in a flying accident, due probably to structural failure, in Albatros DIII 153.69, on 7 March, coming down over Mansu. He was awarded a posthumous Knight's Cross of the Order of Léopold, with War Decoration and Swords.

	1916			2-seater			
1	3 Dec	Caproni	(a)		F19	nr Gorizia	
	1917			Brand CI			
2	11 May	Nieuport Sct	(b)	27.77	„	Sober-Vertojba	
3	14 May	Nieuport Sct	(c)		„	nr Gorizia	0730
4	3 Jun	Nieuport Sct	(d)		„	nr Sober	0930

5	26 Jun	Caudron	(e)		„	Sober	0930
				Alb DIII			
6	28 Sep	Balloon	(f)		F51J	N Plava	
7	29 Sep	Nieuport Sct	(g)		„	S Plava	
	1918						
8	21 Feb	Sopwith	(f)	153.127	„	Casa Zonta	

Pilots: (a) Fw H Mahner and shared with Hptm A Heyrowsky and Fhnr S Wagner; (b) Korp E Heinz and shared with Zugs. K Reithofer and Zugs. J Schmidt; (c) Zugs Stefan Fejes; (d) Korp J Szeikovics and shared with Hptm Heyrowsky and Zugs. K Reithofer; (e) shared with Hptm Heyrowsky and Oblt L Hauser; (f) shared with Korp Eugen Bönsch; (g) shared with Bönsch and Oblt G Kenzian, Flik 53J.

TEICHMANN Karl   Feldwebel   FLIK 42J, 60J, 14J

Born of Sudeten-German parents in 1897, in the town of Rabersdorf, Schlesien, Teichmann pre-war had been a motor mechanic but joined up in 1915 and assigned to the Austro-Hungarian Infantry Regiment Nr.1, but due to his background was sent as a mechanic to Flik 5 on the Russian Front in February 1916. By the late summer he had applied for pilot training and was awarded his pilot's badge in May 1917. Posted to Flik 42J and after securing his first (shared) victory, received the Silver Bravery Medal, 2nd Class. Fighting over the Battle of Caporetto he gained his second and third victories, and then came the award of the Silver Bravery Medal 1st Class. Teichmann was then posted to the new Flik 60J under Linke-Crawford. Although he only scored one victory with this unit, his work was recognised by the Gold Medal for Bravery. In August he was assigned to Flik 14J at Feltre and gained his fifth victory. Although he survived the war he died in Graz, Austria, in 1927, from natural causes.

	1917			Scout			
1	26 Sep	Spad Scout	(a)		F42J	Ronchi	
2	27 Oct	Nieuport Sct			„	Lake Doberdò	
3	23 Nov	Sopwith	(b)		„	San Dona di Piave	
	1918			Phönix DII			
4	3 Feb	Nieuport Sct		228.25	F60J	Monte Nuoval	
5	22 Aug	BF2b	(c)	422.30	F14J	Monte Asolone	

(a) shared with Oblt E Strohschneider and Zugs F Udvardy; (b) shared with Oblt K Patzelt; (c) D8075 139 Sqn.

UDVARDY Ferdinand   Stabsfeldwebel   FLIK 42J

Born in 1895, in the city of Pozsony, later Bratislava, of Hungarian parents, Udvardy joined up in 1915. Assigned to the 72nd Infantry Regiment he then volunteered for the Air Service and completed flight training in September 1916 with the rank of korporal. Sent to Flik 10 he very quickly requested a fighter pilot assignment. After more training he was posted to Flik 42J in May 1917, where he stayed till the Armistice. He scored eight victories and received the Gold Bravery Medal twice and the Silver Bravery Medal, 1st Class, three times. After the war he became a Hungarian citizen and served in the 8th Squadron of the Red Air Force, scoring a ninth victory in 1919 against the Romanians. It is believed he died some time after the Second World War.

	1917			KD DI			
1	10 Jul	Spad Scout		28.42	F42J	Monte Sabotino	1745
2	„	Nieuport Sct	(a)	„	„	„	1750
3	23 Sep	Spad Scout	(b)	„	„	Nova Vas	
4	„	Savoia-Pomilio	(b)	„	„	nr Kostanjevica	
5	26 Sep	Spad Scout	(c)	„	„	nr Ronchi	
6	26 Oct	Seaplane	(b)	„	„	Grado	
	1918			Alb DIII			
7	20 May	Hanriot HDI			„	Montello	
8	20 Jun	Hanriot HDI		153.165	„	Nervesa	
	1919						
9	12 Jun	UC.I	(d)				

(a) shared with Fw J Risztics; (b) shared with Oblt E Strohschneider; (c) shared with Strohschneider and Korp K Teichmann; (d) Obs: Keisz, an a/c of Flik 42.

URBAN Karl   Offizierstellvertreter   FLIK 10, 14J

Urban was born in Graz, Austria, on 29 December 1894 and served with the army when the war started. Volunteered for the Air Service and was sent to Flik 10 on the Russian Front, flying recce and bombing sorties. He was awarded the Silver Bravery Medal 1st Class in March 1916, followed in June by another, then a third Silver Medal in July. He and his observers claimed at least four enemy aircraft although he was wounded by AA fire on 28 August 1916. He then received the Gold Bravery Medal and was sent to Flik 27, and later in 1917 to Flik 66D, in the Tyrol. Finally he became a fighter pilot with Flik 14J at Feltre, gaining his fifth victory on his first fighter sortie. In July 1918 he was rested and given the job as a test pilot but on the 12th of that month the wings of a Phönix fighter — 20.22 — collapsed and he crashed to his death. He was posthumously promoted to his final rank.

	1916			Alb BI			
1	5 May	Sikorsky?	(a)	22.10	F10	nr Koryto	0900
2	7 Jun	Farman	(b)	„	„	Ostrosez	0730
3	„	Farman	(b)	„	„	Olyka	0735
4	2 Aug	Farman	(a)	64.15	„	E Szelwow	0700
	1918			Phönix DI			
5	19 May	Hanriot HDI		228.19	F14J	Cismon	

Pilots: (a) Ltn Otto Jäger; (b) Jäger and shared with Zugs. Fritz Rottmann and Oblt P Graf Grunne.

WEBER Rudolf   Oberleutnant   FLIK 25, 2

Of Saxon stock, born in Segesvar, Transylvania (Romania) in 1890, Weber joined the army in 1911, serving with the 31st Austro-Hungarian Regiment on the Russian Front when war came. Already a commissioned officer, he received the Bronze Military Merit Medal and was then promoted to oberleutnant in the field. Decided to fly at the end of 1915 and became an observer with Flik 25. With this unit he and his pilot scored a victory in June but he was wounded in the face by an AA shell fragment which caused him pain and disfigurement. So upset by this he never allowed his picture to be taken and as far as is known, none of him exists. Awards of the Military Merit Cross, 3rd Class with War Decoration and the German Iron Cross 2nd Class were little compensation. He now became a pilot and was assigned as deputy commander to Flik 2 on the Isonzo Front, flying both two and single-seat aircraft. In a few short weeks between August and October 1917 he gained five victories and was awarded the Order of the Iron Crown, 3rd Class, with War Decoration and Swords. Leaving Flik 2 in January 1918, he was later given command of Flik 102G in northern Italy, mainly operating as night bombers. He saw out the war with this unit, but in taking his machines to Yugoslavia they were confiscated and he and some of his men began the trek home. At a checkpoint he was mistakenly shot by a militiaman, and died from his wound.

	1916			Brand CI			
1	12 Jun	Voisin	(a)	26.21	F25	Zbaraz	1930
	1917			C-type			
2	11 Aug	Nieuport Sct	(b)		F2		1100
3	„	Nieuport Sct	(c)		„		
4	12 Aug	2-seater	(d)		„	nr Kambresko	1000
5	14 Sep	EA	(e)		„		
				Scout			
6	26 Oct	Spad			„	Podlesce	

(a) Pilot: Zugs V Magerl; Obs: (b) Ltn F Schutz; (c) Oblt B Kainz; (d) Ltn A Kratochwill; (e) Ltn E Goth.

WOGNAR Franz   Offizierstellvertreter   FLIK 2

Born 6 January 1890, in Nagyszombat, Hungary, Wognar's family was Slovakian and pre-war he was a mechanic. In 1913 he enlisted in the army and later volunteered to join the Air Service. With Flik 2 on the Isonzo Front and in late 1915 received the Silver Bravery Medal, 2nd Class, and a few months later, the Silver Medal 1st Class. In gaining his second victory he was wounded in the back but was soon back in action and quickly raised his score to five. In March 1917 came a second Silver Medal, 1st Class, and in May came the Gold Bravery Medal. At the end of the year Wognar was assigned as a test pilot but apart from knowing he received a third Silver Medal, 1st Class, little else is known of his life.

	1917			Brand CI			
1	26 Jan	Nieuport Sct	(a)	29.75	F2	St Florian	am
2	1 May	Nieuport Sct	(b)	27.64	„	Monte Sabotino	0825
3	20 May	Spad Scout	(c)	229.20	„	„	0920
4	4 Sep	EA	(d)	329.07	„		
5	16 Sep	Balloon	(e)	39.69	„	Liga	eve

Obs: (a) Kad J Mastijevic; (b) Ltn S Frimmel; (c) Ltn F Gräser; (d) not known; (e) Ltn O Patz.

PART FIVE

ABOVE THE STEPPES

I   The Russian Aces

d'ARGUEFF Paul Vladimirovich   Capitaine   N48, 12TH, 19TH, SPA124

Born Pavel Argeyev, in Yalta (Crimea) on 1 March 1887, the son of an army officer, he gallicized his name to Paul d'Argueff in 1915. He joined the army and completed his training at the Odessa Military Academy in 1907, commissioned in 1910, and served with the 184th and 29th Infantry Regiments. He was on detached service in France when the war started and was assigned to the French army with the 331st Infantry Regiment, but wounded on 23 September. Returned to the 5th Company of the 131st Regiment in October and took command of this company the following month with the rank of capitaine. He received the Croix de Guerre and was made a Chévalier de la Légion d'Honneur, having been slightly wounded again in April 1915, and once more on 2 May. The latter was more serious and made him unfit for further front-line duty. He therefore joined the Aviation Service and was awarded his brevet (No.2573) on 30 January 1916 and assigned to N48 on 1 June. Two months later he transferred to the Russian Front and reinstated into the Russian Army. He flew with the 12th Fighter Detachment and then the 19th, under Aleksandr Kozakov. He gained his first victory in January 1917, although wounded in the action, and was awarded the Order of St Vladimir, 4th Class with Swords and Bow. The 19th was then moved to Jassy, Romania and later to Stanislav. In April he received the Golden Sword of St George after his second victory. Often flying with Kozakov, several more victories came his way and in November he was awarded the Order of St George, 4th Class. After the Revolution, d'Argueff returned to France and assigned to Spa124 in May 1918. He brought his score to 15 in October. After the war he flew with the Compagnie Franco-Romaine airline but was killed in a bad weather crash in mountainous country near Trutnow, on the German-Czech border, on 30 October 1922.

	1917						
1	10 Jan	Albatros C		Nieuport	19th		
–	8 Apr	Fokker		„	„	Mitau	am
2	21 Apr	2-seater		„	„		pm
3	6 May	Brandenburg CI	(a)	„	„	Brezezany	0945
4	17 May	LVG C	(b)	„	„	Jakobstadt	
5	8 Jun	Brandenburg CI	(b)	„	„	Nr Kozova	
6	20 Jun	Rumpler C	(b)	„	„	Nr Nejnokov	
	1918						
7	1 Jun	LVG C		Spad XIII	Spa124	Puisieux-Beaumont	
8	13 Jun	Rumpler C		„	„		
9	14 Jun	2-seater		„	„		
10	26 Jun	2-seater		„	„		
11	27 Sep	Fokker DVII		„	„	N Cerny	
12	28 Sep	2-seater		„	„	Sechault	1010
13	„	2-seater		„	„	Sechault Laval	1520
–	5 Oct	2-seater		„	„	NE Autry	1125
14	„	Pfalz D		„	„	Orfeuil	1815
15	30 Oct	2-seater		„	„	E Quatre Champs	1540

(a) shared with Capt A A Kozakov, 2/Lt Zhabrov and Ens E K Leman; (b) shared with Capt A A Kozakov,

FEDEROFF Viktor Georgievitch   Lieutenant   c42, N26, SPA89

Only flew with the French: see *Over the Front*, pages 158-9 for biography and victory list.

GILSHER Juri Vladimirovich   2nd Lieutenant   7TH

Gilsher came from a family of the Russian nobility, born in Moscow on 27 November 1894. He trained to be a civil engineer rather than a soldier and although he graduated in 1914, the war soon ended his dreams in this direction. As a cavalry cadet he decided to transfer into aviation in 1915, becoming a pilot in September. Assigned to the 4th Army Aviation Air Company, his immediate operational career was cut short following a hand injury, struck by a propeller blade. Gilsher returned to the front in March 1916, with the 3rd Army Air Company and flew recce sorties, but after a combat on 9 May he crashed. His observer was killed and he suffered serious injuries, losing his lower left leg. He refused to be discharged, returned to duty in November, was given temporary command of the 7th Fighter Detachment, and within days was back over the Front. He began scoring in 1917 and later took full command of the 7th following the death of his CO in July. However, on 20 July, in a fight with 15 enemy aircraft in company with just one other Russian, his aircraft was seen to break up and Gilsher fell to his death. It was in this battle that he secured his fifth victory. A machine of FA41 claimed a Russian Nieuport on the Romanian Front on this date. Gilsher had been earlier awarded the Order of St George, 4th Class, the Golden Sword of St George and the Order of St Vladimir, 4th Class.

	1917					
1	13 Apr	Brandenburg CI	(a)	Nieup XXI	7th	Nr Posetch, Galicia
2	„	Brandenburg CI	(a)	„	„	Nr Stanislau
3	15 May	Oeffag CIII	(b)	„	„	Boshovze
4	17 Jul	EA	(c)	„	„	SW Posuchov
5	20 Jul	EA	(d)	„	„	Tarnopol

(a) a/c from Flik 7, shared with Lt D Makeenok and Ens V Yanchenko; (b) a/c of Flik 11; (c) crash-landed and destroyed by artillery fire; (d) shared with Ens V Yanchenko.

KOKORIN Nikolai Kirillovich   Ensign   4TH

Born in Khlebnikovo on 21 May 1889 to a working-class family. He volunteered for the army in late 1910 and the following year he requested a chance to learn to fly and was accepted, only to be almost immediately rejected and assigned to the training school's motor section. Nevertheless he continued to apply for training and was finally accepted in early 1914. He became a pilot in August with the rank of sergeant-major and was posted to the 4th Corps Air Detachment, flying Moranes and Henry Farmans. For his aggressive actions he received the Cross of St George, 1st Class, in April 1916, and in August went to the Army's 1st Combat Air Group under Kozakov, flying defensive sorties for the cities north of Tarnopol. At first he flew Spad two-seaters but then Nieuport Scouts. After his first victory he received the Golden Sword of St George, followed by the Order of St George, 4th Class, after his next victory, followed later by the Order of St Anne, 4th Class. His unit then served in Romania, where he scored victory number three. With two more kills secured, he fell in combat on 28 May 1917 in a fight with five hostile aircraft. Ltns Crybski and Quest of FA242 claimed a Nieuport near where Kokorin crashed.

	1916					
1	25 Nov	EA		Nieup X	4th	Rozitze
	1917					
2	2 Jan	2-seater		Morane H	„	Nr Luzk
3	14 Apr	Albatros CIII	(a)	Nieuport	„	Uvse
4	25 May	Brandenburg CI	(b)	Nieup XXI	„	Shabalin
5	26 May	Brandenburg CI	(c)	„	„	NW Kosovo

(a) shared with Fw Zemblevich; (b) a/c from Flik 11; (c) a/c from Flik 9 and shared with Fw Zemblevich.

KOZAKOV Aleksandr Aleksandrovich   Major   4TH, 19TH

The Russian ace of aces, Kozakov (also spelt Kazakov) was born on 15 January 1889, in the Kherson province of Russia, and his family sent him to military schools at an early age. In 1908 he graduated as a cavalry Cornet and appointed to the 12th Belgorod Uhlan Cavalry Regt.

He transferred to aviation in 1913 and by late 1914 was with the 4th Corps Air Detachment in Poland, flying recce and bombing sorties with Morane-Saulnier machines. His first victory, scored on 31 March 1915, was due to ramming the enemy; he had been experimenting with an explosive device attached to a line which he dangled below his machine. His first awards followed soon afterwards: the Order of St Anne, 4th Class, and then the 3rd Class. In September 1915, Kozakov was posted to the 19th Corps Detachment, taking command with the rank of staff cavalry captain. They flew Moranes and later Nieuports. Flying and fighting continued for the next year, although victories were few, but in August 1916 Kozakov was placed in command of the 1st Combat Air Group, comprising the 2nd, 4th and 19th Corps Air Detachments, operating on the Lutsk area. The Group moved to Romania in February 1917. His personal victories slowly grew although he was wounded on 27 June. However, he continued to score, and his total reached 20 by October. Given the rank of colonel by the Soldiers' Revolutionary Committee in December, and holding temporary command of the 7th Air Division, his fighting war was over, and he resigned his commission in January 1918. He joined the British Joint Military forces at Murmansk in June 1918, and was given the rank of major, commanding the Slavo-British flying detachment at Benezniky. He flew numerous sorties but was badly wounded in January 1919, being in hospital till March, but he received the British DFC. When he returned to his unit, the Bolshevik forces were making progress and in July the British began to evacuate. He was offered a job in England but he could not leave his native country in the hands of the communists. On the evening of 1 August 1919 he took off in a Sopwith Snipe and appeared to stall deliberately into the ground, being killed instantly. His score has been given variously as between 17 and 20 with several more probables.

	1915						
1	31 Mar	Albatros C		Morane	4th	Nr Guzov-Volja	
	1916						
2	27 Jun	Albatros C		Nieup X	19th	Lake Drisvjaty	1600
3	29 Jul	Albatros CIII		,,	,,	Dvinsk	1500
4	6 Sep	2-seater		Nieup XI	,,	Kovel	
5	21 Dec	Brandenburg CI	(a)	,,	,,	Lutsk	1500
	1917						
6	6 May	Brandenburg CI	(b)	,,	,,	Brezazany	0945
7	10 May	Fokker	(c)	,,	,,	Sarniki	
8	17 May	LVG C	(d)	,,	,,	Podgaitsy	
9	25 May	EA		Nieup XVII	,,	W Konjukhi	
10	8 Jun	Brandenburg CI	(e)	,,	,,	W Kozov	0800
11	20 Jun	Rumpler C	(f)	,,	,,	Podgaitsy (FTL)	0900
12	27 Jun	EA		,,	,,	Lipazodoluo	1700
13	,,	Rumpler C	(g)	,,	,,	Stavetyn	2100
14	27 Jul	Brandenburg CI		,,	,,	Obertyn	
15	2 Aug	Brandenburg CI	(h)	,,	,,	Dolinyany	
16	8 Aug	EA	(i)	,,	,,	Ivane-Pusto	
17	29 Aug	Albatros CIII	(j)	,,	,,	Lapkovtsy	1100
18	11 Sep	Brandenburg CI	(k)	,,	,,	Nr Gusyatin	1600
19	23 Sep	Brandenburg CI	(l)	,,	,,	S Gusyatin	
20	26 Oct	EA	(m)	,,	,,	Scalat	

(a) a/c from Flik 10; (b) shared with Capt P V d'Argueff, 2/Lt Zhabrov and Ens E K Leman, a/c of Flik 1; (c) shared with Ens E K Leman and Capt Polyakov; (d) a/c from FAA242, shared with d'Argueff; (e) shared with d'Argueff, a/c from Flik 25; (f) a/c from FA24, shared with d'Argueff; (g) a/c from FA29, shared with Leman; (h) a/c from Flik 20 and Flik 26 respectively, shared with Capt Shangin; (i) shared with Shangin; (j) a/c FA24; (k) a/c Flik 18; (l) a/c Flik 36, shared with Lt Shrinkin from the 7th Det; (m) shared with Lt I V Smirnov.

KRUTEN Yevgraph Nikolaevich   Captain   2ND, N3, 2ND

Born in Kiev, on 29 December 1890, Kruten was the son of a Russian army colonel, while his maternal grandfather was also a colonel. In 1901 he went into the Kiev Military Cadet Corps, going into the mounted artillery division in 1908 as an ensign, but was commissioned in 1911. He became an air observer in 1913, and served with Captain Petr Nesterov, who recommended

Kruten for flight training. He graduated in September 1914 and went to the 21st Corps Detachment flying Voisins, to fly recce and bombing missions. He received the Order of St Anne, 4th Class, in 1915 following his first victory on 6 March. He was now flying with the 2nd Army Air Detachment and for further brave sorties, was given the Order of St Vladimir, 4th Class with Swords and Bow. With the arrival of some Nieuport Scouts, he undertook to produce booklets on useful hints for aerial fighting, and by May 1916 was commanding the 2nd Air Combat Group which went to the Front in July. In November, Kruten went to France to study tactics, attached to Escadrille N3, with whom he shot down one German aircraft and received the Croix de Guerre. He returned to Russia in March 1917 and took command of the 2nd Air Combat Group on the Tarnopol sector. After bringing his score to seven, his machine suddenly went into a spin whilst returning from a flight on 19 June and he crashed by his airfield. He died soon after being taken from the wrecked machine, Nieuport Scout No.2252. He was given the posthumous rank of Lt Col (Podpolkovnik) and the Order of St George, 3rd Class. Score varies between six and eleven.

	1915						
1	6 Mar	EA		Voisin LA	2nd		Ravka
	1916						
2	11 Aug	Albatros CIII		Nieup XI	„		Svoyatichi
3	14 Aug	Rumpler C		„	„		Nesvich
	1917						
4	Feb	EA		Spad VII	N3		France
5	31 May	Brandenburg CI		Nieup XVII	2nd		NE Brezezany
6	5 Jun	2-seater		„	„		Tarnopol
7	6 Jun	Brandenburg CI	(a)	„	„		Tarnopol

(a) aircraft of Flik 18.

LEMAN Ernst Krislanovich   Ensign   19TH

Leman was born in Lithuania in 1894, of a middle class family. When war came he enlisted as a private in November 1914, was sent to the aviation school at Odessa and by the spring of 1915 he had progressed to flight cadet. He eventually became a pilot in June 1916 with the rank of warrant officer and the following month Leman was posted to the 19th Corps Fighter Detachment, which became part of the 1st Combat Air Group in August. He engaged in several combats and was given the Cross of St George, 4th Class, in January 1917, shortly before the unit moved to Romania, and in April he became an ensign. He scored his first success in May and then his second and third, for which he received the Order of St Anne, 4th Class. Following his fourth (shared) victory he was awarded the Order of St Stanislav, 3rd Class, with Swords and Bow. He was wounded on 26 September while downing his fifth victim. Whilst in hospital he married, and then received the Order of St George, 4th Class, in November. While still weak from his wound, he returned to the Front but with the coming revolution, seriously wounded himself attempting to commit suicide on 17 December, and died a few days later.

	1917						
1	6 May	Brandenburg CI	(a)	Nieuport	19th		Shebalin
2	10 May	Fokker	(b)	„	„		Sarniki
3	27 Jun	2-seater	(c)	„	„		Tsmenitzi
4	17 Aug	EA		„	„		
5	26 Sep	2-seater	(d)	„	„		Nr Gusiatina

(a) a/c of Flik 1, shared with Capt A A Kozakov, Capt P V d'Argueff and 2/Lt Zhabrov; (b) shared with Kozakov and Capt Polyakov; (c) shared with Kozakov; (d) shared with Ens Krisanov, who was killed.

LOIKO Ivan Aleksandrovich   Lieutenant   9TH

Born in the city of Minsk on 6 February 1892 and entered military service in 1909. He graduated as a warrant officer from the Alekseyevsky Military School in 1912 and was sent to the 59th Infantry Reserve Battn. being promoted to ensign the following summer. He was commissioned in October 1914, saw action at the Front, then decided to fly. On his being made a pilot he was assigned to the 30th Corps Detachment for recce work flying Henri Farman and Voisin aircraft, in May 1915. A year later he was commander of the 30th but then assigned to the 9th Fighter Detachment on the Romanian Front, gaining his first victory in October. With four victories by September 1917, Loiko received the Order of St Vladimir, 4th Class, with Sword and Bow. This was followed by the Order of St George, 4th Class, with his fifth victory. In all he scored six victories, with several more unconfirmed, but it is not known what happened to him after late 1917 and the revolution. His other awards included the Order of St Anne, 4th Class, 3rd Class and 2nd Class, the Order of St Stanislav, 2nd Class and the Romanian Order of the Star.

	1916					
1	26 Oct	EA		Nieup XI	9th	Mamalyga Stn
2	27 Dec	Brandenburg CI	(a)	„	„	Oneshty
	1917					
–	18 Jul	2-seater		Nieup XVII	„	Vermeshty
3	4 Sep	2-seater	(b)	„	„	Nr Radautz
4	6 Sep	2-seater	(c)	„	„	Teodoreshty
–	7 Sep	2-seater		„	„	Radautz
–	8 Sep	2-seater	(b)	„	„	Gorodniki
5	12 Sep	Brandenburg CI	(b)	„	„	Radautz
6	3 Oct	EA	(d)	Nieup XXIII	„	Yaslovets

(a) Flik 13 a/c; (b) shared with Ens G Suk; (c) shared with 2/Lt Karklin; (d) shared with WO Sapozhnikov.

MAKEENOK Donat Aduiovich   Lieutenant   7TH

Donat Makeenok was born on 19 May 1890, in the small village of Dambovka situated near the Polish-Russian frontier. He enlisted into the Russian Army towards the end of 1911 and went to the 97th Livland Infantry Regt. Within a few weeks he had the chance to volunteer for pilot training. A year later he was accepted and by June 1912 he was starting his tuition. He graduated with the rank of sergeant-major in April 1914 and in early 1915 was flying combat sorties with the 3rd Corps Detachment using Morane Parasol machines. Decorations quickly followed: the Cross of St George, 4th Class, the Cross of St George, 3rd and 2nd Classes, plus promotion to warrant officer. Requesting fighter action, Makeenok was assigned to the 7th Detachment with the rank of second lieutenant at the end of 1916. Often flying in company with Vasili Yanchenko and Juri Gilsher, Makeenok made his first kill in March 1917 and by the end of April had four victories plus another which was unconfirmed. He had to wait until June to make acedom. The following month Gilsher was killed and on 5 August Makeenok himself was wounded, returning to the Front in November. However, hostilities had now ended but in 1919, having returned to German-occupied Poland, he was given the task of finding factories to produce aircraft. By the next year he had been given command of the 3rd Polish Squadron and he saw action in the Russo-Polish war, continuing to command his unit into 1921 but little is known of his life or career after that date. Although he fought with the Russians in WWI and gained eight victories, he is the only Polish-born ace from WWI flying against the Central Powers*. In addition to the above decorations, he also received the Order of St Vladimir, 4th Class, the Order of St Anne, 3rd and 4th Class as well as the Order of St Stanislas, 2nd Class with Swords.

	1917						
1	7 Mar	EA	(a)	Nieup XXI	7th	Nr Svistelniki	
2	13 Apr	Brandenburg CI	(b)	„	„	Bogorodchany	0900
3	„	Brandenburg CI	(b)	„	„	„	0900
4	16 Apr	EA		„	„	Yamritsa Kozeyarki	
–	27 Apr	EA		„	„	Kosjarko	
5	29 Jun	EA		„	„	Potootory Stn	
6	6 Jul	EA	(a)	Nieup XVII	„	Nr Brzezhany	
7	11 Jul	EA	(a)	„	„	Brzezhany	
8	5 Aug	2-seater	(a)	„	„	„	

(a) shared with Lt V I Yanchenko; (b) shared with Yanchenko and Cornet J Gilsher — a/c of Flik 7.

* M S Garsztka was a Polish-born ace who served with the Germans in France and gained six victories with Jasta 31 on the Western Front.

ORLOV Ivan Aleksandrovich   Lieutenant   7TH, N3

Of noble birth, Ivan Orlov was born in St Petersburg on 19 January 1895. He developed a desire to fly at a young age and even built himself gliders in his youth, followed by a powered monoplane in 1913, which he named 'Orlov No.1'. He joined the Russian Aero Club and held licence No.229, dated 13 June 1914. He also studied law and went to the local university, but when war came he joined the Russian Air Service and was assigned to the 5th Corps Air Detachment, as a private, despite his experience and social position. However, he soon gained promotion and decorations as a fearless pilot, flying Voisins on recce sorties. Finally he was commissioned in December 1915 and in the New Year became a fighter pilot. Not long after this he went to the 7th Fighter Detachment in Galicia, gaining his first victory in June 1916. With three victories, Orlov was sent to France to become acquainted with French tactics, being assigned to N3 of Cigognes, flying in company with both Georges Guynemer and Alfred Heurtaux. With this unit he downed his fourth victory in January 1917. Returning to Russia in March, he scored his fifth victory in May. During a combat with four enemy scouts on 4 July, the lower starboard wing of his Nieuport Scout tore away and Orlov crashed to his death. His decorations included the Order of St George, 4th Class; the Golden Sword of St George; Order of St Vladimir, 4th Class; Order of St Anne 3rd and 4th Class; Order of St Stanislas, 3rd Class, with Swords and Bow and the French Croix de Guerre avec Palme.

	1916					
1	8 Jun	Lloyd CII	(a)	Nieup XI	7th	Petlikovze
2	25 Jun	Aviatik BIII	(b)	„	„	Podgaitsy
3	4 Oct	2-seater	(c)	„	„	Zlota-Lipca
	1917					
4	24 Jan	EA		Spad VII	N3	France
5	21 May	Albatros C	(d)	Nieup XVII	7th	Nr Prysup

(a) a/c from Flik 9; (b) shared with Lt V I Yanchenko — a/c from Flik 27; (c) shared with Yanchenko; (d) a/c of FAA242.

PISHVANOV Aleksandr Mikhailovich   Ensign   10TH

From the Crimean region, Pishanov was born on 21 October 1893, in Novocherkassk, one of a dozen children of a farming family. He decided to attend engineering school where he became interested in aviation, so much so that he was taken up in an aeroplane in 1912, and by October of that year had become a pilot. When war came he joined as a private in the army and was decorated with the Cross of St George before taking formal pilot training in 1915. Attached to the 27th Corps Detachment in May 1916, he later took fighter instruction and may well have returned to the 27th had not his skill been noted. Instead he was posted to the 10th Fighter Detachment in August, operating on the Romanian Front. Enemy aircraft were not plentiful and it was not until March 1917 that he downed his first opponent, gaining a second kill on the 28th. He was promoted to ensign and awarded the Order of St Anne, 4th Class. During a desperate battle on 26 June he out-fought several opponents, at one period with a jammed gun, but scored his third kill and received the Order of St Stanislas, 3rd Class. With two more victories, the Order of St George, 4th Class and the Order of St Vladimir, 4th Class with Swords and Bow, he was then wounded on 11 July, losing some fingers from his right hand in a fight with an enemy aircraft. This effectively ended his war flying but later he served with the White Russian forces under General Denikin. Some time after the end of that episode, he flew with the RAF but then emigrated to America in 1926, working for the Sikorski company as an engineer, and later, having become an American citizen, worked for the Seversky Aircraft Corporation. Pishvanov died in 1966 and his son is now a retired American military officer.

	1917					
1	21 Mar	2-seater		Nieup XXI	10th	Nr Galatz
2	28 Mar	2-seater		„	„	S Galatz

–	15 Apr	EA		,,	,,	Nr Galatz	u/c
3	26 Jun	2-seater		,,	,,	Nr Galatz	
4	4 Jul	Brandenburg CI	(a)	,,	,,	Endependanze	
5	7 Jul	2-seater		,,	,,	Latinul	am

(a) enemy a/c serial No.68.54.

PULPE Eduard Martynovich   Second Lieutenant   MS23, N23, 10TH

Pulpe was born in Riga, Latvia, on 22 June 1880, studied at Moscow University, became a teacher, but had taken an interest in aviation. He travelled to France in 1912 and learnt to fly the following year, gaining civil licence No.1571. Still living in France when war came, he joined the French air service, despite his 34 years, and was assigned to MS23 on 1 May 1915, flying over Verdun. He gained four victories over France, winning the Croix De Guerre with four Palmes, and the Medaille Militaire. With promotion to commissioned rank, he was part of a group of pilots selected to proceed to Russia in the spring of 1916, where he was posted to the 10th Fighter Detachment. Here he gained his fifth victory but was shot down and seriously wounded on 2 August, and later succumbed to his injuries. He received the posthumous award of the Order of St George, 4th Class. A two-seater crew of Kampfgeschwader II, Ltns Erwin Böhme and Lademacher, claimed a Russian Nieuport XII shot down in the Rodzyze area on this date. Böhme later became a 24-victory ace, mostly with Jasta 2 in France.

	1915					
1		EA		MS L	MS23	Verdun
2		EA		,,	,,	Verdun
	1916					
3	20 Mar	EA		Nieup	N23	N Maucourt
4	31 Mar	2-seater		,,	,,	Consenvoye
5	1 Jul	EA		Nieup XI	10th	Lutsk-Kovel area

SAFONOV Mikhail Ivanovich   Lieutenant   GLAGOL, 2LFD

Like the Austro-Hungarian Gottfried Banfield, Mikhail Safonov flew seaplanes, at least initially. Born in Ostrogozhsk on 13 November 1893, he came from a noble family and entered the Imperial Russian Naval Academy at St Petersburg, in September 1909. Over the next four years he served on several naval ships and graduated in 1914 with the rank of warrant officer. At the start of the war he served on the battleship *Sevastopol*, but in September 1915 he requested a transfer to aviation. By early 1916 he was with the Baltic Fleet's 3rd Air Division on the coast of the Gulf of Riga and then the 2nd Air Division's First Air Detachment (Glagol). Safonov was engaged in several air fights and was awarded the Order of St Anne, 4th Class, and the Order of St Vladimir, 3rd Class, with Swords and Bow, then commissioned in July 1917. Soon after this he took command of the Glagol Detachment. During a leave period in October, he was married and in November he commanded the 2nd Land Fighter Detachment. Safonov was now flying Nieuport scouts and added three kills to his two scored whilst flying seaplanes, but by the late autumn the war was over and in March 1918 he was discharged. In April 1918 he was one of several airmen to fly aircraft to Finland as defectors, Safonov actually taking his wife with him. During the Finnish Civil War, Safonov flew recce sorties but later left to join the White Russian Forces under Denikin, in 1919. Later still, he and his wife travelled to Persia and India, and here he joined the RAF. Then in 1924 he and his family went to China where he started to organise flying schools for the Chinese navy but was killed whilst testing a flying-boat on the Ming River in May. Occasionally listed with 11 victories, or as low as three.

	1916					
1	9 Sep	Seaplane	Grig M9	Glagol	Gulf of Riga	
	1917					
2	14 Jul	EA	Grig M15	,,	Gulf of Riga	1140
3	7 Sep	2-seater	Nieup NR1	,,	Arensburg	

| 4 | 16 Nov | EA | „ | „ | Moon Island | 0915 |
| 5 | 17 Nov | bomber | „ | „ | „ | 0900 |

de SEVERSKY Aleksandr Nikolaivich Prokoffiev   Captain

2ND BALTIC   2 NFD

A Georgian, de Seversky was born in the city of Tiflis on 7 June 1894. His father had been among the first Russian pilots to own his own aircraft, and by 1908, he had taught his son to fly. It was during this year that the young de Seversky entered the Naval Academy in St Petersburg, graduating in early 1914, and was sent for sea duty. When the war began he requested aviation as his means of going to war and by late June 1915 he was commissioned and assigned to the Baltic Fleet as a pilot. Operated with the 2nd Bombing and Recce station in the Gulf of Riga but on his first sortie to attack a German destroyer, flying a French FBA flying boat, his machine was hit. Coming down to land his bombs exploded, killing his observer and injuring him. Luckily he was rescued but had to have one leg amputated below the knee. His flying career seemed over and he was refused front line duty but in order to show everyone he could still fly he took off on an unauthorised flight at an air show and carried out a spectacular display. Arrested after he had landed, the story soon came to the attention of the Czar. Eventually this led to a return to front line flying, which commenced in July 1916. Three days after his return he downed his first hostile aircraft. For an action fought on 15 August in which he out-fought three enemy machines, he received the Golden Sword of St George, presented to him by the Czar himself. Assigned to command the 2nd Naval Fighter Detachment in February 1917, he was injured when slipping beneath the wheel of a horse-drawn vehicle, which broke his good leg, thus putting paid to his new command. In May he was in Moscow as a technical advisor but by July he was commanding a fighter unit back on the Gulf of Riga. In combat during a German offensive, he scored a number of victories but their confirmation was lacking due to the Russian troop withdrawals, but finally in October his final two claims were confirmed. He was then forced down behind enemy lines on 14 October but successfully negotiated his way back through the front. For this he received the Order of St George, 4th Class and promoted to Captain. de Seversky was then made assistant naval attaché at the Embassy in America, where he assumed his duties in March 1918. Following the revolution, de Seversky remained in the USA, becoming a citizen in 1927 and began a career as an aircraft designer and had his own company. He was voted out of office in 1939 and his company became the famous Republic Aircraft Co. He then became a freelance aeronautical consultant and towards the end of WW2 was a special consultant to the American Government. He remained active in aviation until his death in 1974. Score variations — between 4 and thirteen.

	1916				
1	4 Jul	Scout	Grig M9	2nd	Gulf of Riga
2	13 Aug	Seaplane	„	„	Lake Angern
3	„	Seaplane	„	„	„
4	„	Seaplane	„	„	„
	1917				
5	10 Oct	Scout	Nieup XXI	„	Zerel Island
6	„	2-seater	„	„	„

SMIRNOV Ivan Vasilievich   Lieutenant   19TH

Born 30 January 1895, to a farming family in the province of Vladimir, he was of peasant stock but his situation changed with the coming of war and having joined up, served with the 96th Omsk Regt. Private Smirnov received his first decoration in October 1914, the Soldiers Cross of St George, 4th Class, although his regiment almost ceased to exist. On 8 December he was himself badly wounded in the leg and was out of the war for five months. He decided to transfer to aviation and by August 1916 he was a pilot with the 19th Fighter Detachment, and began his combat career in December, flying Nieuport two-seaters. On 2 January 1917 he shared his first victory and was made sergeant and in April he received the Cross of St George, 3rd Class, followed a few days later by the 2nd Class, for his second victory. He continued in action through the summer, becoming an ensign and achieving a third kill in August; by September he had scored his sixth. He was now flying Nieuport Scouts and later Spads. In November he received the Order of St George, 4th Class, the month in which he raised his score to 11. Following the revolution, Smirnov felt it wise to leave Russia, and with the White Russians, served in Paris as an assistant air attaché and test pilot, also as a pilot with the RAF in England (major). In 1920 he joined the Belgian airline SNETA, which later became Sabena and two years later began a long and illustrious career with KLM — Royal Dutch Airlines. During WW2 he flew with the Dutch East Indies Army Air Corps, with the rank of captain and was shot down and wounded in one leg and both arms by Japanese Zero fighters which attacked his DC3 (serial PK-AFV) on 2 March 1942 while evacuating civilians from Java to Australia. He crash landed on the beach near Carnot Bay and was strafed; one of his crew was killed. The bullets taken from his own body were later made into cuff-links which he always used. Having become a naturalized Dutchman, he was awarded the Dutch DFC, the Croix de Guerre and made a Knight of the Order of Orange Nassau. His flying came to an end in 1949 at which time he had flown over 4,000,000 miles during 28,750 flying hours. He died on the island of Majorca in October 1956.

	1917					
1	2 Jan	Aviatik CI	(a)	Nieup X	19th	Galicia-Lutsk
2	2 May	Albatros C	(b)	MS I	„	W Zavaluv
3	16 Aug	EA		Nieup XVII	„	Melnitsy
4	23 Aug	2-seater	(c)	„	„	Gusyatin
5	8 Sep	2-seater		MS I	„	Gusyatin
6	25 Sep	2-seater	(d)	Spad VII	„	Balin-Prilip
7	24 Oct	Scout		„	„	Kowel
8	10 Nov	Brandenburg CI	(e)	„	„	S Zielona
9	„	Brandenburg CI	(e)	„	„	Zelyonaya
10	23 Nov	Lloyd CV	(f)	„	„	Letovo
11	26 Nov	EA	(g)	„	„	Scalat area

(a) observer Capt Pentko; (b) a/c from FA220; (c) shared with Lt Huber; (d) a/c from FAA240; (e) a/c from Flik 9, shared with Ens L Lipsky; (f) Flik 18; (g) shared with Capt A A Kozakov.

STRIZHEVSKY Vladimir Ivanovich   Ensign   9TH

Yet another of noble birth, Strizhevsky (sometimes spelt Strishzhevskii) was born on 26 December 1894 in the Mogiljevsky Province, and attended the Petrograd Institute where he studied electro-mechanical engineering. Soon after the war began he volunteered for the air service and by mid-1915 had become a pilot with the 16th Corps Squadron, beginning operations in September. With the rank of warrant officer he received all four classes of the Soldier's Cross of St George by early 1916, and was then promoted to ensign, but was injured in a crash on 9 March. He did not return to the Front until August, at which time he was assigned to the 9th Fighter Detachment, although he had a ground job until December when he was fit to return to operational sorties. His first victory came just over a year after his crash and in April he downed three more with another unconfirmed. His fifth came in May, his sixth and seventh in June, but these were his last, although he had an unconfirmed on 18 July. However, in this combat he was wounded in the right leg by two bullets, and by the time he was fit to return to duty, the Russian war had ended. For some unknown reason, Strizhevsky did not receive any decorations nor promotions for his fighter combat work, although Romania awarded him the Order of the Romanian Crown, with Swords.

	1917						
1	7 Mar	EA		Nieup XXI	9th	Herzh region	
2	11 Apr	LVG C		Spad VII	„	Siret	
–	16 Apr	Brandenburg DI		„	„		0915 u/c
3	17 Apr	EA	(a)	Nieup XVII	„	Rakosa Forest	
4	23 Apr	LVG C		„	„	Nr Siret	
–	11 May	EA		„	„		u/c
5	17 May	Brandenburg DI		Spad VII	„	Bacau	

6	17 Jun	Fokker E		„	„	Uzel Valley	1230
7	18 Jun	Brandenburg CI	(b)	Nieup XVII	„	Okna region	
–	18 Jul	2-seater	(c)	„	„	Vermeshty	u/c

(a) shared with 2/Lt G E Suk; (b) Flik 39 a/c; (c) in company with 2/Lt I A Loiko.

SUK Grigori Eduardovich   Ensign   9TH

Born into the nobility on 12 December 1896, of Russian and Czech parents, his uncle Vyacheslav Suk was the well known conductor at the Bolshoi Theatre in Moscow. Suk volunteered for the air service upon the outbreak of war. Becoming a pilot he was sent to the Front, assigned to the 26th Corps Detachment, in March 1916, flying Henri Farmans. After flying combat, he was promoted to warrant officer, sent for fighter training, and then posted to the 9th Fighter Detachment in August. Promoted to ensign he scored his first victory in January 1917, which was not confirmed, but the first confirmed kill came in March. Over the summer of 1917, Suk's score slowly mounted, his fifth victory coming in September. Unusually, Suk flew many combat sorties in a Vickers FB.19 (not unlike a Camel at first glance), a type not used by the British except in Palestine and Macedonia, even then only in small numbers. By November, now flying a Spad, his score had risen to nine but he was then killed in a flying accident on 28 November, while coming in to land at his airfield.

	1917						
1	26 Mar	Brandenburg CI		Nieup XI	9th	Nedzy-Vozargal	
2	17 Apr	2-seater	(a)	„	„	Rakosa area	
3	8 Aug	Oefflag CII	(b)	„	„	Okno area	
4	4 Sep	2-seater	(c)	VFB19	„	Vermeshty	
–	8 Sep	2-seater	(c)	„	„	Seret	u/c
5	12 Sep	2-seater	(d)	„	„	Nr Radautz	1800
6	14 Oct	2-seater		Spad VII	„	SE Radautz	
7	4 Nov	Scout		„	„	Goura-Seltche	
8	8 Nov	EA		„	„	N Raduatz	
9	10 Nov	Brandenburg CI	(e)	„	„	Nr Radautz	

(a) shared with Ens V I Strizhevsky; (b) Flik 44; (c) shared with 2/Lt I A Loiko; (c) Flik 44, shared with Loiko and 2/Lt Sapozhnikov; (d) a/c of Flik 44; (e) a/c of Flik 49.

VAKULOVSKY Konstantin Konstantinovich   Captain   1ST

Of noble birth, Vakulovsky came into the world on 28 October 1894 and in his youth was an army cadet and later attended an engineering school. He graduated with the rank of second lieutenant just before the war erupted and decided to go into aviation, which he did before the year was out. By the spring of 1915 he was a pilot with the Novo-Georgievsky Rampart Squadron, part of the defence system of this fortress near Warsaw, Poland. The fortress fell to the Germans in August, Vakulovsky being one of the last to fly out, to receive the Order of St George, 4th Class. The surviving aircrew became the 33rd Corps Detachment, a recce unit, and for his work here he received the Golden Sword of St George. Commissioned in July 1916, he was given command of the 1st Fighter Detachment and downed his first opponent in September. Despite being severely shocked by a near miss AA shell this same month, which caused him to be absent from the Front until October, he gradually increased his score of victories, became a captain, and even survived being shot down by ground fire in June 1917, although he suffered some injuries. He was then awarded the Order of St Vladimir, 4th Class, with Swords and Bow. Vakulovsky raised his score to six at the beginning of September but nothing is known of him after the revolution. He was also the recipient of the Order of St Anne, 2nd Class, with Swords, two 3rd Class awards of this Order, and three 4th Class; two Orders of St Stanislas, 2nd Class with Swords, and a 3rd Class with Swords and Ribbon.

	1916					
1	7 Sep	EA	Nieup XI	1st	Lake Krakshta	
2	28 Oct	Albatros	„	„	Lake Vishnevsky	

	1917						
3	14 Apr	2-seater		Morane-S	„	NE Budslav	
–	12 May	EA			„	Kabilnichachby A/F	u/c
4	21 Aug	Scout		Nieup XVII	„	Riga Sound	
5	1 Sep	EA		Nieup XXIII	„	Iskul Area	
6	„	EA		„	„	„	

YANCHENKO Vasili Ivanovich　　　Ensign　　7TH, 32ND

With 16 victories, Vasili Yanchenko was the second highest scoring Russian pilot of the war. Born on New Year's Day 1894 he studied engineering pre-war during which time he became interested in aviation. Soon after the war began he volunteered to join the Russian Air Service as a private, then went through the various training organisations and by the late summer of 1915 was a pilot, assigned to the 12th Corps Detachment as a sergeant. On his first recce sortie on 15 September, his engine blew up and caught fire. Although he got down safely he suffered burns, but he received the Soldier's Cross of St George, 4th Class, for saving his machine and observer. In early 1916 he transferred to the 3rd Corps Detachment but did not get on with his CO so requested a transfer to the 7th Fighter Detachment in March, arriving at his new unit on 7 April, on the Tarnopol Front. Yanchenko gained his first victory in June and although he flew numerous sorties, did not score again until October, but his daring had caused his promotion to ensign and he had been awarded the Soldier's Cross of St George, 1st Class. The Order of St Anne, 4th Class, followed and so did his third victory. In January came the Order of St Vladimir, 4th Class, with Swords and Bow. Following injuries in a crash, he teamed up with Donat Makeenok and Juri Gilsher and by the end of June he had achieved seven victories. He scored five kills in July, although Gilsher was killed during one of their combats. Yanchenko landed near the crash site, removed his dead friend's body from the wreck and arranged for it to be taken back to Tarnopol. Makeenok was wounded in August, which left Yanchenko the only ace with the 7th, but then, on 20 September, he was assigned to the 32nd Corps Detachment. With this unit he brought his score to 16 by mid-October but then the war was over, and fearing reprisals from the Bolsheviks he left his unit in November and joined Denikin's White Army early in 1918. He commanded the 2nd Air Squadron from August 1918 until August 1920, and later that year went to America where he worked as an engineer under Igor Sikorski, and became a US citizen. In the 1930s he moved to Syracuse, New York, working as a design enginer until he retired in 1952.

	1916						
1	25 Jun	Aviatik BIII	(a)	Nieup XI	7th	Podgaitsy	
2	4 Oct	2-seater	(a)	„	„	Zlota-Lipa	
3	18 Oct	EA		„	„	Lipitsa	1605
	1917						
4	7 Mar	2-seater	(b)	„	„	W Lipitsa	
5	13 Apr	Brandenburg CI	(c)	Morane-S	„	Bogorodchani	0845
6	„	Brandenburg CI	(c)	„	„	„	0845
7	27 Jun	EA		Nieup XVII	„	Shumlany	
8	2 Jul	Brandenburg CI		Nieup XI	„	Nr Brzezhany	
9	6 Jul	EA	(b)	„	„	N Brzezhany	
10	11 Jul	EA	(b)	„	„	Brzezhany	
11	18 Jul	EA		„	„	Brzezhany	
12	20 Jul	2-seater	(d)	„	„	Tarnopol	2030
13	5 Aug	2-seater	(b)	„	„	Brzezhany	
14	23 Sep	Albatros DIII		„	„	Gusyatin	1120
15	8 Oct	Aviatik C		Nieup XXI	32nd	Zbrizh area	
16	14 Oct	Albatros DIII	(e)	„	„	Gorodok	1630

(a) shared with Ens I A Orlov; (b) shared with Ens D A Makeenok; (c) a/c of Flik 7, shared with 2/Lt J V Gilsher and Makeenok; (d) shared with J V Gilsher; (e) a/c from Flik 30.

Over the years there have been a number of pilots in the Russian Air Service named as WW1 air aces, but where information is either lacking or they have been wrongly listed. Among them have been:

Tadeusz Grochowalski, from Poland. Claimed five victories with the 7th Fighter Detachment but only one seems to have been confirmed.

Viktor Komorovski, a Russian noted with at least five victories.

Jaan M Majhlapuu, an Estonian, supposedly with five victories.

Antoni E Mrochkovski, from Poland; one victory with the 24th Corps Detachment in 1915, also noted with five in some sources.

S S Puzh, with five.

Boris Sergeievich Sergievski, 25th Corps Detachment and 2nd Fighter Detachment. A score as high as 11, including three balloons, has been recorded but not substantiated. Probably not more than two or three victories actually confirmed.

Olgerdis J Teteris, from Latvia, 13th Corps Detachment. Listed in some sources with six victories before his death by AA fire on 28 February 1917, he only achieved two official kills.

Peter Martinovich Tomson, 1st Corps Detachment. Scores of between five and eleven must include unconfirmed and/or actual engagements as he was only credited with one official victory.

Viktor Viktorovich Utgoff, often listed with five but this is incorrect. Flew seaplanes and flying boats with the Black Sea Fleet.

F T Zveriev, sometimes noted with ten victories, none being known.

Bibliography

In Volo per Vienna, Gregory Alegi, Trento/Rovereto, Museo Caproni/Museo Storico Italiano dell
a Guerra, 1993;

L'Asso degli assi, Gregory Alegi & Cesare Falessi, Roma, Bariletti, 1992;

Vita eroica di Ernesto Cabruna, Tomaso Cartosio, Roma, Stato Maggiore Aeronautica, Vercelli,
1972;

La grande guerra 1915-18, Paolo Ferrari (ed.), Valdagno, Gino Rossato Editore, 1994;

Gli amici di Marcon, Francis Lombardi, Associazione Arma Aeronautica, Vercelli, 1978;

Nieuport Macchi 11 & 17, Maurizio Longoni, Milano, Intergest, 1976;

L'idea meravigliosa di Francesco Baracca, Vincenzo Manca, Roma, Dell'Ateneo, 1980;

Air Aces of the Austro-Hungarian Empire 1914-18, Martin O'Connor, Flying Machine Press, 1994;

The Imperial Russian Air Service, Alan Durkota, Thomas Darcey & Victor Kulikov, Flying
Machines Press, 1995;

La guerra nell'aria, Felice Porro, Corbaccio, 1935;

Impressioni e ricordi di guerra aerea, Silvio Scaroni, Roma, Danesi, 1922;

Battaglie nel cielo, Silvano Scaroni, Milano, Mondadori, 1934;

Die k.u.k. Seeflieger, Peter Schupita, Koblenz, Bernard & Graefe, 1983;

Air Aces of the 1914-1918 War, Edited by Bruce Robertson, Harleyford Publications, 1959.